BEYOND THE CONTRACT STATE

Ideas for social and economic renewal

in South Australia

T0363972

BEYOND THE CONTRACT STATE

Ideas for social and economic renewal
in South Australia

Edited by
JOHN SPOEHR

WAKEFIELD PRESS

Wakefield Press
Box 2266
Kent Town
South Australia 5071

First published 1999

Designed and typeset by Clinton Ellicott
Printed and bound by Hyde Park Press, Adelaide

National Library of Australia
Cataloguing-in-publication entry

Beyond the contract state: ideas for social and economic
renewal in South Australia.

ISBN 1 86254 465 4.

1. South Australia – Economic conditions – 1990–   .
2. South Australia – Social conditions – 1990–   .
3. South Australia – Social policy. 4. South Australia –
Economic policy – 1990–   . I. Spoehr, John.

339.5099423

Wakefield Press thanks Wirra Wirra Vineyards and
Arts South Australia for their continued support.
Promotion of this book has been assisted by the
South Australian Government through Arts South Australia.

CONTENTS

PART 2: TRANSFORMING THE CONTRACT STATE

CHAPTER 1

BEYOND THE
CONTRACT STATE

JOHN SPOEHR

Forget any imbalance of power, of knowledge, of financial muscle, or of wider social consequences which make contracting unstable and inefficient. Contract is King. But the extravagant claims made for the results of all this free contracting – from the financial system to the National Health Service – do not bear close scrutiny. Britain has grown less rapidly and the gains from the lower growth are bitterly unequally distributed ... A new value system has grown up on which everything can have a price put on its head and is potentially up for sale. Concepts which civilised community hold dear – the ethic of care in medicine, of justice in the courts, of service in the public sector – have been threatened by the overarching ethic that they must be on the market ...

Will Hutton (1997) *The State to Come*, pp. 2–3

We must reply we will intervene – we will intervene to retain our right to a say in our own future, to temper the market place by action to provide services and social justice, to retain institutional safeguards and provide needed development in the community interest, for we know that we intervene or we sink.

Don Dunstan (1998) *We Intervene or We Sink*, **Whitlam Oration**

In South Australia we are witnessing the consolidation of a 'contract state'[1] – a society transformed by privatisation, deregulation and contracting-out. This is taking place in the context of a broader, neoliberal economic transformation of the global economy, popularised as 'globalisation'. These changes are bringing about a major shift in geopolitical, class and gender relations and increasing inequality within, and between nations. While small regional economies like South Australia remain exposed to an unregulated global economy, the prospects for social and economic renewal are extremely limited, as former Professor of the Harvard Business School, David Korten illustrates (1998, p. 1), 'An unregulated global economy dominated by corporations that recognise money as their only value is inherently unstable, egregiously unequal, destructive of markets, democracy, and life, and is impoverishing humanity in real terms as it enriches a few in financial terms'.

The contract state does little to protect its citizens from predatory corporations in the global economy; instead, it attempts to position itself to compete as a player in global and local bidding wars for footloose firms. This is a 'game' where the dice are loaded against smaller and less wealthy nations or regions. In this respect the odds are not in South Australia's favour! South Australia already has a history of spending more on attracting firms than other mainland states (Industry Commission 1996). This trend is neither desirable nor sustainable over the medium term. South Australia cannot hope to compete with the wealthier eastern states in bidding wars over business locations. The results of this approach so far suggest that the high technology vision set by the Brown/Olsen government will not be met by these means. It appears the main benefits so far are the establishment of a number of back office call centres. If this trend continues, South Australia risks becoming the low-tech centre of mainland Australia – an information-rich, but knowledge-poor state. This is not the road to prosperity in a world where higher-order knowledge and skills are primary determinants of future job security, satisfaction and prosperity.

More broadly, it is not in South Australia's or Australia's interests to support unfettered corporate mobility within the global economy. The logic of competitive advantage in an unregulated global economy will produce more losers than winners, for this is a world where the rich and powerful thrive, and the poor and marginal struggle to survive, as Korten (1998, p. 2) illustrates:

Increasing the global competitiveness of one country by using public subsidies to increase private profit – to the extent it works – simply draws investment away from others and creates new losers. If indeed we are to have a world that works for everyone, we must come to terms with the dark side of global capitalism's competitive dynamic ... Fortunes change quickly in a global capitalist economy of excess productive capacity, massive unemployment, an unconscionable gap between rich and poor, and large amounts of speculative money looking for quick profits ... The glory is fleeting and for each winner, it seems there are many more losers.

This may seem an overly pessimistic reading of the changes taking place, but it seems clear that the contract state will not lead to a more just or democratic society. It will instead exacerbate inequality and sharpen social, economic and spatial divisions, just as it has in the heartland of the neoliberal economic experiment – the United States and Britain.

The consolidation of the neoliberal contract state in the 1990s is as revolutionary a change as the rise of the social democratic 'welfare state' in the 1950s. The driving ideological forces behind this shift are the neoliberal economic ideas transported from two of the most wealthy but socially fractured nations on earth. These are hardly socially just models upon which to base the future development of South Australia. The legacies of poverty and inequality which have arisen from the ideological zealotry of Reaganomics and Thatcherism should be cause for alarm rather than comfort. There is nothing relaxed and comfortable about the contract state.[2] In the contract state the terms of the contract are heavily weighted in favour of the wealthy and powerful. When the major players in the contract state are multinational corporations with budgets bigger than state governments and shareholders with few allegiances to local community goals or expectations, it is easy to see who the big winners will be. For this is the nature of the contract state – a clash between the public interest and shareholder interests, a clash between collective aspirations and private self-interest.

The contract state is a state which is prepared to dismantle collective institutions in an attempt to attract domestic and international capital. It is an end game in the neoliberal economic experiment as it pits nation against nation in an endless race to the bottom to attract investment. In this race to the bottom, the contract state renounces the use of debt as a source of underpinning future growth, deregulates the labour market and marginalises unions to push down real wage levels, sells public utilities and contracts-out public services to create new opportunities for corporate profitability. Through this, the contract state is facilitating a major redistribution of public wealth to private interests. Not surprisingly, the net effect is growing inequality, unemployment, insecurity and poverty.

The signs of social and economic distress are clear in South Australia as this book reveals. Poor economic performance is fuelling this distress as Frank Gelber and Matthew Jones outline in chapter 3. As a consequence unemployment rates in South Australia are ratcheting upwards. Related to this is a disturbing increase in the number of 'prime age' people leaving the state. This represents a significant erosion of the future skill, knowledge and economic base of the state. This and growing dependency of South Australians upon government transfers or financial assistance is demonstrated graphically by Graeme Hugo in chapter 4. Recent trends indicate that South Australia has 'a heavier reliance on government transfers than any other state or territory'. Over the five years to 1997, the number of 'income units' dependent upon income support measures increased by nearly 12 per cent. In chapter 7 Ray Broomhill and Rhonda Sharp indicate that, 'despite increasing levels of participation by women in the labour market, occupational and industry sex segregation has remained largely static'. In addition they find that if 'hidden' unemployment is taken into account, 'real' rates of unemployment for women are around two-thirds higher than those for men. Focusing on industrial relations issues in chapter 14, Barbara Pocock and Anthony Psarros demonstrate that South Australian workers are reporting higher levels of work-related stress than other Australian workers and they feel more pessimistic about promotional prospects. They also demonstrate that overall employee earnings have fallen behind other states. Relative to Australia, South Australian ordinary-time earnings reached a fourteen-year low in 1997. In chapter 18 Adrian Vicary and Mark Henley indicate that the number of South Australian households living below 60 per cent of average weekly earnings increased by 62 per cent over the ten years to 1996. These are some of the social and economic consequences of the contract state. Equally important are the broader political consequences of the contract state for the health of democracy in South Australia.

The contract state undermines the institutions of government and democracy. There are few places for community participation in the policy-making process of the contract state unless you are a member of the corporate community. Unions and community organisations are constantly on the defensive in the contract state. As advocacy organisations, they face the threat of defunding, and in the case of unions, the threat of legal sanctions. The contract state represents the 'hollowing-out' of the state (Jessop 1994), a process that erodes public institutions and collective needs and aspirations and replaces them with private institutions and individual aspirations. The contract state is a client state where shareholders of international corporations compete unfairly with citizens to shape the public interest, and governments hide behind 'commercial confidentiality' to obscure the public interest.

The contract state can also be regarded as a response to a crisis of accumulation within capitalism. In the search for new markets and opportunities for increased profitability, international capital is becoming more sophisticated and more predatory. In the global economy this is made possible by contract states which pursue neoliberal restructuring agendas. The first wave of this restructuring in Australia involved financial and trade liberalisation. Combined with a revolution in electronic communications technology there are few obstacles left in the way of unfettered capital mobility. This is not to say that citizens in the contract state are powerless and unable to determine their destiny in the global economy, for this ignores the capacity of communities to organise for change. In this respect one of the most important victories in the international arena has been the success of the global campaign against the introduction of the Multilateral Agreement on Investment. This augers well for those who oppose the neoliberal restructuring agenda.

In South Australia the second wave of neoliberal restructuring is now taking place. Embodied in the concept of the contract state, this agenda is facing growing hostility from citizens and communities throughout Australia. The rise of Pauline Hanson and One Nation, and growing volatility within the electorate sound political warnings about the negative consequences of neoliberalism.

The emergence of the global financial crisis in the late 1990s has also undermined the neoliberal restructuring agenda by exposing the inadequacies and dangers of deregulated financial markets. The proponents of this deregulation must now face their critics. Among the critics is Californian-based author of *Miti and the Japanese Miracle*, Chalmers Johnson:

These famous tenured professors of economics, who never once faced a 'market force' in their own lives, were hired to preach the beauties of 'globalisation', in this case meaning American institutions. Concretely, these include total laissez faire, destruction of unions and social safety nets, staffing of regulatory agencies with retired financiers, indifference to pay differentials between CEOs and the ordinary labor force, moving manufacturing to low-wage areas regardless of the social costs, and totally unregulated flows of capital in and out of any and all economies. *Australian Financial Review*, 18 November 1998, p. 22

Even free market purists are acknowledging the need for new forms of financial regulation to regain some stability and predictability in the global economy. This convergence around the necessity for some form of regulation represents a critical turning point in the debate on globalisation. New political spaces are likely to emerge over the next few years as this debate intensifies. As they do, opportunities to reflect critically on the merits of the contract state are likely to increase.

In arguing the case against the contract state in South Australia we need to be aware of both the consequences of pursuing neoliberalism and the alternatives available to it. There are important lessons to be learnt from South Australian history and international experience.

Before providing a brief historical overview of recent political and economic issues surrounding the emergence and operation of the contract state in South Australia, it is useful to reflect on international experience. By failing to learn from history, the advocates of neoliberalism are doomed to repeat the mistakes of the past.

Much is made in Australia of the virtues of the neoliberal economic policies of the United States. It is worth building further upon Chalmers Johnson's criticisms of the US 'free market' model and its role in advocating a neoliberal globalisation agenda. Perhaps one of the most persuasive critiques of the US model comes from the authors of the international best selling novel, *The Global Trap*.

Globalisation, understood as the unfettering of world-market forces and the removal of economic power from the state, is for most nations a brute fact from which they cannot escape. For America, it is a process that its own economic and political elite deliberately launched and keeps in motion.

Martin & Schumann 1996, p. 216

In this context the debate surrounding the US model of labour market deregulation should be understood, for it is the archetype for the neoliberal contract state – a key element of the broader neoliberal globalisation agenda. It has also proved to be the most difficult element to introduce into the Australian context. The greater strength of unions in Australia and the relationship between unions and the Australian Labor Party (ALP) in government have helped to prevent complete labour market deregulation, although much has happened at a state and federal level to lay the foundations for this as Barbara Pocock and Anthony Psarros demonstrate in chapter 14. (See also Spoehr & Broomhill 1995.) Indeed the tactics used by Patrick Stevedores and the federal Coalition government during the Webb Dock dispute suggest that labour market deregulation will be a primary objective of the second term of the Howard government.

While the low level of official unemployment in the US is causing many to investigate labour market policies in that country, it is a grave mistake to herald labour market deregulation as the solution to unemployment. There is no shortage however, of advocates of total deregulation in Australia, as five prominent Australian neoliberal economists demonstrated after the 1998 federal election. The 'Five Economists' as they have come to be known, advocated the replacement of Living Wage adjustments with tax credits for families on low incomes (Dawkins et al 1998). This is a formula for further erosion of 'real' wage levels as the US approach to labour market deregulation illustrates.

Behind the 'hype' surrounding the US labour market 'miracle' is a disturbing story of growing job insecurity, industrial unrest and corporate thuggery. Martin and Schumann (1996, pp. 115–17) provide a vivid illustration of this in action in the US town of Peoria.

It doesn't get much worse than this. Jack Hayes sits ashen-faced in his narrow broken kitchen and struggles to maintain his composure. He has worked for twenty-nine years as a lathe operator and mechanic at Caterpillar, the world's largest producer of construction machinery and bulldozers. He has been through all the ups and downs of his firm's history at its main factory and head offices in Peoria ... including the terrible 1980s when 'Cat' nearly went bankrupt. Hayes voluntarily put in hours helping to redesign work routines, to install new computer-controlled machinery ... Then in 1991, Hayes recalls, when turnover and profits reached an all time high, management declared war on the workforce. Wages had to drop as much as 20 per cent, and two hours would be added to the working week.

Four years on, Hayes still does not know the answer. The organised Cat workers held a number of strikes ... keeping up their last action for eighteen months. Now came Fites' [Caterpillar CEO] hour. Wages in Japan and Mexico were lower than in Peoria, he explained to his people, so any new hiring could only be at below union rates ... When the strikers finally gave in, Fites imposed on them terms and conditions that had not been seen in decades. These require them to work twelve hours a day when necessary, including at weekend and with no extra pay.

These and less draconian industrial campaigns by employers have resulted in the US becoming the largest low-wage economy in the

OECD. One illustration of this has been the sharp decline in real wages in the US. Around 80 per cent of all male employees and workers are earning '11 per cent less an hour in real terms than they did in 1973' (Martin & Schumann 1996, p. 117). Inequality has grown dramatically in the US with the top one per cent of 20 million households doubling their income over the fifteen years to 1996. The average net income of corporate executives rose by around 66 per cent over the same period. By 1996 the income ratio between corporate executives and ordinary employees was 120:1 (Martin & Schumann 1996, p.118). These are the consequences of US-style, labour market deregulation. They are hardly glowing references for the US model. Indeed, the broader OECD experience suggests 'that the more deregulated the labour market, the worse the fate of low-paid workers' (ACIRRT 1999, p. 99).

In a low-wage, high-unemployment state like South Australia, US-style labour market deregulation is a particularly draconian response to unemployment. It would fuel the growth of the working poor in South Australia. Proceeding down this path sets South Australia on the way to becoming the Mexico of Australia – a low-wage sweat shop, serving the needs of a more affluent north.

THE EMERGENCE OF THE CONTRACT STATE

To understand the emergence of the contract state we need to review the recent political and economic history of South Australia. The emergence of the contract state in South Australia can be traced back to the 1970s when the legitimacy of Keynesian economic ideas were undermined by the global economic crises precipitated by the OPEC oil crisis. Led by the United States and Britain, Australian governments joined the retreat from 'Keynesian' style economic and social policies. At first the retreat in Australia from these welfare state policies was tempered by Labor governments under pressure by community organisations and the broader labour movement to retain a commitment to their social democratic traditions. By the mid-1980s the collectivist ideals of the welfare state were overtaken by the rise of 'economic fundamentalism' (Langmore & Quiggin 1994) or 'economic rationalism' as it is more popularly understood. The major tenets of economic fundamentalism have been driving economic and social policy in Australia and South Australia for nearly twenty years. At a national level the Keating Labor government laid the foundations for the ascendancy of economic fundamentalism by deregulating the banking and financial system, advocating accelerated trade liberalisation, privatising the Commonwealth Bank and embarking upon enterprise bargaining (Spoehr & Broomhill 1995). The first of these policy shifts was to have dire consequences for state Labor governments during the early 1990s.

Responding to cuts in Commonwealth financial assistance and the general climate of fiscal austerity at the time, the South Australian Labor government of John Bannon began a process of public sector 'downsizing' and outsourcing in mid-1990. A 'razor gang', the Government Agencies Review Group, began a process which led to the loss of hundreds of public sector jobs (Parkin 1992). On top of this painful period of public sector restructuring came the collapse of the State Bank and State Government Insurance Commission in 1992. The Hawke Labor government's deregulation of the financial system in conjunction with the South Australian Labor government's hands-off approach to the management of the State Bank proved calamitous (Parkin 1992; Spoehr 1990). The political consequences for Labor of the State Bank and SGIC financial losses were abundantly clear as the state election loomed in 1993. Labor responded to the crisis by developing a blueprint for managing the higher public sector debt that resulted. While the crisis was an enormous setback, Labor did manage to construct a credible debt management strategy to help recover from the financial losses (Regional Research Network 1994). Although Premier John Bannon resigned in 1992 taking full responsibility for the crisis, the political damage to Labor was irreparable in the short term. Riding on a political tidal wave of public outrage, a newly elected Liberal government wasted no time unleashing a strident 'free market' approach to social and economic development in South Australia.

The financial crisis caused by the collapse of the State Bank and SGIC provided the political context in which to launch a radical program of neoliberal economic reform. In the absence of its own blueprint for reform, the incoming Liberal government, like its conservative counterparts in other states, appointed external consultants to lead a commission of audit investigation of public sector finances and reform. This tried-and-true formula for manufacturing a climate of financial crisis made the neoliberal economic objectives of privatisation and outsourcing more achievable. A privatised policy development process in the form of an audit commission provided predictable policy prescriptions. Ultimately, the membership of the commission ensured an outcome favourable to the government (Spoehr & Broomhill 1995). A 'debt crisis' was duly 'manufactured' and radical public sector spending cuts announced (Broomhill et al 1995).

The commission of audit provided the intellectual foundations, such as they were, for the state government to pursue a path of radical reform in the wake of the financial crisis. The ideological pragmatism that often characterised government policy-making during much of the post-war period was displaced by a more ideologically zealous neo-liberal agenda. For the first time in South Australian history a state government renounced debt as a tool for underwriting social and economic development. This represents a dangerous new direction in South Australian financial management as Paul Chapman and I illustrate in chapter 8. In South Australia this sort of zealotry is rare, and even rarer is the capacity within the Liberal government to sustain it intellectually.

To uncover the intellectual foundations of the neoliberal ascendancy in South Australia we need to examine the contribution of external consultants to Liberal government policy development. The Liberal government has relied heavily upon consultants to help legitimate its political inclinations. With the abandonment of the tripartite and community consultative structures established by the Labor government to help inform policy development, the processes of decision-making within government are now more than ever subject to the influence of private consultants.

The *Report of the SA Commission of Audit* remains the most comprehensive set of reform policies to emerge from the Liberal government since it was first elected. In the absence of a broader economic and social development strategy, it remains the government's only comprehensive policy blueprint. As a consequence there is a significant policy vacuum in South Australia. While the development of economic and social policy has been patchy in South Australia over the last fifteen years, the Bannon and Arnold Labor government's A.D. Little report, *Future Directions for the South Australian Economy*, the Planning Review, Social Justice and Women's Budget statements and attempts to develop a Social Development strategy represented significant attempts to generate policy coherence during the 1980s. Little of this work survived a change of government.

Institutions established by the Bannon/Arnold Labor government in areas such as manufacturing industry development and health and social welfare were dismantled by the Brown Liberal government. The Economic Development Board established within the Economic

Development Authority by the Labor government was replaced by the SA Development Council (SADC) based in the Premier's Department. These changes had more to do with territorial leadership conflicts within the Liberal Party than a commitment to new and effective institutional structures. Indeed leadership rivalry between Premier Dean Brown and Industry Minister John Olsen nearly paralysed the industry development structures of government. Not surprisingly, this institutional rivalry only ended when the leadership struggle came to an end. The rise of John Olsen as Premier of South Australia is significant to the extent that he is more ideologically tied to the tenets of neoliberalism than his predecessor appeared to be. Certainly he has driven a much more vigorous privatisation and debt reduction agenda.

Most of the institutional structures which were attempting to provide a focus for policy development and analysis were axed, including such key bodies as the Manufacturing Advisory Council. The more recent losses of regional Health and Social Welfare Councils continues this trend. In the place of these institutionally embedded structures are poorly resourced and short-term consultative structures like the Premier's Partnership for Jobs Forum, the Regional Development Taskforce and Job Workshop consultations.

The failure of the Brown/Olsen government to introduce well-resourced institutional structures that actively engage industry, unions and community organisations in policy development and implementation is a serious setback for social and economic renewal in South Australia. The presence of strong institutional structures linking industry, unions, the education sector and communities together is likely to be one key to maintaining local integrity in a deregulated global economy as Ray Broomhill in chapter 6 and Rodin Genoff and Graeme Sheather in chapter 12 illustrate (see also Amin & Thrift 1994).

This new period in South Australian political and economic history can be regarded as a time in which the contract state is being consolidated. It is a period characterised more by the ideological zealotry of Thatcherism than the pragmatism of former Liberal Premier, Tom Playford. The pragmatism of 'wets' within the Liberal Party has been displaced by a 'dry' economic liberalism. The rise of what can be described as a radical, free market agenda in South Australia can be attributed more to the influence of a small but influential conservative intelligentsia than a strong commitment to, or understanding of economic liberalism within the Liberal government. In this context, the influence of the University of Adelaide and Flinders University-based South Australian Centre for Economic Studies (SACES) on policy-making in South Australia has been profound. The close relationship between the SACES and the government was institutionalised through significant funding and other commitments to assist the growth of the SACES. A symbiotic relationship appeared to develop between the SACES and the state government, particularly in the public pronouncements of the Centre's Director, Professor Cliff Walsh who remained a close advisor to the government after his appointment to the South Australian Commission of Audit. It is no doubt useful for the Liberal government when the SACES consistently articulates a more conservative policy position than that of the government. This has often had the political effect of making the government's policy pronouncements look moderate compared to the SACES neoliberal policy prescriptions.

After a dream run with local media, the advice provided by Professor Walsh is now under challenge. Matt Abraham of the *Australian* has emerged as one of the most courageous critics.

For the past five years, the reassuring message has been one of economic rationalism. Sell assets, shed debt, outsource and, above all, downsize; and the private sector jobs and economic growth will follow.

How unsettling then, when the people plotting this course begin to express nagging doubts about their once-confident plans for a brave new world.

In Adelaide early this month, one of the nation's most ardent economic rationalists, Professor Cliff Walsh, ... reached for the ripcord ...

So what's gone wrong?

After all, have not the Brown-Olsen Liberal governments followed the formula of downsize-outsource-privatise pretty much to the letter? Over the past five years, the state government has wiped out 12 000 secure, middle class public service jobs, blowing an enormous confidence crater in the local landscape.

But last week Walsh rejected any suggestion that such a brutal strategy could have a significant effect. Instead, he argued the problem with sluggish growth had to be due to 'something more fundamental about the South Australian economy'.

But what? Well that's the problem. He doesn't know. 'In virtually any other set of circumstances, the sort of data you see portrayed in here would have been pulling employment levels up", he said. "It hasn't been ... it's still a puzzle.

Abraham 1998, p. 15

This sort of scrutiny of neoliberal economic advice creates new spaces for a more robust and full debate around alternatives to economic fundamentalism.

NEW IDEAS AND NEW SPACES FOR DEBATE

The dominance of neoliberal economic ideas in South Australia is starving the state of ideas to drive sustainable growth. It is also undermining the pursuit of a more equitable and prosperous society. This stranglehold must be broken by a more vigorous and sophisticated debate canvassing new ideas for social and economic renewal.

South Australia is at a critical juncture in history. Growing inequality, poverty and unemployment linked to the dismantling of the welfare state are denying citizens their right to participate meaningfully in society. This hardship is set to intensify as the pressures of competing in the global economy compromise the pursuit of broader social objectives. Already, a widening gap between the performance of the South Australian economy and Australia as a whole, suggests that we have entered a period of sustained decline. As Frank Gelber and Matthew Jones demonstrate in chapter 3, South Australia's share of the nation's economic and employment growth is likely to further contract ensuring that unemployment remains stubbornly high. The South Australian labour market is in crisis and the prospects for improvement are bleak as detailed in chapter 5. The high standard of living and lifestyle enjoyed by many is likely to become the luxury of fewer and fewer people as full-time employment becomes more difficult to obtain and maintain. Fewer people in full-time jobs means less purchasing power to sustain local businesses and more pressure on government to provide relief for a growing pool of long-term unemployed people. As a consequence, more people are likely to leave South Australia in search of work elsewhere. As they do the revenue base of the state contracts along with the capacity to provide the services required by those who remain.

The pursuit of 'level playing fields' and 'free markets' in a predatory global economy has local effects that Australians are increasingly beginning to identify, question and reject. The neoliberal economic agenda of unleashing global capital in the name of 'globalisation' is contributing to chronically high rates of unemployment, poverty and inequality in Australia. All of these combine to generate social exclusion. To overcome this hardship it will be necessary to confront the legitimacy of the contract state and restore the right of communities to take action through government to ensure justice and prosperity for all sections of society.

As the failures of financial deregulation are increasingly exposed, opportunities are likely to emerge for broader debates about the role of government and the need for strategic planning and public investment. As the cracks widen in the neoliberal economic agenda, new political spaces are opening up for debate on the role of government, the costs and consequences of privatisation and deregulation and the need for new strategies to tackle unemployment. Some ground has been gained on these fronts over the last few years as the result of strong community-based campaigns and alliances. Victories against privatisation of electricity utilities in New South Wales, South Australia and Tasmania represent significant setbacks for neoliberalism. So has the campaign against the sale of the remainder of Telstra.

New political spaces are opening up as communities begin to challenge economic fundamentalism. This is translating into electoral politics. Significant support in the 1998 federal election for One Nation and the success of the Australian Democrats in the Senate and a near win for the Democrats in the seat of Mayo in South Australia illustrate an increasingly volatile electorate. There is deep disillusionment within the electorate about the impact of economic fundamentalism and the failure of the Coalition or the ALP to pursue alternative ideas. This disillusionment is grounded in the experiences of many communities confronting chronically high rates of unemployment, population loss and service cuts.

While rationalisation and privatisation of services in Australia is fueling job losses and service cuts, drought and declining commodity prices have broken the spirit of many regional communities. The obsession with smaller government has ripped thousands of public sector jobs out of already struggling communities. As a consequence, small towns are dying as many leave in search of work in regional centres and capital cities. These are the sort of political, economic and social conditions that right-wing nationalism thrives in. They are also the conditions for the emergence of other political alternatives. Indeed the Left may now be entering a period more open to social democratic and socialist ideas.

The recent electoral successes of the Social Democrats and Greens in Germany, socialists in France and the Left Party in Sweden suggest that the long years of conservative political ascendancy may be coming to an end – at least in Europe. The success of the Swedish Left Party is of particular significance given the explicit feminist and environmentalist program that has underpinned its resurgence. The Left Party doubled its vote in the 1998 national election from six per cent to around 12 per cent. South Australia can learn a great deal from the partnership-based models of social and economic development currently being implemented in Europe. The spectacular success of the 'Partnership 2000' program of the government of the Irish Republic is one illustration of the importance of collaborative strategic planning and good government.

Voices which assert the right of communities to collectively determine social and economic priorities and which argue for social democratic and socialist alternatives are attracting strong community support. This was starkly illustrated in South Australia in 1998 when over five thousand people gathered at the Adelaide Entertainment Centre to hear former South Australian Premier, Don Dunstan, give the first South Australian Whitlam Oration. His inspiring 'We Intervene or We Sink' was a timely reminder that there is a growing number of South Australians looking for inspired leadership and alternatives to economic fundamentalism. This is now forcing the ALP to rethink its policies. While Labor's rhetoric always tends more to the Left when in opposition, a shift to the Left is nevertheless welcome. South Australian Labor leader, Mike Rann recently made the bold claim that the next Labor government in South Australia will be a government that Don Dunstan will be proud of. This is an accurate reading of widespread support in Adelaide for Don Dunstan's vision of social democracy. At a national level, Kym Beazley during the 1998 federal election campaign made important and welcome commitments to no further privatisation, to a more vigorous assault on unemployment and assistance to distressed regions. He also promised a more activist government. In opposition to the prevailing neoclassical economic orthodoxy, commitments like these do help to create new political spaces in the mainstream for a more progressive policy debate. Recent history tells us however, that significant social democratic and structural reform within the ALP should never be overestimated. Any progressive policy reform within the ALP is likely to require a great deal of internal and external pressure. It is difficult to see how this will be achieved without reform to some of the alienating structures prevailing within the ALP. In the end, strong and effective social movements, unions and new broad Left alliances will all be necessary to generate the political momentum necessary to successfully challenge the consolidation of the contract state.

If the ALP fails to make a clear break with economic fundamentalism, other political forces will fill the political vacuum that remains on the Left. In the absence of any coherent Left alternatives, the rise of parties like One Nation is assured. The prospect of One Nation becoming the dominant voice of dissent in Australia should be enough to motivate social democrats, socialists and indeed true liberals to reject economic fundamentalism. Enlightened social democratic governments at a state and national level are likely, in the current political and economic context, to attract growing community support if they are prepared to make a serious commitment to countering growing inequality, poverty and unemployment.

The challenge of securing a prosperous and just future for South Australians will not be met by governments locked into the pursuit of a neoliberal contract state. This book provides some of the tools to understand and challenge the contract state. It is written with the explicit intention to promote a vigorous debate around social and economic alternatives to the contract state.

This book is divided into two parts. Part 1 – Trends and Issues in the Contract State provides an overview and expert analysis of key economic and social trends. In addition, a number of key political and economic issues confronting South Australia, such as public debt, privatisation, gender inequity and the nature and impact of globalisation are discussed and analysed. In Part 2 – Transforming the Contract State a range of prominent South Australian academic and community-based commentators analyse policy debates and new ideas for social and economic renewal in a wide range of areas including industry development, urban planning, health, housing, education and community services.

The book begins with a call for a social democratic transformation of the role of government. The following chapter, based on Don Dunstan's Whitlam Oration, offers us inspiration in the struggle for the pursuit of a more just and prosperous society. It opens up new political spaces for critiques of economic liberalism while offering the prospect of revitalising the debate surrounding democratic socialist ideas and practice.

REFERENCES

Abraham, M. 1998, 'Irrational numbers', *Australian*, p. 15.

ACCIRT 1999, *Australia at Work*, Prentice Hall, Sydney.

Amin, A. & Thrift, N. (eds) 1994, 'Living in the global', in *Globalization, Institutions and Regional Development in Europe*, Oxford University Press, Oxford.

Broomhill, R., Genoff, R., Juniper, J. & Spoehr, J. 1995, ' The debt made us do it', in *Altered States – The Impact of Free Market Policies on the Australian States, Adelaide*, eds John Spoehr & Ray Broomhill, University of Adelaide, Centre for Labour Studies.

Dawkins, P., Freebairn, J., Garnaut, R., Keating, M., & Richardson, C. 1998, 'Dear John: how to create more jobs', *Australian*, October 26, p. 13.

Industry Commission 1996, *State, Territory and Local Government Assistance to Industry – Draft Report*, July.

Hutton, W. 1997, *The State To Come*, Vintage, London.

Jessop, B. 1994, 'Post Fordism and the State', in *Post Fordism: A Reader*, ed Ash Amin, Blackwell, Oxford.

Korten, D. C. 1998, 'The global economy: Can it be fixed?', paper presented to the Bellerive/Globe International Conference on Policing the Global Economy, Geneva, March 23–24.

Langmore, J. & Quiggin, J. 1995, *Work for All – Full Employment in the Nineties*, Melbourne University Press, Melbourne.

National Economics 1998, *State of the Regions*, report to the Australian Local Government Association 1998 Regional Cooperation and Development Forum.

Martin, H.P. & Schumann, H. 1996, *The Global Trap – Globalization and the Assault on Democracy and Prosperity*, Zed Books, London.

Parkin, A. 1992, 'Looking back on the Bannon decade', in *The Bannon Decade – The Politics of Restraint in South Australia*, eds Andrew Parkin & Allan Patience, Allen & Unwin, Sydney.

Spoehr, J. & Broomhill, R. (eds) 1995, *Altered States – The Impact of Free Market Policies on the Australian States*, University of Adelaide, Centre for Labour Studies, Adelaide.

Spoehr, J. 1990, *From Lending Binge to Credit Squeeze – The Failure of Bank and Finance Sector Deregulation*, United Trades and Labor Council of SA, Adelaide.

NOTES

1   The use of the term 'contract state' was first comprehensively applied in Australia by John Alford and Deidre O'Neil (1995) in their edited study on the emergence of the 'contract state' in Victoria.

2   During the 1998 federal election campaign, Coalition leader John Howard used the term 'relaxed and comfortable' to describe how Australians would feel under a future Coalition government.

CHAPTER 2

WE INTERVENE
OR WE SINK

DON DUNSTAN

In charting a course for the Labour movement it is vital to do two things – to analyse and understand the dynamics of the national and global economies, and to do so with a proper appreciation of our history of dealing with the problems of a market economy.

Labor in this country never accepted the utopianism of the Marxist philosophy of dialectical and historical materialism, which held as doctrine, that if all privately owned means of production, distribution and exchange were expropriated to the state, then all cause of exploitation, all existence of classes in society would end – that the state would in fact wither away and there would be left merely an 'administration' – a process owned and controlled by the whole people. In Engel's lyrical phrases towards the end of his pamphlet, *Socialism: Utopian and Scientific*, 'Men, at last masters of their own mode of socialisation become thereby masters of nature, masters of themselves – free ... It is humanity's leap from the realm of necessity into the realm of freedom.' Marx and Engels were severely limited by their training in Hegelian philosophy and so were led to reject the minor proposals for Utopian experiments – spewing out the Utopian minnows and swallowing a Utopian whale! And as we have seen, the systems founded upon their ideas have collapsed spectacularly after periods – not of freedom – but of bitter repression characterised by the inhumane and cruel regimes from Stalin to Ceaucescu, by the emergence of institutionalised privilege within the system, and by a failure to provide to citizens, either the services, the goods or the environment, which as human beings they were entitled to demand.

But the great misfortune that has occurred on the collapse of the system is that Soviet citizens, denied under their controlled education system, an adequate knowledge of economic history, have tended, in sweeping away a centrally planned system to leave the market and the growth of a capitalist economy largely uncontrolled, resulting in the very problems which gave rise to the whole communist theory in the first place.

The conditions of uncontrolled capitalism were for the working people of England and Western Europe and, later, of America, some of the worst conditions known in modern human history. It is quite clear that the treatment of such people by those who saw the only virtue in economic activity as being economic gain and riches, came to be widely condemned. Marx's chapters on the Working Day and Industrial Capital in *Das Kapital* were vivid and accurate, and taken from official records which set out the pitiful conditions workers laboured under through uncontrolled capitalist development. The chaotic conditions now developing and providing misery for millions in former Soviet countries, and where a class of crooked exploiters of that chaos is emerging, were utterly predictable.

Labor in Australia and Social Democrats everywhere have always accepted that we had to maintain the discipline of the market place as the only effective general method of meeting the needs and wants of the people. It was accepted that we would maintain a *rentier* society in which development occurred and capital for development raised by borrowing money and paying interest or dividends on it. But in those circumstances we have also rightly believed that the state must intervene to ensure that market forces do not prevent the social needs of the community being met.

And Labor has been clear what those social needs are. In this respect I recount from my political memoirs, my own reasons for entering political life in Australia and working through the Australian Labor Party as the great reform party of this country.

I believed then, as now, that it is possible to build a society in which individual citizens have security of food, shelter, work and services; which will celebrate their worth as individuals and that peoples are made many, their differences their strength, where all citizens have an equal and effective say in their own governance and an opportunity to participate in and to influence decisions affecting their lives. It is possible to build a social democracy – a dynamic society in which there would be equal opportunity to act creatively within a social context..

Dunstan 1981

It has been Labor's proud accomplishment that great progress has been made in Australia towards the goal of that kind of society. Those accomplishments are now all under severe threat.

We are faced presently with political opponents who have adopted a policy which largely advocates and advances unrestricted capitalism. We have schools of economics where the history of economic thought is but little taught, and universities where history studies are regarded as economically unimportant. The return to the advocacy of simplistic *laissez faire* policies in economics belies the experience of history. Rational economic analysis has been superseded by the economic teaching of the Chicago School, calling itself oxymoronically 'economic rationalism'. Their thesis is: that faced with a globalised economy we must reduce government provision of services to the barest minimum and ensure that services as far as they are provided to the community, whether public utilities or social services, are only provided through organisations operating in the interests of private profit. Further, that competition and the operations of an unregulated market can produce the optimum pattern of production and development of our resources, and that in the interests of incentive and international competition the public sector must eschew raising money by way of loan for long-term infrastructure development. And finally, redistributive taxes must disappear as a means of social justice and that we must totally deny ourselves in all circumstances of the fiscal flexibility to run a deficit budget.

To examine and expose the absurdity as well as the enormity of the above I need to revisit history a little. I do so, not to advocate the politics of nostalgia, but to show that there have been proven ways to deal with the wrongs, the social injustices, the failures of the private sector to produce needed results. We have established institutions which continue to serve the purpose of serving the community. The institutions and policies of the past can be adapted and built upon to make sensible policy to deal with current challenges. It is vital to learn the lessons of history. If we don't know where we have come from, we cannot make intelligent judgments about where we are going.

Firstly, there are considerable limitations to relying on the unregulated market place alone to produce optimal results socially and economically. Keynes exposed the baselessness of *laissez-faire* theories in his lectures in 1924 and 1926 entitled 'The End Of Laissez Faire'. As he said then:

The world is not so governed from above that private and social interest always coincide. It is not so managed here below that in practice they coincide. It is not a correct deduction from the principles of economics that enlightened self-interest always operates in the public interest. Nor is it true that self-interest generally is enlightened; more often individuals acting separately to promote their own ends are too ignorant or too weak to attain even these. Experience does not show that individuals when they make up a social unit are always less clear-sighted than when they act separately.

Historically, Labor (and at times as I shall show, non-Labor) governments have proved it necessary to intervene in various ways in the market place to ensure socially desirable results. Sometimes the traditionally termed Left–Right divide in these interventions has been characterised as a fight between public and private ownership. This is quite an inadequate analysis. Labor has not held the view that there is any particular virtue of the public over the private, as long as the needs of the public are adequately served. In the case of basic services, this means delivery on the basis of social justice. Intervention involves more than nationalising assets or undertakings. It may involve meeting community needs by setting up a publicly owned enterprise where the private sector will not operate. A government enterprise may itself force better service by competition with the private sector. Intervention may also occur through licensing or regulating, or it may mean providing assistance to the average citizen to place them on an equal footing with wealthier interests. The forms of intervention are necessarily empirically chosen, but as I shall show through the example of South Australia, intervention has been vital to produce a productive, fair and just society.

BUILDING INDUSTRIES FOR THE FUTURE

South Australia, at its founding in 1836, had poorer natural timber resources than any other state. Much of the woodland that existed was quickly cleared in the province's first forty years. Timber was used for fuel, fencing, in the mines, or often wasted. In 1875 the *Forest Act* was passed and a board appointed. The board established a number of nurseries and trialed many species of trees. Outstanding results were obtained from *Pinus radiata* which appeared to grow more rapidly here than in its native environment. In 1883 the board was replaced by the first government Woods and Forests Department in the British Empire, and in 1902 the first state sawmill established. Australia's first course in Forestry was initiated in 1910 and became a degree course at Adelaide University where it remained until its transfer to Canberra in 1925. Problems with die-back in *Pinus radiata* were solved by the use of zinc sulphate and bipartisan political support led to the establishment of a large state-owned forestry industry. While 'thinnings' provided a considerable resource, calls to the private sector to make use of it drew no response by 1930. It was only much later that private sector operations began to be involved. The state sector has remained the driving force in providing a timber resource to this state, and of proving the usefulness of a non-indigenous timber to communities elsewhere in Australia. By 1975, state-owned forest in South Australia covered 73 000 odd hectares; the private sector forest 16 500 hectares; the department had created 6000 jobs and paid $19.9m to state revenue. The whole enterprise had provided a cheap timber resource which has been a factor in keeping housing costs down. The state forestry enterprise is on the Olsen government's privatisation list. The whole pine forestry enterprise and the pine resource of this nation would not exist if the task had been left to the enterprise of the private sector – indeed we would not have developed *Pinus radiata* as a resource in this country at all.

THE IMPORTANCE OF POWER

In the depression years of the 1930s, this state was a largely agricultural area with a declining mining sector and small production in motor body building and was hardest hit of all mainland states. Adult male unemployment stood at 33 per cent and farmers were walking off farms in droves. Former Premier Tom Playford who presided over the tough administration of the Lands Department was determined to see that the economy diversified and industrial development undertaken. That would not happen on its own – the necessary infrastructure support must be created. At that time the electricity supply was provided by the Adelaide Electric Supply Company, a body incorporated by statute but wholly privately owned and financed, and which in its early years had regularly paid a dividend of 12 per cent, and although this fell to seven per cent for a time was restored to ten per cent by the time Playford was embarking on his industrialisation program. Electricity production in South Australia was also subject to uncertainty resulting from problems with coal supply from the eastern states. However, the company refused to be involved in the costly exercise of exploiting the soft brown coal deposits within South Australia, where supplies could be assured. Nor would they do special deals to assist the establishment of industry here. To deal with these issues Playford appointed a royal commission into the South Australian electricity industry. The key findings of the commission were:

(11) It is essential that the Company should endeavour to fix its charges for industrial purposes at a rate sufficiently low to meet competition for industry by other states.

(18) Over the period of the last 24 years the Company has paid in dividends and interest nearly 2 000 000 pounds more than if the Treasury rates had been paid. Future capital costs at Treasury rates would result in reduced capital costs and so lower charges.

(19) An adequate supply of electricity at reasonable charges is of the utmost importance to the community particularly for the development of industry. The interests of the public in this regard have so far been largely at the discretion of the directors of the Company. Its claim that the public interest has been and will continue to be studied tends to conflict with the directors' duty to shareholders.

(20) The Company supplies a large area of the more densely populated portion of the state. If it is to expand its area of supply or refuse supply entirely in accordance with its own decisions founded to a large extent on its own interests the development and coordination on sound lines of electricity supplies throughout the state will be very difficult.

Accordingly, the royal commission recommended that the assets of the company be acquired and that from then on electricity supplies be the responsibility of a statutory trust owned by the state. With the support of the Labor Party, Tom Playford pushed the legislation through the parliament, and the Electricity Trust of South Australia (ETSA) was established. ETSA became a vital factor in South Australia's economy, owning and running its own soft brown coal mine at Leigh Creek, financing its operations through semi-governmental loans, providing good deals for industry, and ensuring not only reasonable costs to consumers generally, but also ensuring delivery to the poor and the remote on a basis of social justice. The royal commission had pinpointed the fact that there is real conflict between the aims required of directors of companies in the private sector: their primary concern must be to maximise returns to their shareholders, while the board members of a publicly owned trust must endeavour to operate efficiently and economically with the best return possible to the government, subject to the objective of providing the service that the community needs on a just and reasonable basis.

ETSA is a government undertaking which has been wholly funded by its clients – the consumers of electricity. It has not cost the Treasury a thing. It has, as was proposed by the royal commission, raised capital for its plant and development by loans approved at semi-governmental loan rates which are well below the cost of dividends sought by investors in share capital. Those loans have been largely repaid, so the users have already paid the capital cost of the undertaking. ETSA has not only paid the government the normal state taxes and charges and a notional amount equal to Commonwealth Company tax, but also amounts as 'dividends' as John Spoehr and John Quiggin illustrate in their chapter on the ETSA privatisation debate.

Mr Olsen, at the last election solemnly promised the people that there would be no sale of ETSA. After the election he became aware, he says, that the auditor-general had warned that the state risked the loss of up to $1 billion in Commonwealth 'Competition Policy' compliance payments if it retained ETSA in public ownership. This warning was communicated to the Premier's Department at least four months prior to the election. Mr Olsen, on the other hand, had assured us with a straight face, that he was 'unaware of' the auditor-general's warnings before the election. Essentially the warning involved certain identifiable risks to the state's finances arising from South Australia's participation in the national electricity grid.

Mr Olsen claimed that this 'new' advice meant that the electricity undertaking must be sold. If it is sold this does not mean that South Australia has conformed to national competition policy. Mr Olsen has said that we are facing a loss of over $1 billion. How? The auditor-general has said no more than that the risks identified in the negotiations for South Australia's entering the national grid must be properly managed.

The electricity undertaking will still be subject to the requirements of national competition policy and subject to competition in the operation of the national grid. Non-compliance will affect South Australia's payments whether the undertaking is privately or publicly owned. Privatising is not a condition of national competition policy, so the question of compliance with that policy and the effect of non-compliance still faces us. Compliance with the policy has been on track for some time. The auditor-general is merely warning us that non-compliance will carry costs.

In addition, the raising of share capital for the electricity undertaking will mean that dividends to shareholders will have to be paid by the consumers. For shares to be sold they must have the promise of dividends at a higher level than semi-government bond interest payments. As the Playford royal commission pointed out, electricity charges would be much lower if governmental loan rates are payable for capital development rather than dividends on shares.

So all Mr Olsen is doing with his ploy to make the Treasury books look better (with a one-off addition of money from the sale) is to increase substantially rather than decrease, the effective burden on South Australian taxpayers. For the taxpayers and the consumers of electricity are the same people – virtually every South Australian is a consumer of electricity.

This course of action is being pursued as an ideological commitment to privately provided services – a belief that social needs will inevitably be met if everything has as its sole object the making of private profit. The results of that belief are only too vividly demonstrated in New Zealand. There the previously government-controlled electricity supply in Auckland was transferred to a corporation where four of the nine-member board were elected by the consumers but the control was in the hands of a five-member majority. The task of the latter group was to prepare the undertaking for a share float where those five would thereafter be elected by the subscribing shareholders. This was the road to effective privatisation after which the government had no control, and the consumers merely token and minority input. The regime of management, which subsequently operated to reduce costs of the undertaking, saw capital investment in upgrading the existing works put on hold and the staff and maintenance reduced in order to make the share float attractive. Subsequently, the entire electricity network system collapsed disastrously when core elements of the network burnt out, causing massive losses to business and private individuals, and dire discomfort to Auckland residents.

The negative consequences of government withdrawal from strategic intervention in the economy have been amply demonstrated in South Australia in recent times, as the mismanagement of our most precious commodity, water, illustrates. South Australia is the driest state in the driest continent on earth. The provision of water has always been a matter of crucial public importance. It was one of the great successes of the Playford regime that we did it so effectively. While other states have, from time to time, had to impose water use restrictions, this has not occurred in South Australia since 1957. The Engineering and Water Supply Department of South Australia took over the whole water and waste water management of the state – not operating on a series of local water boards but operating under central management and using governmental loan money to build efficient catchments to store and supply natural rainfall and to hold waters pumped from the Murray River. Pipelines were built across the state and water was made available to the poor and the remote at prices they could afford. The rating system ensured that the more valuable properties subsidised the poor and the average householder. Adelaide was effectively sewered ahead of any other Australian capital. The only criticism that could be made of the water supply was that it was alkaline and its taste was unattractive.

When Gough Whitlam commenced his program to improve the quality of life in the poorer suburbs of metropolitan areas by offering money to the states under section 96 grants to undertake sewerage of their unsewered urban areas, he argued that South Australia didn't qualify for these grants because Adelaide was already fully sewered. I agreed that we were, but also made the point that we suffered a different disability – our water needed filtration. Following one of those arguments he and I seemed to have with considerable regularity, it was agreed that we could get money to commence the filtration of the metropolitan water supply. The department operated efficiently but was subjected to repeated scrutiny of its operations, and its structure and management went through revision from time to time to ensure that that efficiency was maintained.

Enter Mr Brown. No mention was made at the 1993 elections of any move to privatise the water supply. Mr Brown embarked however upon a program that he said would deliver great results to South Australia. The plant and equipment of the water supply would still continue to be owned by SA Water – the department downsized and 'corporatised' – but the management of water and waste water would be outsourced to a consortium which would bring international expertise to South Australia. It was claimed that the consortium would base its research operations for the whole of South East Asia and the Pacific in South Australia and tender for projects for water and waste water in that region to provide employment for South Australians. It would also be required to draw on South Australian suppliers of equipment in the areas of international operations, thus creating a great water industry for

South Australia. There was also a provision that within twelve months the company formed by the successful consortium would become at least 60 per cent Australian-owned.

The successful consortium was formed by Thames Water (one of Mrs Thatcher's privatisation beneficiaries), Compagnie Generale des Eaux (a French corporation also running privatised water operations throughout the world) and Kinhill, a local engineering company well known in Australia. The details of the contract with the consortium were not revealed publicly on the grounds of 'commercial confidentiality'. That excuse in relation to state assets and money is entirely without justification. When South Australia made an agreement with BHP to set up an iron-ore smelter and later a steelworks and shipyard at Whyalla it was done under indenture properly scrutinised by parliament. In due course the agreement with the United Water consortium was leaked. It did not contain the assurances and enforceable guarantees Mr Brown had claimed for it. The company, United Water, has not only made no attempt to involve Australian ownership, but the Kinhill interest has been sold to another international company. The management of South Australia's water supply is now entirely in foreign hands, and hands which are concerned only with the provision of returns to their foreign shareholders and the payment of much larger salaries to their executives than are ever paid in the public sector. Water is not cheaper – its price has gone up more than inflation. Employment in the industry has significantly decreased. The reality is that, far from the principal companies working through their local subsidiary here to attract contracts in developing countries in our region, they are in fact in competition with that company for contracts. The research facilities of the principal companies have not been transferred from France or England. The great water industry is a mirage.

The objectives of the Engineering and Water Supply Department were not to make money for the government (although at the time of outsourcing it was providing revenue above its costs). The key objectives of the department were:

- to ensure optimal use of the state's water resources for the greatest benefit of the community
- provision of water-related services to the extent and standards established by government in consultation with the community
- efficient provision of services

- full recovery of expenses from recipients of services except where explicit government subsidies apply
- provision of services in a socially responsible manner.

It can be seen that those objectives are very different from a concentration on maximising returns to foreign shareholders. And the result? In 1997 the reduced maintenance staff of United Water failed adequately to monitor the operation of the sewage treatment plant at Bolivar. A sewerage pond gate leaked, was not repaired, and for weeks raw sewerage poured into the bio-mass and killed it. The sewerage system, functioning efficiently until then, ceased to function, and Adelaide, which can normally proudly boast its clean air by comparison with other cities, had its north-western suburbs – nearly one-third of the whole metropolitan area – invaded by the smell of hydrogen sulphide for months. Was the great international expertise of our foreign management able to cure the problem? No, they had to call back a former E&WS employee who had shifted interstate and whose investigation put the blame squarely on them.

Clearly the substitution of maximising returns to shareholders for the stated aims of social justice in the function of public utilities in South Australia does not produce optimal outcomes, let alone just outcomes. Nor can the market place always satisfy economic demand or community need, as the development of the arts industry in South Australia illustrates. To secure a nationally recognised centre for the arts, it was necessary to develop a multifaceted employment base for workers in the arts industry. In order to give actors and technicians reasonable employment opportunities, we needed to have, amongst other things, a film industry. There was no film industry in South Australia in the mid-1970s. With the help and advice of Phillip Adams I was shown the basis on which we might proceed. We set up, not the limited film units attached to the government which some other states had done, but a statutory corporation with full entrepreneurial capacity. The corporation was given exclusive rights to making government films which provided it with a basic run of work and enabled it to go into production itself to demonstrate to producers the advantages of working here. Historically it became a prime factor in the re-establishment of the Australian film industry which had been destroyed by the uncontrolled market place – the dumping of American films here in theatre chains controlled by the internationals. Among the early successes of the venture were – *Sunday Too Far Away*,

Picnic at Hanging Rock, *The Last Wave*, *Storm Boy* and *Breaker Morant*.

None of that would have happened but for the community enterprise in setting up the corporation. And its success has persisted. The film, *Shine*, of significant international acclaim and commercial success, was made by Scott Hicks, a man who got his start at the Film Corporation and who chose to make *Shine* with the corporation. Those who say that this would have happened as the result of market place initiative are absurdly refusing the evidence.

MOVING BEYOND THE DEBT FETISH

In planning our future it serves neither economic efficiency nor social justice to destroy the institutions that society from experience has created, and that are efficiently meeting the social needs of the community. They are not impediments to progress but foundations for it. But the economic rationalists and Mr Olsen adduce a further argument for selling off the family silver. That argument centres around debt. According to its proponents we must rid ourselves of all public debt. Australia, like most of the market economies of the world, has, for sound reasons, borrowed money to build its infrastructure. We would not have a town hall, a general post office, roads and railways, schools and hospitals if we had not done this. It is always important, of course, to be careful to ensure that the level of borrowing does not get to a stage where debt can not be serviced from current income. People are constantly encouraged to borrow money for the major investment most families make in their lives – the purchase of a home. Rightly, banks do not lend to those who require more than 30 per cent of their current income to service the interest and principal repayments on their home loans. Nor should South Australia's debt servicing go beyond that figure, and in fact it is far lower, as Paul Chapman and John Spoehr illustrate in their chapter on public debt. But with public debt it must be remembered that loans do not have to be repaid within thirty years. Public infrastructure lasts far longer and services normally not one, but three or four generations. It is reasonable, and has always been the practice, that the cost of major public works is shared over the generations that make use of it. Loans can be rolled over and in history have been.

The debt burden in South Australia in world terms is quite low. At the time the Liberal government took over in 1993, after the so-called State Bank disaster, the public debt of South Australia in real terms was less than in Tom Playford's day or in the early years of my government. We reduced it quite markedly by selling our railways to the Commonwealth and having the Commonwealth assume the railway debt obligation.

Are we really in a desperate situation? In 1992 South Australia's public debt per capita was less than that in Belgium, Italy, Ireland, Greece, Netherlands, Canada, Spain, Austria, United States, United Kingdom, Denmark and France, and well below the average. That position obtains today. Why do we have to have a fire sale of community assets, including assets which are revenue-producing? It is only for ideological and irrational reasons that this is proposed.

We must retain our right to intervene through state action to create undertakings to temper the market place or to remedy its failures. Moreover, we must retain our right to exercise community judgment about the depredations of international footloose capital and investment in relation to meeting the social aims of justice and ensuring a fair go in our community. We must retain the protections which have been historically built to insulate the working people and to right the wrongs of the disadvantaged and underprivileged. All of these are now under threat. Witness the fact that South Australia had, under successive governments, the most extensive public housing program of any state. With over 30 per cent of housing built from public funds, the state government kept housing, and therefore industrial and business costs, low and provided South Australia with both the most affordable housing and the lowest housing prices in the market place. The federal and state economic rationalists are reducing the program and are selling off the public housing stock. In South Australia we had under my government the best health and hospitals establishment in Australia and the best public education system. Both have been starved of the money needed to maintain those standards. The hospital system, once our proud boast, is in dire straits. And it is no excuse to say that the tax base has declined and we can't afford it. An Australia which sees more and more of its people falling below the poverty line while its wealthy have increased their wealth exponentially is not taxing fairly. Wealthy Australians gained a huge benefit from the introduction of imputation credits on franked-share dividends. In the first six years of the operation of dividend imputation, shareholders received tax benefits amounting to around $13 billion. The well-off are also avoiding tax by the use of private family trusts. Overwhelmingly these are fictional arrangements where family members have income notionally distributed to them to bring them below a tax threshold.

The intervention that I have been concerned about in this chapter is intervention for social justice. The present state governments and the federal government are certainly intervening – intervening to demolish rights and protections of citizens to make them completely subject to the greedy manipulators of the market place, to have governments abdicate the role of providing social justice and to prevent intervention in it in the future. I will end with three examples of this.

The Aboriginal people of this country have been denied their rights from the beginning of European settlement here. The repeated instruction of the Westminster government that the land rights of Aborigines must be preserved was ignored in every state. Aboriginal people have at last established in law that they have land rights here, and that Australia was not, contrary to the judgement of Mr Justice Blackburn, 'terra nullius'. The courts have ruled that, in most cases of title in Australia, the clock cannot be turned back. But in lands not alienated from the Crown with exclusive land rights to the grantee (as in the case of freehold land), if there is a remaining connection with the land, Aboriginal descendants of the original owners have rights to it subject to the specific, overriding rights granted under leaseholds. This is a right established by Aboriginal citizens in law – our law. Mr Howard proposes to effectively deprive them of this right in support of pastoral lessees – to grant to this group of people, an enhancement of their existing rights – and Mr Howard describes this as a 'fair compromise'. He's saying to Aboriginal people: 'I'll fix the market place and fix it against you'. Although he insists he's not racist, he feels that it's appropriate to extinguish the rights of Aboriginal people to negotiate in relation to their land not provided for in the pastoral leases, in order to support the impoverished pastoral interests of this country.

To the trades' unions he says he is not against trades unions. Nevertheless, he appears determined to destroy them for the 'benefit' of the working class who can subsequently negotiate on his kind of level playing field. His level playing field displays an unevenness of Himalayan proportions. But his catch cry: 'The market place will provide' prevails. The protection of workers' conditions established by years of struggle must go out the window. Like the Labor movement, the trades' unions in this country were established because of the unfairness of the unregulated market place and the rapacity of employers driven by the same motive as is now hallowed by economic rationalism; that is, the greed to maximise personal returns regardless of the needs of others. The government has clearly involved itself with private interests in a plot to break the Maritime Union of Australia (MUA) – and the way they have achieved this is just a beginning. Mr Howard says he is not against unionists or individual members of the MUA, but he hails as 'historic' the unloading of cargo by non-union labour. He strongly argues for citizens' obeying the law, but backs with the taxpayer's money, a scam by which Patrick Stevedores have emptied their subsidiary companies of assets, so that when waterside workers have sought orders against unlawful dismissal, as they are entitled to do, they find that the companies they are suing are empty shells. The Howard government is pursuing Mr Skase over that kind of crookery but involves itself in a similar kind of operation.

Most threatening of all is the Howard government's enthusiastic involvement in the plans for the Multilateral Agreement on Investment (MAI), an agreement negotiated under the auspices of the OECD. The core concept of the agreement is 'non-discrimination' – non-discrimination in relation to foreign investors and the operations of multinational corporations. Under the MAI, foreign investors and their investments must not be treated less favourably than the host country's investors. Investment-related payments, including capital, profits, and dividends must be permitted to move freely to and from the host country. Investors and key personnel must be granted permission to enter and stay to work in support of the investment. Requirements specific only to foreign investors are to be prohibited. The OECD offers as an example of a prohibited requirement, a minimum target of export goods and services. However, not mentioned by the OECD is that a requirement for job creation would also be prohibited. And this is what is proposed.

Furthermore, an international tribunal will be established with the power to enforce the treaty, which allows an investor to sue a state or one state to sue another. However, no state can sue an investor!

While it is possible under negotiations for the treaty to have exceptions from its provisions, the treaty requires that these be rolled back over a limited period and ultimately eliminated. Once a party to the treaty, we are committed to it for at least five years. If we withdraw after this period however, its effects in relation to dealings enacted during the five-year period will be in force for a further fifteen years. In the context of exclusions, the Howard government has made an exception in regard to indigenous people. Whether this exclusion can in fact cover the range of Aboriginal rights is unclear.

The treaty typically has opposed legal enforceability of labour rights, and as far as the environment is concerned, the treaty has no legally enforceable provisions. The treaty appears to be fulfilling the claim made for it by the President of the United States Council for International Business that 'The MAI is an agreement by governments protecting international investors and their investments and [is designed]to liberalise regimes. We will oppose any and all measures to create or even imply obligations by governments or business related to environment or labor.'

Mr Howard and his government already appear determined to demolish protection checks and balances against market place injustice in Australia. By adopting the MAI, we will be cast into a position where there are no internationally enforceable means to limit market place injustices, no representative or accountable body with any power, no protection of any kind. This proposal will hand us over to the international financial market place with no recourse and no say in what happens. We have already seen that the International Monetary Fund (IMF) insists that developing countries must institute economic rationalist policies in order to continue receiving ongoing support for their loan structures. Such policies have abolished help for the poor and the underprivileged, downsized government services, abolished redistributive taxation and imposed flat-rate value-added taxes. Only the prospect of a total breakdown in society in Indonesia has forced the IMF to modify its demands there, and to admit reluctantly that a problem is created by the selling-down of the currencies of South East Asia. The rupiah has, in this uncontrolled market place, clearly been sold down to far below its real value – with dire effects on the lives of ordinary people in Indonesia. And it is into this uncontrolled environment it is proposed that we move the Australian economy. Such a move would be a total abdication of democratic rights to the manipulators of the market place.

Mr Howard is inviting us to pursue the policy of lemmings – to rush over a cliff and find ourselves free in the market place, in a sea in which we will drown.

Our response must be that we will intervene; we will intervene to retain our right to a say in our own future, to temper the market place by action, to provide services and social justice, to retain institutional safeguards and provide needed development in the community interest, for we know that we intervene or we sink.

REFERENCES

Dunstan, D. 1981 *Felicia – The Political Memoirs of Don Dunstan*, Macmillan, South Melbourne, Vic.

PART 1

TRENDS AND ISSUES IN THE CONTRACT STATE

CHAPTER 3

STATE OF STAGNATION, INVESTMENT REQUIRED

FRANK GELBER AND MATTHEW JONES

INTRODUCTION

South Australia is experiencing economic stagnation with low economic growth generating low employment growth. The resulting weakness of job opportunities has caused high net interstate migration outflow with lower population growth feeding back into lower growth in demand for services. Much of the workforce in general, and young people in particular, have to leave the state in order to get a good job. The consequence is a state unable to provide sufficient jobs for its people and as a result losing population (see figure 1).

South Australia's employment growth averaged only 0.8 per cent per annum, 1.0 per cent below Australia's during the ten-year period to June 1997 (see table 1). Why has South Australian employment growth been so low? Employment growth is output growth less productivity growth.

- Output growth was 0.7 per cent lower with a –0.7 per cent contribution to lower South Australian employment growth. Of that there was:
  - A negative contribution of 0.1 per cent due to industry structure, reflecting the extent to which industries with relatively lower growth are relatively concentrated in South Australia; that is, if South Australian industries grew at the average Australian rate, what would South Australian growth be? The outcome is a minor negative to growth.
  - A negative contribution of 0.6 per cent due to relative industry performance indicating weak growth by comparison with the rest of Australia. This is the main contribution to weak growth.

- Productivity is a double-edged sword, with strong productivity adding to competitiveness but reducing employment for a given output growth. Productivity growth was faster than the Australian average, contributing to the weak employment growth with a negative contribution of 0.3 per cent. Of that:
  □ Industry structure contributed negatively to employment growth by 0.3 per cent; that is, South Australian industry has a relative concentration of industries where productivity improvements have been greater.
  □ There was a negligible contribution from relative industry performance.

Table 1 demonstrates that the main contribution to South Australia's low employment growth is weak economic growth, although augmented by greater productivity improvements in industries concentrated in South Australia.

TABLE 1: OUTPUT AND EMPLOYMENT GROWTH INDICATORS 1987–97 (ANNUAL AVERAGE PER CENT)

	South Australia	Australia	Difference
Employment growth	**0.8**	**1.8**	**–1.0**
• Output growth	2.6	3.3	–0.7
• Contribution to SA growth – industry structure		–	–0.1
• Contribution to SA growth – relative industry performance	–	–	–0.6
• Productivity growth	1.8	1.5	
Contributions to South Australian employment growth			–0.3
• Contribution to SA employment growth – industry structure			–0.3
• Contribution to SA employment growth – relative industry performance	–	–	0.0

*The contributions to growth are calculated as follows: the contribution of 'industry structure' is the growth rates that the State economy would have achieved if the growth rates of its constituent industries had equalled the relevant Australian industry growth rates. The contribution of 'relative industry performance' is the difference between the 'industry structure' contribution and the actual growth rate of the state economy. This then reflects that part of the state's growth which is due to its industries performing differently to the Australian average.

Over the decade, South Australia has been unable to attract sufficient investment to generate the industrial capacity required to underwrite higher economic growth. Here too, South Australia has under-performed.

There are no quick solutions. The usual approach taken by other states has been to attract investment in whatever is the fashionable industry at the time – currently, call centres – where competition between states is fierce. Often, however, it is better to build on the strengths of the existing industrial base. For South Australia, alternative opportunities exist in building on the current industrial structures and infrastructure, focusing on the shift from primary to secondary processing and strengthening industrial clusters. The question as to whether South Australia continues to stagnate will hinge on the ability to attract enough investment to develop its industrial base.

One element of this is the provision of infrastructure, effectively reducing the costs to industry and improving the financial feasibility of development projects in the state. In this respect South Australia has been hampered for almost a decade by the consequences of the financial excesses of the 1980s. It is a careful balancing act. The state government's temptation is to play the financially respectable citizen and appease the ratings agencies (and also reduce the cost of funds) by reducing expenditure, but the cost of this is to constrain infrastructure spending. And we include here constraints on training expenditure aimed at building the skills base of the workforce, perhaps targeted towards developing sectors.

In terms of the impact of the overall economic environment, Australia is at the end of a mining boom and there will be limited opportunities for the state to exploit secondary processing of minerals. Already there is substantial over-capacity in base metals, and external conditions will continue to affect demand. Current problems in agriculture are less fundamental. The potential to develop secondary processing is still present. The strongest potential remains in the manufacturing sector.

In the short run, the recent improvement in Australia's competitiveness has improved the financial feasibility of projects. The depreciation in the Australian dollar has improved the competitiveness of both exports and import-competing industries, providing an opportunity to expand markets and develop new ones. But manufacturing has struggled with low growth for over thirty years, and we regard this as a problem for

South Australia. At the national level we regard the current account deficit as a symptom of structural imbalance in the Australian economy. Australia's manufacturing sector is too small. At some stage in the next decade, there will be a phase of growth in manufacturing Australia-wide. South Australia must position itself to ride this growth phase.

South Australia will find it difficult to break out of the vicious cycle of under-investment and poor employment growth when part of the problem exists at a national level as well. A relatively small state will find it hard to overcome national problems. The eastern states in particular, have shown themselves able to attract alternative investment in new industry sectors and South Australia needs to follow by example. The main tasks for South Australia are to attract more investment and to build up the industrial and employment base of the state.

THE STATE SUFFERS FROM LOW ECONOMIC GROWTH

South Australia's economic growth has been under-performing when compared to the rest of the nation. Lower growth means lower employment growth. Lower employment growth feeds back into lower growth in demand for goods and services. Overall growth has averaged 2.6 per cent over the ten years to 1997 compared to 3.3 per cent for Australia. South Australia has under-performed, relative to Australia, in 13 (of the 18) Australian and New Zealand Standard Industry Classification (ANZSIC) industry sectors representing 62.4 per cent of total state product as can be seen in table 2. The five sectors which have performed above average (agriculture, manufacturing, electricity, gas and water, transport and storage, and communications) make up the remaining 37.6 per cent of gross state product (GSP) but only 29.1 per cent of total state employment. The fastest growing sectors are in less labour-intensive sectors of the workforce.

VICTORIA SUFFERED SIMILAR PROBLEMS BUT APPEARS TO BE OVERCOMING THEM . . .

South Australia does not compare well with Victoria, a state which has suffered many similar economic problems. Victoria, like South Australia, was hit by the 1990 to 1992 recession as well as suffering financial and debt crises. Overall Victorian economic growth through the decade was a little lower than South Australia's at 2.4 per cent, while Victoria's employment growth was only slightly stronger at 1.1 per cent for the period, although weaker than the national average. Nevertheless,

TABLE 2: SOUTH AUSTRALIA – OUTPUT, EMPLOYMENT AND PRODUCTIVITY GROWTH 1987–97

Industry Sectors	Proportions of Employment – 1997		Annual Employment Growth 1987–97		Proportions of GDP – 1997		Real Annual Growth 1987–97		Productivity – Absolute GDP per employee in 1997		Productivity Growth 1987–97	
	SA %	Aus %	SA %	Aus %	SA %	Aus %	SA %	Aus %	SA	Aus	SA %	Aus %
Agriculture, forestry, fishing	7.5	5.1	0.6	0.1	5.6	4.0	2.4	2.4	36.9	42.6	1.8	2.3
Mining	0.5	1.0	-9.1	-1.5	2.1	4.3	-0.8	4.6	201.1	222.9	9.2	6.2
Manufacturing	14.9	13.5	-0.2	0.0	19.5	13.6	3.9	2.0	65.2	54.2	4.1	2.0
Electricity, gas and water	1.0	0.8	-5.4	-6.7	3.4	3.2	4.5	2.7	177.1	213.8	10.5	10.1
Construction	5.4	7.0	-1.7	1.6	5.4	6.2	0.6	2.4	50.3	47.9	2.4	0.9
Wholesale trade	5.2	5.9	-0.7	1.3	7.9	10.2	2.1	2.4	76.3	93.1	2.8	2.3
Retail trade	14.2	14.8	1.5	2.4	7.1	7.0	1.0	2.5	25.1	25.5	-0.4	0.1
Accommodation, cafes and restaurants	4.5	4.8	4.3	4.9	1.4	1.8	0.9	2.4	15.9	20.7	-3.2	-1.3
Transport and storage	4.1	4.7	0.2	0.4	5.8	5.4	4.6	3.6	71.5	61.7	4.4	3.2
Communication	1.6	2.0	-2.6	0.9	3.3	3.9	8.3	2.4	100.3	107.7	11.3	9.2
Finance and insurance	3.3	3.8	-0.3	0.3	5.4	5.8	4.0	4.7	82.2	82.2	4.3	4.3
Property and business services	9.2	9.9	4.8	5.6	6.9	8.2	2.9	4.2	37.6	44.7	-1.8	-1.3
Government administration and defence	3.7	4.4	1.7	1.0	2.6	3.3	1.0	2.2	36.0	40.7	-0.7	1.2
Education	7.5	7.0	1.7	2.1	4.7	4.2	2.0	2.5	31.8	32.2	0.3	0.4
Health and community services	11.2	9.2	1.7	2.8	6.5	5.2	3.0	3.6	29.0	30.1	1.3	0.8
Cultural and recreational services	2.2	2.3	2.2	3.9	1.6	2.0	-0.2	3.2	35.4	47.0	-2.3	-0.7
Personal and other services	4.0	3.8	1.7	2.9	2.1	1.8	1.9	3.8	26.4	25.7	0.3	0.9
Ownership of dwellings	n/a	n/a	n/a	n/a	n/a	n/a	1.4	3.1	n/a	n/a	n/a	n/a
TOTAL	100.0	1.0	0.8	1.8	100.0	1.0	2.6	3.3	50.0	53.8	1.7	1.5

FIGURE 1: NET INTERSTATE MIGRATION

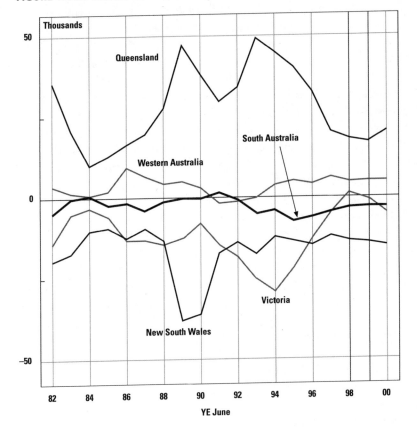

Source: BIS Shrapnel, ABS data

Victoria is recovering better, with growth over the past five years to 1998[1] of 3.6 per cent against a weak 3.0 per cent in South Australia. Over the same period, the national economy grew by 4.3 per cent per annum.

BUT IN SOUTH AUSTRALIA THE RESULT IS LOW EMPLOYMENT GROWTH ...

The key element of South Australia's stagnation is dismal employment growth (table 2). Employment growth over the ten-year period to 1997 has averaged 0.8 per cent, less than half the Australian average of 1.8 per cent. This is true across nearly all sectors with only three (agriculture, electricity, gas and water and government administration) out-performing the national average. Some sectors have been particularly poor with communications employment shrinking at an average of 2.6 per cent despite the national growth average. Of the productive sectors, mining, construction and wholesale trade employment are all notably poor performers, shrinking over the ten-year period, while all the sectors except mining, grew at the national level.

Even South Australia's largest industry sector, manufacturing, shrank by an annualised 0.2 per cent in employment terms against zero growth across the country. On the services side, education, health and community services and cultural and recreational services have all under-performed.

South Australian employment is not only growing slowly but has been doing so from a low base. Despite eight years of economic growth, South Australia has still not recovered its employment level to that achieved at the peak, before the recession, in 1990. Across Australia, total employment is estimated for 1998 to be 7.9 per cent above the 1990 peak. But more importantly, full-time employment growth has stalled. Full-time employment in South Australia is about nine per cent below its pre-recession peak, compared to only one per cent in total Australia.

AND HIGH UNEMPLOYMENT ...

A consequence of poor levels of employment creation is a stubbornly high unemployment rate which has remained well above the national average (table 3). The state hit an unemployment rate of 10.3 per cent in August 1998 against 8.2 per cent nationally. But South Australia's unemployment rate would have been considerably worse had there not been net interstate emigration and had not many people been encouraged to leave the workforce, as is reflected in the state's low participation rate (60.8 per cent compared to the national average of 64.2 per cent). In addition, there remain strong indications that there is a high proportion of people with jobs who are under-employed. The productivity figures in some sectors reinforce this notion when compared to the national average.

TABLE 3: SOUTH AUSTRALIAN LABOUR FORCE AND EMPLOYMENT

	Civilians 15 and over		Labour Force		Partici-pation Rate	Employed Persons		Unem-ploym't Rate
	000s	% Ch	000s	% Ch	%	000s	% Ch	%
1988	1108	1.4	677	1.6	61.1	619	1.8	8.6
1989	1118	0.9	699	3.1	62.5	644	4.0	7.8
1990	1131	1.1	710	1.6	62.8	659	2.2	7.2
1991	1143	1.1	717	1.0	62.7	649	−1.5	9.5
1992	1153	0.9	710	−0.9	61.6	624	−3.8	12.1
1993	1159	0.5	713	0.3	61.5	638	2.2	10.5
1994	1165	0.6	713	0.0	61.2	638	0.0	10.5
1995	1170	0.5	726	1.8	62.0	656	2.8	9.6
1996	1176	0.5	727	0.1	61.8	858	0.3	9.4
1997	1183	0.6	729	0.3	61.6	659	0.2	9.6
Forecasts								
1998	1192	0.8	739	1.4	62.0	668	1.4	9.6
1999	1201	0.8	747	1.1	62.2	680	1.8	8.9
2000	1210	0.7	765	2.4	63.2	704	3.5	7.9
2001	1219	0.7	778	1.7	63.8	712	1.1	8.4
2002	1227	0.6	772	−0.8	62.9	697	−2.1	9.7
2007	1264	0.6	815	1.1	64.5	746	1.4	8.5
2012	1294	0.5	874	1.4	67.5	817	1.8	6.5

WITH THE RESULT BEING THAT PEOPLE LEAVE

If employment growth had not been so weak, people would have been able to stay in the state rather than migrate. The total population of South Australia is around 1.5 million (mid-1997) and has been growing at or under 0.5 per cent for the last five years which is considerably below the equivalent five-year Australian population growth figure of 1.2 per cent. But South Australia's low population growth figure is not the result of poor immigration or a low birth rate but is due to large out-flows of people to the other states (figure 1).

The level of net interstate migration has offset strong population growth and overseas migration (figure 2). People are less mobile in Australia than they are, for instance, in the United States and this is

FIGURE 2: SA COMPONENTS OF POPULATION INCREASE

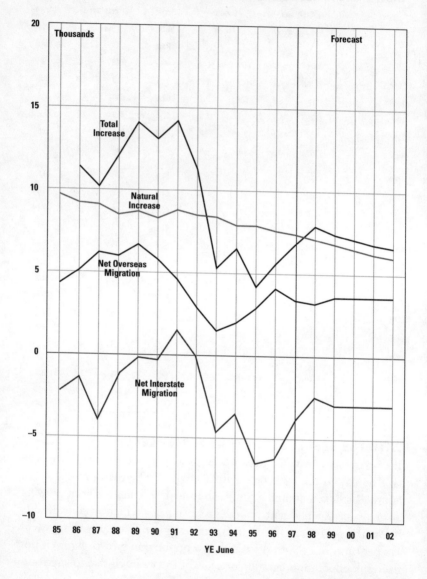

Source: ABS and BIS Shrapnel

mainly due to the tyranny of distance which characterises a large, but sparsely populated country. Of course people have strong ties to their home state often related to family, friends and upbringing, thus making the idea of leaving difficult and unappealing. Nevertheless, people have been leaving the state and they do so because they have a stronger reason to leave rather than to stay to find work. In South Australia net interstate emigration has been continuing from the time of the financial crisis of the early 1990s. The problem has been a lack of employment opportunities and the result is that people have to travel beyond the boundaries of their home state for work.

SO WHAT IS THE CAUSE OF THE MALAISE?

South Australia's economic growth has under-performed Australia by 0.7 per cent, yet the state's employment growth has under-performed by 1.0 per cent. Why the difference and what is the connection? Employment growth is output growth less productivity growth. We examine the influences of aggregate output and productivity growth to understand why South Australia has under-performed.

. . . LOW GROWTH

Over the decade to 1997, South Australia grew by 2.6 per cent compared with an Australian average of 3.3 per cent (see table 1). What are the contributors to the economic growth shortfall? Lower economic growth has two components: firstly, industry structure and secondly, relative industry performance.

In terms of industry structure, the question centres on the extent to which stronger growth takes place in sectors of relative importance in South Australia. If the sectors are of a similar relative size, and if each sector grew at the same rate as the national average, the state aggregate rate would be the same or similar to the Australian rate. In the event, when tested we found a contribution of only –0.1 per cent to the growth shortfall. Industry structure was only a minor cause.

The lower South Australian growth is largely attributed to relative industry performance, with a negative contribution of 0.6 per cent. While the comparatively larger sectors (manufacturing, health and community services) performed well in terms of growth compared with the Australian average, many small sectors lost ground. Some sectors have been growing too slowly when compared to the rest of Australia.

... AND HIGHER AGGREGATE PRODUCTIVITY GROWTH

To a small extent, lower employment growth was a attributable to a negative contribution of 0.3 per cent (table 1), related to faster productivity growth in South Australia.

Like economic growth, productivity has two components: firstly, industry structure and secondly, relative industry performance. The –0.3 per cent difference indicated in table 1 is due to industry structure with a negligible contribution from relative industry performance. South Australia has a concentration of industries where more rapid productivity improvements have been achieved.

The key is that four sectors – manufacturing, retail trade, health and community services and personal and other services have achieved relatively rapid productivity improvements both in South Australia and Australia-wide (table 2). All of these represent a greater proportion of South Australian gross product than they do Australia-wide. Hence the higher aggregate productivity growth and lower employment growth in South Australia.

These four sectors represent a cross-section of industry and employ almost half of the workforce. Of these sectors, manufacturing is the only sector with above-average productivity. The others are relatively labour-intensive. However because of its size, manufacturing employed 14.9 per cent of the South Australian workforce in 1997 against 13.5 per cent nationally. The machinery and equipment manufacturing subsector, which makes up 51 per cent of this sector's gross product, and is dominated by vehicle manufacturing, has experienced considerable restructuring and industry change in the last ten years, so accelerating the state's productivity performance. Retailing employed 14.3 per cent of the workforce in 1997 with only 7.1 per cent of gross state product while health employed 11.3 per cent with only 6.5 per cent of gross state product.

Combined, these four sectors represent 35.2 per cent of South Australian industry but employ 44.3 per cent of the workforce. High productivity growth in these sectors has underpinned the strong industry structure contribution to South Australia's productivity growth and hence lower employment growth.

TOO LITTLE INVESTMENT HAS UNDERCUT GROWTH . . .

Over the decade, South Australia has been unable to attract sufficient investment to generate the industrial capacity required to underwrite higher growth. Both private and public investment as a percentage of gross state product have been below the Australian average, as table 4 shows.

TABLE 4: TOTAL INVESTMENT IN SOUTH AUSTRALIA AND AUSTRALIA AS A PERCENTAGE OF GROSS STATE PRODUCT (1996/97)

	Dwellings	Non-dwelling construction	Equipment	Total private	General gov'ment	Public enterprises
South Australia	3.0	2.2	7.2	13.4	1.9	2.3
Australia	4.3	3.5	7.8	16.7	1.8	2.7

Source: ABS, BIS Shrapnel

Private investment in South Australia has performed relatively poorly in the decade to 1997 (see figure 3), with growth often driven by single large projects. These projects are often narrowly based and focused on a small number of industries which do not bring wider benefits.

Poor levels of private investment (figure 4) keep economic growth low and inhibit employment growth. This only serves to limit the expansion of consumer demand for basic necessities such as private housing. The housing market has displayed a number of unusual features. For instance between 1989 and 1994, while the rest of the country suffered a recession, South Australia was experiencing very mild upturns and downturn trends in its building cycle. However, immediately after this period, a build-up of excess stock depressed housing commencements which halved over the four-year period to 1996/97 to the lowest levels since the 1950s. The state government has responded with a revised subsidy scheme to encourage first-time buyers, and this has boosted activity a little. But with land and house prices lower in South Australia than in other states, it only serves to emphasise that the real problem is security and availability of employment and not housing cost. The real problem for the housing market is lack of demand, again associated with net interstate emigration and slow employment growth.

FIGURE 3: STATE PRIVATE INVESTMENT

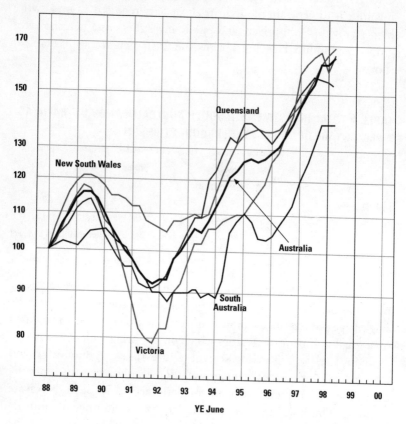

YE June

Source: BIS Shrapnel, ABS data

Public investment has dwindled as the state government has focused on balancing the budget rather than developing an infrastructure base. Public sector investment by the state government has shrunk across most sectors. For instance, the government has virtually withdrawn from investment in public sector dwellings with only 59 in 1996/97 way down from 1524 in 1989/90. In health and education, investment levels are dominated by a few large projects with both sectors showing decline in terms of new construction. During 1995/96, activity halved in the education sector and in 1994/95, new commencements declined some 51 per cent in the health sector to the lowest levels since 1982/83.

FIGURE 4: SOUTH AUSTRALIA – PRIVATE INVESTMENT

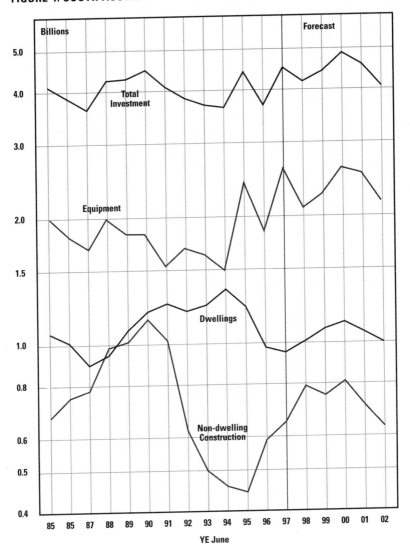

Source ABS and BIS Shrapnel

The one bright spot has been the readiness of the government to spend on transport infrastructure, including new roads, highways and public transport projects. In 1996/97, spending in the roads sector was some 20 per cent up on 1992/93 levels.

Nevertheless, spending will be constrained both by the limited expansion of the tax base which will remain dependent on population growth, and a continuing determination to reduce state debt.

In this context the federal government's and state governments' approach of privatising public assets in order to reduce public debt, by selling a portion of the assets to overseas interests, diverts effort from the problem. The size of the state debt is an overhang from the financial excesses of the late 1980s. But a continuing preoccupation with it is damaging the state's long-run economic development. Too much time, effort and resources are being spent on the reduction in total debt and too little on building an infrastructure base. What is needed is a careful balance between the conflicting goals of sound financial management and state economic development.

THE STATE'S PROBLEMS ARE THOSE OF AUSTRALIA – THE NEED TO DEVELOP MANUFACTURING AND STOP THE WORSENING CURRENT ACCOUNT DEFICIT ...

South Australia's experience is typical of the nation's wider problems relating to the development of a strong and diversified manufacturing base in order to remove pressure on the current account deficit (CAD). It is a problem visible at the national level through a balance of payments constraint and a current account deficit cycling around 4.5 per cent of GDP. The deficit remains Australia's number one economic problem and this macro-level problem begins at the state and local level, with South Australia a classic example.

The fundamental issue is that after approximately two to three years of solid economic growth, domestic industry runs out of capacity in key manufacturing sectors. Imports then escalate to fill the gap left by constrained domestic production. A blow-out in the current account deficit leads to a monetary tightening, as the government attempts to slow the growth in domestic demand and imports. A domestic economic downturn follows, with lower imports and an improvement in the current account deficit. Monetary policy is then eased leading to a pick-up in demand and stronger economic growth after which the cycle begins again.

The reason for industry constraints, escalating imports and associated current account/foreign debt problems is insufficient investment in the manufacturing sector, both now and over the past 25 years. Manufactures are the fastest-growing component of world merchandise trade, and account for around 85 per cent of Australia's merchandise imports, but only 28 per cent of merchandise exports (both including simply transformed goods and metals commodities). The ability of the manufacturing sector to either increase exports and/or substitute for imports is critical to the trade account/current account deficit, and, given the usual policy response, is therefore critical to sustained economic growth.

South Australia's large manufacturing sector at 19.5 per cent of GSP in 1997 (against 13.7 per cent nationally) conceals its heavy dependence on the machinery and equipment subsector at 50.8 per cent of total manufacturing in 1997, as opposed to 27.2 per cent for all Australia. The other strong manufacturing subsector is secondary processing of food and beverage. Without these subsectors, South Australia's manufacturing performance would be dismal. With the exception of Queensland, South Australia's manufacturing turnover per person employed is the lowest (in the 1996–97 ABS Manufacturing Survey) of any state.

Australia's manufacturing industry has ample spare capacity now, but the current pause in investment means that, apart from minerals processing, there is little new capacity coming on stream. Moderate-to-strong growth in manufacturing product forecast for the next two years will soon use up current spare capacity, and production constraints in some key sectors are likely to emerge by the end of the decade. The underlying structural problem of insufficient capacity remains. Manufacturing industry plays a vital role in the economy and its performance has an impact on the current account.

The Australian economy is now a more open economy, with both exports and imports increasing their shares of GDP, particularly over the last decade. In 1984/85 exports constituted 12.3 per cent of GDP while imports accounted for 18.2 per cent of GDP. In 1997/98 exports comprised 24.6 per cent of GDP while imports accounted for 26.0 per cent. (Note all shares calculated in constant 1989/90 prices.) The cause of this has largely related to government policy as well as widening consumer tastes for overseas products.

These trends constitute a major impact on the balance of payments, summarised as follows:

- The extreme cyclicality of the goods and services balance (exports minus imports).
- The underlying trend in the goods and services balance showing a long-term structural improvement through the 1990s.
- The long-term deterioration in the net income and transfers deficit, which mainly represents net interest payments on the increasing foreign debt and repatriated profits on foreign equity in Australian businesses. The dominance of the net income deficit on the overall current account deficit underlines the fact that the goods and services balance needs a substantial long-term improvement to offset the increasing income and transfers deficit.

AND REVERSE THE GROWING STRUCTURAL IMBALANCE . . .

Industry across Australia as well as in South Australia needs investment, and the flow of interest payments, repatriated profits and dividend income overseas is symptomatic of this need to source investment from overseas due to insufficient domestic funds.

Offsetting the long-term deterioration in the current account deficit have been structural and efficiency improvements to the Australian economy over the past decade. This has triggered long-term improvements to the goods and services balance, a situation likely to continue. However, a significant part of this improvement in net exports leaks back overseas in the form of repatriated profits, dividends and retained earnings, offset only partially by profits earned by Australian companies in overseas operations. In 1997/98 this was estimated at $6.2 billion compared to an estimated $14.2 billion repatriated from Australia. These net equity service payments of $8.8 billion represented 1.5 per cent of GDP, while net interest payments accounted for 2.3 per cent of GDP.

A LOWER CURRENCY IS A GOOD TIME TO BEGIN TO REBUILD MANUFACTURING . . .

Manufacturing industry has now been given the opportunity it needs to build much needed capacity. The recent depreciation in the Australian dollar has improved the competitiveness of manufacturing exporters, providing them with an opportunity to expand market share and develop new markets. In particular, the fall in the dollar has improved competitiveness against US and European competitors for export markets in South East Asia. But the general currency re-alignment that accompanied the depreciation of the dollar has also given manufacturers the opportunity to build domestic market share through import substitution.

Improved competitiveness has already lifted manufacturers' margins, encouraging them to develop overseas markets as well as focus on domestic opportunities. Improved margins should also encourage a more determined approach to expanding capacity. Nevertheless, whereas strong margins may encourage expansion, dependence on a fluctuating exchange rate will not encourage long-term thinking. At US76 cents, the Australian dollar was overvalued making it difficult for industry to sell overseas, whereas at US60–65 cents this situation is transformed. But there remains the risk that this situation will be short-lived.

A strong manufacturing base needs a competitive currency, and a currency driven by world commodity prices will not always provide such competitiveness. Commodity prices are currently weak but, once they pick up, the impact on competitiveness could again hurt manufacturing. Clearly there are risks with expanding capacity, but improved margins offer the cushion, and greater competitiveness, the opportunity.

MANUFACTURING INDUSTRY INVESTMENT REMAINS SOUTH AUSTRALIA'S BEST SHORT-TO-MEDIUM-TERM SOLUTION

South Australia will find it difficult to break out of the vicious cycle of under-investment and poor employment growth when many of the components of the problem exist not just at a state level but at a national level as well. A relatively small state will find it hard to overcome national problems. The other states, particularly the eastern states, have shown themselves able to attract alternative investment in new industry sectors, a road which South Australia needs to pursue as well.

The main task for South Australia is to attract more investment and build up the industrial and employment base. Given the high level of competition between the states in attracting business investment, the South Australian government has a limited ability to offer incentives to companies in order to attract them. This problem is compounded by the state's limited natural advantages in many industries and its remote location in relation to the bigger eastern states.

So the challenge for South Australia is to stop the rot in terms of sluggish employment growth, build on the state's strengths and to develop a skills base which will attract industry expansion back to the state. Infrastructure investment would be a key component of any economic development strategy, including improved road and rail links to the eastern states. In this context, the Alice Springs to Darwin rail link is an expensive red herring, missing the point in terms of industry investment. Instead, South Australia's manufacturing, which remains heavily dependent on one subsector, machinery and equipment, needs to develop a more diversified structure.

The presence of industry clusters in the state supporting manufacturing provides the base. The success of policy initiatives using that base to attract investment will determine whether South Australians will be able to find jobs at home or will continue to move interstate to seek suitable employment.

NOTE

1   The figure for 1998 is an estimate based on the latest available national accounts data.

CHAPTER 4

SOUTH AUSTRALIA'S POPULATION AT THE TURN OF THE CENTURY

GRAEME HUGO

INTRODUCTION

South Australia's population represents its most important resource, yet our understanding of how it is changing in the late 1990s and the implications of this change is limited. As the slowest growing of Australia's mainland states it is assumed that the population is a static and unchanging backdrop against which economic forces are played out. The truth is quite different. The state's people have changed substantially over the last 15 years and it is important for policy-makers to be aware of these changes and to anticipate likely future changes. All policy development should be designed to meet the needs of people, and a sound knowledge of how those people are changing is an essential ingredient for effective policy development and planning.

This chapter seeks to chart and explain the major changes which have taken place in the state. Impending change in the population and its likely implications are discussed. Firstly, an examination of the overall change in numbers of the population and the processes shaping that change is undertaken. The chapter then considers the changing characteristics of the South Australian population. Changes in relation to age structure, family structure and functioning, ethnicity, work/living arrangements, health and poverty are examined over the 1981–96 period and some indications of future trends are discussed. Thirdly, the chapter examines the changing spatial distribution of South Australia's and Adelaide's population. Throughout this discussion two themes are developed. It is argued that the state's population is changing in relation to its diversity: the population is becoming more diverse in its characteristics and segmentation. This has considerable implications for planning and service provision. Secondly, it is argued that there is increasing inequality within the South Australian population. In common with other OECD populations, South Australia has seen a hollowing-out of the middle class and a growth of both high-income and low-income households, especially the latter. This presents many new challenges to policy-makers but also represents a significant shift in South Australian society.

The bulk of information used here is derived from the Australian Census of Population and Housing. I will especially compare the situations in 1981 and 1996 which were census years. Australia has one of the most accurate censuses of all countries, but it is somewhat limited in the socially relevant data it collects. Most such information is collected in other ABS data collections, particularly the ABS annual publication on Australian social trends.

POPULATION GROWTH IN SOUTH AUSTRALIA

Although Australia's current rate of population growth (around 1.2 per cent per annum) is less than half that of the boom years of the 1950s and 1960s, it remains among the highest in the OECD nations and not much lower than the world average (1.48 per cent). Nevertheless, in the nineties, South Australia's rate of population growth (around 0.4 per cent per annum) has been lower than the other mainland states and territories. The state's population grew faster than that of the nation during the long boom period of the post-war period up to the early 1970s and grew more slowly than the national average in the subsequent period when Australia's overall growth was reduced. Hence both the Australian post-war population boom and the subsequent bust were exaggerated in South Australia, and this has had a number of significant effects on South Australia's population structure. It also should be noted that South Australia's share of the national population has declined from 9.2 per cent in 1961 to 8.1 per cent in 1996.[1]

It is important to disaggregate these trends in terms of the processes actually creating them. Population growth is the function of three basic processes: mortality, fertility and migration, and each of these needs to be considered separately. The components of the state's population growth show a clear pattern. Natural increase (that is, births minus deaths) has changed very little in South Australia over the post-war period in absolute terms (although not as a rate). On the other hand, net migration (excess of migration gains over losses) gain was consistently high during the boom period but subsequently has fallen dramatically with there even being more people moving out of the state than into it in a number of years.

As in the rest of Australia there has been a major improvement in mortality in South Australia over the post-war period. Between 1947 and 1996, Australian males have increased their average span of life from 66.67 years to 75.22 (8.55 years) and women from 70.65 to 81.05 (10.4 years). This has been a substantial improvement involving both major therapeutic advances and lifestyle developments. One of the major features of this has been an improvement in life expectancy among the older population. Between 1970–72 and 1996 the improvement was 4.22 years for men and 4.23 years for women, due largely to an unanticipated greater degree of survival of our elderly population. This has proved especially significant in South Australia where, as is shown later, the aged are a larger proportion of the resident population than in the other states. Moreover, service providers have been dealt a 'double whammy' since not only have they been confronted with a situation in which there is an unexpectedly large number of older people surviving but the survivors are 'sicker' than in the past. The people 'rescued from death' by the new developments in medicine who previously would have died, are generally not rescued in full health. Accordingly, the incidence of illness and disability among the elderly population has increased. Hence table 1 indicates that the incidence of disability and hardship among the older population has increased in Australia between 1981 and 1993. From a South Australian perspective it is worth noting that South Australians over a long period have had above-average life expectancy compared with Australia as a whole (Hugo 1983).

Turning to fertility, the data show a sharp increase in fertility in the state during the early post-war years taking the average number of children per woman up to over three. This was followed by a steep decline between the early 1960s and the mid-1970s which saw fertility fall below replacement level (total fertility rate [TFR] of 2.1).[2] The subsequent period however has seen stability in fertility levels around a TFR of 1.7. This level of fertility is somewhat lower than that of Australia as a whole and there has been a consistent pattern of South Australia's fertility being substantially lower than the national level. For example in 1996, 1986 and 1976 the state levels were 1.75, 1.76 and 1.86 respectively compared to 1.8, 1.87 and 2.05 nationally. While it is clear that the current fertility is low by historical standards it is significantly higher than in many European countries.

TABLE 1: PROPORTION OF THE POPULATION WITH DISABILITIES AND HANDICAPS

Age group (years)	1981 %	1988 %	1993 %
With a disability			
65–74	35.5	44.2	48.8
75 & over	53.1	63.5	66.7
All people	13.2	15.6	18.0
With a handicap			
65–74	24.1	35.0	39.3
75 & over	45.4	58.1	61.0
All people	8.6	13.0	14.2

Source: Australian Bureau of Statistics 1995, p.55

The causes of the decline and subsequent stability of fertility at a low level are complex. They relate to a number of significant changes in South Australian society. On the one hand, the position of women has changed considerably. This is reflected for example, in an increase in participation in the workforce outside the home among the state's women. This is depicted in figure 1 which shows clearly how the level of participation has increased at all ages since World War II but especially in the child-bearing and post-child-bearing years. Only between 1991 and 1996 has there been a decline, and this is undoubtedly due to some 'discouraged-worker' effect in the down-turn of that period. Similarly figure 2 shows a substantial increase in participation in the upper years of secondary school and post-school education among Australian young women over the post-war period.

The trends in figures 1 and 2 are both a cause and consequence of low fertility in the state. There are also other factors involved. The incidence of abortion in South Australia since the liberalisation of abortion laws in the early seventies indicates that in recent times there has been a consistent pattern of around one in five pregnancies in the state resulting in an abortion. Clearly abortion is being used as a form of contraception as well as a way of protecting the rights of women. There is thus a need for improvement in birth control education, although a 1995 survey showed that 66.7 per cent of Australian women aged between 18 and 49 were taking some form of contraceptive (ABS 1998, p.30). The

FIGURE 1: SOUTH AUSTRALIA: FEMALE LABOUR FORCE PARTICIPATION RATES BY AGE, 1911–96

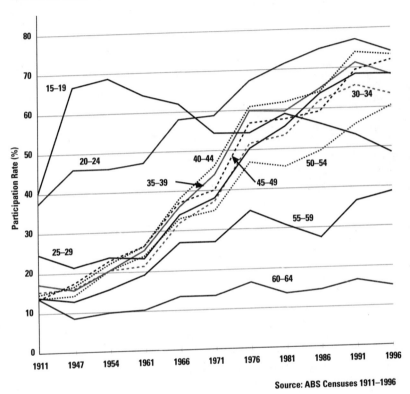

Source: ABS Censuses 1911–1996

introduction of the contraceptive pill in the early 1960s undoubtedly has been of great importance in providing women with the ability to control the number of children they have and when they have them.

Net migration has been the most volatile element in the state's population growth. This comprises two components: the net gain or loss in exchanges with other states and territories and the net migration from overseas. Both elements were substantial in the state's population gains in the quarter century following the war. Nevertheless, net migration with other states has been negative for most of the last quarter century and international migration net gains are much smaller than they were in the 1950s and 1960s.

FIGURE 2: AUSTRALIA: PER CENT OF MALES AND FEMALES AGED 15–19 IN FULL-TIME EDUCATION, 1947–1996

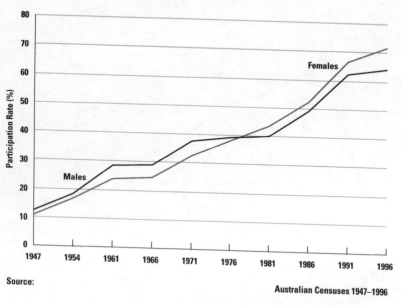

Source:

Australian Censuses 1947–1996

The pattern is especially striking with respect to interstate migration. Bell (1997a) has analysed recent trends in this movement and figure 3 shows that interstate migration net gains were recorded in the 1947–66 and 1971–96 periods with consistent net losses being experienced subsequently.

In the last inter-censal period the net losses reached record proportions with a net loss of 21 016 persons in 1991–96. As with other states, South Australia's net losses have been to Queensland. The downturn in the state's economy since the fall of the State Bank has been a major factor in the record outflow of South Australians. Moreover the flow has been selective of particular groups (Bell 1997a):

- young adults aged 15–29, especially young women
- to a lesser extent those aged 40–64
- predominantly singles and couple families
- overseas born (especially those born in mainly English-speaking countries) over-represented; most of them had been in Adelaide a fairly long time

FIGURE 3: SOUTH AUSTRALIA: COMPONENTS OF POPULATION CHANGE, 1947–54 TO 1991–96

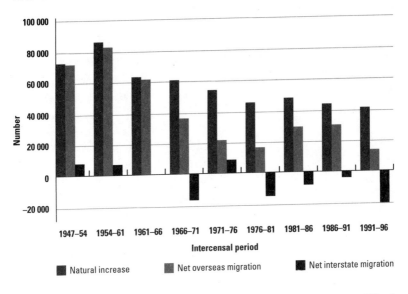

Source: Bell 1997b, p.6

- the largest net outflows were of professionals, managers, sales and service workers and clerks
- substantial net losses of those in the middle ($30 000–$50 000 per annum) and high-income groups (more than $50 000) and gains of households earning below $14 000 per annum.

Hence, the effect of the net loss interstate was amplified by the fact that it disproportionally contained the young workforce and economically productive groups.

Turning to international migration, figure 3 shows a slightly different pattern with heavy gains in the 1947–71 period being replaced with smaller gains over the next quarter century. Table 2 shows the pattern of national and state net gain of migrants from overseas. This shows a clear pattern not only of reduction in the overall intake, but also in the proportion of the national intake coming to live in South Australia. In recent years this has fallen below four per cent, substantially below its current share of the national population (eight per cent).

Indeed the reduction in international migration net gain has meant that, in the mid-nineties, for the first time since World War I, the net overseas migration gain has not been enough to compensate for the net loss of people through interstate migration.

TABLE 2: NET OVERSEAS IMMIGRATION*, TOTAL AUSTRALIA AND SOUTH AUSTRALIA, 1966–97

Year (ending Dec 31)	Australia	South Australia	SA percentage of Australian net migration gain
1966–70	643 351	64 766	10.1
1971–75	343 372	28 169	8.2
1976–80	293 860	10 517	3.6
1981–85	419 297	27 733	6.6
1986–90	591 770	26 570	4.5
1991–95	411 630	17 420	4.2
1996–97	182 529	6851	3.8

*Overseas immigration: 1966–73 = Permanent movement

1974–97 = Permanent and long-term movement

Source: ABS Overseas Arrivals and Departures Bulletins and Australian Demographic Statistics Quarterlies, various issues

The pattern of international migration has greatly shaped the ethnic composition of the state's population. The fact that the state received more than its proportion of migrant settlers in the period 1947–71 and substantially less than its share subsequently, has meant that groups dominant in the early post-war national intake (for example British, Greeks, Italians, Poles, Dutch, etc.) are over-represented in the contemporary population, while those which have dominated more recent migrant flows (New Zealanders, Chinese, Filipinos, Malaysians, Indians, Hong Kong-born) are substantially under-represented. Indeed 1996 was an interesting year from the perspective that for the first time since 1954, South Australia had a smaller proportion of its population born overseas (21.2 per cent) than was the situation for the nation as a whole (21.8 per cent). Of the eight largest overseas-born groups in South Australia in 1996, only the Vietnamese-born population grew over the last five years while seven declined. The latter was due to the dying-off of some of the ageing migrants from Europe who had moved to the state in the 1950s and 1960s, the re-migration of these interstate (Bell 1997a) or who returned to their home country as they grew older (Hugo 1994).

International migration has had a profound effect on the composition of the state's population. Despite the downturn in the level of migration, the post-war transition to a multicultural society is evident in table 3. This indicates that in 1947, 93.3 per cent of the state's population was born in Australia and more than 98.6 per cent born in an English-speaking country, but by 1996 these proportions had been reduced to 75.5 and 85.4 per cent respectively. The table clearly shows how in recent years the UK/Ireland and other European-born groups have experienced decline in numbers compared with massive growth in the 1947–76 period. While the Asian-born group has grown significantly since 1976, this has been both upon a small base and has been significantly slower than in other mainland states. Only the Vietnamese-born have grown strongly to number more than 10 000 and they are under-represented compared with the Australian-born as are all Asian-born groups. In 1996 almost three-quarters of the state's migrants (73.2 per cent) had been in Australia since before 1981, and 46.4 per

TABLE 3: SOUTH AUSTRALIA: BIRTHPLACE OF POPULATION 1947, 1976, 1986, 1991 AND 1996

Birthplace	1947	1986	1991	1996	Per cent change			
					1947–76	1976–86	1986–91	1991–96
Australia	602 521	1 029 470	1 065 286	1 077 533	+57.9	+8.0	+3.5	+1.1
	(93.3%)	(76.5%)	(76.2%)	(75.5%)				
New Zealand	1459	8287	10 020	9681	+180.9	+102.2	+21.0	–3.4
	0.2	0.6	0.7	0.7				
UK/Eire	32 718	146 403	145 440	131 624	+382.6	–7.3	–0.7	–9.5
	5.1	10.9	10.4	9.2				
Other Europe	6687	105 462	106 618	101 118	+1625.8	–8.6	+1.1	–5.2
	1.0	7.8	7.6	7.1				
Asia	1443	23 309	32 720	37 386	+448.6	+194.4	+40.4	+14.3
	0.2	1.7	2.3	2.6				
Other	1085	33 014	38 661	70 594	+680.5	+289.9	+17.1	+82.6
	0.2	2.5	2.8	4.9				

Source: ABS, 1947, 1976, 1986, 1991 and 1996 Censuses

cent are aged 50 years or over compared with 27.9 per cent of the total state population. Accordingly, there has been a reduction in the numbers of South Australians unable to speak English at all or who cannot speak it well: from 18.1 per cent in 1981 to 17.7 per cent in 1996.

Many of the overseas-born have a distinctive spatial distribution (Hugo 1993; Beer & Cutler 1995; ABS 1997a) and with the overseas-born disproportionally concentrated in the Adelaide metropolitan area and within Adelaide, some groups are significantly concentrated. For example, figure 4 shows the distribution of the mainly English-speaking-country origin migrants (predominantly from the UK and Ireland) and they are strongly concentrated in the northern, and to a lesser extent, southern suburbs developed in the 1960s and 1970s when the peak migration of this group occurred. The distribution of those from non-English-speaking countries however, is quite different, with a more east-west distribution reflecting the preference of these groups for market-gardening land along the River Torrens, and the then-cheap rental housing of the inner suburbs in the 1950s and 1960s. Hence, Italians have settled along the Torrens west and east of the city, Greeks in the western and southern suburbs, Vietnamese in the north east, etc.

CHANGING AGE STRUCTURE

The demographic trends outlined above have had profound effects on the age structure of South Australia. This is important because the level and nature of demand for virtually all goods and services is influenced by the state's age structure. The declines in fertility and immigration discussed above have meant that South Australia's population was younger than that of the nation in the 1950s and 1960s when Australia had a young population, but also that the state's population was older than the nation in the 1980s and 1990s when Australia's population has been ageing. South Australia, as a result of its lower fertility, disproportionately low immigration gain and net interstate migration loss has an older population than that of the nation as a whole with 13.8 per cent aged 65 years or over in 1996 compared with 12.0 per cent nationally. Moreover, the state received a disproportionately large number of young adult, interstate and international migrants in the 1950s and 1960s. Most of these have remained in South Australia and 'aged in place' resulting in an exacerbation of the national ageing trend in the state. This is reflected in figure 5 which shows the age structure of the state in several census years since the war and the projected population in 2011. This indicates how

FIGURE 4: POPULATION DISTRIBUTION OF THE MAINLY ENGLISH-SPEAKING OVERSEAS-BORN IN ADELAIDE, 1996

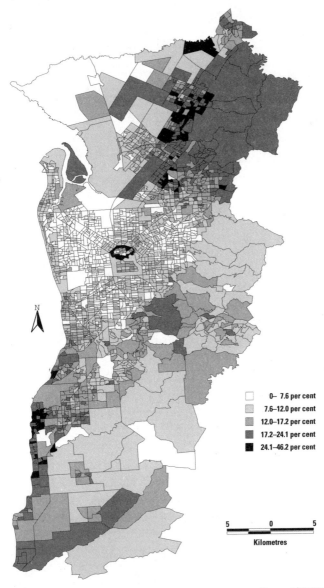

0– 7.6 per cent
7.6–12.0 per cent
12.0–17.2 per cent
17.2–24.1 per cent
24.1–46.2 per cent

Kilometres

Source: ABS 1996 Census

FIGURE 5: SOUTH AUSTRALIA: AGE AND SEX STRUCTURE OF THE POPULATION, 1961–96 AND PROJECTED 2011

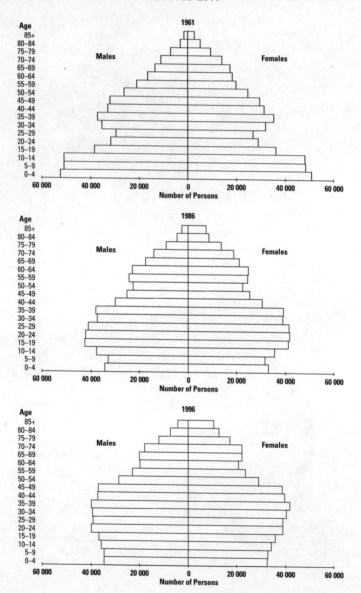

Source: ABS 1961–1996 Censuses and ABS 1996a

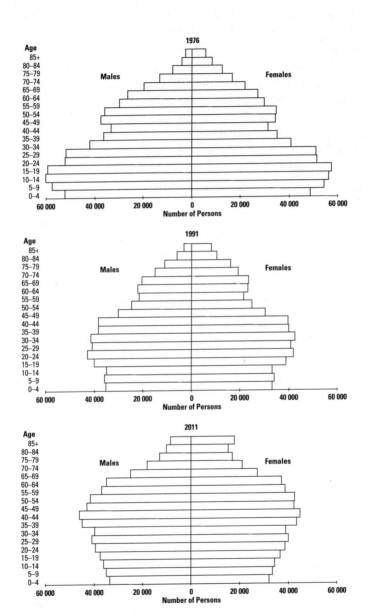

the pyramid has been dominated by the high fertility of the post-war baby boom years which has produced a 'bulge' which has moved inexorably up the age pyramid followed by the smaller numbers of the baby bust years born in the 1970s, 1980s and 1990s. Hence, the state's age structure is being transformed from a pyramid to a pillar in shape. This of course will mean considerable change in the number over time entering education, entering the workforce, needing housing etc.

The past, present and impending age structure situation in South Australia is shown in table 4 which shows that the state's median age has increased from 23.9 in 1911 to 35 currently and will be 43.2 by 2031. Meanwhile, the percentage aged 65 years and over has increased from 4.6 to 13.8 and will increase to 23.1 in 2031. The table shows that the ratio of dependent population (aged 0–14 and 65+) to that in the working ages (15–64) has in fact decreased progressively from 61.1 per cent in 1954 to 52.8 per cent currently and will continue to decrease to 49.9 per cent in 2011. Thereafter however, the passage of the baby-boom cohort into the older age groups will see a rapid growth of the dependency ratio in the population.

TABLE 4: SOUTH AUSTRALIA: SUMMARY MEASURES OF AGE AND SEX COMPOSITION 1911–96 AND PROJECTED MEASURES 2001–31

	Census Year								
	1911	1954	1976	1986	1991	1996	2001	2011	2031
DEPENDENCY RATIO (percentage of population 15–64 years)									
Youth (0–14 years)	48.3	46.6	41.2	33.1	31.8	31.3	29.2	26.7	26.8
Elderly (65 years and over)	7.3	14.4	14.2	17.4	18.9	21.2	21.2	23.1	37.3
Aged (85 years and over)	0.3	0.7	1.0	1.4	1.4	2.1	2.4	3.4	5.0
Total (0–14 and 65+)	55.6	61.1	55.3	50.5	50.7	52.8	50.4	49.9	64.1
MEDIAN AGE (years)	23.9	30.7	28.7	32.0	33.5	35.0	37.0	39.8	43.2
PERCENT AGED 65+	4.6	8.9	9.1	11.6	12.5	13.8	14.1	15.4	22.7
SEX RATIO (Males per 100 females)									
Age group (years)									
0–14	102.4	104.8	105.5	104.9	104.7	105.3	105.4	104.5	104.5
15–24	102.9	109.6	102.0	103.8	103.3	103.6	103.8	104.1	102.8
65 and over	96.4	80.0	66.9	71.9	74.3	74.6	77.0	79.6	81.3
85 and over	76.5	60.1	17.1	37.3	41.2	40.2	45.2	49.6	52.5
Total	104.4	102.7	99.3	97.9	97.4	96.8	98.3	98.1	96.9

Source: ABS 1911, 1954, 1976, 1986, 1991 and 1996 Censuses and ABS 1996a, p.84

Figure 6 shows that, in the middle of the second decade of next century, the number of elderly dependents will outnumber the number of children in the state for the first time in history. The ageing of the population has bought with it a change in the sex ratio of the population. While males outnumber females in the state in the entire period since the initiation of white settlement, this was changed in the mid-1970s when women now outnumber men.

FIGURE 6: ACTUAL AND PROJECTED YOUTH AND ELDERLY DEPENDENCY RATIOS, 1954–2031

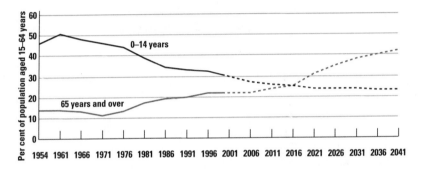

Source: ABS Censuses; ABS 1996a

While relative proportions between various age groups are important, the actual numbers are of particular significance since they are relevant to the numbers demanding particular types of services. Table 5 for example, shows what will happen to the number of persons in South Australia aged 0–14 years if current trends continue. This sees a progressive decrease over the next half century. Similarly with numbers aged 15–24 although a small increase is projected in the early years of next century.

On the other hand, the outlook for the aged population presented in table 6 shows a pattern of recent and impending consistent growth of the elderly although there will be a slow-down in the late 90s and first decade of the next century as the impact of the low-fertility years of the 1930s and early 1940s is felt. However, after 2011 the post-war baby-boom groups begin to pass age 65 and there will be rapid growth of the

TABLE 5: SOUTH AUSTRALIA: PROJECTED GROWTH OF DEPENDENT CHILD AND YOUTH POPULATION 1996–2051

Year	Age 0–14 No. (000)	Per cent	Age 15–24 No. (000)	Per cent
1996	294.1	20.7	195.1	13.7
2001	295.7	19.4	200.8	13.2
2006	291.5	18.6	205.4	13.1
2011	285.8	17.8	203.6	12.7
2021	280.2	16.8	198.8	11.9
2031	278.8	16.5	192.2	11.3
2041	272.9	15.9	192.3	11.2
2051	268.7	15.7	188.7	11.1

Source: ABS 1996 Census and ABS Projection Series C (ABS 1996a)

elderly population. A trend to note in table 6 is that there is a clear 'ageing of the aged' population in that the 'old-old' aged 75 and over are projected to grow faster than the 'young aged' between 65 and 74 years. This is due to the improved longevity of the older population discussed earlier and has implications for service provision, since the 75+ population are by far the heaviest users of health, welfare and specialised housing services for the aged. Hence the outlook is that, while the state's population as a whole is expected to grow by less than a fifth over the next 35 years, that of the elderly will almost double.

It is important to realise that while the elderly of today share some characteristics with the elderly of earlier and later generations, they differ from them because of the differences in the contexts which they have lived through. For example, when the baby boomers enter the older age groups, the average level of education of the elderly will be significantly higher than that of earlier generations. Despite the fact that unemployment has increased among mature members of the workforce, most current retirees have not suffered any significant period of unemployment, so have been able to accumulate assets such as houses.

Table 7 shows how migrants are forming an increasingly large proportion of our older population. This is because the bulk of the state's migrant population arrived as young adults in the 1950s and 1960s and are now ageing into the older age groups. Hence an increasing proportion of our elderly will not be able to speak English fluently, have

TABLE 6: SOUTH AUSTRALIA: ACTUAL AND PROJECTED CHANGE IN THE OLDER POPULATION 1981–96, 2001–31

Age group	Number (in thousands)								% change		
	1981*	1986*	1991*	1996*	2001	2006	2011	2031	1991–1996	1996–2006	2006–2031
55–64	125.0	131.7	123.4	122.4	147.2	181.0	203.5	214.9	−1.2	+47.9	+18.7
65–74	86.5	96.2	105.5	112.6	112.2	113.0	130.4	198.2	+6.7	+0.4	+75.4
75–84	38.3	47.1	56.9	65.5	78.4	84.3	80.7	137.3	+15.1	+28.7	+62.9
85+	10.1	12.5	13.2	19.2	24.8	30.2	36.6	51.9	+45.5	+57.3	+71.9
Total 65+	134.9	155.8	175.6	197.3	215.4	227.4	247.7	387.4	+12.4	+15.3	+70.4
Total persons	1285.0	1345.9	1400.7	1427.9	1524.8	1567.0	1603.1	1704.8	+1.9	+9.7	+8.8

*Census count population

Source: ABS Censuses 1981, 1986, 1991 and 1996, ABS, 1996a: Series C

different cultural practices and not have as many family members available locally to support them etc. (Hugo 1984).

It is important to realise that the various age groups making up the population are not distributed spatially in the same way as the total population. For example, the elderly population distribution in metropolitan Adelaide is shown in figure 7 and this indicates that they are strongly

TABLE 7: SOUTH AUSTRALIA: POPULATION AGED 65+ BY BIRTHPLACE, 1971–96

Year	Australia-born			Overseas-born			Non English-speaking-born			Mainly English-speaking-born		
	No.	%	% Growth	No.	%	% Growth	No.	%	% Growth	No.	%	% Growth
1971	79 711	8.9		19 889	7.1		6 570	5.1		13 319	8.8	
1976	87 859	9.2	+2.0	25 527	8.7	+5.1	n/a	–		n/a	–	
1981	99 816	10.2	+2.6	32 854	11.2	+5.2	13 382	10.2	+7.4*	19 472	11.9	+3.9*
1986	110 963	10.5	+2.1	40 820	13.6	+4.4	17 801	12.9	+5.9	23 019	14.3	+3.4
1991	119 469	11.2	+1.5	53 594	17.1	+5.6	26 025	17.3	+7.9	27 569	17.0	+3.7
1996	124 035	11.5	+0.8	63 980	21.1	+3.6	33 382	22.1	+5.1	30 598	21.2	+2.1

*% Growth 1971–81

Source: ABS 1971–96 Censuses

concentrated in the middle suburbs of the city where they settled as young families in the 1950s and 1960s. The stereotype of the aged being concentrated in the inner suburbs is clearly no longer relevant in Adelaide.

While public attention is focused on the growth of the aged population, in fact the fastest-growing age group in the Australian population over the next decade or so will be the population in their 50s. This of course represents the ageing of the baby boom cohort which will produce unprecedented growth of the elderly age group in the second and third decades of next century. This rapid growth typifies all of Australia but is exaggerated in South Australia because of the factors discussed earlier. In the United States marketers refer to this rapidly growing group as 'mid youth' and see the growth of this group as a significant development opportunity.

THE CHANGING SOUTH AUSTRALIAN FAMILY

No change in post-war South Australia has been more substantial and wide-reaching in its influence than the change in size and functioning of the family in the state. South Australian households have become progressively smaller due to reduced fertility, ageing and increased divorce. Table 8 shows that the average size of households in the state has declined by a full person to 2.6 persons in 1996.

It is of the utmost importance to appreciate that in the state, households have increased significantly faster than the population over the entire population period. This has been due partly to age structure factors (a relatively large proportion of the population being in the age groups leaving the parental home), older people staying living independently longer and marriage break-up. This differential between growth in population and households is evident in figure 8. It also shows that the personal mobility of the state's population has greatly increased. Indeed the number of South Australians per motor vehicle has decreased from 5.6 in 1947 to 1.5 in 1996. These trends have significant implications for South Australian society. On the one hand, the differential in the growth rate of households and population has meant that the demand for many things which are household rather than individual-based (housing, furniture, appliances) has increased faster than the population. Of course the increased motor vehicle ownership has also changed the way in which many services are provided, suburbs are developed etc. which assume motor car ownership. Yet at the 1996

FIGURE 7: ADELAIDE STATISTICAL DIVISION: DISTRIBUTION OF PERSONS AGED 65 YEARS AND OVER, 1996

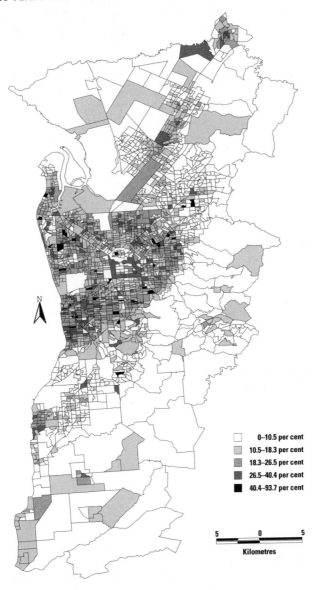

0–10.5 per cent
10.5–18.3 per cent
18.3–26.5 per cent
26.5–40.4 per cent
40.4–93.7 per cent

5   0   5
Kilometres

Source: ABS 1996 Census

TABLE 8: SOUTH AUSTRALIA: GROWTH OF POPULATION AND HOUSEHOLDS, 1947–96

Census	Population number[a]	Growth rate[b]	Household number[c]	Growth rate	Mean household size[d]
1947	646 073		166 118		3.65
1954	797 094	+2.86	212 095	+3.55	3.49
1961	971 487	+2.87	259 344	+2.91	3.54
1966	1 094 984	+2.42	299 933	+2.95	3.48
1971	1 173 707	+1.40	342 064	+2.66	3.30
1976	1 244 755	+1.18	390 514	+2.68	3.07
1981	1 285 033	+0.64	432 137	+2.05	2.88
1986	1 345 945	+0.93	475 985	+1.95	2.74
1991	1 400 630	+0.80	509 771	+1.38	2.63
1996	1 427 936	+0.39	549 518	+1.51	2.60

a Full-blood Aboriginals were excluded from census in 1947, 1954 and 1961 and they were not included in official results until 1971

b Average annual percentage growth since previous census

c Heads of private occupied dwellings

d Population in private occupied dwellings divided by the number of private occupied dwelling.

Source: ABS Censuses

FIGURE 8: SOUTH AUSTRALIA: GROWTH OF POPULATION, HOUSEHOLDS AND VEHICLES: 1961–96

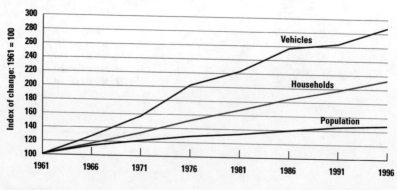

Source: ABS Censuses

census 11.9 per cent of households had no car while 46.0 per cent had more than one vehicle.

One of the most significant changes in South Australia's population over recent years has been an increase in diversity. This has already been seen in the discussion of increased ethnic diversity but also applies in a number of areas, especially in the family. In the 1950s, the bulk of South Australian families comprised a two-parent (with the male working) family with dependent children. This accounts now for around one-tenth of households in the state. Hence in both the private sector and public sector we must rid ourselves of often implicit assumptions that the unit we are dealing with and planning for is the 1950s typical household. Table 9 shows the changes that have occurred in family and household composition in the state over the last decade. It must be commented that in 1996, 2.7 per cent of the state's population (39 239 persons) lived in non-private households such as aged-care institutions, prisons etc. This has decreased since 1986 when 41 099 persons were in such situations (3.1 per cent of the total). The ABS (1996b) defines a family as 'two or more persons, one of whom is at least 15 years of age, who are related by blood, marriage (registered or de facto), adoption, step or fostering, and who are usually resident in the same household'. Hence, persons living alone and in group households (unrelated persons living together) are not considered as families. It will be noticed from table 9 that single-person households have increased by over 50 per cent in the 1986–96 period and are second only to single-parent families (in terms of living arrangements) to have grown fastest over the last decade. This is almost four times faster than the increase in the total number of households. Group households have increased much more slowly. The growth of single-person households is a function of the ageing of the population, growth of divorce and separation and delayed marriage.

Table 9 indicates a major change in South Australian families over the last decade. Couples living without children are the most common category of living arrangement. Indeed couples and singles account for more than a half of all households in the state. The couple household growth is partly due to the ageing of the population and the expansion of the numbers of 'empty nesters' although there has been a tendency for young adult children to stay at home with parents much more than in the past. The number of two-parent families with dependent and/or non-dependent children actually declined between 1986 and 1996 (from 198 200 to 181 113). This reflects ageing, the decline in fertility and

TABLE 9: SOUTH AUSTRALIAN FAMILIES AND HOUSEHOLDS: SUMMARY, 1996, 1991 AND 1986

Family type	1996		1991		1986		Change 1986–96
	No.	%	No.	%	No.	%	%
Couple without children	145 235	26.6	129 672	25.7	122 743	25.5	+18.3
Couple with dependent children	129 222	23.7	132 222	26.2	125 652	26.2	+2.8
Couple with non-dependent children	34 690	6.4	37 621	7.5	42 704	8.9	−18.8
Couple with dependent and non-dependent children	17 201	3.2	20 797	4.1	29 844	6.2	−42.4
Total couple families	326 348	59.8	320 312	63.5	320 943	66.8	+1.7
Lone parent with dependent children	34 417	6.3	29 299	5.8	22 528	4.7	+52.8
Lone parent with non-dependent children	16 667	3.1	14 773	2.9	n/a	n/a	+6.0*
Lone parent with dependent and non-dependent children	3 806	0.7	4 121	0.8	5 703	1.2	−33.3
Total lone parent families	54 890	10.1	48 193	9.6	n/a	n/a	+22.8*
Other Families	6 336	1.2	6 210	1.2	21 633†	4.5	n/a
Single Persons	138 995	25.5	110 432	21.9	92 137	19.2	+50.9
Group Households	18 748	3.4	19 034	3.8	17 524	3.6	+7.0
Total	**545 317**	**100.0**	**504 181**	**100.0**	**480 468**	**100.0**	**+13.5**

*Includes 'Other' category

†In 1986 'Other' comprises 'Related Adults' and includes lone parents with non-dependent children.

Source: ABS 1986, 1991 and 1996 Censuses

especially increased marital break-up rates since 1976. Hence the number of single-parent households increased substantially, so that by 1996 they made up 10.1 per cent of all households, 14.2 per cent of families and 23.2 per cent of those with children. Some 17.2 per cent of children aged between 0 and 14 years lived in single-parent families. Of course if a longitudinal perspective is adopted we can state that well over one-third of children in South Australia can expect to live in a single-parent family at some stage in their childhood. It is interesting that in 1996, of the 181 113 two-parent families with children, 53.5 per cent had two incomes and in 15 per cent neither parent was employed, yet among single parents 57.1 per cent did not have a job. It is not surprising then that single-parent families are very highly represented among low-income families. Hence 51.6 per cent of single-parent families earned less than $400 per week while this applied to only 9.1 per cent of two-parent families with children. On the other hand, only 6.7 per cent of single-parent families earned $1000 or more per week compared with 37.7 per cent of two-parent families.

The increase in diversity of families and households is evident in table 9. In 1992 there were some 19 000 blended families in the state; that is, children with different parents living in the same family. In 1992 in all of Australia eight per cent of all couples were in a de facto relationship compared with five per cent in 1982 (ABS 1995, p. 38) but more than half (56 per cent) of all couples who married in that year had cohabited compared with 16 per cent in 1975 (ABS 1997b, p. 28). About half of de facto families had children. Some 25 per cent of families with dependent children include children who are not living with both of their natural parents. Some three per cent of families are blended families and four per cent are step families.

Paradoxically, while households have been getting smaller in South Australia, the size of houses has become larger. Around one-third of single-person households have more than two bedrooms in their houses and this applied to two-thirds of two-person households. Nevertheless there has been a significant increase in the diversity of housing in the state with an increased proportion of medium and higher-density housing, as table 10 shows.

TABLE 10: SOUTH AUSTRALIA: HOUSING TYPE, 1976, 1986 AND 1996

	1976	1986	1996	Per cent change 1976–96
Separate house	333 144	367 423	419 980	+26.1
Semi-detached, row or terrace house, townhouse, flat unit or apartment	86 964	95 655	113 293	+30.3
Other dwelling	2 630	7 276	4 330	+64.6
Not stated	7 544	5 633	4 740	−37.2
Total	430 282	475 987	542 343	+26.0

Source: ABS 1976, 1986 and 1996 Censuses

WORK PATTERNS

There have been significant changes in the nature and conditions of work among South Australians. It was notable at the 1996 census that for the first time since the Second World War there was an absolute decline in the numbers employed between censuses. There was a 1.9 per cent fall in the number of persons employed in the state between 1991 and 1996 although the proportion of all workers made up of women increased from 43.5 to 44.4 per cent. Table 11 shows that labour force participation rates declined in all ages for men over the last two decades while that of females has increased, although male participation rates are higher than for females except in the 15–19 age group. Clearly, increased levels of higher education are important in reducing rates at the younger male ages while the discouraged-worker effect and involuntary and voluntary earlier retirement are responsible in the older ages. The shedding of workers by the government sector saw the proportion of workers employed by the state government declining from 17.4 per cent in 1991 to 13.4 per cent in 1996 while the declines for the federal government were from 5.8 to 4.6 per cent and local government from 1.5 to 1.4 per cent. The downturn in the state's economy following the crash of the State Bank is clearly apparent in the employment figures.

TABLE 11: SOUTH AUSTRALIA: LABOUR FORCE PARTICIPATION RATES OF MEN AND WOMEN BY AGE GROUP, 1976, 1986 AND 1996

Age Group	1976		1986		1996	
	Males	Females	Males	Females	Males	Females
15–19	58.3	54.4	56.8	56.1	48.2	48.6
20–24	89.3	67.0	89.8	75.0	82.9	74.0
25–34	96.5	51.1	93.8	61.4	88.7	65.7
35–44	96.7	60.6	93.4	65.5	88.6	70.5
45–54	94.3	52.0	88.7	53.7	85.0	66.8
55–64	80.6	26.1	59.8	21.1	55.6	27.6
65+	15.4	4.5	7.6	2.5	7.8	2.6

Source: ABS 1976, 1986 and 1996 Census

The census data also reflect the major changes which have occurred in the nature of work in the 1990s. In 1996 some two-thirds of workers worked 35 hours or more, some 3.6 per cent less than in 1991. A quarter of the workforce was working on a part-time basis, some three-quarters of them female. This reflects the increased casualisation of the workforce which is occurring along with decreasing unionisation and increased out-of-hours work. Moreover, table 12 shows the shifts which have occurred over the last decade with the reduction in manufacturing employment and increasing involvement in the service industry.

TABLE 12: SOUTH AUSTRALIA: INDUSTRY OF THE POPULATION 1986 AND 1996

Industry	1986	1996	Per cent change
Agriculture and mining	45 959	36 613	−20.3
Manufacturing	90 351	88 645	−1.9
Electricity, gas, water	9 811	4 630	−52.8
Construction	34 845	29 301	−15.9
Wholesale, retail trade	108 966	112 588	+3.3
Transport, storage	26 147	21 782	−16.7
Communication	11 165	10 551	−5.5
Finance, property, business	48 679	69 184	+42.1
Government administration, defence	27 816	24 994	−10.1
Community services	112 416	110 499	−1.7
Recreation, personal, other	34 732	61 373	+76.7
Not classifiable, not stated	17 871	22 347	+25.0
Total	**568 758**	**592 507**	**+4.2**

Source: ABS 1986 and 1996 Censuses

INCOME

One of the most distinctive characteristics of Australian cities in the 1990s is the increasing polarisation between rich and poor (Gregory & Hunter 1995a; 1995b; Badcock & Browett 1997). The 'hollowing out' of the middle class in OECD countries and the corresponding increase in the well-off and the poor groups also appears to be accompanied by an increasingly sharp spatial separation of the better-off and poor areas of major cities. In 1995/96 the top 20 per cent of income earners earned 37.4 per cent of the total income and the bottom 20 per cent, 7.8 per cent (ABS 1998, p. 121). This situation has deteriorated a little since 1990 when 36.5 per cent of the income was carried by the top-income earners and 8.2 per cent by the low-income earners (ABS 1994, p. 133). Over that period the percentage of income units who relied upon government benefits increased from 30.6 to 33.5 per cent. In 1996 when the national average was 29 per cent, the state had the largest proportion of income earners reliant on government transfers of any of the states and territories. Moreover, in that year less than a half of income units (49.6 per cent) had wages and salaries as their main source of income compared with 55.5 per cent nationally. Household disposable income per capita increased from $14 200 in 1991 to $16 200 in 1996, while the national average increased from $14 900 to $17 300. Female incomes among full-time workers are four-fifths the size of males.

INDIGENOUS POPULATION

The Aboriginal and Torres Strait Islander population of South Australia is one of the most important and distinctive groups in the population. Table 13 shows that the indigenous population of the state has grown considerably faster than the population of the state as a whole. This has been a function of two major factors: firstly, it will be noted that the growth of the population has been somewhat erratic. This has been due to the fact that there has been increasing willingness among the people of indigenous extraction to identify themselves at the census as Aboriginal or Torres Strait Islanders (Taylor 1997). The Aboriginality question in the census is a self-identification question, and with increasing pride among people of indigenous origin, more people are classifying themselves in this category. Moreover, indigenous people have significantly higher fertility than the population as a whole (Gray 1997). However, even allowing for these factors there has been some concern about explaining the unexpectedly rapid growth of the indigenous population between 1991 and 1996 which grew by one-third nationally – twice the level of the previous inter-censal period.

It has been suggested (Hugo 1986) that the Aboriginal population is a distinctive subgroup in the Australian population in almost every respect. In the 1970s it was described as a demographically Third World population living in a developed country. While the gap between the indigenous and non-indigenous population has narrowed, table 14 shows that the contrast remains considerable. Most dramatic of all are the differences in mortality. Aboriginal men can expect to live over 18 years less than the population as a whole, while the difference for

TABLE 13: SOUTH AUSTRALIA: INDIGENOUS POPULATION CHANGE, 1971–96

	Population at end of period	Net change	Per cent change	
			Intercensal	Annual
1971–76	10 714	+3 415	+46.8	+8.0
1976–81	9 825	−889	−8.3	−1.7
1981–86	14 291	+4 466	+45.5	+7.8
1986–91	16 429	+1 958	+13.7	+2.6
1991–96	20 444	+4 195	+25.8	+4.7

Source: ABS 1971–1996 Censuses

women is 14 years. Indigenous babies are twice as likely to die before their first birthday than are the babies of the whole population. These inequalities reflect the disadvantage that this group face. For example, the chance of an indigenous person in the state being in a prison in the state is six times that of the total population. A quarter of them are unemployed compared with a tenth of the total population and they are more highly represented among low-income and low-status occupations. They are four times more likely to live in public rental accommodation and a third as likely to have a tertiary qualification. They are less likely to live in Adelaide than the state's total population and have twice as high a proportion of their population aged under 15 years than is the case for the total population. Clearly, the indigenous population must remain a major target for government policy to attempt to redress the gaps which exist in the quality of life and standard of living.

EDUCATIONAL ATTAINMENT

One of the most significant changes which has occurred in the state's population since World War II relates to educational attainment. This is dramatically shown in figure 9 which depicts the change in the proportions of South Australians aged 15 to 19 years who have been recorded as having been in full-time education between 1954 and 1996. Over this period, the proportion in education has increased four times and the situation has gone from when the rate was higher for males than females to the opposite being the case. Hence there has been a substantial improvement in the level of training of the human resources of the state.

TABLE 14: SOUTH AUSTRALIA: COMPARISON OF VARIOUS DEMOGRAPHIC AND SOCIAL CHARACTERISTICS OF THE INDIGENOUS AND TOTAL POPULATION, 1996

Characteristics	Indigenous population	Total population
Expectation of life at birth (years) male*	56.4	74.7
Expectation of life at birth (years) female*	66.4	80.5
Infant mortality rate	12.6	4.9
Total fertility rate	2.1	1.7
Percentage in major urban	44.3	68.5
Percentage aged less than 15	39.5	20.6
Unemployment rate	24.5	10.4
Percentage employed as managers, administrators, professionals	25.2	37.2
Percentage labourers and related workers	22.1	10.1
Percentage with diploma, degree or higher	4.3	14.2
Individual income $199 or less per week	53.0	41.2
Individual income $600 and over per week	7.7	17.2
Percentage of households living in public rental accommodation	39.4	9.7
Percentage of persons in prisons, corrective and detention institutions (for adults)†	0.6	0.1

*1986–91 data for indigenous and 1991 data for total population

†1991 data

Source: ABS 1991 and 1996 Censuses, ABS 1997c

Nevertheless there remain significant inequalities in gaining access to higher education and in the quality of education available to particular groups. To take one example, there are clear differences in Adelaide in the extent to which children from different groups proceed to tertiary education. Figure 10 shows the proportion of state school students in Year 12 in 1995 enrolling or deferring in a tertiary institution in 1996. The north-western and southern suburbs stand out as having very low continuation rates. Moodie (1995) has shown that, although 37 per cent of Year 12 students are from low socio-economic status, only 24.2 per cent of applications to enter university were from people from such backgrounds and represented 22.7 per cent of offers. Moreover, the rate of lower socio-economic status groups dropping out before Year 12 is much greater than those in the better-off groups.

FIGURE 9: SOUTH AUSTRALIA: PER CENT OF MALES AND FEMALES AGED 15–19 IN FULL-TIME EDUCATION, 1954–96

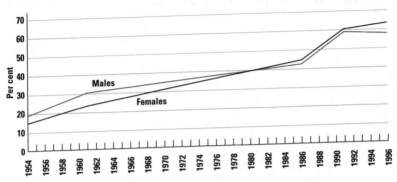

Source: ABS 1954, 1961, 1986, 1991 and 1996 Censuses

SOCIO-ECONOMIC STATUS

It is apparent from earlier analyses in this chapter that the gap between poorer groups and those who are relatively well off has increased in South Australia in recent years. This is a function of:

- an increased proportion of the population being reliant on government transfers increasing their vulnerability to poverty
- a higher level of unemployment
- an increase in two-income families leading to an increase in the better-off segments of the population.

Some have argued that the widening of the gap between the better-off and poorer segments of society has led to a sharpening of the spatial differences between different areas in Adelaide according to the socio-economic status of their inhabitants. Glover et al (1996, p. 357) have carried out a cluster analysis based on a number of socio-economic variables designed to classify postcode areas in metropolitan Adelaide on the basis of their socio-economic characteristics. Figure 11 shows the spatial distribution of areas classified as low and high socio-economic status. These show a clear pattern of differentiation, with the north-western and southern suburbs having generally low socio-economic status and the eastern suburbs being relatively well off.

This important east/west division does have some minor exceptions but it is reflected in a number of other aspects of service provision

FIGURE 10: ADELAIDE METROPOLITAN AREA: PERCENTAGE OF 1995 YEAR 12 STUDENTS FROM STATE SECONDARY SCHOOLS ENROLLING OR DEFERRING IN A TERTIARY INSTITUTION, 1996

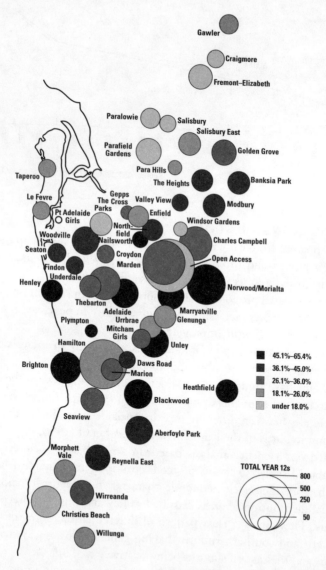

Source: Calculated from DECS 1996 and SATAC 1996

and well-being of the population; for example the north-western and, to a lesser extent the southern, suburbs show out as areas of low-health status.

CHANGING POPULATION DISTRIBUTION

While the state's population has grown only marginally in the last decade there continues to be some dynamism in the distribution of population within the state (Bell 1997b). Firstly, with respect to the comparison of population living in the Adelaide metropolitan area and that living in the remainder of the state, figure 12 shows an interesting pattern. It is evident that in the century leading up to the 1970s there was a clear pattern of increase in the proportion of population living in Adelaide. This progressive concentration of the population in the capital was due to the shedding of labour from non-metropolitan areas due to mechanisation and capital substitution for labour in agriculture and improved transportation which made many non-metropolitan services uncompetitive with Adelaide-based counterparts. In addition, industrial development and expansion of the tertiary areas of the economy focussed on Adelaide.

However, it is notable that, since the 1970s, there has been a levelling-off in the balance of population between metropolitan and non-metropolitan areas. Indeed, in the eastern states there has been a reversal or counter-urbanisation in which the non-metropolitan population has expanded faster than that in the capital cities (Hugo 1996). There is some debate as to whether this is a true 'turnaround' or whether it is a new form of more diffuse urbanisation with substantial population growth in a peri-urban mixed urban/rural area on the edges of the major cities. Although non-metropolitan population growth is spatially concentrated in Australia, it is not restricted to peri-urban areas in the eastern states. In South Australia however, as table 15 shows, the only statistical division in South Australia to experience a net migration gain was outer Adelaide – the peri-urban area of Adelaide. Although all other non-metropolitan areas experienced net loss, it was especially heavy in the northern, south-east and Murraylands divisions. The population growth in the outer Adelaide statistical division between 1991 and 1996 was equivalent to half of the total growth in the Adelaide statistical division (Ford 1997). Migration flows into Adelaide are predominantly from the five, other non-metropolitan statistical divisions while the main gain in outer Adelaide is from the metropolitan area (Bell 1997c).

FIGURE 11: SOCIO-ECONOMIC CLUSTERS BASED ON POSTCODES, METROPOLITAN ADELAIDE, 1991: CLUSTERS OF POSTCODES WITH GENERALLY SIMILAR SOCIO-ECONOMIC CHARACTERISTICS

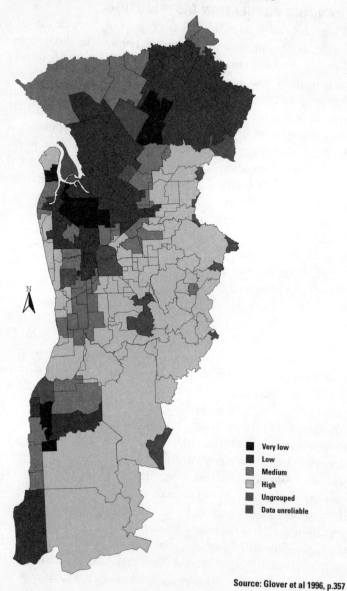

Very low
Low
Medium
High
Ungrouped
Data unreliable

Source: Glover et al 1996, p.357

FIGURE 12: CHANGING DISTRIBUTION OF THE POPULATION OF SOUTH AUSTRALIA BETWEEN METROPOLITAN, OTHER URBAN AND RURAL AREAS, 1844 TO 1996

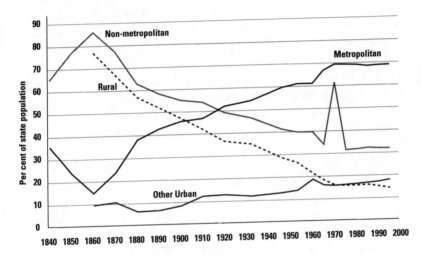

Source: Hugo 1971; ABS 1971, 1976, 1981, 1986, 1991 and 1996 Censuses

TABLE 15: SOUTH AUSTRALIA: NET MIGRATION BY STATISTICAL DIVISION, 1986–91 AND 1991–96

Statistical division	Population change		Net migration	
	1986–91	1991–96	1986–91	1991–96
Adelaide	53 359	22 023	25 250	−5 535
Outer Adelaide	11 306	11 206	8 266	8 155
Yorke & Lower North	289	190	−465	−341
Murray Lands	1 923	34	−586	−2 336
South East	−38	−137	−2 656	−2 547
Eyre	−1 770	−137	−3 336	−1 472
Northern	−1 320	−5 089	−6 021	−8 909
Total	63 749	28 090		

Source: Geodemographic Research Group, University of Adelaide

In relation to population change within the Adelaide statistical division, there has been a substantial change over the last decade. Until recently, a population growth map of Adelaide resembled a doughnut, with a central area of population decline and concentric rings of progressively more rapid population growth as the growing edge of the metropolitan area is approached (Division of National Mapping, and ABS 1984). However, the most recent social atlas of Adelaide (ABS 1997a) shows a quite different pattern. Certainly growth is still occurring on the periphery but there is significant growth in the centre and in parts of the inner and middle suburbs. This is due both to the life-cycle effects of the generation of first-home owners dying off or moving into other accommodation, and to deliberate growth attempts to thicken the population density of inner and middle urban suburbs.

CONCLUSION

South Australia's population has changed dramatically in recent years despite a slow-down in overall population growth. In the medium term it could well be that the state's population will grow faster than over the last decade. This could occur as the effects of the debt created by the State Bank collapse of the early 1990s recede and the low-cost and life-style advantages of Adelaide as opposed to Sydney and Melbourne lead to a flow of people from the major national concentrations of population. This would be assisted by the increasing role of information technology in rendering major city locations less necessary for many economic activities. However, even if the low growth or stable regime is maintained in the longer term, the population will continue to change dramatically in its composition and spatial distribution. This has certainly been the case over the last decade of slow growth.

Knowledge of the patterns of change in population can greatly inform decision-making by planners and policy-makers in both the public and private sectors. It does not, however, provide them with a totally accurate window on the future. Nevertheless, contemporary trends in population growth, structure and distribution do indicate a number of changes occurring in the population which are altering and will continue to alter the level and nature of demand for goods and services. It has been argued here that the greatest changes occurring to the contemporary population of South Australia are in the structure, composition and, to a lesser extent, distribution of the population rather than in its size and growth. Yet this has equally profound implications for planning as would rapid growth of population. The 1990s have seen the state's population become both more diverse in its composition and more unequal. Both of these trends will present considerable challenges to government and to the private sector over the next decade.

REFERENCES

Australian Bureau of Statistics (ABS). *Australian Demographic Statistics Quarterly*, various issues, Catalogue No. 3101.0, ABS, Canberra.

—— *Births Australia*, various issues, Catalogue No. 3301.0, ABS, Canberra.

—— *Deaths Australia*, various issues, Catalogue No. 3302.0, ABS, Canberra.

—— 1986, *Australian Demographic Trends*, Catalogue No. 3102.0, ABS, Canberra.

—— 1994, *Australian Social Trends 1994*, Catalogue No. 4102.0, ABS, Canberra.

—— 1995, *Australian Social Trends 1995*, Catalogue No. 4102.0, ABS, Canberra.

—— 1996a, *Projections of the Populations of Australia – States and Territories, 1995–2051*, Catalogue No. 3222.0, ABS, Canberra.

—— 1996b, *1996 Census Dictionary*, Catalogue No. 2901.0, ABS, Canberra.

—— 1997a, *Adelaide ... A Social Atlas*, Catalogue No. 2030.4, ABS, Canberra.

—— 1997b, *Australian Social Trends 1997*, Catalogue No. 4102.0, ABS, Canberra.

—— 1997c, *Demography South Australia 1996*, Catalogue No. 3311.4, ABS, Canberra.

—— 1998, *Australian Social Trends 1998*, Catalogue No. 4102.0, ABS, Canberra.

Badcock, B. A. & Browett, M. H. (eds) 1997, *Developing Small Area Indicators for Policy Research in Australia*, monograph series 2, National Key Centre for Social Applications of GIS, Adelaide.

Beer, A. & Cutler, C. 1995, *Atlas of the Australian People* – 1991 Census, South Australia, AGPS, Canberra.

Bell, M. 1997a, *Interstate Migration: The South Australian Experience*, Department for Transport, Urban Planning and the Arts and the University of Adelaide, Adelaide.

—— 1997b, *South Australia at the 1996 Census: Population Change and Distribution*, Department for Transport, Urban Planning and the Arts and the University of Adelaide, Adelaide.

—— 1997c, *Population Movement in South Australia: 1986 to 1991*, Department for Transport, Urban Planning and the Arts and the University of Adelaide, Adelaide.

Commonwealth Bureau of Census and Statistics (CBCS), *Demography*, various issues, Government Printer, Canberra.

Department of Education and Community Services (DECS) 1996, *Mid Year Census 1996: Student Enrolment Data*, DECS, Adelaide.

Division of National Mapping and Australian Bureau of Statistics 1984, *Adelaide – A Social Atlas*, Division of National Mapping and Australian Bureau of Statistics, Canberra.

Ford, T. 1997, *Population Trends in Adelaide's Peri-urban Region*, Department for Transport, Urban Planning and the Arts and the University of Adelaide, Adelaide.

Glover, J., Shand, M., Forster, C. & Woollacott, T. 1996, *A Social Health Atlas of South Australia*, 2nd ed, Policy and Budget Division, South Australian Health Commission, Adelaide.

Gray, A. 1997, *The Explosion of Aboriginality: Components of Indigenous Population Growth 1991–1996*, Centre for Aboriginal Economic Policy Research, discussion paper no. 142/1997, Australian National University, Canberrra.

Gregory, R. G. & Hunter, B. 1995a, 'The macro-economy and the growth of ghettos and urban poverty in Australia', National Press Club Telecom Address, discussion paper no. 325, Centre for Economic Policy Research, Australian National University.

—— 1995b, 'Further remarks on increased neighbourhood inequality', *Social Security Journal*, June, pp. 20–8.

Hugo, G. J. 1971, Internal migration in South Australia, 1961–1966. Unpublished M. A. thesis, Flinders University of South Australia, Adelaide.

—— 1979, 'Some demographic factors affecting future housing demand in Australia,' *Australian Quarterly*, vol. 51, no. 4, pp. 4–25.

—— 1983, 'South Australia's changing population', *South Australian Geographical Papers*, no. 1, Royal Geographical Society of Australasia (SA Branch), Adelaide.

—— 1984, 'The ageing of ethnic populations in Australia with special reference to South Australia', *Occasional Paper in Gerontology*, no. 6, National Research Institute for Gerontology and Geriatric Medicine, Melbourne.

—— 1986, *Australia's Changing Population: Trends and Implications*, Oxford University Press, Melbourne.

—— 1993, 'The changing spatial distribution of major ethnic groups in Australia, 1961–1986', revised version of a report prepared for the Office of Multicultural Affairs, April.

—— 1994, *The Economic Implications of Emigration from Australia*, AGPS, Canberra.

—— 1996, 'Counterurbanisation', in *Population Shift: Mobility and Change in Australia*, eds M. Bell & P. Newton, AGPS, Canberra, pp. 126–46.

Moodie, G. 1995, An instrumental approach to equity, quality and opportunities for learning, paper presented at second National Conference on Equity and Access in Tertiary Education.

South Australian Tertiary Admissions Centre (SATAC) 1996, *Nineteenth Annual Report to 30 June 1996*, SATAC, Adelaide.

Taylor, J. 1997, *Changing Numbers, Changing Needs? A Preliminary Assessment of Indigenous Population Growth, 1991–96*, Centre for Aboriginal Economic Policy Research, discussion paper no. 143/1997, Australian National University, Canberra.

NOTES

1   The other states experiencing a decline were NSW (37.3 to 33.8 per cent), Victoria (27.9 to 24.9 per cent) and Tasmania (3.3 to 2.6 per cent) while those recording an increase were Queensland (14.5 to 18.3 per cent), Western Australia (7.0 to 9.6 per cent), ACT (0.6 to 1.7 per cent) and the Northern Territory (0.3 to 1 per cent).

2   The Total Fertility Rate (TFR) 'indicates the number of children that will be born alive to a woman during her lifetime if she were to pass through all her childbearing years conforming to the age specific rates of a given year' (Hugo 1986, p.43). More simply it indicates approximately the completed total number of children women are having on average at a particular time

CHAPTER 5

A LABOUR MARKET IN CRISIS?

JOHN SPOEHR

Draw a map of Australia in 1998 charting the distribution of incomes and occupations, and you will see a nation fracturing along class, residential and ethnic lines. Globalisation has fragmented the Australian labour market, dividing its cities and regions into districts of success and districts of failure. The centrifugal forces of the global economy are tearing at the ties that bind the citizenry, bestowing greater wealth and privilege on the most skilled and educated, while scuppering the job prospects and living standards of the less skilled. Some peoples' boats are rising. Some people's boats are sinking. And the old solutions don't work any more.

Stephen Long, *Australian Financial Review*, 24–25 October 1998, p. 21

Globalisation is fragmenting the Australian labour market, creating 'work rich' and 'work poor' districts in our cities and regions. Regions like South Australia are part of a periphery in the Australian labour market. This periphery has a greater share of national unemployment, poverty and inequality and a declining share of population and employment. That the ratio of people employed per thousand resident population declined significantly in South Australia between 1991 and 1996 illustrates this (Stimson, Fikreth, & O'Connor 1998). This suggests increasing dependency in South Australia, with a larger proportion of the population reliant upon the state for support. Disturbingly, just as dependency has increased, the ratio of people employed in industries that typically provide such support has declined significantly in South Australia and Australia as a whole.[1]

In 1991 South Australia had a relatively high employment to population ratio, ranking the second highest of the states and territories. By 1996 it had fallen to second lowest and was the only state or territory to experience a decline. Within the state, the areas to experience the most significant decline were Northern SA, South Eastern SA and Yorke and Lower North SA.[2] Not surprisingly, these areas have some of the highest unemployment rates in Australia. Given the likelihood of continued slow jobs growth in South Australia the outlook for many of these regions is bleak.

The greatest immediate threat is that unemployment will rise substantially as the full impact of global financial instability dampens Australian growth prospects. Excluding the effects of this downturn, the decline in the national unemployment rate to around eight per cent (trend) at the end of the current recovery period is a poor outcome compared to six per cent in 1990 and 6.1 per cent in 1980 (at the end of previous recovery periods). Unemployment has ratcheted upwards over the last ten years. This is particularly evident in states like Tasmania, Victoria, Queensland and South Australia. Unemployment rates in these states are 30 to 40 per cent higher than those recorded in 1980 and 1990. It is worth remembering that South Australia's unemployment rate was around seven per cent in 1980 and 1990.

The Australian unemployment rate fell by just 0.4 per cent from 8.6 per cent to 8.2 per cent over the twelve months to August 1998. With annual economic growth rates likely to slow over the short term, unemployment is set to rise steadily early in 2000.

The South Australian labour market is now at a critical juncture. Unemployment remains stubbornly high and is set to remain around nine per cent for the remainder of the century. If the labour force participation rate (the total number of employed and unemployed) had held steady at around 62 per cent rather than falling to around 60 per cent over the twelve months to September 1998, the unemployment rate would have been significantly higher. Disturbingly, the number of South Australians in employment declined by 17 000 over this period against the national trend. While men have borne the brunt of the steady decline in manufacturing industry jobs, around 12 000 jobs held by women were lost in the twelve months to September 1998 (ABS Cat. 6202). These are indications of a crisis in the South Australian labour market.

This chapter provides an overview of recent trends in the South Australian labour market. In the absence of significant policy change, the prospects for any significant reductions in unemployment are poor. This poor outlook will place great pressure on many struggling regional labour markets. South Australia's regional labour markets are now poised to experience the highest unemployment rates since the Great Depression.

INDUSTRY EMPLOYMENT

The impact of global economic and industry restructuring is reflected in changing patterns of industry employment. Declining industry protection and world commodity prices, public sector job cuts and the introduction of labour-displacing technologies have led to significant job losses in a range of South Australian industries. Over the ten years to September 1997, the mining; manufacturing; electricity, gas and water; construction; finance, insurance and communications industries contracted by around 16 800 persons (see table 1). This contrasts with growth of around 54 600 persons in industries including agriculture; wholesale and retail; accommodation, cafes and restaurants; government administration; and health and community services. It should be noted that much of this growth has been in lower-skilled, part-time and casual positions in industries where women are over-represented. The disproportionate growth of casual and part-time jobs in the service industries, while supporting the increasing participation of women in the labour market, represents growth at the cost of job security. Recent industry employment growth trends signal the deterioration of a core of full-time jobs and the growth of an insecure periphery of low-wage jobs.

JOB VACANCIES AND UNEMPLOYMENT

A graphic illustration of the crisis in the SA labour market can by obtained by comparing the number of job vacancies advertised on a monthly basis with the number of unemployed people measured on a monthly basis. At the beginning of 1998 there were around 58 unemployed people for every job vacancy advertised in South Australia. The number of job vacancies available has not recovered to levels experienced during the last economic recovery. In January 1998 they were around 45 per cent below the peak in job vacancies in January 1990. If rates of under-employment are taken into account, the competition for job vacancies is fierce.

UNEMPLOYMENT

South Australia was the only mainland state in Australia to make no significant inroad into unemployment over the twelve months to September 1998. All mainland states except South Australia experienced a reduction in unemployment. In South Australia unemployment remained stuck at 9.7 per cent from May through to December 1997 before steadily rising to 10.2 per cent in September 1998 (see table 2).

TABLE 1: EMPLOYMENT BY INDUSTRY, SOUTH AUSTRALIA, SEPTEMBER 1987 TO SEPTEMBER 1997

Industry	Number of persons employed (000s)		Change over ten years %	Contribution to total employment (%)	
	12 months to Sept 1987	12 months to Sept 1997		12 months to Sept 1987	12 months to Sept 1997
Agriculture	46.2	50.8	9.9	7.6	7.7
Mining	8.8	3.5	-60.2	1.5	0.5
Manufacturing	100.8	97.8	-2.9	16.6	14.8
Electricity, gas and water	10.8	5.9	-45.4	1.8	0.9
Construction	42.3	36.0	-14.9	7.0	5.5
Wholesale and retail trade	116.3	126.7	8.9	19.2	19.2
Accommodation, cafes and restaurants	19.3	30.7	59.1	3.2	4.6
Transport and storage	25.6	26.1	2.0	4.2	4.0
Finance, insurance and communication services	35.8	32.9	-8.1	5.9	5.0
Government administration, defence and education	63.4	73.8	16.4	10.5	11.2
Health and community services	63.4	73.8	16.4	10.5	11.2
Cultural, recreational, personal and other services	35.0	40.9	16.9	5.7	6.2
Total	**605.6**	**659.6**	**8.1**	**100.0**	**100.0**

Source: ABS Ausstats

One of the starkest illustrations of the current jobs crisis in South Australia is the tendency for unemployment to ratchet upwards with each recession. At the end of the economic recovery periods of the late 1970s and 1980s, unemployment had declined to around seven per cent.

EMPLOYMENT AND UNDER-EMPLOYMENT

Official unemployment figures obscure the full dimensions of the jobs crisis. Changes in the structure of the labour market resulting in the growth of part-time and casual positions, often at the expense of secure, full-time positions, have produced a large pool of under-employed people.

Of particular concern is the recent sustained decline in full-time employment in South Australia. The number of full-time jobs declined

FIGURE 1: SA UNEMPLOYMENT AND JOB VACANCIES JAN 1989–JAN 1998

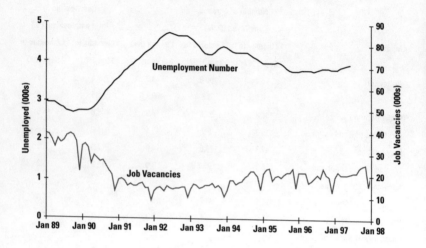

Source: ABS Labour Force Cat. 6202 and ANZ Job Vacancies

TABLE 2: UNEMPLOYMENT RATES, AUSTRALIA AND STATES, JANUARY 1980, 1990, 1997–SEPTEMBER 1998 (TREND)

	Qld	WA	NSW	Vic	Tas	SA	Aust
Jan 1980	6.5	7.2	5.6	5.7	6.5	7.4	6.1
Jan 1990	6.9	6.7	6.1	4.7	8.6	7.1	6.0
Jan 1997	9.8	7.6	7.9	9.1	10.6	9.4	8.7
April	9.6	7.3	8.1	9.2	10.8	9.6	8.7
June	9.4	7.2	8.1	9.2	10.9	9.7	8.7
Sept	9.3	7.0	8.0	8.8	11.4	9.7	8.5
Dec	9.1	7.0	7.6	8.4	11.2	9.7	8.3
Jan 1998	8.9	7.0	7.5	8.3	11.0	9.8	8.2
April	8.6	7.0	7.5	8.4	10.6	10.0	8.0
June	8.7	7.1	7.5	8.4	10.8	10.1	8.1
Sept	9.0	7.2	7.5	8.2	10.8	10.2	8.2

Source: ABS Cat. 6202 and unpublished data

by 1.5 per cent or around 7000 in South Australia over the three years to 1998. This reflects the combined effects of the significant job losses in the South Australian and Commonwealth public sectors over this time, the impact of declining tariff protection measures upon manufacturing employment and low prevailing economic growth rates. Part-time job growth has increased by nearly 15 per cent over the same period. These trends are of great concern as they translate into lower-quality, lower-paid and more insecure jobs for South Australians.

South Australia has the highest proportion of under-employed people in Australia. Nearly eight per cent of the South Australian labour force or around 52 000 people would prefer to be working more hours than they currently are. If added to the number of people currently unemployed, the combined number of people seeking work or more work could increase the competition for available job vacancies by up to 75 per cent.

LONG-TERM UNEMPLOYMENT

Perhaps one of the most disturbing features of the current crisis is the very high level of long-term unemployment (LTU) in South Australia (those people unemployed for more than 12 months). South Australia has the highest levels of long-term unemployment in mainland Australia as table 3 and figure 2 indicate. Nearly 30 000 unemployed people in SA in December 1997 had been out of work for twelve months or more. This represents around 43 per cent of unemployed people. Disturbingly, levels of LTU have remained high throughout the economic recovery period and have shown no significant improvement over the last four years. At the end of the 1980s recovery period, LTU was ten per cent lower as a proportion of total unemployment than currently is the case.

AVERAGE DURATION OF UNEMPLOYMENT

Adding to concern about the growth in long-term unemployment are data on the average duration of unemployment (ADU) in South Australia. The ADU for SA in December 1997 was 69 weeks. This is 23 per cent higher than the national average of 53 weeks. For unemployed men, the ADU was more than a year and a half (81 weeks). This is the highest mainland ADU for unemployed men, and 20 per cent higher than the national average of 60 weeks. The ADU for unemployed women in SA was 51 weeks, the highest mainland ADU for a state and 16 per cent higher than the national average of 43 weeks.

TABLE 3: LONG-TERM UNEMPLOYMENT AS PERCENTAGE OF TOTAL UNEMPLOYMENT, AUSTRALIAN STATES, OCTOBER 1988–OCTOBER 1997

Year	Qld	WA	NSW	Vic	Tas	SA
Oct 88	25	21	37	25	43	32
Oct 89	24	17	28	18	37	30
Oct 90	16	16	26	16	29	30
Oct 91	24	24	27	26	31	34
Oct 92	30	30	36	39	41	37
Oct 93	31	31	35	41	39	43
Oct 94	29	27	39	42	48	42
Oct 95	25	23	37	33	45	36
Oct 96	27	20	30	35	34	31
Oct 97	29	20	35	37	38	43

Source: ABS unpublished

FIGURE 2: LONG-TERM UNEMPLOYMENT RATE – SOUTH AUSTRALIAN AND AUSTRALIAN AVERAGE (1987–97)

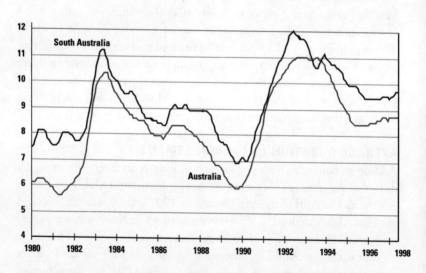

RETRENCHMENTS AND LAY-OFFS

The number of people employed in South Australia declined by around 20 000 over the two years to August 1998. The foundation of secure jobs in South Australia is being undermined by the loss of around 700 full-time jobs per month. In addition to public sector workforce reductions averaging more than 6000 per annum over the last four years, nearly 14 000 people per year were laid off or retrenched. Over the 1994–98 period, the annual average number of people laid off or retrenched has steadily increased. Towards the end of the last recovery period the average number of retrenchments and lay-offs was significantly less than the average over the four years to 1998. Over the 1989–90 recovery period the number of laid-off or retrenched persons ranged between 9000 and 11 000 persons per annum. Over the 1994–98 period it has been approximately 21 per cent higher.

PUBLIC SECTOR EMPLOYMENT

One of the most significant contributors to the loss of full-time employment in South Australia has been the loss of secure positions within the public sector. Continuing a trend which began in the early 1990s, and accelerated in the mid-1990s, the state and Commonwealth public sector workforces are in rapid decline due to privatisation, downsizing and outsourcing. The public sector workforce in South Australia has declined steadily since 1990 (see table 4). The rate of decline accelerated in 1993. There were 16 per cent or around 22 500 employees less in the public sector workforce in August 1997 compared to August 1993 (ABS Cat. 6248.0).

Given its relative dependence on public sector employment, it is worrying that South Australia has been more adversely affected by public sector workforce reductions than Australia as a whole over the course of the mid-1990s. The rate of decline in public sector employment in South Australia has been higher than the Australian rate. This is particularly evident in 1995 when the rate of decline was five times greater than the Australia rate of 0.5 per cent.

STATE PUBLIC SECTOR

State public sector employment has historically made a vital contribution to the provision of secure employment to South Australians. This contribution has been eroded significantly in recent years. In 1991, around 18 per cent of employed people in South Australia were in state

TABLE 4: PUBLIC SECTOR EMPLOYMENT, SOUTH AUSTRALIA AND AUSTRALIA, 1986–97, PERSONS (TREND)

Month/Year	Employees – SA	% change on previous year	Employees – Australia	% change on previous year
Aug 90	152 600		1 733 100	
Aug 91	148 300	–3%	1 715 200	–1%
Aug 92	144 700	–2%	1 674 300	–2%
Aug 93	141 800	–2%	1 641 200	–2%
Aug 94	133 900	–6%	1 570 500	–5%
Aug 95	127 100	–5%	1 564 500	–0.5
Aug 96	121 900	–4%	1 505 600	–4%
Aug 97	119 300	–2%	1 476 400	–2%

Source: ABS Cat. 6248.0

public sector employment. Over the 1992–97 period the state public sector share of total employment declined to 14 per cent, representing a 22 per cent change in just four years.

The state government's target of a reduction of 12 400 full-time equivalent positions was met and exceeded by June 1997. Reflecting this policy direction, the number of employees in the state public sector began to decline dramatically in 1994 (see table 5). The rate of decline varied from six per cent between 1993 and 1994 to two per cent between 1996 and 1997. Over the 1993–97 period, the public sector workforce contracted by around 19 000 persons.

HIDDEN COSTS OF PUBLIC SECTOR RESTRUCTURING

The proportion of secure 'ongoing' positions within the public sector is declining at the same time as overall levels of public sector employment. The number of ongoing positions declined by four per cent or 2777 people between June 1995 and June 1997. The proportion of contract positions has increased dramatically in the last three years from 9.8 per cent in June 1995 to 15.3 per cent in June 1997. Women are over-represented in less secure contract and casual positions within the public sector. While women represent more than half of those employed in permanent positions, they represent two-thirds of contract and casual positions.

TABLE 5: STATE PUBLIC SECTOR EMPLOYMENT, 1986–97, PERSONS

Year	Persons	% annual change
1986	108 064	
1987	110 122	1.9
1988	108 892	−1.1
1989	110 476	1.5
1990	116 208	5.2
1991	115 700	−0.4
1992	111 025	−4.0
1993	110 781	−0.2
1994	105 836	−5.5
1995	102 899	−2.8
1996	94 808	−7.9
1997	91 812	−3.2

Source: Annual Report of Commissioner for Public Employment, 1997

YOUTH UNEMPLOYMENT

One of the most disturbing characteristics of unemployment in South Australia is the chronically high rate of youth unemployment. For 15–19 year olds youth unemployment in South Australia was the highest in Australia over the twelve months to September 1998 (see table 6). Over the twelve months to September 1997 it averaged 35 per cent. Over the next twelve months the average had increased to around 37 per cent. This is 28 per cent higher than the national average.

Youth unemployment rates vary considerably throughout South Australia, with rates well above the state average recorded in southern and northern Adelaide. Unemployment rates in many of South Australia's metropolitan and regional areas have been double the state unemployment rate for many years. Youth unemployment has been at chronically high levels for the last ten years (see table 7). While young men experience consistently higher youth unemployment rates in urban South Australia, young women in the rural area of southern and eastern South Australia have significantly higher rates of unemployment compared to young men.

TABLE 6: YOUTH UNEMPLOYMENT RATES BY STATE, PER CENT, 15–19 YEAR OLDS SEEKING FULL-TIME EMPLOYMENT, AVERAGE OVER 12 MONTHS TO SEPTEMBER 1998

Western Australia	23.9
New South Wales	27.6
Victoria	34.3
Queensland	30.3
Tasmania	35.1
South Australia	**37.3**
Australia	30.4

Source: ABS Cat 6202

TABLE 7: AVERAGE YOUTH UNEMPLOYMENT RATES IN REGIONAL SOUTH AUSTRALIA, 15–24 YEAR OLDS, 1988–96

Rank	Region	Females	Males	Persons
1	Western Adelaide	16.8	25.8	21.7
2	Northern and Western SA	21.7	20.6	21.2
3	Eastern Adelaide	18.7	21.8	20.1
4	Northern Adelaide	16.5	22.1	19.4
5	Southern Adelaide	18.6	16.7	19.4
6	Southern and Eastern SA	22.2	13.6	17.5

Source: ABS Labour Force, unpublished and Social Justice Research Foundation

The average youth unemployment rate for 15–24 year olds in the worst-affected areas of South Australia ranged from between 17 and 22 per cent over the 1988–96 period. Of particular concern are the very high rates of unemployment among young women in rural South Australia and young men in western and northern Adelaide.

REGIONAL UNEMPLOYMENT

There is considerable variation in unemployment throughout the state. Nearly 35 per cent of all statistical local areas (SLAs) in June 1997 had unemployment rates higher than the state rate of 9.1 per cent (Spoehr 1998). Over 40 SLAs recorded unemployment rates higher than the state rate. The number of SLAs recording increases in unemployment rates for June 1997 was eight per cent higher than that recorded for June 1996. Unemployment rose in 69 SLAs and fell in 57 SLAs over the 1996–97 period.

The 20 SLAs with the highest rates of unemployment in June 1997 are detailed in table 8.

TABLE 8: STATISTICAL LOCAL AREA UNEMPLOYMENT RATES, SOUTH AUSTRALIA, JUNE QUARTER, 1996–97

	Statistical Local Areas	1997 rate %	1996 rate %
1	Elizabeth (C)	21.8	16.7
2	Enfield (C) – B	21.7	20.8
3	Coober Pedy (DC)	16.7	11.3
4	Hindmarsh (M)	16.4	15.3
5	Wallaroo (DC)	15.6	14.7
6	Thebarton (C)	15.2	14.7
7	Munno Para (C)	15	12.1
8	Enfield (C) – A	14.3	13.9
9	Peterborough (M)	13.8	13.2
10	Port Pirie (DC)	13.6	12.7
11	Dudley (DC)	13.4	6.7
12	Adelaide (DC)	13.1	10.6
13	Morgan (DC)	12.6	9.5
14	Port Adelaide (C)	12.5	12.4
15	Port Elliot & Goolwa (DC)	12.4	11.1
16	Port Augusta (DC)	12	11.1
17	Riverland – Unincorporated	12	10.1
18	Mannum (DC)	11.8	9.7
19	Whyalla (DC)	11.7	10.8
20	Willunga (DC)	11.3	13.2
	South Australia	**9.1**	**9.1**

Source: DEETYA Small Area Labour Markets, June 1996–97

In June 1997, 17 per cent fewer metropolitan SLAs in South Australia experienced a reduction in unemployment compared to June 1996. There was no improvement in the number of country SLAs recording a fall in unemployment over the same period.

CONCLUSION

The outlook for the South Australian labour market is bleak if recent trends persist. In the absence of significant domestic policy shifts and an improvement in the international economic outlook, double digit unemployment will persist in South Australia well into the next century. Many regions throughout South Australian may be confronted with the highest unemployment rates and poorest job prospects since the Great Depression.

Reliance on insecure, part-time and casual job growth in the service industries will fuel population loss and contribute to a vicious cycle of self-reinforcing decline in South Australia. The loss of population which flows from job seekers moving interstate in search of more secure, higher-quality, higher-paid jobs denies South Australia the skills, dynamism and purchasing power necessary for revitalisation.

APPENDIX A: RATIOS OF INDUSTRY EMPLOYMENT PER 1000 RESIDENT POPULATION IN SOUTH AUSTRALIA AND AUSTRALIA, 1991 AND 1996

INDUSTRY	South Australia		Australia	
	1991	1996	1991	1996
Extractive Activities	**26.27**	**25.75**	**24.12**	**23.10**
Agriculture, Forestry and Fishing	23.42	23.28	19.00	18.27
Mining	2.85	2.47	5.12	4.83
Transformative activities	**92.17**	**86.16**	**85.65**	**84.99**
Manufacturing	62.59	62.30	55.27	54.40
Elect/Gas/Water	5.22	3.26	5.41	3.31
Construction	21.36	20.60	24.97	27.28
Distributive activities	**100.48**	**101.81**	**105.46**	**110.62**
Wholesale-Retail*	78.14	79.16	79.24	83.60
Wholesale		23.61		25.17
Retail	55.55		58.43	
Transport Storage	16.20	15.23	19.26	18.56
Communication	6.14	7.42	6.96	8.46
Producer services	**41.46**	**48.65**	**46.68**	**58.98**
Finance, Property and Business*	41.46	48.65	46.68	58.98
Finance and Insurance	13.58		16.71	
Property and Business Services	35.07		42.27	
Social services	**105.52**	**95.26**	**98.43**	**92.10**
Public Admin/Defence*	20.72	17.57	23.83	20.79
Community Services*	88.40		74.60	
Educational Services	30.54		30.44	
Health and Community Services	47.15		40.87	
Personal services	**28.42**	**43.14**	**29.34**	**46.06**
Recreational/ Personal Services*	28.42		29.34	
Cultural & Recreational Services	9.02		10.10	
Personal and Other Services	16.51		15.66	
Accommodation, Cafes and Restaurant Services	17.61		20.30	

(Note: For the 1996 Census data, wholesale and retail were recorded separately; finance, property and business services were recorded separately; public administration/defence was renamed as government, administration and defence and community services were recorded separately as education services and health and community services; recreational/personal services were recorded separately as cultural and recreational services and personal and other services)

Source: Derived from Stimson, Fikreth, & O'Connor, K. 1998.

REFERENCES

Australian Bureau of Statistics Cat. No. 6202.0 *Labour Force, preliminary*
—— Cat. 6203.0 *Labour Force*
—— Cat. 6248.0 *Survey of Employment and Earnings*
—— Austats

Commissioner for Public Employment 1997, *Annual Report*, Government of South Australia.

DEETYA Small Area Labour Market Database, 1990–98

Stimson, R. J., Shuaib, F. & O'Connor, K. 1998, 'Population and employment "Hotspots" and "Coldspots" in the Australian Space Economy, 1986 to 1996', Australian and New Zealand Regional Science Association, Annual Conference, 21–23 September.

Spoehr, J. 1997, *South Australian Labour Market Briefing*, vol. 2, no. 2., Centre for Labour Research, University of Adelaide.

NOTES

1   Appendix A details industry employment to population ratios for Australia and South Australia for the 1991–96 censuses.

2   These areas are ABS statistical divisions.

CHAPTER 6

SURVIVING IN THE GLOBAL JUNGLE

The implications of global restructuring and neoliberalism for South Australia

RAY BROOMHILL

In the past two decades a very significant process of economic, political and social restructuring has occurred throughout the capitalist economies, including of course, Australia. These changes have created major problems and challenges for many regions and local economies. This is particularly so for those economies, such as South Australia's, which have to a degree been marginalised and bypassed in the global economic restructuring process. At the same time, we have also seen significant restructuring of the local political sphere as subnational governments themselves have been forced to adjust to a very different global economic environment. However, understandings of the nature and significance of these are currently underdeveloped and many issues and questions remain unresolved. The aim of this chapter is to consider a number of questions about the changes that local communities like South Australia confront in the context of global restructuring. In particular, this chapter seeks to investigate the relationship between 'globalisation' and local economic welfare. It is also concerned with the nature of the nexus between global economic restructuring and neoliberal policies at the local level. Finally, the chapter discusses whether states improve local economic fortunes through any form of institutional intervention. These are important questions for state policy-makers to seriously consider as they attempt to redefine the boundaries of the possible alternatives to neoliberalism and those economic fundamentalist policies which have been adopted as a response to economic restructuring.

THE IMPACT OF GLOBAL RESTRUCTURING ON LOCAL ECONOMIES

In both academic and political discussions over the past couple of decades, there has been considerable debate on the impact of economic restructuring and globalisation on local regions and economies. In academic debates on the one hand, there has been something of a polarisation between those who see these changes as potentially positive, at least for localities prepared to take advantage of the opportunities available, and those who view them as fundamentally negative, or at least containing severe dangers and problems (Lovering 1995). On the other hand, within the political discourse surrounding policy in Australia, there has existed an almost hegemonic domination by the advocates of the 'positive localisation' story who emphasise that the dynamic forces supposedly associated with globalisation provide an increased potential for local economies to greatly benefit from the growth opportunities provided by the dramatic changes currently taking place through globalisation. However, not only is this good news story about the positive potential of globalisation a grossly exaggerated one for most local communities, it has also reinforced pressures on state governments to compete with each other and to adopt policy approaches which have worsened the negative impacts of globalisation.

Within the 'positive localisation' debate, the potential benefits of globalisation and localisation are frequently overstated by proponents on both the social democratic Left and the fundamentalist Right (Axford 1995; Hirst & Thompson 1992; Ruigrok & van Tulder 1995). In reality, in most regions throughout the world, the processes of restructuring are more commonly producing 'fractured local economies, disempowered regions and fragmented local cultures' (Amin 1994, p. 27). Manuel Castells argues that cities and regions are now being structurally transformed in a very uneven process. In particular, those cities which are able to use their informational potential to extend and deepen their global reach will become dominant. We will simultaneously see the decline of many former industrial centres which are unable to make a transition to the informational economy since only some cities and regions will be able to make this transition. There will emerge new dynamic economic centres in developing areas such as in the Asia Pacific region. These 'informational' cities will be 'global' cities connected to a network of decision-making and information-processing centres. However, they will also be 'dual' cities with polarised communities.

The simultaneous growth of wealth and extreme poverty will produce strong social tensions between the global cosmopolitanism of the elite and the black holes of the urban ghettos. The violence of this confrontation will awaken our deepest 'psychic terrors' and lead to a 'structural urban schizophrenia' (Castells 1993). Saksia Sassen, in examining the consequences for cities of the emergence of a global economy, similarly argues that the processes of economic change are leading to a growing polarisation of the occupational and income structures resulting in absolute growth at both the top and bottom ends of the distribution and a decline in the middle of the distribution (Sassen 1991).

While the current phase of profound capitalist restructuring has generated a series of problems and crises for local economies everywhere, the impact has created havoc, particularly within older 'peripheral' industrialised economies, such as the South Australian, which have been bypassed in the dramatic re-organisation currently occurring in the global economy. As many researchers have demonstrated, a key aspect of the current restructuring process is that it is impacting in an extremely uneven manner on local economies. Two key characteristics of 'post-Fordist' global restructuring are firstly, a decline in many of the old industrial centres and secondly, associated growth in those cities and regions which multinational capital perceives as being able to adapt to, and foster new and more profitable forms of investment. Consequently, what we are witnessing is a growing polarisation between different economic regions and the exacerbation of spatial inequalities as shifting global markets produce winners and losers in the international competitive arena. Clearly, some regions and specific social groups are benefiting from the globalisation and restructuring process as wealth and resources are increasingly concentrated in a small number of cities and regions which host the most dynamic and expanding industries, particularly finance and informational technology. Meanwhile, other regions wither and decline as they become increasingly vulnerable to changes in the global economy and increasingly dependent upon the changing investment patterns of footloose globalising capital.

The South Australian economy is particularly vulnerable in the current restructuring scenario partly because, historically it has occupied a somewhat peripheral position within the overall Australian economy, which itself of course has occupied a peripheral and vulnerable position within international capitalism (Schedvin 1987). For over a hundred years after its foundation in 1836, the local economy was dominated by agricultural production. The 25-year period following the Second World War saw the rapid development of manufacturing in the state to the point where the economy became heavily reliant upon it for employment and economic growth (Rich 1986, p. 212). However, the manufacturing sector provided a brittle and limited base for the local economy. In the first place, investment came primarily from outside the state, and the sector increasingly became composed of branch offices of interstate and transnational firms. When economic globalisation hit South Australia during the mid-1970s, the effect was to cause many of these firms to restructure, rationalise or relocate their production. Secondly, investment in manufacturing was focused on a rather narrow range of goods, especially white goods and the motor vehicle industry. With the downturn in these areas which occurred in the 1970s, the state economy was left without a broad range of manufacturing activity which could act as the base for diversification.

The traumatic consequences of the impact of global restructuring on South Australian communities is evident not only in the decline of industry and the increasing numbers of unemployed, but equally as important, in the emergence of severe social problems and inequalities, and in the breakdown of the processes of social cohesion and reproduction. Many households and families suffered greatly increased stress – evidenced by rising poverty levels, crime, violence and gambling. It is increasingly evident also that restructuring has caused a major crisis of political and social alienation and exclusion (see chapter 7). This crisis is occurring throughout Australia and has been most clearly evidenced in the rise of Pauline Hanson and the One Nation phenomenon. Even in those regions and cities which appear to be flourishing, the growth of poverty, inequality and social problems has been exacerbated as the benefits of restructuring are distributed with increasing unevenness. For example, although Sydney is experiencing a building and finance boom which is providing benefits to a core group of workers and property owners, an increasing percentage of the population, especially those located in the peripheral western suburbs, is experiencing a widening of the gap between the haves and have-nots (Oakley 1994; Gregory 1993; Gregory & Hunter 1995).

The processes of global restructuring have also produced enormous pressures on state governments in Australia, as elsewhere, and created a far harsher economic policy environment whereby governments are under extreme pressures to redefine their approach and role. These changes have profound implications for future political governance. State governments in Australia are clearly facing significant difficulties in formulating an adequate policy response to the challenges raised by globalisation. In Australia as in other countries, this confusion has so far produced a hotchpotch of policy approaches, ranging from the creation of science parks, industrial districts and a 'Multifunction Polis' to the building of gigantic shopping centres and high visibility public relations ventures such as theme parks and international sporting events. These energetic, sometimes frantic attempts at making a particular local economy stand out in the crowd of competing regions can only be seen as desperate bids for development by means of local 'boosterism' – providing a great deal of hype but little substance (Amin & Malmberg 1994, pp. 242–3; Lovering 1995; Jessop 1997).

Under global restructuring, the flexibility and mobility of global capital has created a situation whereby it is increasingly possible to create a bidding competition between regional governments and workforces – a phenomenon which has been approvingly described within the discourse of mainstream economics in Australia as 'competitive federalism'. This increased competitiveness between states has resulted in the adoption of beggar-thy-neighbour policies as states have competed ferociously for available sources of investment funds. For example, the newly elected Queensland Coalition government in March 1996 announced that it intended to engage in 'open warfare' to poach business from the other states (*Advertiser* 9 March 1996, p. 8). The pressures on state governments have also been exacerbated as a result of the restrictionist fiscal policies of the federal government which has itself been dramatically affected by the impact of restructuring on its own financial capacity. Because the states have had financial responsibility for many of the welfare and social aspects of government activity in Australia, the fiscal crisis passed on to them from the federal level of government has placed them under further strain and greatly contributed to their shift to a far narrower and more 'economistic' approach to governance.

Policy prescriptions adopted at the state level have generally been based upon a 'free market' approach which have stressed the need for the local economy to develop 'global competitiveness' (Bryan 1995). There has been a strong shift in the approach taken by most Australian state governments towards what might be termed a more entrepreneurial state role. Alain Lipietz identifies the ideological underpinnings of this shift as the adoption of a culture of 'liberal-productivism' whereby all decisions are determined on the basis of their contribution to growth and productivity (Lipietz 1994, pp. 343–5). The adoption of such a liberal-productivist approach by government has occurred at the expense of social coherence and political democracy. This approach has been firmly endorsed by both major political parties in South Australia, and to varying degrees has been accepted by both local business and the trade union movement. Bob Jessop has characterised this change of policy direction by local governments as representing a significant shift from local Keynesianism to what he terms a 'workfare state' model in which the primary goal is the development of local competitiveness and in which 'redistributive welfare rights take second place to a productivist reordering' of policy (Jessop 1994, p. 263). Although Jessop sees this shift as representing a long-term change associated with the end of the post-war Fordist era to a state role more geared to the demands of fundamental economic restructuring within capitalism, he argues that the workfare state could well take neoliberal, neocorporatist or neostatist forms depending on local circumstances. Other researchers have been more inclined to see opportunities and spaces for more progressive approaches to remain on the political agenda and some of these will be examined shortly. Nevertheless, the dominant direction taken by the new local workfare state within Australia, as in many other countries, has clearly been towards the neoliberal form and warrants some further discussion.

THE GROWTH OF LOCAL NEOLIBERALISM

Since the mid-1970s, national governments in virtually all western capitalist countries have increasingly responded to the impact of global restructuring by implementing a range of neoliberal policies. These have included deregulation, privatisation, attacks on labour and, wherever possible, a privileging of the private sector over the public. The political Right has promoted neoliberalism as providing a successful transition to a restructured economy and economic regeneration via a market-guided strategy. While the Right has focused attention on restructuring the nation–state, it has also regarded it important to restructure the policies of the state at the local level. Such a strategy has received official endorsement from the OECD which has encouraged the reduction in specific regional industry development programs and the shift to 'actions aimed at improving the general business environment' at the local level (Bureau of Industry Economics 1994, p. 2).

Economic fundamentalists portray the adoption of neoliberal policies by governments as being simply an inevitable acceptance of the
failure of Keynesianism and the restoration of the proper (that is, far
more limited) role of government. Some neoliberal proponents of the
benefits of globalisation have tended to see the decline of the
nation–state and the shift to a more regional unit of governance as one
of the positive elements of the spread of multinational corporations
and the growth of global markets. At the extreme 'free market' end of
the 'positive localisation' position resides the influential Japanese management consultant and guru Kenichi Ohmae who has boldly predicted
the imminent death of the nation–state (Ohmae 1995). Ohmae sees the
growth of 'region–states' as being of more relevance in a world where
borderless transnational (as distinct from multinational) corporations
relate 'not to the artificial political borders of countries but to the more
focused geographical units'. Region–states are 'the right size and scale to
be the true, natural business units in today's global economy' (Ohmae
1995, p. 5). Naturally, neoliberal approaches to the form of strategy to
be adopted by local states have been based upon a 'free market' approach
and stress the need for the local economy to develop 'global competitiveness' (Peck & Tickell 1994a; Bryan 1995).

Throughout the world, local governments have been told by mainstream economists and a wide range of international political institutions
and business organisations that there is no alternative available to implementing the shift to a more market-oriented approach to state policy-
making and to the effective dismantling of the public sector. The
powerful message of neoliberalism has been that global restructuring and
the rapid internationalisation of the world economy has made it imperative that, in order to survive, local economies simply must become
internationally competitive and the role of government totally reshaped.
In this process, every corner of society and the economy must be
brought into the market sphere. This argument so far has been a very
successful one politically, and the promoters of neoliberalism, by and
large, have achieved a great victory selling this message. Bob Jessop has
argued that the discourse around economic policy-making has been
dramatically changed by recent restructuring in the global economy
(Jessop 1997). Emphasising the constitutive role of discourse in determining the parameters of economic strategies, Jessop argues that
the 'image' of the local economy and its place in the world has been
itself restructured, or 're-imagined', primarily through the emerging

hegemony of neoliberalism. In fact, the discourse of neoliberalism no longer 'imagines' the local region as a political, economic and cultural community, but rather as a narrowly economic entity which, in order to survive, must undertake entrepreneurial activities to achieve competitiveness.

In this neoliberal 're-imagining of the local', the processes of governance are also construed in a very different way from those operating in the Keynesian era. Consequently, there have recently been very dramatic changes in the economic policy approaches employed by subnational governments under the influence of neoliberal ideology. At the local level, policy-makers influenced by neoliberalism have generally sought to increase competitiveness via market mechanisms in order to create a favourable climate for business investment. The policies introduced have typically included attempts to lower wages especially at the lower end, to lower business taxes, to ease planning and environmental controls, to deregulate business controls and, particularly, to weaken employment legislation and to reduce the power of local unions. A common neoliberal argument has been the need for a decentralisation of the wage system to tailor wages to local and regional market conditions. This strategy has been applied especially in areas of industrial decline where it is argued that greatly increased 'flexibility' is required in wage levels in order to create investment and employment. Local industry policy has typically been non-interventionist, focusing on opening up new industries to the private sector via privatisation rather than through any form of active state coordination. While the Right has typically expressed strong support for local small business, this has tended to translate in practice into the removal of 'state-imposed burdens' rather than through genuine positive support. On the other hand, some forms of direct assistance to business have occurred in the form of ad hoc subsidies aimed often at marginal enterprises or used as incentives to attract multinational or national investment. This approach has led governments into adopting practices which in some cases have bordered on the corrupt and in others on the foolish. One such example of the latter might well be a recent South Australian government plan to 'kick-start the local economy' by head-hunting thirty rich Asian millionaire businessmen eager to escape the Asian economic meltdown (*Advertiser* 8 June 1998). Peck and Tickell see the pressures currently imposing themselves upon governments as creating a great deal of confusion as we enter a period of 'institutional searching'. But as Alain

Lipietz reminds us: 'the history of capitalism is full of experiments which led nowhere ... abandoned prototypes and all sorts of monstrosities' (Lipietz 1987, p. 15).

The imperatives of the shift to an entrepreneurial state model of governance have produced a marked decline in concern with democratic processes in public policy-making by government. An example of this process can be seen in the South Australian government's rejection of the call for a referendum on its proposed sale of the Electricity Trust of South Australia. Their disarmingly frank reason was that such a referendum would certainly be lost. The imperatives of the market's demand for privatisation of public assets has simply overridden any democratic concerns. One of the key aspects of the neoliberal approach has been to restructure the process of economic decision-making to enhance the involvement of local business personnel in state decision-making frequently to the exclusion of other groups, especially unions and representative community organisations. Hence in Australia we have seen the emergence of economic development boards and authorities comprising primarily, local business interests as the main vehicles for the provision of policy advice to state governments. To an increasing degree also, state governments have been inclined to 'outsource' public policy-making by making use of private consultancy firms to develop economic strategy. The shift to a more entrepreneurial culture within universities has also drawn many entrepreneurial academics into the policy-making arena as paid consultants. Much of the South Australian conservative government's neoliberal agenda has been developed in consultation with Professor Cliff Walsh, the Director of the Centre for Economic Studies of the Adelaide and Flinders Universities. As Professor Richard Blandy has pointed out, Walsh has continued to vociferously advocate and defend these policies in the daily newspaper without his key role in the development of those policies being made explicit by that newspaper (*Advertiser* 7 July 1998, p. 18). These individuals and organisations who have been employed as policy consultants have not been inclined to see the incorporation of broader social and equity goals as central to economic policy-making and have tended to favour the boosterism approach to local economic development. Hence we have seen the decline of governance processes designed to generate coherent and systematic approaches to promoting community welfare, and instead have seen the predominance of 'consultants' reports, outline proposals, non-binding agreements, glossy brochures ... cultural exchanges, databases and information centres' (Jessop 1997, p. 40). As John Lovering has whimsically commented in relation to these partly privatised policy-making institutions which are under considerable pressure to 'spectac-ularise' policy: 'if there is not much going on, there are a large number of actors involved in pretending there is' (Lovering 1997, p. 117).

What has actually been 'going on', however, is a quite dramatic decline in the role of state governments in relation to broader socio-economic and social reproduction activities. The neoliberal policy approach has produced a severe down-grading of social policy and the transfer of social and welfare services to the private sector as the focus of the local state, as with the nation–state, is shifted towards 'capital accu-mulation' at the expense of 'social reproduction' (Eisenschitz & Gough 1993, pp. 59–75). From the late 1980s the role of government and state in South Australian social policy development, as in other Australian states, has undergone a fundamental change (Broomhill et al 1995). From that point the state government began to adopt a far more market-oriented approach to policy-making while simultaneously downgrading broader social policy goals. Janine Brodie has characterised this process as shifting the boundaries of the public and private spheres (Brodie 1994, p. 55). Neoliberalism is engaged in a powerful discursive and political struggle to shrink the defined boundaries of the public sphere so that areas of social reproduction which were previously undertaken by the state are increasingly being redefined as being the responsibility of the private or household sphere (see chapter 7) Therefore, economic restructuring is placing the burden of economic 'adjustment' on house-holds – and on women in particular. Many of the so-called increased 'efficiencies' associated with the shift to a restructured, leaner state simply amount to a shifting of the costs of restructuring onto the unpaid household.

CAN LOCAL NEOLIBERALISM WORK?

There is considerable debate within progressive discourses about the likely success and sustainability of neoliberal policies at the local level. A significant body of international research produced by critics of neo-liberalism naturally emphasises the negative effects of the globalisation process and has identified numerous ways in which neoliberalism has badly disappointed local economies by failing to deliver either eco-nomic or employment growth. For example, British geographer Mike Geddes has argued that in 'the context of overall levels of unemployment, neoliberal industrial policy has ... been associated with the collapse of many local economies' (Geddes 1994, p. 157). Many Left analysts also suggest that the application of such policies exacerbates and further distorts the imbalance of power which has developed between global corporations and local state policy-makers, communities and citizens. In a study of the impact of restructuring strategies in Europe, Ash Amin and Anders Malmberg conclude that policies of the entrepreneurial model of local economic development have exposed 'local communities to the horrifying prospect of becoming the playing field for a thousand-and-one different entrepreneurial ventures, bound together by nothing more than the profit-seeking adventurism of the private sector' (Amin & Malmberg 1994, p. 244). The capacity of neoliberalism to solve the problems of local economies is also dismissed by Jamie Peck and Adam Tickell who argue that evidence of its failure to produce recovery can be found even in the showcase regions of neoliberalism such as Britain's M4 corridor and the Californian technopoles (Peck & Tickell 1994b, p. 295). These policies have also been demonstrated to contribute significantly to a loss of local economic autonomy and political control by regional governments as well as to a general erosion of social and economic living standards, cultural identity and self-confidence within communities.

However, from another Left perspective, pointing to the failures of neoliberalism to restore growth and reduce unemployment really misses the point about the role these policies play in the restructuring process, and why such policies have been widely embraced by both capital and governments. In many instances, critics of neoliberalism have underestimated the logic and achievements of such economic fundamentalist policies and of the restructuring of the state for capital (Gough 1996, p. 392). The rise of neoliberalism and its adoption at the local level can better be understood as the result of the changing political goals of large capital in the context of a period of rapid restructuring. For this reason it is important to consider a number of aspects of the political, economic and social context from which neoliberal policies emerged.

The fifty-year period of relatively steady economic growth which occurred throughout the post-war capitalist world has now ended. The period of instability and global restructuring which we are now experiencing is characterised by a much harsher economic environment. What has occurred over the past two decades within most industrialised economies results largely from a major breakdown in the previous growth cycle of capitalist accumulation. The period of growth and rapid capital accumulation that occurred during the long boom of the post-war period was based upon a stable economic regime of mass industrial production and mass consumerism (Lipietz 1987). Successful accumulation was supported by Keynesian macroeconomic policies, the development of a welfare state, corporatist class arrangements between capital, labour and the state, and government intervention to promote investment, stability and consumption. It was, of course, also based upon a set of social relations and gender arrangements which were also underpinned by the state and which provided the social and economic stability required to sustain economic accumulation (McDowell 1991).

By the late 1960s the strain was beginning to show in the post-war Fordist model. Historically, periods of restructuring are periods of fairly severe and traumatic change during which capital re-invents itself, often at the expense of large sections of the community and, indeed, of sections of capital itself. In the radically changed circumstances of our current phase of capitalist restructuring, capital has increasingly perceived the liberal Keynesian political framework and policies of the post-war era as impediments to its desire and need to have unrestricted free movement in and out of national economies. This phase of capitalist restructuring is in fact 'global' in scope. Consequently, the restructuring that has occurred in the structure of transnational capital and the global marketplace has in turn resulted in enormously increased pressure on governments to adopt 'free market' public policy approaches. This of course is nothing new. The regular re-emergence of crises within capitalist economies has invariably produced a dramatic change in the sort of policy approach adopted by governments. This was evident in the restrictionist and harsh policies adopted by governments during the Great Depression.

Consequently, neoliberalism has gained such widespread support from capital because it seeks to facilitate and reinforce the processes of restructuring and its therapeutic role following the 'bust' period of the cycle of capitalist development. By reducing all forms of government regulation, by reducing government ownership, and by lifting all geographical restraints on the free flow of capital and commodities, free market strategies seek to maximise the ability of (at least some sectors of) capital to restructure. In particular, deregulation and privatisation permit key sections of capital to shift investment focus out of areas of declining profitability while creating new areas for potentially profitable investment. At the same time, labour market deregulation, the abandonment of corporatist compromise arrangements between capital, labour and the state, and the reduction of state welfare expenditures all reinforce the disciplining of the workforce which is occurring naturally as a result of increased unemployment and labour market competition.

At the subnational level, the local state itself also played a crucial role during the post-war Fordist period both in promoting successful capital accumulation and in facilitating political stability and social reproduction (Kratke & Schmoll 1991, p. 543). South Australian post-war development has been perceived as involving a high level of local state intervention in the economy (McFarlane 1986; Chapman 1993). The economic strategy developed over the post-war period in South Australia involved seeking to gain maximum benefit from federal industry protection policies combined with the extensive provision of public economic and social infrastructure and services in order to attract private investment away from the eastern states and from foreign investors. Significantly, the South Australian state government not only stimulated economic development, but also actively promoted increased social development, coherence and equity, especially in the decade of the 1970s when the actively reformist Dunstan Labor government was in office (see chapter 2).

The end of the post-war Fordist period of growth dramatically changed the political, economic and social context, not only for the national state, but for the local state as well. In fact, the position of the local state in the restructuring process has been construed by some analysts as being in some ways more significant. Jessop has identified a phenomenon described as the 'hollowing out' of the nation–state whereby the power and autonomy of the national state is weakened by a transference of some of its former activities both upwards and downwards. On the one hand, many of its former regulatory activities are increasingly being performed by supranational institutions such as the International Monetary Fund (IMF), the World Bank, the World Trade Organisation and the proposed Multilateral Agreement on Investment (MAI). On the other hand, there is simultaneously occurring a transfer of economic and political authority downwards to the local state in line with the demand by capital for local economies to be more competitive in the new world economic order (Jessop 1994, p. 272). Bob Jessop sees some cause for optimism in this trend as it leads to an increasing emphasis on economic regeneration at the local level. A similar optimism is provided by Margit Mayer who sees the local state as playing a far more active role in a post-Fordist future. She argues that with the breakdown of Fordism there has occurred a proliferation of local economic growth models as local states have become 'direct players in the world economy' (Mayer 1992, p. 263).

While the validity of this metaphor of the 'hollowing out' of the nation–state remains problematic on a number of counts (Hirst & Thompson 1996; Weiss 1998), it is certainly true that governments at the subnational level increasingly face pressures to become more intensely competitive and entrepreneurial. As a result, Keynesian socio-economic interventionism has given way to a policy approach more crudely geared to promoting capital investment and short-term profit-ability and productivity gains (Peck & Tickell 1994; Kratke & Schmoll 1991). Capital increasingly prefers to negotiate directly with a sub-national state than with a more powerful national state. Perhaps even more importantly, in promoting the shift to a more explicitly free market approach, capital is actively fostering regional competition and the adoption of beggar-thy-neighbour economic policies to serve its own interests. Consequently, the shift of policy decision-making from the national to the state level should not be seen as increasing the power of the local state. In fact, in some ways the reverse is true. British geographers Paterson and Pinch develop the view that restructuring has reduced the local state's long-term capacity for autonomy (Paterson & Pinch 1995). They argue that there has occurred a deterioration in the scope and authority of local government itself and that Jessop's 'hollowing out of the nation state' thesis fails to note that restructuring has also meant the reduction in the role and autonomy of subnational governance. While Jessop argues that responsibility for important state functions such as labour market policy, education and training, tech-nology transfer, science parks etc. may be devolving to the local level, Patterson and Pinch argue that, in practice, the capacity to act on these issues is both limited and declining. This is the result of the restruc-turing, and depoliticisation, of local governance that is currently taking place – in particular through privatisation and contracting-out. In prac-tice, the local state is even more vulnerable to pressures from national and global capital to restructure its activities and to redirect them to serving the economic needs of capital rather than the social and welfare needs of the community. Consequently, the real story is not that the nation–state is losing power to the local state but rather that, to some extent, the nation–state and, even more profoundly, the local state, are both losing power to a restructured but increasingly centralised and globally mobile capital. Current global changes are generally resulting in the fragmentation and fracturing of local economies and political institutions in a way which has reduced the 'manoeuvring space' available to both local industry and local governments (Graham 1995, p. 84). As Amin and Malmberg put it: 'If localities are on the march, it is . . . to the tune of globalising forces in the organisation of production: a process in which local economic sustainability is far from guaranteed' (Amin & Malmberg 1994, p. 234). Therefore, the metaphor of 'hollowing out' may be just as appropriately applied to the local state as to the nation–state (Paterson & Pinch 1995).

Consequently, while the immediate, beneficial aspects of the shift to neoliberalism at the local level for capital are clear, the question of the long-term viability and sustainability of the restructured entrepreneurial local state is another matter. While restructuring has led local states increasingly to pursue short-term, beggar-thy-neighbour, neoliberal policies in the face of deregulating global competition which may benefit capital in the short term, it is clearly not a stable or effective long-term political response by the local state to the profound crisis of capitalism precipitated by the end of Fordism. British geographers Peck and Tickell argue that a coherent post-Fordist state structure has yet to emerge or stabilise (Peck & Tickell 1994a). They see the adoption of neoliberal policies as a temporary and unstable 'institutional fix'. In fact, neoliberalism will only prolong the crisis by maintaining systemic instability – the return to the 'jungle' of unfettered national and global markets creating havoc for local communities. Furthermore, the ability of neoliberalism to provide a stable framework for social reproduction is even more problematic. The destructive and fragmenting impact of neoliberal policies on communities and households creates severe doubts about the long-term potential of societies to maintain a structure which permits even capital to flourish. The social chaos engendered by the Asian crisis and the subsequent imposition of draconian free market structural adjustment policies vividly highlights this problem.

Interestingly, there are pessimistic and optimistic scenarios which can be constructed on the conclusion that neoliberalism cannot, in the long term, provide the social, community and household structures required to sustain economic accumulation. Peck and Tickell are themselves essentially sceptical about the capacity of local governments to capture any meaningful degree of political and economic power 'in the context of globalising accumulation and global deregulation' (Peck & Tickell 1994a, p. 325). Instead they see the nation–state remaining the primary focus in the struggle for the establishment of a new equitable and workable social framework since 'this is likely to remain the principal scale at which democratic control and political power can be (re)coupled'. In their view, solutions to the post-Fordist crisis are unlikely to come from increased local competition but must begin with action through national and global coordination. The pessimistic scenario is also dramatically depicted by Josef Esser and Joachim Hirsch who portray a frightening vision of a neo-Fordist society wracked by extreme social polarisation and class divisions (Esser & Hirsch 1994, p. 76–8). On the one hand they predict mass unemployment and a vast underclass of dispossessed and alienated; on the other, they also perceive the continuation of great wealth and privilege accumulated in a small group of beneficiaries sustained by an increasing concentration of corporate power and backed by the development of a repressive neoliberal state. They foresee the emergence of a new authoritarian alliance between the state and capital to create extreme forms of exploitation so that profitability is generated in the context of generalised impoverishment. They report that signs are already emerging in German cities of a new authoritarian post-Fordist society as 'chic shopping precincts and pedestrian zones are planned from the very beginning to accommodate water cannons and commando troops' (Esser & Hirsch 1994, p. 93).

Before we sink too deeply into despair however, it is important to note the existence of other more optimistic analyses concerning the possibilities for local communities in the wake of neoliberalism's failures. A more agreeable scenario is presented by Mike Geddes who argues that the local state played a major role in the regulation of the post-war regime of accumulation and that the current application of neoliberal policies by local governments represents a 'flawed post-Fordism' (Geddes 1994). He then develops the argument that the local state will continue to provide an important forum for contestation by progressive forces because the shift of investment focus by capital to the local level, while containing many dangers, also has the capacity to open up new political spaces for contestation and to produce alternative models for post-Fordist communities (Geddes 1997). Paradoxically, while there has certainly been a strong shift to neoliberal policies at the local as well as the national level, at the same time there has also emerged, albeit in a fairly fragmented way, a range of interventionist local economic policies and approaches which are neo-Keynesian in nature. In fact, while the increasing competition between urban regions since the 1970s pushed many local governments towards the adoption of a more entrepreneurial neoliberal approach, it has also led some to adopt more interventionist strategies (Kratke & Schmoll 1991, p. 545). To what extent then do alternatives to neoliberalism present a viable option for local communities faced with the challenges posed by global restructuring?

THE POSSIBILITIES AND CONTRADICTIONS OF ALTERNATIVE LOCAL POLICIES

A number of reasons for the continuation of forms of state intervention at the local level even within the context of an increasingly neoliberal global world can be identified (Sengenberger 1993, p. 315–6). Of key importance has been the spectacular failure of national governments to resolve problems arising from the end of the post-war boom. Although restructuring has led to the rise of neoliberal economic policies hostile to intervention in the economy at the national level, the failure of these policies has also resulted in greater emphasis on state-led economic growth strategies at the local level in many countries (Sengenberger 1993, p. 315). Moreover, the increasingly uneven impact of global restructuring on subnational regions has itself forced many regions, especially those most severely disadvantaged by it, to adopt a more active state economic strategy rather than relying solely on aggregate national growth.

Even in cases where local governments may have adopted a fundamentally neoliberal approach to policy-making in general, their 'basket' of policies has sometimes included elements which are essentially neo-Keynesian in the sense of seeking to use non-market coordination to address particular market inadequacies and failures (Eisenschitz & Gough 1996, p. 434). These seemingly contradictory policy trends therefore, not only represent different responses to restructuring by different local states, but in many instances exist side by side within the same government's strategy. State and local governments in most industrialised countries have come under pressure from many conflicting sources and have therefore faced increasing difficulties in formulating coherent policy responses to the challenges raised by globalisation. For example, the policy approach of the South Australian government over the past decade, while increasingly influenced by neoliberalism, has continued to display a number of interventionist elements in promoting growth; for example, in relation to maintaining support for tariff protection for the local car manufacturing industry.

Interventionist strategies adopted by local states represent a range of different political approaches from liberal through to Left social democratic. Like the conservative approach, governments influenced by more liberal variants of neo-Keynesianism have identified a very active role for the local state in boosting markets, profits and individual enterprise as the basis for a dynamic local economy. Such liberal neo-Keynesian policies have been based upon a perception of the need for a degree of state coordination and regulation of private capital to promote high growth and increased competitiveness. As such, they perhaps represent a step in the right direction in the search for collective approaches to dealing with the challenges posed by restructuring. However, in many respects they bear a close resemblance to policies promoted by the advocates of neoliberalism. Policies of this type remain fundamentally reliant on a trickle-down effect to benefit the community. To the extent that they are actually likely to be at all 'successful' therefore, they are in danger of deepening the problem of uneven development and exacerbating social and economic inequalities (Eisenschitz & Gough 1996, pp. 444–6). However, as a number of critics of contemporary neo-Keynesian 'boosterism' have noted, the more likely outcome of such an 'entrepreneurial state' policy approach is the expenditure of considerable state resources with little or no result in terms of new investment and employment growth (Lovering 1995; Amin & Malmberg 1994; Jessop 1997).

Recent neo-Keynesian approaches with a more social-democratic flavour have sought to broaden industrial strategies to provide more active industry intervention based upon selective and strategic policies. For example, more interventionist forms of industry assistance have introduced performance contracts for assistance measures and targeted strategic sectors including service and high-technology industries. These strategies require far more economic intelligence and planning by state agencies. Social-democratic neo-Keynesian approaches similarly have been more interventionist in promoting a broader approach to industrial development by the development of social and economic infrastructure; that is, they adopt the view that economic dynamism is not just achieved through individual firms but through a web of economic, social and political institutions and practices as well.

Social-democratic neo-Keynesian policies usually have as their strategic aim the modernisation of the local capitalist economy by making it more productive, internationally competitive and profitable, assuming that faster growth will benefit wages and conditions and that capital needs coordination. This approach actively promotes new forms of production to enhance the region's competitiveness by the introduction of 'flexible specialisation' production techniques, an increased export orientation and the development of public/private partnerships. It may also include the promotion of a variety of government/business networking arrangements such as business clusters, industrial districts, technology innovation centres and science and technology parks. It often involves an attempt to promote the development of cooperation and trust in capital/labour relations not just at the enterprise level but also at the regional level. Many social-democratic neo-Keynesian approaches also include the application of 'new growth theory' which suggests that public policies at the local level can accelerate growth and productivity through state provision of education and training, research and development and local economic infrastructure. They may also include direct job creation and production of public goods, employment subsidies and public works infrastructure development schemes to support private sector investment and to create employment. While some of these strategies have been directed at seeking to attract outside investment into the region, many have adopted an endogenous approach to promoting local growth. A common feature of most neo-Keynesian local strategies is a focus on the goal of maximising and enhancing local resources for economic development – a 'bootstraps' strategy (Eisenschitz & Gough 1993, pp. 10–11).

These policies and strategies have degrees of merit and value as alternatives to the neoliberal approach. Clearly, given the devastating impacts experienced by regions as a result of current global restructuring, increasingly interventionist policies are essential in any local strategy aimed at combating the negative impact of global markets. However, it is important to recognise that a number of quite significant limitations on the likely success of such policies continues to exist – deriving from the significant constraints which exist on the power and autonomy of local/state governments – and including both the powerful nature of the forces of global restructuring and the dependency of localities themselves on the national state.

The 'bootstraps' ideology embraced by many, or perhaps even most,

interventionist policies invariably leads to acceptance of the economistic discourse of the need for local communities to become more
internationally 'competitive'. Much of the debate about the need for
embracing local economic strategies which will promote competitive
advantage ignores the fact that only a few local communities can be
winners in such a competitive race. From the point of view of the
majority of the community there is a great danger that the single-
minded pursuit of competitive advantage will actually involve us in a
global 'race to the bottom'. Similarly, there are great dangers in states like
South Australia becoming entangled in a process of bidding for investment with other regions. This has been a common element within the
economic development policy approach taken by all Australian states
but, as Amin and Malmberg have demonstrated, more often than not
such an approach leads to the state incurring great expense but without
great return (Amin & Malmberg 1994). The blind acceptance of the
rhetoric of interstate competitiveness inevitably paves the way for the
adoption of beggar-thy-neighbour policies. South Australia is clearly not
well placed to engage in bidding wars with the eastern states and would
be far better off seeking collaboration and cooperation with other states
for mutual benefit. Regional differences and inequalities within Australia
make it essential that the federal government play a leading role in
ensuring harmonious national development. Within the Australian
context, it is important to recognise also that the federal nature of the
political system makes it inevitable that state economies and governments are for the foreseeable future going to be significantly dependent
upon the national government. Consequently, the ability of each of
the states to adjust to the impact of global restructuring and resist its
negative impact will depend in large part on the ability of the Australian
national state to do the same. An important component of any state
policy approach is therefore an emphasis on the federal government's
playing a key role in promoting regional development, and by recognising the special needs of different communities in the context of
global restructuring.

One of the elements of optimism about the economic potential
for intervention at the regional level has been the perceived spread of a
number of successful models based on local economic development
strategies. Parts of Sweden, the German Lander and the Third Italy
are frequently promoted by supporters of increased state intervention at
the local level as examples of successful endogenous local economic

development (Perulli 1993). While these regions may indeed offer the basis for an alternative model for other regions, they clearly do not represent the typical product of the adoption of conventional forms of neo-Keynesian interventionism. On the contrary, these examples are rather rare exceptions to the dominant trends in regional development and result from specific local circumstances and policy approaches which demonstrate that successful local economic development is integrally connected to the quality of the region's political, social and cultural infrastructure. These successes are examples of local communities that have retained a degree of resilience and social coherence – qualities which are very much under attack by the forces of global restructuring and neoliberal policy – and which cannot be developed by entrepreneurial and economistic policy approaches.

Policy-makers seeking to develop more progressive policies in response to the challenges of global restructuring would do well to ignore the hype and false promises promulgated by the ideologues of the market and the advocates of local boosterism. The potential of local strategies to develop international competitiveness is similarly frequently overstated and fundamentally serves only the interests of footloose capital (Bryan 1995). South Australia, as a small state with limited resources, is in a vulnerable position in the global marketplace and in relation to the process of global restructuring currently underway. It is not going to become a tiger economy (which is perhaps fortunate given that most of the Asian tiger economies have now been effectively hunted, bagged and mounted by free market hunters) and the South Australian government will remain severely constrained in its ability to restructure the local economy. Nevertheless, there is clearly a tradition of state intervention in South Australia which has served the community well. This is a key reason why the social infrastructure of the state continues to support a living standard and quality of life beyond that which the level of economic activity would seem to suggest possible. Increased state intervention, therefore, undoubtedly should continue to be a key component of a progressive agenda. However, the primary goal of such intervention should be to create greater resilience to the impact of global changes. Intervention should focus on building solid, collective social and economic infrastructure – including respect and increased support for the public sector, for households and for other vital non-market components of our economy. Of course, such policies will not be possible if we continue to reduce the 'public' space for community participation and contestation of the political process. The emergence of neoliberalism as the dominant ethos guiding public policy-making has led to the undermining of democratic process at the state level and the adoption of a discourse which presents economic decision-making as a depoliticised 'no-choice' process. The further down the path to neoliberalism we go, the more difficult it becomes to maintain any form of democratic autonomy over local decision-making.

REFERENCES

Advertiser 9 March 1996, p. 8.

Amin, Ash 1994, 'Post-Fordism: Models, fantasies and phantoms of transition', in *Post-Fordism: A Reader*, ed Ash Amin, Blackwell, Oxford, pp.140.

Amin, Ash & Malmberg, Anders 1994, 'Competing structural and institutional influences on the geography of production in Europe', in *Post-Fordism: A Reader*, ed Ash Amin, Blackwell, Oxford pp. 22748.

Axford, Barrie 1995, *The Global System: Economics, Politics and Culture*, Polity Press, Cambridge.

Brodie, Janine 1994, 'Shifting the boundaries: Gender and the politics of restructuring', *The Strategic Silence: Gender and Economic Policy*, ed I. Bakker, Zed Books, London, pp. 46–60.

Broomhill, Ray, Genoff, Rodin, Juniper, James & Spoehr, John 1995, 'The debt made us do it! The South Australian neoliberal agenda', in *Altered States: The Regional Impact of Free Market Policies on the Australian States*, eds John Spoehr & Ray Broomhill, Social Justice Research Foundation, Adelaide, pp. 213–26.

Bryan, Dick 1995, 'International competitiveness: National and class agendas,' *Journal of Australian Political Economy*, vol. 35, pp. 123.

Bureau of Industry Economics 1994, *Regional Development: Patterns and Policy Implications*, Australian Government Publishing Service, Canberra.

Castells, Manuel 1993, 'European cities, the informational society and the global economy', *New Left Review*, vol. 204, pp. 18–32.

Chapman, Paul 1991, 'Australian industry Surely not no policy,' in *Australian Industry What Policy*, Pluto Press, Sydney, pp. 69–96.

Eisenschitz, Aram & Gough, Jamie 1993, *The Politics of Local Economic Policy: The Problems and Possibilities of Local Initiatives*, Macmillan, London.

Esser, Josef & Hirsch, Joachim 1989, 'The crisis of Fordism and the dimensions of a 'post-Fordist' regional and urban structure', *International Journal of Urban and Regional Research*, vol. 13, no. 3, pp. 417–36.

Geddes, Mike 1994, 'Public services and local economic regeneration in a post-Fordist economy,' in *Towards a Post-Fordist Welfare State?*, eds Roger Burrows, and Brian Loader, Routledge, London, pp. 154–76.

Geddes, Mike 1997, 'Poverty, excluded communities and local democracy', in *Transforming Cities: Contested Governance and New Spatial Divisions*, eds N. Jewson & S. MacGregor, Routledge, London, pp. 205–18.

Gough, Jamie 1996, 'Neoliberalism and localism: Comments on Peck and Tickell', *Area*, vol. 29, no. 2, pp. 392–98.

Gregory, R. G. 1993, 'Aspects of Australian and US living standards: The disappointing decades 1970–1990', *Economic Record*, vol. 69, pp. 61–76.

Gregory, R. G. & Hunter, B. 1995, *The Macro Economy and the Growth of Ghettos and Urban Poverty in Australia*, discussion papers no. 325, ANU Centre for Economic Policy Research, Canberra.

Hirst, Paul & Thompson, Grahame 1992, 'The problem of 'globalisation': international economic relations, national economic management and the formation of trading blocs', *Economy and Society*, vol. 21, no. 4, pp. 357–96.

Hirst, Paul & Thompson, Grahame 1996, *Globalization in Question: The International Economy and the Possibilities of Governance*, Cambridge, Polity Press.

Jessop, Bob 1994, 'Post-Fordism and the state', in *Post-Fordism: A Reader*, ed A. Amin, Blackwell, Oxford, pp. 251–79.

Jessop, Bob 1997, 'The entrepreneurial city: Re-imaging localities, redesigning economic governance, or restructuring capital?', in *Transforming Cities: Contested Governance and New Spatial Divisions*, eds N. Jewson & S. MacGregor, Routledge, London, pp. 28–41.

Kratke, Stefan & Schmoll, Fritz 1991, 'The local state and social restructuring', *International Journal of Urban and Regional Research*, vol. 15, no. 4, pp. 542–52.

Lipietz, Alain 1994, 'Post-Fordism and democracy', in *Post-Fordism: A Reader* ed A. Amin, Blackwell, Oxford, pp. 338–58.

Lipietz, Alain 1987, *Mirages and Miracles: The Crisis of Global Fordism*, Verso, London.

Lovering, John 1995, 'Creating discourses rather than jobs: The crisis in the cities and the transition fantasies of intellectuals and policymakers', in *Managing Cities: The New Urban Context*, eds Patsy Healy, Stuart Cameron, Simin Davoudi, Stephen Graham & Ali Madani-Pour, Wiley, New York, pp. 109–26.

McDowell, Linda 1991, 'Life without father and Ford: The new gender order of post-Fordism', *Transactions of the Institute of British Geographers*, vol. 16, no. 4, pp. 400–19.

McFarlane, Bruce 1986, 'The role of government in the economic life of South Australia', in *The State as Developer : Public Enterprise in South Australia*, ed K. Sheridan, Royal Australian Institute of Public Administration and Wakefield Press, Adelaide, pp. 4–30.

Mayer, Margit 1992, 'The shifting local political system in European cities', in *Cities and Regions in the New Europe*, eds M. Dunford, & G. Kafkalas, Belhaven, London, pp. 255–78.

Oakley, Susan 1994, Industrial Restructuring and the Spatial Equity in Cities: A Case Study of Sydney, Melbourne and Adelaide, Honours thesis, Flinders University of South Australia, School of Sociology, Adelaide.

Ohmae, Kenichi 1995, *The End of the Nation State: The Rise of Regional Economies*, The Free Press, New York.

Patterson, A & Pinch, P L 1995, 'Hollowing out the local state: Compulsory competitive tendering and the restructuring of British public sector services', *Environment and Planning A*, vol. 27, pp. 1437–61.

Peck, Jamie & Tickell, Adam 1994a, 'Jungle law breaks out: Neoliberalism and global-local disorder', *Area*, vol. 26, no. 4, pp. 317–26.

Peck, Jamie & Tickell, Adam 1994b, 'Searching for a new institutional fix: The 'after-Fordist crisis and the global-local disorder', in *Post-Fordism: A Reader*, ed Ash Amin, Blackwell, Oxford, pp. 280–315.

Perulli, Paolo 1993, 'Towards a regionalisation of industrial relations', *International Journal of Urban and Regional Research*, vol. 17, no. 1, pp. 98–113.

Ruigrok, Winfried & van Tulder, Rob 1995, *The Logic of International Restructuring*, Routledge, London.

Rich, David C 1986, *The Industrial Geography of Australia*, Methuen, Sydney.

Sassen, Saksia 1991, *The Global City*, Princeton University Press, Princeton.

Schedvin, C. B. 1987, 'The Australian economy on the hinge of history', *Australian Economic Review*, pp. 20–30.

Senenberger, Werner 1993, 'Local development and international economic competition', *International Labour Review*, vol. 132, no. 3, pp. 313–29.

Spoehr, John & Broomhill, Ray (eds) 1995, *Altered States: The Regional Impact of Free Market Policies in the Australian States*, Social Justice Research Foundation, Adelaide.

Weiss, Linda 1998, *The Myth of the Powerless State: Governing the Economy in a Global Era*, Polity Press, Cambridge.

CHAPTER 7

RESTRUCTURING OUR LIVES

Engendering debates about social and economic policy
in South Australia

RAY BROOMHILL AND RHONDA SHARP

Current Australian policy debates about how state governments can respond to the challenges posed by global restructuring present a narrow and 'economistic' view of the impact of restructuring on a community. In particular, 'mainstream' economic analyses contain what Isabella Bakker has termed 'conceptual silences' in relation to significant sectors of both the economy and society (Bakker 1994, p. 1). Economistic perspectives of restructuring are particularly limited in their capacity to uncover the gendered nature of restructuring. Because the restructuring process currently underway is occurring on many levels, including the economic, social, political and ideological, understanding the linkages between these levels is important in developing not only an adequate analysis of the highly gendered nature of restructuring but also in creating more comprehensive and equitable policy responses by government.

Over the past two decades, in South Australia and elsewhere, economic policy debates have been dominated by the discourses of restructuring. However there remains relatively little awareness that recent profound economic and social changes have had very different impacts on men and women, and a significant impact on gender relations. Most policy discourse assumes that the effects of restructuring are gender-neutral (Bakker 1996, p. 6; Cohen 1994; MacDonald 1995). There also has been scant recognition of the gendered impact of policies adopted by governments themselves in response to restructuring. Moreover, the gender blindness of policy-making has had important consequences for the development of social and economic policy in response to restructuring at all levels of government in Australia – including at the state level. However, the recent shift to neoliberalism has not only further entrenched a policy-making approach which is insensitive in its response to restructuring's gendered impact, but it has also reinforced rather than counteracted the extremely negative impacts of restructuring on large sections of the South Australian community.

To fully comprehend the extent of the impact which restructuring and neoliberalism are having on the position of men and women and on gender relations in South Australia, a few comments on the nature of the state's post-war social and economic dynamic are necessary. During the so-called Fordist era in South Australia from the Second World War to the mid-1970s, growth and stability were underpinned by a set of economic structures and arrangements which were generated and reproduced at both the national and local levels. In South Australia, as in other Australian states, these included the development of a significant manufacturing sector, an active and interventionist role by governments strongly influenced by Keynesianism, a low-cost and highly sex-segmented labour market, a steady and increasing supply of women's labour in the paid economy, and a highly centralised national and state industrial relations system built around the highly gendered concept of a minimum family wage for male workers. Of crucial importance also was a more informal set of social and gender arrangements which, although based fundamentally upon a nuclear family structure and a male breadwinner norm, was undergoing some significant changes throughout the 1950s and 1960s. Within South Australian households, women remained primarily responsible for domestic labour and social reproduction even though increasingly being drawn into the labour market on a part-time basis. Many of these social and gender arrangements were constructed at the national level but were reaffirmed and expanded at the level of the state community.

Historically, South Australian state governments have played an important role in influencing both the pace and direction of economic development as well as ensuring social welfare and social reproduction. In both economic and social policy realms, post-war South Australian governments significantly influenced the position of men and women and the gender relationships that existed between them. While state economic intervention, during the Playford era in the 1950s and 1960s in particular, was not generally motivated by a conscious desire by policy-makers to improve the economic and social position of women, in significant ways women's ability to participate in the labour market was enhanced by state interventionist policies. At the same time the range and types of employment created as a result of state economic development strategies ensured the maintenance of a fairly rigid sexual division of the labour market. Under the Dunstan Labor government of the 1970s, the steady growth of the community services area of the state's economy, largely driven by the public sector, provided an enormous area of growth in women's employment. Both Labor and Liberal governments in South Australia also provided a growing welfare state structure which underpinned individual and family welfare, and social reproduction where the family failed or couldn't cope. Especially during the Dunstan decade of the 1970s, the South Australian government became increasingly active in support of welfare and social equity through involvement in a wide range of social policy areas – including the expansion of housing, health and education.

Throughout industrialised countries from the mid-1970s, the onset of economic crises and the subsequent prolonged period of restructuring resulted in these economic, social and political arrangements becoming increasingly unstable, as Fordist economic growth stumbled (Bakshi et al 1995, p. 1543). While the current process of restructuring can be understood in part as capital's response to the onset of major crises in accumulation and profitability, it can also be seen as the result of a breakdown of Fordist social and political arrangements. Consequently, at the present time, not only are the structures and processes of the South Australian economy being restructured, but a radical restructuring is also occurring in the gender arrangements and household structures which underpinned social reproduction during the post-war Fordist era in South Australia. Because gender relations played such an important role in the structures of Fordism, the restructuring of gender relations is also likely to have a profound effect on the new restructured economy. While the government has been profoundly affected by the impact of economic and social restructuring on South Australia, it has itself exerted very significant impact on the welfare of individuals and households as a result of the shift to a neoliberal policy approach.

In this chapter we attempt to develop an analysis of the impact of restructuring on the South Australian community which more adequately acknowledges the breadth and gendered nature of the changes occurring as a result of restructuring. In particular we examine the gendered impact of restructuring on the spheres of the labour market, the household and government policy-making. We also explore some of the ways in which a more gender-aware analysis of the impact of restructuring on South Australian society provides a different perspective on the issues which need to be addressed by state government policy-makers attempting to deal with the challenges posed by restructuring.

RESTRUCTURING GENDER IN THE SOUTH AUSTRALIAN LABOUR MARKET

Restructuring has had a major impact on the South Australian labour market. However, understanding the significant, but different impact, of restructuring on the position of women and men in the labour market has been very limited. In the dominant political and economic discourse on the employment problems associated with restructuring, and the emergence of the 'rustbelt' phenomenon in some Australian states, the main issue emphasised has been the loss of male breadwinner jobs in the manufacturing sector. A recent report by the Reserve Bank of Australia concluded that 'full-time male workers have borne the brunt of a rising trend in the unemployment rate over the past three decades' (*Australian* 27 May 1998, p. 8). Similarly the *Advertiser* in a report on South Australia's jobs crisis noted that, 'male full-time employment . . . which remains the main source of income for most families, has still not recovered to its pre-recession levels' (*Advertiser* 18 June 1996, p. 34). The economist Bob Gregory has stressed that for huge numbers of men, the consequences of economic restructuring have been negative: 'The Australian job loss has been concentrated on males. After adjusting for population growth, one in four male, full-time jobs has disappeared since 1970' (Gregory 1993, p. 61). At the same time, it has been widely recognised that the labour market participation of women has been increasing – albeit in the areas of part-time work. This has sometimes been interpreted as a causal factor in the decline of full-time male jobs: some analysts have perceived this trend in terms of women replacing men in the secondary labour market and causing a decline in men's position. While restructuring has undoubtedly had a devastating effect on enormous numbers of male workers, this view is one-dimensional and has in fact had a limiting effect on employment and economic development policy responses to restructuring by most governments – including the South Australian.

The gendered impact of restructuring on the labour market has been complex and often misinterpreted. One of the most commonly identified changes has been the continually increasing participation of women in paid employment. Women's labour market participation rate in South Australia increased significantly from 45 per cent to 53 per cent between 1977 and 1997. Similarly, by May 1998 women represented 43 per cent of the total South Australian workforce compared to 37.5 per cent in 1978 (ABS 1998; ABS *Labour Force Australia Historical Summary 1978–89*). However, there is recent evidence that under the impact of federal and state neoliberal policies, women are beginning to be driven from the workplace back into the home. A major ABS study published in mid-1998 reported that women are dropping out of the workforce because of growing work disincentives resulting from government subsidies paid to women staying at home compared to dramatically reduced childcare support (*Advertiser* 23 July 1998, p. 19). The ABS reported that in South Australia, 22 100 women had left work since the Federal Coalition came to office in 1996 (*Advertiser* 22 July 1998, p. 9). Women's labour force participation rate declined quite significantly in July 1998 to only 49.5 per cent – a quite significant reversal of the steady post-war growth trend, and the first time in a decade it had fallen below 50 per cent (ABS 1998).

However, aggregate figures showing women's ever-increasing participation in the labour market reveal only part of the full picture. One of the outstanding characteristics of changing employment patterns throughout Australia over the past twenty years has been the increase in part-time and casual employment. The great majority of all part-time workers are female. Overall, in May 1998, 72.6 per cent of all part-time workers were women (ABS 1998). The percentage of all adult women in South Australia who participate in the labour market on a part-time basis increased from 15.7 per cent to 23.5 per cent between May 1978 and May 1997 although, again, a sharp decline occurred in women's part-time employment in the twelve months from May 1997 to May 1998. In May 1998 48.2 per cent of all women workers in South Australia were in part-time employment. Significantly, however, we find that the participation rate for women in full-time employment has actually remained remarkably steady over the 20-year period 1978–97 – with virtually no growth over that time in the percentage of women occupying full time jobs. The so-called feminisation of work phenomenon is almost totally based upon increasing levels of part-time employment by women.

The labour market experiences of South Australian men have also undergone fundamental changes under restructuring. The male labour market participation rate has declined significantly from 79.8 per cent to 69.8 per cent in the 21-year period 1978–98. In particular, there has been a significant drop in male employment in manufacturing in South Australia from the late seventies through to the nineties, notably in the metal industries. In 1978, 24.6 per cent of male workers were employed in manufacturing (ABS *Labour Force Australia: Historical Summary 1978–89*) compared to only 19.4 per cent in May 1996 (ABS 1997, p. 184). Of most significance, however, male full-time employment has dropped dramatically over the period 1978–98 from 71.1 per cent to 54.4 per cent of the adult (over 15 years) male population. This undoubtedly marks a major shift in overall workforce opportunities for many men. There also appears to be a very significant generational shift – as older workers have prematurely dropped out of the labour market in large numbers and younger males enter the workforce via the peripheral labour market though part-time and casual jobs in the service sector.

Despite these significant changes, occupational and industry sex segregation have remained largely unchanged over the last twenty years, and women generally continue to occupy a disadvantaged labour market position. More than two-thirds of women continue to be employed as clerks, salespersons, personal service workers and professionals (primarily as nurses and teachers). The health and community services sector, the education sector and the retail sector still account for almost 50 per cent of all employed women in South Australia (ABS 1997). Women remain under-represented in all other industry groups, but are most notably absent in manufacturing, mining, construction and transport. The occupational categories and industries in which women predominate continue to attract the lowest rates of pay, are often considered unskilled or low skilled in nature. They are also not easily linked to 'productivity gains' for wage bargaining purposes as male work has been. Between 1995 and 1997 workers in the Australian Bureau of Statistics' 'managerial' classification increased their earnings by 25 per cent, while over the same period the lowest-paid occupational categories earned an increase of just six per cent (*Australian* 17 January 1998, p. 1). As Michael Raper, the President of ACOSS, stated, this 'demonstrates yet again that talk of increased flexibility in the wages system really means greater opportunities for those at the top' (*Australian* 17 January 1998, p. 1). In South Australia in May 1996, women working full-time earned an average of only 80 per cent of full-time working men – a decline from the May 1988 figure of 84 per cent. Even more revealing, however, is that women's total take-home earnings compared to men's dropped from 67 per cent to 64 per cent between 1996 and 1998 (ABS *Average Weekly Earnings, Australia*). These figures suggest that, under restructuring, women's earnings have fallen significantly relative to men's. The increasing number of casual and part-time female workers helps to explain these figures.

Restructuring has produced unemployment rates in South Australia consistently above the national average. For most of the 1980s, officially recorded female unemployment rates were higher than male rates. In the past few years however the male rate of unemployment has risen above the female rate (see table 1). However, hidden unemployment and under-employment have been more significant in the experience of women than men. In September 1997 an additional 67 400 women, compared to 29 500 men without work in South Australia were recorded as being willing and able to work but were not recorded as unemployed in the labour force statistics (ABS *Persons Not in the Labour Force*). As shown in table 1 this suggests that the 'real' level of unemployment amongst women in South Australia, if hidden unemployment is taken into account, was 25 per cent. In addition, a further 11.2 per cent of the female labour force who were in part-time employment were recorded as 'underemployed'; that is, wanting to work more hours than they were able to find employment for (ABS *Underemployed Workers*). Nevertheless, an increasing number of men also have borne the costs of hidden unemployment and under-employment. The 'real' level of unemployment for men in South Australia in September 1997 was 16.2 per cent.

Restructuring has also brought changes to the nature and conditions of work for both women and men in South Australia. In many cases this has produced a significant lowering of standards of employment. In part this can be attributed to the increasing percentages of men and women working part time. Invariably, part-time and casual workers have lower levels of entitlement to sick leave, annual and long service leave and superannuation coverage. An ABS supplementary survey on the nature of part-time work conducted in South Australia in the late 1980s found that the majority (77 per cent) of part-time work was casual in its pattern of hours and conditions. Only a small minority of part-time work situations provided the benefits of full-time pay and conditions

TABLE 1: UNEMPLOYMENT AND HIDDEN UNEMPLOYMENT IN SOUTH AUSTRALIA, MARCH 1986 AND SEPTEMBER 1997

	March 1986		September 1997	
	Males	**Females**	**Males**	**Females**
Number in labour force	398 300	261 300	419 000	314 400
Number of 'official' unemployed	32 600	25 000	43 300	28 200
Rate of 'official' unemployment	8.2%	9.6%	9.6%	7.3%
Number of 'hidden' unemployed	13 500	47 400	29 500	67 400
Rate of 'hidden' unemployment	3.3%	15.4%	6.6%	17.7%
Rate of 'unemployment plus hidden unemployment'*	11.5%	25.0%	16.2%	25.0%

*expressed as a percentage of the total of all those in the labour force plus those classified as 'hidden unemployed'.

Sources: ABS Cat. No. 6220.0 *Persons Not in the Labour Force*

ABS Cat. No. 6203.0 *Labour Force, Australia*

ABS Cat. No. 6265.0 *Underemployed Workers*

(Sharp 1987, pp. 37–8; ABS *Type and Conditions of Part-time Work, South Australia*). Ironically, while restructuring has meant unemployment or reduced employment for many women and men, for others it has meant greatly increased hours of work. In a survey of hours worked by employees during a particular week in South Australia in 1996, just under half (47 per cent) of all full-time workers had worked in excess of 40 hours per week. Almost a quarter (24 per cent) of full-time workers had actually worked in excess of 49 hours during that week (ABS 1997, p. 192). There has also been an enormous increase in persons holding multiple jobs – an increase of 66 per cent in the past decade. Over half of multiple job holders in South Australia are now women and over 40 per cent of multiple job holders worked full-time in one of their jobs (*Advertiser* 21 March 1998).

Under restructuring there has also been an acute intensification of the work process resulting in increased stress and reduced working conditions. A survey of 10 000 Australian workers by the ACTU in 1997 found that 70 per cent complained of increased workloads and more than a quarter had taken time off because of stress in the past year. The increasing pattern of stress was attributed to restructuring of management practices, workloads, hours of work and job insecurity (*Advertiser* 30 March 1998, p. 7). Another survey of 3500 national businesses conducted by Drake International found that South Australia was second only to Queensland as the state with the worst levels of employee stress. The worst areas were identified as banking, the public service, education and the health sector – all areas with high levels of female employment (*Advertiser* 29 August 1998, p. 43). In an ABS study, women were found to have been more likely than male workers to have been given greater responsibilities at work, extra duties and changed hours of work (*Australian* 28 June 1997, p. 3). In addition, it is clear that home-based work (or outwork) is a growing area of employment in South Australia. The precise extent of this form of employment is difficult to estimate due to the lack of official statistics relating to it. However, the incidence of outwork is known to be quite high in the textiles, clothing and footwear industries and is rising rapidly in other areas as employers seek more 'flexible' forms of labour (Tassie 1989, pp. 30–2). A 1998 study reported up to 25 000 women and children working in Adelaide sweatshops some receiving payment of as little as 97 cents per hour (*Advertiser* 13 June 1998; Adelaide Central Community Health Service 1998).

Undoubtedly some women in elite jobs have done very well as a result of opportunities created by restructuring. Restructuring the labour process has in fact further privileged some already skilled workers and this will further marginalise most women unless the gendered nature of the process is acknowledged and rectified by policy-makers. Evidence is also emerging that under restructuring class differences between women and between men have increased. A recent Australian study by Bob Gregory and Boyd Hunter show that for women a change in employment pattern according to socio-economic level of neighbourhood is taking place. In the top 50 per cent of neighbourhoods, the proportion of women employed increased by ten per cent (Gregory & Hunter 1996). However, for the remaining half of all neighbourhoods, employment for women fell by 40 per cent. The polarisation in labour market experiences of different income groups of women has been greatly exacerbated by recent neoliberal policy changes. A study by the National Centre for Social and Economic Modelling conducted in 1997 found that low-income married mothers with young children face considerable policy disincentives to maintain paid employment or to increase their hours of work. The study demonstrated that some low-income women re-enter the workforce only to find that their families would have been financially better off had they stayed at home. On the other hand, women capable of commanding larger salaries face far less of a problem with work disincentives (*Australian* 30 September, p. 3). Clearly, restructuring has produced a widening gap in the labour market experiences of both men and women – leading to a sharp polarisation of class differences. Aggregate employment figures across South Australia as a whole also disguise even greater inequalities when the employment experiences of men and women are disaggregated by locality, race and age. Quite extreme differences exist across local government localities in the distribution of unemployment of both women and men. Men in poorer socio-economic localities had significantly higher unemployment rates than men in the richer local government areas (Centre for Labour Research 1998).

More research on the impact of restructuring and labour market policies which is sensitive to the intersections of gender, race, locality and class is needed. However, the picture that emerges of the labour market experience of women and men in a restructuring South Australian economy is a fairly negative one. While some feminist researchers have argued that on the whole, restructuring has been positive for women, and particularly that the feminisation of work has increased women's capacity to use the benefits of paid work (with all its limitations) to gain economic independence (Hartmann 1987, p. 33), the South Australian experience of restructuring suggests that there is very little evidence that most women have gained significantly from these labour market changes. Clearly, there is small justification for the simplistic view that men have 'borne the brunt' of restructuring and women have benefited. While more women have undoubtedly gained part-time employment opportunities, an assessment of these gains needs to take into account the problems associated with part-time work. Significant also is the impact of restructuring on women's wages, working conditions and unpaid workload.

Also for many men restructuring has had a significantly negative effect. The numbers of men in full-time employment have declined substantially, especially for older men, and the numbers employed in the casualised and part-time sector considerably increased, especially for younger men able to find employment in the growing service sector. Although continuing to occupy relatively segmented positions in the labour market, men and women in some ways therefore appear to be experiencing more similar working conditions as a result of the restructuring of the South Australian labour market. This does not so much reflect any significant improvement in women's position but rather perhaps a 'harmonising down' process whereby the decline in men's overall position has made many men's jobs more like women's jobs.

In response to the powerful impact of the forces of restructuring on the employment experiences of South Australian women and men, state government employment and economic development policies have struggled to find a coherent response which adequately meets the challenges posed. During the two major periods of Labor government under Dunstan and Bannon in the 1970s and 1980s, a number of quite significant reforms aimed at directly improving the position of women in the employment area occurred. Equal opportunity in particular was an area of considerable action during the 'Bannon decade' of the 1980s. A wide network of Equal Opportunity units were established within a number of government departments. Initiatives focused on factors preventing women's entry into the labour market, particularly male-dominated sectors. For example, the Labor government successfully set a target of 50 per cent female participation in all jobs created under the Commonwealth Employment Program (South Australia 1986, pp. 9–10).

Since the early 1990s, state governments throughout Australia, under pressure from the worsening economic crisis, the resurgence of conservative, free market economic ideologies, and policy developments at the federal level, have increasingly adopted a neoliberal policy approach. While the Bannon and Arnold Labor governments of 1982–93 successfully introduced a number of quite significant reforms to improve the position of women in employment, the subsequent election of a Liberal government in 1993 saw the emergence of a significant policy shift towards a more free market approach. In the area of economic development and employment policy the Liberal government placed emphasis on shifting resources into export industries, deregulating labour markets and significantly reducing employment in the public sector. Outsourcing, contracting-out and privatisation in the areas of water, electricity, transport, prisons and health services were seen as leading to 'thousands of jobs' in the private sector (*Advertiser* 1 June 1996, p. 3). However, the more likely outcome of these strategies is the nett loss of jobs, particularly for women, rather than a gain. The transference of public sector jobs to the private sector has resulted in increased part-time and casualised employment in areas which were previously full-time, permanent positions. Over 12 000 jobs in four years, almost a quarter of the total state public sector, have been lost as a result of the Liberal government's cutbacks and contracting-out policies (*Advertiser* 20 October 1997, p. 11). The other area of employment growth in Adelaide has been through the establishment of back office and call centre operations by national companies. This 'back office jobs revolution' was being actively promoted by the government as financial and service companies abandoned the state (*Advertiser* 20 June 1996). Again the picture is one of full-time permanent jobs for both men and women being replaced by part-time, low paid and casualised work.

Under both Labor and Liberal regimes, government and influential industry and union groups have argued that the restoration of economic growth, and hence job creation, depends upon the improvement of South Australia's international competitiveness. However, the notion that South Australia's economic salvation is based entirely on increasing the value of our exports is highly problematic from an employment-creation perspective – particularly for women. There is a tendency to equate the 'wealth-generating' sectors of the economy with those which produce goods and services traded on the world market and valued in dollar terms. This refers to that very narrow section of the economy which is geared to private sector export production. Many of the goods and services produced by women's paid and unpaid labour do not fit into this orthodox conceptualisation of 'productive' economic activity. Even within the paid economy, women are more likely to produce services, often within the public sector, which are not easily quantified in monetary terms, except as a debit in the form of wages paid by the state. These areas of economic activity are, nonetheless, vital to the South Australian economy. The role of the public sector in contributing to the accumulation of national wealth has been ignored by the majority of economists and by capital.

However, the different and unequal labour market outcomes for men and women under restructuring also need to be understood in the broader context of changes occurring within the organisation of family life and households. The 'private' realm of the family and household is taken as a given and not subjected to scrutiny by conventional economic analyses of restructuring and by policy-makers. The organisation of the family and households has, amongst other things, a marked impact on the capacities of men and women to participate in paid work. Being disproportionately responsible for the unpaid activities of households, women enter the labour market with 'domestic baggage' with the result that the 'labour market is no level playing field' (Humphries 1998, p. 223). Policies aimed at redressing the negative impact of restructuring on men and women in the 'public sphere' will be very limited without an equal focus on the profound changes simultaneously occurring in the 'private' spheres of the household and gender relations.

GENDER RESTRUCTURING IN THE SOCIAL AND HOUSEHOLD SPHERES

Two central dynamics are relevant to the impact of restructuring on household spheres. Firstly, a greatly increased burden has shifted to individuals and families, both as a result of the restructuring process itself and the accompanying withdrawal by the South Australian government from many of the activities it had previously undertaken in support of household welfare and social reproduction. Secondly, restructuring, and neoliberal policies adopted in response to it, have themselves undermined the resilience of many households and reduced their ability to adjust to these new challenges. An examination of continuities and changes in these realms is central to understanding the gendered dimension of restructuring and to broadening the debate about policy responses to meet the challenges of restructuring.

Among the many significant transformations which capitalism is undergoing with the end of the post-war Fordist era is the emergence of a new gender (dis)order. The restructuring of gender relations has profound implications for other elements of the restructuring process and will be a very important factor in determining the shapes of all post-restructuring societies. Gender relations under the Fordist regime of capital accumulation supported the use of women's unpaid labour for the undertaking of a range of productive and reproductive activities within households and communities. Men's paid labour, in turn, was remunerated at levels which could support the household/family system. With the end of Fordism the existing unequal structure of gender relations has come under extreme pressure. The old 'father and ford' social compact which existed between male workers, manufacturing capital and the (Keynesian welfare) state has severely broken down (McDowell 1991). Because the leading spokespersons of capital in the now-dominant finance and service sectors have been so intently focused upon achieving their own short-term economic goals in the restructuring process, they have largely discarded previous concerns for the maintenance of a stable workforce and the need to socially reproduce that labour force. Capital has been far more interested in enforcing greater labour market discipline within the economy, in particular by removing safety net and welfare provisions which were so important in underpinning the increasing bargaining power of workers, trade unions and other groups (including women) during the post-war boom. Hence, under overwhelming pressure from capital to refocus far more directly on facilitating corporate 'economic' goals, the state too has virtually lost interest in providing welfare support for family and household structures.

The impact of restructuring has been exacerbated by the shift to neoliberal state policies which have greatly reduced or abandoned the traditional support provided by the state governments and federal government for social welfare and reproduction. This is most directly reflected at the state level in reduced expenditures on public health, education, housing, transport and community services. In 1993 the new South Australian Liberal government in 1993 quickly adopted a policy approach which was very heavily influenced by economic rationalist ideas in both economic and social policy areas. South Australia's debt situation and an 'unexpected' discovery of a so-called budgetary 'black hole' of $10 billion were used as justification for the introduction of a series of 'dry' economic policies aimed at rapid reduction of debt. The policies adopted included a series of harsh cutbacks in public spending in activities which were described as being areas of 'overspending', as well as a program of asset sales. Large cuts initially were made to education ($40 million) and health ($65 million) expenditures (*Advertiser* 1 June 1994). Further significant cuts were applied in these and other areas in subsequent budgets. Increased charges were introduced for power, water, public housing and transport. This shift to a neoliberal policy regime has very significantly reduced the support traditionally available for households to undertake social reproduction and has commodified services previously provided collectively by the state.

The changes by capital and the state to the support of the family/household system have undermined the Fordist arrangements whereby women provided their unpaid labour within the context of a family wage (Smith 1998, p. 12). Many working class households now depend on two income earners. The rising number of single-parent households require women to seek paid employment to support their dependent children. At the same time the demand by employers for 'flexible' work patterns is reducing women's capacity to provide unpaid productive and reproductive labour. Ironically, these changes are occurring simultaneously with a resurgence of rhetoric from right wing governments about the importance of the nuclear family and family values. However, in so doing, the state is effectively attempting to shift the burden of welfare and social reproduction during the restructuring process back on to the 'private' realm of the household and the individual. Clearly, the rhetoric of family and individualism is being used to facilitate a quite deliberate attempt to restructure gender relations in a very significant way.

Economic restructuring and neoliberal policy approaches therefore are reshaping the responsibilities and the organisation of the household/family system and are having a profound impact on everyday life and gender relations within many households. This impact has important consequences both for individual and family welfare and for the broader process of social reproduction within the economy and society. A number of Australian household time-use studies are now available which clearly indicate that a large part of our community's work takes place outside the market or paid sector of the economy. The unpaid production of goods and services by households is a crucial component of the ways individuals and households in our society achieve their standard of living. It also is a vital component of economic production and of the ways in which our society reproduces itself. The unpaid work of households is enormously productive or value-adding, and thereby contributes significantly to the total output of an economy. In 1992 the Australian Bureau of Statistics valued household production at between 48 and 64 per cent of conventional gross domestic product (ABS 1994). Estimates, which include both the capital and labour inputs utilised in household production, indicate that the aggregate value of goods and services produced in the household sector is 98 per cent of goods and services produced in the market or paid sectors (Ironmonger 1996, p. 43). Moreover, the household sector collectively utilises significantly more labour hours than the market sector. In 1992, 380 million hours of unpaid work in households and communities and 272 million hours of work in paid employment in the business and government sectors (or 40 per cent more unpaid than paid labor hours) was undertaken by Australians (Ironmonger 1996, p. 43). The combined labour hours of men and women are therefore spread between paid and unpaid work in roughly equal proportions.

The work of households is, however, highly gendered, with women remaining responsible for 70 per cent of household labour activities

(Bittman & Pixley 1997, p. 90). Restructuring is significantly impacting on the allocation between the paid and unpaid work of men and women, but in a way which continues to assign the major burden of unpaid productive work and social reproduction to women. A comparison of the 1987 and the 1992 time-use studies by Michael Bittman and Jocelyn Pixley shows that women, under pressures emanating from the restructuring process, are reshaping the gender division of labour in the household by reducing the amount of time they spend on unpaid activities by about three hours per week (largely through a reduction in cooking time). However, while women's unpaid household work has reduced marginally, women remain responsible for the overwhelming proportion of the domestic workload even where their participation in the paid labour market has increased. While men have increased their hours of parenting work, in general their overall level of household work has not increased. While women's unpaid labour is undergoing restructuring and moving towards the traditional male model, any adjustments between paid work and unpaid household labour have been primarily made by women.

The full impact of restructuring on the organisation of the household/family system and the process of social reproduction which includes emotional care work, however, is only partially captured by the measurable aspects of household work. The caring and nurturing activities of households are largely unmeasurable but are vital not only for producing and maintaining the labour force, but also for our existence as social beings, contributing to our ability to operate both as autonomous individuals and as interdependent and dependent members of communities and families. Restructuring is profoundly impacting on the capacity of many households (that is, primarily women) to provide that emotional support. It is of course important to recognise that the impact of restructuring on different groups in the South Australian community has been very uneven. In particular, it is important to understand the differential impact of restructuring on households by class. Belinda Probert in a study of Melbourne households has shown that the social reproductive activities of households and strategies for survival under restructuring vary significantly by social class, reflecting a growing polarisation of experience and opportunities (Probert 1996, p. 44). Working class households in which the male breadwinner is in a low-skilled job and the female is engaged in full-time, unpaid household work appear to be holding on to a Fordist set of gender relations based upon a strict sexual division of labour. Children remain the focus of identity for these women, and paid work and the care of children are perceived as incompatible. In contrast, further up the socio-economic scale women are more likely to combine work with parenting. In these cases an increasing degree of negotiation around household work occurs resulting in less rigid sexual divisions of labour (Probert 1996, p. 42–4). In short, different households are engaged in different strategies of adjustment in response to the impact of restructuring. It appears however, that the scope for transforming the Fordist gender relations underpinning men and women's paid and unpaid work within working-class households is less than their middle-class counterparts.

Although not all households have been negatively affected by the changes associated with the restructuring of gender relations in the home, the impact has been traumatic for many. In South Australia there is considerable evidence of widespread social disintegration and household stress resulting from the impact of restructuring. The number of South Australian households whose incomes were below 60 per cent of average weekly earnings, for example, rose from 25.8 per cent to 41.7 per cent between the 1986 census and the 1996 census (*Advertiser* 23 May 1998, p. 33). A 1996 national report on poverty, the first since 1975, found that the percentage of the population living below the poverty line had increased from 12.5 per cent in 1975 to 16.7 per cent in 1996. The total numbers categorised as either 'rather poor' or 'very poor' increased from 20.6 per cent to 30.4 per cent (Fincher & Nieuwenhuysen 1998, p. 4). In 1996 the publication of *The Social Health Atlas of South Australia*, a major study of income distribution and health, revealed that 'Adelaide has more people on low incomes than any other city in Australia and the gap between rich and poor is widening' (*Advertiser* 7 December 1996, p. 27; Glover 1996). The report found that economic polarisation has increased as suburbs like Elizabeth, Salisbury, Munno Para and Noarlunga have experienced severe declines in income while wealthier areas such as Happy Valley and Stirling are relatively better off.

In this period of restructuring, as an increasing number of nuclear families disintegrate, the numbers of single-parent families have risen substantially, and with them the numbers of families experiencing varying levels of poverty. One-parent families represented 20 per cent of all families in South Australia in 1997 – up from 14 per cent in 1989 (*Advertiser* 10 March 1998, p. 19). The 1996 census shows that the number of single-parent households living in poverty doubled between 1991 and 1996 (*Advertiser* 1 November 1997). Women still comprise 87 per cent of all heads of single-parent families (*Advertiser* 10 March 1998, p. 19). By 1996 social security payments were being paid to one-third of the population and South Australia had the highest percentage of welfare recipients of the mainland states (*Advertiser* 6 April 1996). As publicly provided welfare services are downsized, the state is facing a 'welfare crisis' as rising numbers of needy people turn to private community agencies already stretched to capacity and increasingly unable to cope. The major private welfare agency, the St Vincent de Paul Society, reported an 80 per cent increase in the demand for emergency assistance over the five years to 1996 (*Advertiser* 19 May 1998). A nationwide survey found that in 1997, 11 800 South Australians experienced at least one bout of homelessness, These included 3600 children and 3700 women. Meanwhile, at the same time as the government announced a further 'crackdown' on access to public housing, the numbers on the Housing Trust waiting list expanded to 30 000 (*Advertiser* 2 March 1998, p. 12).

There is evidence of increasing levels of domestic violence within families (*Advertiser* 8 February 1996) and the numbers of confirmed cases of child abuse increased by 58 per cent between 1994 and 1995 (*Advertiser* 25 August 1995, p. 3). A conference held in Adelaide in November 1996 on the 'overwhelming social problems' facing social workers heard 'stories of poverty, domestic violence and desperation' being poured out by their rapidly increasing clientele. South Australia has experienced one of the biggest rises in bankruptcies of any Australian state. The Inspector General in Bankruptcy reported that most SA bankrupts were not business people but workers affected by excessive use of credit cards, unemployment, domestic break-ups and the lack of adequate health insurance (*Advertiser* 11 March 1996). One of the impacts of declining economic security has been a dramatic rise in gambling activity amongst working class households. Gambling turnover in South Australia increased by 50 per cent between 1993 and 1998 rising to 3.3 billion dollars in 1998 (*Advertiser* 30 October 1998, p. 9). The state also experienced the highest rate of robberies in the country with these crimes almost trebling over a decade from the mid-1980s to the mid-1990s (*Advertiser* 3 June 1996).

Consequently, the combined impact of restructuring and the neo-liberal policies of the current Liberal government have put enormous pressures on the capacity of the household/family system to undertake productive and reproductive activities. These activities are essential both to the overall economic well-being of the community and to the welfare of individuals and households. They are vital therefore in ensuring the maintenance of a society which is resilient to the potentially devastating impact of restructuring. Support for households' ability to undertake these productive and reproductive activities should also be a priority for policy-makers concerned about social equity. The current political rhetoric of the importance of the family fits uneasily with the evidence of social disintegration and household stress in South Australia resulting from restructuring. By increasingly privatising individual and family welfare and shifting the burden of social reproduction to the private realm of the individual and household, South Australian policy-makers are exacerbating these problems.

CONCLUSION

We are only just beginning to uncover the complex nature of the impact of restructuring generally and its gendered outcomes in particular. The lack of theoretical and empirical work in the area of gender and restructuring ultimately limits policy prescriptions. Nevertheless, some broad policy lessons can be deduced from the above analysis. Firstly, the current neoliberal direction of state policy is undesirable as it exacerbates, rather than ameliorates, the negative effects of restructuring on the lives of the majority of women and men and households. The deregulation of labour markets has made employment more tenuous. Cutbacks in public expenditures which previously supported the welfare and social reproductive activities of households have produced enormous economic hardship and social disintegration. The gender-blindness of the neoliberal approach results in a failure to address the existing unequal position of men and women in society. Instead it is assumed that free and equal individuals pursue self-interested economic goals, reap rewards commensurate to their individual choices and efforts within a self-regulating marketplace (Sharp & Broomhill 1988, p. 40). In reality, however, there is no 'level playing field' for the large numbers of women and men who face deep-rooted and worsening inequalities as a result of the impact of the restructuring process. When the distribution of economic resources is left to the market place there will always be winners and losers and the winners will consistently be those who are already in a privileged position.

Secondly, the current neoliberal policy discourse has shifted the boundaries between the 'public' and the 'private'. Neoliberal policies, steeped in a discourse of the primacy of selfish individualism over community, markets over government and efficiency over equity, have contributed to a narrowing of the state's responsibilities in the 'public' domain and a (re)privatising of responsibilities to the 'private' realm. As a result, costs are increasingly being shifted to the private sphere of the household and family. Women are bearing a disproportionate share of these costs because of their greater contribution to unpaid household production and social reproductive activities. Apart from the equity issues which arise from this there are also efficiency issues. There is no strong household on which to shift the burden of restructuring. South Australian households (like many restructuring communities elsewhere) are showing signs of pressure and disintegration. Moreover, there is little sign that gender relations, particularly in working class households, are capable of readily adjusting to the new demands. In this context, a policy approach which is better geared to supporting the welfare of those households most under pressure from restructuring is desperately needed.

Thirdly, neoliberal policies have served to reduce the public realm of political negotiation. In the past, the state public sector was where significant decisions about social and economic infrastructure, health, education and welfare were made. By shifting these decisions to the market and to the individual decisions of households, governments are undermining the capacity for involvement by groups who have struggled to alter the gendered nature of these policies. Importantly, the development of the welfare state in the post-war period created a space for contestation over gender issues to occur within the political sphere. This increased capacity for political contestation fundamentally changed gender relations in the post-war community. As feminist researchers have shown, the development of the welfare state in post-war capitalist societies, while clearly producing very complex and contradictory outcomes for women, also fundamentally changed the position of women by creating the conditions for increased labour market participation, by providing a secure safety net and support services and by reducing their dependency on individual men (Sharp & Broomhill 1988, pp. 15–20). Even more significantly, the development of the welfare state fundamentally re-aligned the boundaries between the economy and the state in relation to gender. It shifted the boundaries of gender politics and opened up spaces for political contestation about gender issues which did not exist formally (Brodie 1994, pp. 53–4). The expansion of the 'public' realm into areas previously defined as 'private', and therefore not open to political contestation, effectively 'democratised' gender relations and empowered women, and men, to negotiate around welfare, social reproduction and quality of life issues in ways not possible before. In the context of a public discourse dominated by neoliberalism, it is increasingly difficult to talk about women, gender and the public good. The need for deregulation is presented by neoliberals as a depoliticised discourse. A repoliticised public process in which women and men seeking to change the existing gender order can participate is needed in South Australia.

Finally, reform of the policy approach is not possible without state mechanisms to generate new policies. Under Labor in the 1980s, a range of social and economic reforms was achieved in relation to gender equity. These reforms were made possible within a context which no longer exists. An important element in the success of these reforms was the existence of political support for social improvements within the government. Important also was the establishment of social justice and women's policy units within the bureaucracy. Femocrats within the state public service were very successful in introducing reform initiatives from within the bureaucracy – often with strong resistance from within the patriarchal structures of the organisation. However, the way the state has devised and implemented its policies has been dramatically restructured. In the name of 'mainstreaming', women's policy units and gender equity and social justice structures within the state have now been all but eliminated by the Liberal government. Without these structures, the primary economic departments within the state bureaucracy continue to systematically ignore the specific position of women and men within the South Australian paid and unpaid economies. Consequently, the need for active policies both to counteract the inequitable social and economic impact of restructuring and to meet the special needs of those women, men and households most disadvantaged by market forces must be a high priority for future policy-making in South Australia.

REFERENCES

Adelaide Central Community Health Service 1998, *Outwork – Reaching an Invisible Workforce*, Adelaide.

Advertiser various references.

Australian various references.

Australian Bureau of Statistics (ABS) 1987, Cat. No. 6203.4, *Type and Conditions of Part-Time Work*, South Australia, occasional paper

—— 1994, Cat. No. 5240.0, *Unpaid Work and the Australian Economy*, occasional paper.

—— 1997, *South Australian Year Book 1997*.

—— 1998, Cat. No. 6201.4, *Labour Force, South Australia*.

—— 1998, Cat. No. 6203.0, *Labour Force, Australia*.

—— Cat. No. 6203.4, *Type and Conditions of Part-time Work, South Australia*.

—— Cat. No. 6204.0, *Labour Force, Australia: Historical Summary 1978–89*.

—— Cat. No. 6220.0, *Persons Not in the Labour Force*.

—— Cat. No. 6265.0, *Underemployed Workers*.

—— Cat. No. 6302.0, *Average Weekly Earnings, Australia*.

Bakker, Isabella 1994, 'Introduction: Engendering macroeconomic policy reform in the era of global restructuring and adjustment', in *The Strategic Silence: Gender and Economic Policy*, ed Isabella Bakker, Zed Books, London, pp. 1–30.

Bakker, Isabella 1996, *Rethinking Restructuring: Gender and Change in Canada*, University of Toronto Press, Toronto.

Bakshi, P., Goodwin, M. et al. 1995, 'Gender, race and class in the local welfare state: Moving beyond regulation theory in analysing the transition from Fordism', *Environment & Planning A*, vol. 27, no. 10, pp. 1539–54.

Bastalich, Wendy & Broomhill, Ray 1993, 'Women and industry policy', in *Making the Future Work: Crisis and Change in the South Australian Economy*, eds Roy Green and Rodin Genoff, Allen & Unwin, Sydney, pp. 78–94.

Bittman, M. & Pixley, J. 1997, *The Double Life of the Family, Myth, Hope and Experience*, Allen & Unwin, Sydney.

Brodie, Janine 1994, 'Shifting the boundaries: Gender and the politics of restructuring', in *The Strategic Silence: Gender and Economic Policy*, ed Isabella Bakker, Zed Books London, pp. 46–60.

Centre for Labour Research 1998, *South Australia Labour Market Briefing*, vol. 2, no. 2, September, University of Adelaide, Adelaide.

Cohen, Marjorie Griffen 1994, 'The implications of economic restructuring for women: The Canadian situation', in *The Strategic Silence: Gender and Economic Policy*, ed Isabella Bakker, Zed Books, London, pp. 103–16.

Fincher, Ruth & Nieuwenhuysen, John (eds) 1998, *Australian Poverty: Then and Now*, Melbourne University Press, Melbourne.

Glover, John et al 1996, *A Social Health Atlas of South Australia*, South Australian Health Commission, Adelaide.

Gregory, R. G. 1993, 'Aspects of Australian and US living standards: The disappointing decades 1970–1990', *Economic Record*, vol. 69, pp. 61–76.

Gregory, R. G. & Hunter, B. 1995, *The Macro Economy and the Growth of Ghettos and Urban Poverty in Australia*, discussion paper no. 325, ANU Centre for Economic Policy Research, Canberra.

Hartmann, Heidi I. 1987, 'Changes in women's economic and family roles on post-World War II United States', in *Women, Households and the Economy*, L. Beneria & C. R. Stimpson eds, Rutgers University Press, New Brunswick, pp. 33–64.

Humphries, Jane 1998, 'Towards a family-friendly economics', *New Political Economy*, vol. 3, no. 2, pp. 223–40.

Ironmonger, Duncan 1996, 'Counting outputs, inputs and caring labor: Estimating gross household product', *Feminist Economics*, vol. 2, no. 3, pp. 37–64.

MacDonald, Martha 1995, 'The empirical challenges of feminist economics: The example of economic restructuring', in *Out of the Margin: Feminist Perspectives on Economics*, E. Kuiper & J. Sap eds, Routledge, London, pp. 175–97.

McDowell, Linda 1991, 'Life without father and Ford: The new gender order of post-Fordism', *Transactions of the Institute of British Geographers*, vol. 16, no. 4, pp. 400–19.

Probert, Belinda 1996, 'The riddle of women's work', *Arena Magazine*, vol. 23, pp. 39–45.

Sharp, Rhonda 1987, 'Perils for Part-Timers', *Australian Society*, November, pp. 37–8.

Sharp, Rhonda & Broomhill, Ray 1988, *Short Changed: Women and Economic Policies*, Allen & Unwin, Sydney.

Smith, Dorothy 1998, 'The underside of schooling: Restructuring, privatisation, and women's unpaid work', *Journal for a Just and Caring Education*, vol. 4, no. 1, pp. 11–29.

South Australia 1986, The 1986/87 Budget and its impact on women, information paper presented with the 1986/87 budget papers, South Australian Government, Adelaide.

Spoehr, John & Broomhill, Ray (eds) 1995, *Altered States: The Regional Impact of Free Market Policies in the Australian States*, Centre for Labour Studies/Social Justice Research Foundation, Adelaide.

Tassie, Jane 1989, *Out of Sight Out of Mind: Outwork in South Australia*, Working Women's Centre of South Australia, Adelaide.

CHAPTER 8

PUBLIC DEBT AND THE SOUTH AUSTRALIAN GOVERNMENT

PAUL CHAPMAN AND JOHN SPOEHR

INTRODUCTION

Any attempt to revitalise the South Australian economy requires a reassessment of the implications of public sector debt. There is a broadly held but mistaken view that public debt, in South Australia and elsewhere, is associated with hard times and poor economic performance. The opposite more often applies. Those who argue for the elimination of South Australian public debt appear to be unaware of its importance. Debt has always been part of the process of South Australian economic development. Raising debt was one of the first tasks of the South Australian Company which founded the colony, and it has been with South Australia ever since.[1]

A review of debt and views expressed about it are important for a number of reasons. Firstly, debt provides government with many billions of dollars that can be put to a variety of developmental purposes. It is therefore significant in any consideration of the revitalisation of the South Australian economy. Secondly, a particular perspective on debt reveals much about a particular perspective on the role of government. Can government be trusted to borrow and invest wisely? Answers to that question are central to gaining an understanding of the politics of the debt debate. In the end, perspectives on debt significantly prescribe the economic role of the state government.

The Olsen Liberal government believes that the public sector should not hold debt. The Premier therefore, is publicly committed to the elimination of public debt in South Australia (*Advertiser* 10 October 1998). This means that the role of government, especially in a rejuvenated and developing South Australian economy, will be more limited than it has been in the past. To be anti-debt is to wish for significantly less government. Conversely, we will argue here that the South Australian government cannot play its part in economic development and rejuvenation without continuing to maintain large debts.

This chapter examines the issue of public debt from a broad, developmental perspective. It begins with an overview of South Australia's current public debt: how big and what shape it is and its broad role in the net financial accounts of South Australia. The following section then summarises some of the prominent views expressed in the debate over debt in South Australia. We then extend the debate, describing the developmental role and importance of debt more broadly. Debt is seen to be associated with growth, both as a cause and a consequence.

While some conservative analysis recommends doing away with debt so as to unleash the private sector, the view which emerges here is that South Australian economic development will not be enhanced by large-scale reduction of public debt. If it were not offset by an equal increase in private debt (which is in some ways less desirable, for reasons to be explained), or an increase in investment and control by outsiders (which is undoubtedly less popular), it would directly create a reduction in South Australian economic activity and growth.

The final section offers some conclusions. It is argued that there is no debt crisis in South Australia, nor is there a debt reduction imperative. This chapter does not propose that debt should be accumulated imprudently or that any level of debt is sustainable. However, public sector debt has made, and can continue to make an important contribution to economic growth in a small, regional economy such as that of South Australia which lacks both the centripetal pull of larger centres and the local entrepreneurial leadership needed for sustained growth. Government has a positive role to play in revitalising South Australia and this leads directly to the proposition that public debt can have a positive purpose.

UNDERSTANDING SOUTH AUSTRALIAN PUBLIC SECTOR DEBT

Public debt can initially be understood in relation to the macro-economy of South Australia. Like Australia as a whole, South Australia has a continuous need for an inflow of funds. This is to say that, like the nation as a whole, South Australia has a current account deficit: what it earns from the rest of the world (through trade and our interstate and overseas investments) is less than what it receives (for imports and as income on investments made in South Australia). By rest of the world, is meant both interstate and overseas.[2]

It is not possible to calculate the size of this deficit for South Australia because states do not record the trade and investment flows among themselves or between themselves and overseas. However, it is clear that the prevalence of current deficits is not simply the case of South Australians being reckless or wasteful. Rather, as for Australia as a whole, the ongoing need for an inflow of funds should be conceived as a deficiency in local savings relative to local investment opportunities or, equally well, as a surplus in local investment possibilities relative to savings.

In short, if the disparity in South Australian saving and investment rates continues at least at present levels, the net financial position of the state will remain one that requires an ongoing inflow of funds. South Australia then faces three possibilities: to allow outsiders to invest and hence lose control of local assets (so called 'foreign' direct investment); to have local private interests borrow money from outsiders (which increases private debt); or, to have the government borrow the funds.

In reality, the strategy in the past wisely has been to opt for a combination of all three methods. Hence, some of the local current deficit is covered by investment funds from outside firms like General Motors and Mitsubishi which then control some local assets; some is raised by resident firms which borrow from national and international financiers; and, some by governments who do the same. Seen in this light, public sector debt is one means of acquiring funds from interstate and overseas to finance the desired level of current expenditure. The question here is to determine if this remains a desirable means of doing so.

One aspect of the answer to that question concerns the relative cost of public sector debt. There are a number of cogent reasons to believe that if the capital inflow which South Australia needs is raised by the public sector, it will be raised at lower interest rates which reflect the lower risks associated with public borrowers. The reasons are worth reviewing.

Firstly, democratic and constitutional governments are relatively stable entities. There is little possibility of their disappearing into bankruptcy or of their running illegal or immoral scams and, hence, no need to charge extra interest to cover such risks. Similarly, because governments are long-lived, their reputation in credit markets is especially important. They will act to preserve a good reputation and this further reduces the risk of public sector default. Governments also generally invest in assets they control outright (rather than as minority owners) and this too reduces risk. Their assets are also generally located within their jurisdiction (although a prime contra-example is part of the debt accumulated in the late 1980s by the then State Bank of South Australia in the US, London and elsewhere) and tend to be physical assets which, because they are verifiable and immovable, can act as collateral for the loans taken out to build them. Generally, public debt is openly recognised and mutually guaranteed.

For all these reasons (and for others we will consider below) public sector debt tends to be cheaper than debt contracted by the private sector. In addition, one other special consideration applies in South Australia. When it comes to debt, it is important to recognise that South Australia lacks the large and long-lived, indigenous private sector corporations which financiers prefer. If the government does not borrow to finance expansion, the local private sector will not be a potential alternative. Hence, doing away with public debt means a concomitant increase in outside ownership and control in the South Australian economy, unless it means less capital inflow and less activity overall.

Having conceived public debt in broad terms, it is important now to describe the current debt position of the South Australian government. South Australia's public sector debt is the amount of accumulated borrowing undertaken by the state government. In overall terms, the liabilities of the state government amount to $25 billion. This includes not just borrowings but also accumulated indebtedness due to superannuation obligations and the like. To get an overall view of debt *per se*, we must also add that the large amount of state liabilities is more than offset by the state government's assets of $33.3 billion (*Budget Paper no. 2*, 1998/9, table 7.1). This healthy net position is largely the result of the investments made by public trading enterprises (like ETSA, the SA Housing Trust etc.) in infrastructure and land. It establishes the first point: the state government has significant net worth. Even when judged on the basis applicable to the private sector, the state government is in a strong financial position. If it were a private company, it would be seen to have modest levels of net debt. On the basis applied to private corporations, there is simply no debt crisis in South Australia.

A more common measure of debt obtains by examining only financial assets and liabilities (by ignoring the largest of the state government's assets and excluding the financial sector).[3] By this measure the state government's liabilities ($15.7 billion) far outweigh its assets ($2.7 billion), giving a net public debt of $13 billion which is the oft-quoted source of concern (*Budget Paper no. 2*, 1998/99, table 7.4). A less common but sometimes quoted figure for South Australia's public debt focuses solely on the liabilities of the state's financial institutions, which stood at $8.4 billion in June 1997 (table 7.2).

The size of South Australia's current debt can also be judged on the basis of projections relating to its future size and shape under current policies. Public sector debt is falling under current policies. By June 1998, it had fallen to below 20 per cent of gross state product (GSP) for the first time since June 1990. Further, in its most recent budget papers, the state government projects that the current, steep decline in net debt will continue and that, without major assets sales, it will fall to 15.7 per cent of GSP by 2001/02 (*Budget Paper no.2*, table 2.3). That result comes from large falls in gross debt (from the current 30.1 per cent of GSP to 24.6 per cent by 2001/02). It would be a level comparable to the lowest of Australian states and would be the lowest level of public sector debt recorded in South Australia since proper accounting began. As previously stated, the current government also wants to conduct massive public asset sales to eliminate public debt completely by the next state election. By historical comparison, both the current reductions and this more ambitious and extreme program appear to be unwarranted.

THE DEBT DEBATE

Having established a conceptual framework for, and considered the size of public sector debt in South Australia, we are now in a position to examine the major elements of the debt debate. The debt debate in South Australia has been generally of poor standard. It has proceeded on the too simple, and therefore mistaken view that public sector debt acts as a continuous drain on current spending. It shows little appreciation of debt as it is understood in relation to private corporations, as a means of financing balance sheet growth by accumulating liabilities and assets. The fact is that with less debt there would be fewer public assets and the benefits which presently flow from them would need to be paid for from current sources of income. The net effect on current savings is then problematic and depends in part on the relative efficiency with which the public sector accumulates and manages its assets. While this important matter of relative efficiency is outside our consideration of debt *per se*, we would only say that there is no reason to judge *a priori* that the public sector is inefficient or the private sector more efficient. A preference for the private sector is then ideological. It is not a self-evident truth and is not a convincing argument against public sector debt.

We can discern this confusion and ideological content in the views of the current government. It is likely that the Olsen Liberal government is the most strongly opposed to debt of any South Australian government. However, the sophistication of their view does not match its degree of conviction. There is no shortage of public comments by government ministers on the government's position but nowhere are the arguments made in great detail. We have seen that the Premier has made inopportune public statements about eliminating debt and the overall anti-debt position is also reflected in the following: 'we can secure the financial future of South Australia, by reducing debt ...' (Premier Olsen, Ministerial Statement on ETSA, 30 June 1998).

It is as if the government believes the benefits of debt reduction were both substantial and obvious. However, the crucial considerations are those of the size of the debt in relation to assets and of debt-servicing in relation to income. On both these measures the government is overreacting. There is simply no debt crisis in South Australia and the lack of an empirical basis for the government's concerns suggests either that the issues are not well understood or that the government sees political advantage in obfuscation behind ideology.

Judging from the stated position of South Australia's two major opposition parties, confusion seems rife in the political debate over debt in South Australia. Both the ALP and the Australian Democrats support substantial debt reduction, although neither have been explicitly in favour of its elimination. The ALP parliamentarians have drafted what they call a 'Government Financial Responsibility Bill' and a strategy for debt reduction is the first of its five parts (ALP Election 1997 document, 'Government Financial Responsibility'). The strategy calls for debt reduction in real terms, in nominal terms and as a percentage of GSP (although under any but the most unusual circumstances, the second condition will make the first and last redundant).

The ALP's position makes little more sense than the government's. It sets no limits on debt reduction and implies it is to continue until the debt is fully repaid. There is no recognition of the importance and positive role that debt can play. There is also a lack of recognition that most of the debt has been incurred to purchase income-earning assets and that repaying that majority will merely change the composition of the state's assets and liabilities but will not change its net position. The

ALP appears to be more interested in making politically motivated points than in addressing debt in a sophisticated manner. So, for example, it points out that the auditor-general has criticised that part of the government's privatisation program already concluded on the grounds that 'after $2 billion of asset sales, the public interest saving only exceeded the dividends they replaced by $4 million, indicating they did not get good prices for the assets they sold'.

On the one hand, it is important for the ALP to point out that the impact of current sales has been small and it is right for them also to note that this has something to do with the net effect of any loss of dividends. However, it shows a lack of understanding to think this all indicates that poor prices have been secured. The net effect of debt reduction on the interest bill might be low simply because the interest rate charged on the retired debt was low. Indeed, data provided by the South Australian Financing Authority (SAFA) to the Australian Democrats show that significant parts of the current debt are held at rates as low as 4.95 per cent. Further, if the retired debt were partially rolled over because the government organisation involved wanted to retain some of it, then the net interest effect will depend on the relative rates of interest charged on the new debt. Then again it could be that some of the debt was retired early and attracted penalties as a result. In short, the effect of debt retirement on debt-servicing costs is a matter for which much information is required.

The Australian Democrats also oppose the government's apparent preoccupation with debt and, like the ALP, they are not pro-debt. Their position was summed up by Ms Kanck, MLC. It emphasised the size of the debt and the apparent ideological nature of the government's position stating that 'while the Democrats support the continued reduction of debt it should be noted that state debt as a ratio of GSP is at its second lowest level of the past 30 years. This suggests the government has an ideological obsession with the level of debt rather than a coherent strategy to reduce [it] . . .' (Kanck 1998).

The observation that the government lacks a coherent debt reduction strategy is valuable. However, it is confusing for the Democrats to support further debt reduction, despite the current level being modest, and to charge the government with being ideological for doing the same. But then this seems typical of the debt debate. Confusion and over-simplification seem also to characterise the views of a number of leading local academics.

Professor Cliff Walsh (Executive Director of the South Australian Centre for Economic Studies) is a long-time advocate of a strategy to cut drastically and, ultimately, eliminate the debt. Professor Walsh's views are particularly influential with the Olsen government with which he has a close financial relationship.[4] Professor Walsh has also been very public in his views as a columnist for the *Advertiser* newspaper.

Professor Walsh contends that the increase in public debt during the early 1990s to one-third that of the Playford era was 'unsustainable' (SACES 1998, p. 66). But to support that argument Professor Walsh has been disingenuous. Firstly, he has argued that, in Playford's time, '[i]nterest rates were much lower … than those we bear today' (Walsh, *Advertiser* 30 June 1998). However, South Australia's debt is actually held at a range of interest rates, some of which are lower than today's lending rates and, if we compare current real market rates with those of the Playford era, we find that, at some four per cent, they are little different. Certainly, they were not 'much lower' in Playford's time.

Professor Walsh has also argued that, if the debt were reduced, we would get back our AAA credit rating. However, it is important to realise that, to the extent that the debt is reduced, the improved rating is of less value, and if the debt were eliminated, the AAA rating would be of no value at all. The only advantage to an improved credit rating applies to new loans and, even here, comparisons made between South Australia and other states suggest that the gain is likely to be small. Indeed, anecdotal evidence has it that when South Australia had a AAA rating like Victoria and NSW, its government was still charged higher interest rates. Further, the difference between the current AA rating and the much lauded AAA has been described as 'very fine' by the director of one ratings agency. On assumptions generous to the anti-debt argument, a return to the AAA rating has been estimated to be worth a mere $1.5 million p.a. (SA Commission of Audit 1994, p. 18). Clearly, it is easy to overstate the importance of the AAA rating.

Perhaps because of this, Professor Walsh has proposed in his newspaper articles that the real importance of the improved rating would be that it would send a desirable signal to potential investors. This is to be doubted. A government willing to cut back its own commitments to the state is unlikely to instill confidence in potential private sector investors. In any case, given the costs of early debt retirement, it is not at all obvious that getting AAA rating would provide more incentive to potential investors than incurring the same cost to, say, build more infrastructure like the Alice-to-Darwin rail link.

The only argument provided by Professor Walsh and the SACES that seems to make sense is the observation that, unlike in Playford's day, a significant part of South Australia's debt is being used to cover the losses from the State Bank and not to do anything productive. There can be no doubt that the State Bank losses are an ongoing drain on the state's resources. However, the situation has arisen because of the lack of prudential supervision by the Reserve Bank and the lack of control exercised by previous Labor governments. It is not an argument against debt *per se*.

Finally, it has been argued that, despite the important and beneficial role that has been played by the government in South Australian economic development, now it should 'get out of the way' (Walsh, *Advertiser* 20 Jan 1998). Walsh contends that, unlike the situation in Playford's day, the manufacturing industries he spent much time and debt attracting are past their heyday and that 'it needs to be understood that what ... is require[d] is to turn much of what Playford did on its head'.

We doubt that a practical man, as Premier Playford was, would agree with the abstract reasoning which forms the basis of that criticism. There is little to support Professor Walsh's contention and much to suggest the opposite: that the similarities with the Playford era are more important than the differences. Consider that, while many manufacturing jobs are being lost, some important parts of manufacturing (like food processing and rare earths refining) would have a bright future were they to receive government support as the motor vehicle industry and others did under Playford. Secondly, the state government has an important role in encouraging growth outside of manufacturing (such as in wine, IT or back office activities). This also requires government planning, support and the accumulation of debt.

These points are fundamental to the role of the state government in the South Australian economy. They refer to long-term aspects of South Australian growth which began long before Playford's time and which will continue into the future. There is a long and strong association between public debt and private prosperity in South Australia which Professor Walsh apparently does not understand and which his policy advice would break. This is the next issue for consideration.

PUBLIC DEBT AND ECONOMIC GROWTH IN SOUTH AUSTRALIA

Clearly, there is no obvious reason to believe that South Australia's debt should be drastically reduced or eliminated. However, this begs the question of whether debt might not have a positive role to play by, for example, funding a package of moves aimed at economic and social rejuvenation. To answer that question we begin by examining the historical evidence on the relationship between of debt and growth in South Australia. Then we construct a simplified framework for understanding the parameters of South Australian economic growth and hence, for assessing the way in which public debt responds to them.

In assessing the historical role that public debt has played it is important to recognise the sophisticated efforts that have been made to accumulate it. South Australia has always needed to borrow money and South Australian governments have always gone to considerable lengths to seek out debt. In the nineteenth century, they borrowed heavily in London, offering so called 'colonial consuls' with a sophistication and at interest rates said to have been 'a source of envy' among borrowers from other British colonies (Butlin 1964, p. 337).

After Federation, when the Commonwealth government assumed some of the functions of the previous colonial governments and began to accumulate debt itself, the borrowing activities of the state government were reduced but not eliminated. In the period after 1918, the South Australian government entered a number of innovative arrangements, (sometimes including the British government) which involved foreign loans to provide the jobs, housing and other infrastructure required for the arrival of assisted immigrants. The state's forestry industry and prime Riverland irrigation areas were developed on this basis, as was the draining of the South East and the extension of the road and rail network. Very few would argue that these were poorly made investments, or that the state would have been better off had the debt to finance them not been incurred.

In the post-1945 period under Premier Playford, debt grew very quickly but so did the economy. It is highly unlikely that South Australia would have grown as strongly if Playford had believed, as does the state's current government, that public debt was a constraint to growth.

On the other side of the account, there have been times in which the debt burden on South Australia has been heavy. The depression years of the 1890s and the 1930s showed how, in hard times, debt-servicing costs could be a significant drain on the public purse. This is a major problem with debt and one reason why South Australia must pursue all three of the previously mentioned means of importing capital. Whereas direct investment by outsiders requires the remittance of funds only if the investments are profitable, debtors (public or private) carry the risk of the investments they make and, in times of general or global recession, this can be seriously debilitating to the local economy. Prudence suggests that the debt-servicing burden must be subject to critical scrutiny and overall restraint. This is especially true in the current era of deregulated financial and foreign exchange dealings which add volatility to funding flows.

Nonetheless, the historical record makes clear that there is a broadly positive association between debt and growth. This is confirmed by the following figure which examines the post-war performance and public debt levels of the South Australian economy. It shows that high growth can coincide with high debt. However, the situation is complex. Increased debt does not always mean immediately higher growth and decreased debt does not necessarily mean slower growth.

The complexity of the situation can be illustrated. Firstly, some of the investments made by governments, with borrowed funds are of long gestation and hence are not immediately associated with higher growth. Investments made through education and health are in this category: we reasonably anticipate that they are good investments but do not expect we can calculate directly the rate of return or the impact on growth. The picture is further complicated by the fact that, at times, debt is incurred not for productive purposes but to cover mistakes as has been the case with the recent increase in debt to cover the State Bank losses. Not only was the collapse of the State Bank a drain on the liquidity of the state government which was the ultimate owner, but they were also losses made on loans outside South Australia and therefore were of no value at all to the state when they became non-performing.

Considering the historical role of debt raises a second consideration: that of the relationship between public debt and profit. To be sustainable, private debt must turn a private profit. This is not so with public debt which can be desirable even if it is not profitable. Of course, this is not always the case and government properly incurs debt to fund a range of projects. For example, the debt used to build up the assets of ETSA has generated profits to the public sector far in excess of the cost of that debt and so can be justified in simple business terms.

However, there are other investments such as those in roads, tunnels and bridges from which the government does not seek to make a book profit but for which it is not difficult to find a strong economic rationale. Such investments add to the asset base of the economy and enhance the productivity of both private and public activity. These too are then readily justified. Less obviously, but nonetheless rationally justified, is government debt acquired to achieve non-economic purposes. For example, debt might be incurred to save an area of wilderness by compulsory acquisition and proclamation of a conservation park, or it might be used to fund the operation of the Art Gallery of South Australia. These too are legitimate uses of borrowings, despite their lack of profit return. Furthermore, such activities would not be undertaken by private interests. In short, public debt serves a variety of purposes and must be judged by a variety of criteria. Its contribution to growth cannot be gauged by whether or not it is profitable.

Of course, this is not to say that public debt is always wisely used. Public enterprise can readily stray outside prudent bounds if left inadequately attended. However, the point being made here is that the role of debt cannot be so easily circumscribed as to limit it to only those

FIGURE 1: DECLINE IN DEBT AND SOUTH AUSTRALIAN GSP GROWTH

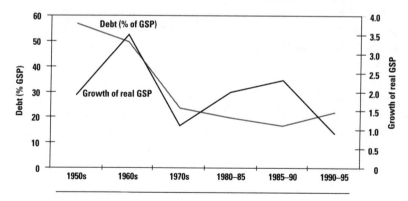

instances that have a direct, financial justification. Government, especially if it is to complement the private sector, must do more than undertake profitable activities.

To understand more deeply the role and importance of debt to social and economic revitalisation requires an appreciation of the parameters of South Australian growth. We have already described how

South Australia runs a current account deficit and has an ongoing need for outside capital. We can add further that economic growth in an isolated and small state basically requires the ability to attract both private capital and labour. As Graeme Hugo's analysis shows in chapter 4, South Australia is failing to attract and keep labour. We contend that without public sector borrowings, South Australia is also unlikely to attract all of the capital it requires. This holds out the possibility of self-reinforcing decline. Firstly, growth slows and less labour is attracted, then less debt is sustainable and growth slows again, more labour is lost and the process continues on a downward spiral.

In this, perhaps the critical consideration is that of expectations. Growth is largely just a confirmation of the expectation of growth. That is to say that growth breeds growth by generating a self-fulfilling optimism among participants. Now, in the late 1990s, with a stagnant economy and lacking the stimulus provided by significant population growth, expectations of South Australian growth are modestly pessimistic. It is not certain that the natural and inherent advantages of South Australia are sufficient to induce the private investment and other commitments that are necessary to generate further growth.

This is not the first time South Australia has suffered a crisis of confidence. Each time it happens, those involved find good reason to believe that growth has reached some limit. Despite that, the growth performance of South Australia over the last 160 years has been creditable by world and historical standards. Looking back, such growth may have seemed assured and inevitable; in previous times however, it has been the subject of considerable uncertainty. The reluctance of the present Liberal government to persevere with debt is a result of a recurrence of this uncertainty. It not only threatens to reduce directly the amount of economic activity, it also proposes to be a self-fulfilling pessimism. This then illustrates the more subtle and indirect ways in which an aversion to public debt can have undesired and undesirable consequences for growth.

To summarise the complex relation of debt and state growth: the anti-debt argument is that the debt build-up in periods of fast growth is merely a consequence of growth and the result of the profligacy and economic foolishness of the public sector. It is even thought to be the cause of any subsequent downturn. In general, the anti-debt view is that debt accumulates when economic performance is poor. We argue the contrary, that public debt is primarily a cause of growth and its accumulation in bad times is generally a precondition for private recovery. The elimination of debt will not unleash the initiative of the private sector. Instead, it will make less provision for private growth and provide fewer incentives for private sector expansion. More broadly, by denying much-needed, new investment in social and physical infrastructure it will erode the standard of living of ordinary South Australians.

CONCLUSIONS

The debt debate in South Australia is, in many ways, over-simplified. This chapter has sought to add substance to that debate. It has found that South Australia is facing no debt reduction imperative. Public sector debt has been and continues to be a key ingredient in promoting South Australian economic development.

The problem with the Olsen government's commitment to eliminating debt is not simply that government revenues might be used unwisely for that purpose. It is also that the government has been led to believe that public asset sales are essential because of the debt. This is doubly wrong. It not only threatens to reduce the total funds available to the South Australian economy, it will needlessly shift control and revenue from the public to the private sector.

That the government appears to be panicking needlessly over its debt is apparent in its arguing that the sale or lease of publicly owned electricity assets are essential. While the national electricity market places competitive pressures on some of those assets (particularly generation and retailing), overall, they are likely to remain profitable and some of them (such as the transmission activities) are likely to be very profitable. There is no good argument for the majority of electricity assets not to stay in public hands.

None of this is to imply that debt is costless or that any level of debt is acceptable. However, debt and growth are linked in a complex, but largely positive fashion, so that radical public debt reduction is a sub-optimal growth strategy for South Australia. The proposition that debt should be reduced to zero is extreme and ill-advised. This represents a new and dangerous turn in the politics of South Australian development.

It is to be hoped that this chapter provides part of the antidote to the simplistic notions which lie behind the anti-debt position. We acknowledge that some of the debt growth has been forced upon South Australia as a result of its exposure to the losses of the State Bank and has therefore been raised at interest rates higher than those which would have been chosen in more ideal circumstances. This provides good argument to refinance the debt portfolio progressively (and for prudently supervising all state assets) but not for doing without it. Just as there is a need to refinance the debt, so there is a need to reaffirm its importance and positive benefits. This, we believe, is an essential ingredient in revitalising the South Australian economy.

REFERENCES

Butlin, N.G. 1964, *Investment in Australian Economic Development*, Cambridge University Press, Cambridge.

Main, J.M. 1986, 'The Foundation of South Australia', in *The Flinders History of South Australia Political History*, ed D. Jaensch, Wakefield Press, Adelaide, chapter 1.

Olsen, J. 1998, 'Ministerial Statement on ETSA', 30 June.

SACES (South Australian Centre for Economic Studies) 1998, *March Economic Briefing*, p. 66.

SA Commission of Audit 1994, *Report*, v. 2, p. 18

NOTES

1   In 1834 the South Australian Commissioners were authorised by the Colonial Office to raise the first loans of the new colony: £50 000 to send initial emigrants and £200 000 for initial infrastructure spending. By 1840, the first criticism of the debt burden had emerged (Main 1986, pp. 9–19).

2   However, it is likely that South Australia runs a lower deficit than the nation as a whole. This is because the state has an older population and older people tend to run surplus budgets. Further, younger and growing populations in other states have higher current investment needs. Finally, unemployment is relatively high in South Australia and so aggregate demand is not growing as quickly. Nonetheless, as our objective here is to consider the conditions for economic renewal, we will regard the South Australian deficit as no less pressing than elsewhere.

3   We exclude the financial sector because, if we didn't, when SAFA borrows money and lends it to, say, ETSA, the debt would be double-counted; once as a liability of SAFA and again as a liability of ETSA.

4   The South Australian government is a long-term financial supporter of the Centre and Professor Walsh is employed two days per week as adviser to the Premier.

CHAPTER 9

ETSA AND THE PRIVATISATION PANACEA

JOHN SPOEHR AND JOHN QUIGGIN

During the mid-1990s South Australia became a laboratory for large-scale outsourcing experiments. A number of these experiments proved to be politically explosive, contributing to a significant swing against the Liberal Party in the 1997 state election. Emboldened by electoral survival, the Liberal government initiated a further round of privatisations in 1998. The centrepiece of this second wave of privatisation was the proposed sale of the state electricity industry.

The privatisation program of the Liberal government gained considerable momentum during the mid-1990s. It began with the largest information technology outsourcing projects ever undertaken in Australia. This involved outsourcing the management and maintenance of all government information technology services to the United States transnational firm, Electronic Data Services. In 1995 Adelaide's metropolitan water and sewerage treatment services were outsourced to the French/Anglo/Australian United Water consortium for around $1.5 billion, while northern metropolitan bus services were outsourced to the British multinational, SERCO. In addition, the management of Modbury Hospital was outsourced to US firm, Healthscope. There has been considerable controversy surrounding these cases. The most spectacular example was the 'Big Pong' in 1997, where lack of maintenance on the privately operated Bolivar Sewerage Treatment works led to a mechanical failure which resulted in the release of millions of litres of untreated effluent. A sulphurous stench hung over much of metropolitan Adelaide in the lead-up to the 1997 state election.

The Big Pong seriously damaged the case for outsourcing. Other important but less spectacular problems with outsourcing included widespread reports of cost over-runs in the delivery of government information technology services and financial difficulties threatening the viability of Healthscope. This experience fueled the recent voter backlash against the Liberal Party in the 1997 election.

Despite its near defeat, and commitments to the contrary made during the 1997 election campaign, the Liberal government revived proposals for privatisation in 1998. The proposed sale of the Electricity Trust of South Australia and Optima Energy (ETSA/Optima), HomeStart, Ports Corporation and WorkCover was the most ambitious asset sales program in South Australian history.

The proposed asset sales are likely to ensure that the backlash against outsourcing and privatisation grows. The warning signs are clear for any political party that advocates the sale of electricity assets. The defeat of the Liberal Party in the 1998 Tasmanian election was attributed by many commentators to the proposed sale of the Tasmanian Hydro Electric Commission. A similar result may be in store for the Olsen government (using arguments almost identical to those put forward by defeated Tasmanian Premier Tony Rundle) if it continues its campaign to sell ETSA.

There is no precedent in South Australian history to the Brown/Olsen government's radical program of privatisation. For much of the post-war period there was bipartisan political support for public provision and ownership of key utilities and services. We argue that government ownership of strategic assets has been, and will remain essential to the development of South Australia. The nationalisation of the electricity industry in 1945, the creation of the *Pinus radiata* timber industry and the development of water and sewerage infrastructure were among many examples of the South Australian government investing in growth in the post-war period. Similarly, the growth of the passenger motor vehicle industry was facilitated by government provision of land and infrastructure to the fledgling industry and through public investment in urban development and low-cost housing to enable the industry to attract and maintain a skilled workforce. Without this intervention and investment, it is likely that South Australia would have experienced slower economic and employment growth. The provision of infrastructure services to regional South Australia would also have proceeded more slowly and the costs to consumers would have been higher in the absence of intervention.

Those who advocate a retreat from public intervention and investment in the 1990s are too dismissive of the critical role that the government has played in the history of South Australia's development. They argue that South Australia has entered a new phase of economic development that does not require the strategic public investments of the past. They reject the idea that public investment can play a critical role in promoting higher rates of economic and employment growth. Indeed they advocate less public investment as a precondition for growth. There is, as we shall demonstrate, a growing body of evidence to suggest that higher rather than lower rates of strategic public investment will produce higher rather than lower rates of productivity and growth. There are equally powerful social and political arguments that demonstrate that privatisation of key assets often leads to a trade-off between shareholder interests and service access, quality and cost.

The proposed sale of ETSA represents an important turning point in the debate on the role of government in South Australia. If successful the sale would be a great victory for advocates of economic rationalism. It is likely that this success would pave the way for the privatisation of other key state assets.

Privatisation is neither inevitable nor irreversible. High levels of community opposition to the sale of ETSA are just the most recent illustration of the growing dissatisfaction with privatisation of core assets. It is unlikely that this opposition will diminish, as privatisation is no panacea for an ailing economy and labour market.

This chapter discusses some of the economic and political motivations behind the recent wave of privatisation in South Australia. In particular we focus on the debate surrounding the proposed sale of the electricity industry. The arguments put forward by the state government and its ETSA sale consultants are challenged and an alternative analysis of the financial impact of the sale provided. We conclude that the sale of the industry will result in a substantial net loss to taxpayers while also undermining the capacity of future governments to strategically utilise the industry to pursue social and economic development objectives. We conclude that privatisation of the electricity industry in South Australia will not halt the deteriorating economy and labour market.

THE STATE FOR SALE

Since the election of the Liberal government in 1993, nearly $1.5 billion worth of South Australian public enterprises have been privatised. This represents a dramatic acceleration of the privatisation program of the previous Labor government. The sale of the South Australian Gas Corporation by Labor set a precedent that the incoming Liberal government drew upon continually to justify its privatisation objectives. Indeed, it is likely that some of the privatisations proposed by the

Liberal government in 1998 would have been on the agenda had a Labor government been in power during the mid-1990s.

TABLE 1: PRIVATISATION IN SOUTH AUSTRALIA SINCE 1993

SOUTH AUSTRALIA	Proceeds	Sale type
1993/94		
SA Financing Trust	$5 m	Trade sale
SAGASCO	$29 m	Trade sale
SAGASCO	$417 m	Trade sale
1994/95		
Austrust Trustees	$44 m	Trade sale
Enterprise Investments	$38 m	Trade sale
Island Seaway	$2 m	Trade sale
Pipelines Authority of SA	$304 m	Trade sale
State Bank of SA	$10 m	Trade sale
1995/96		
Forwood Products (Timber)	$123 m	Trade sale
Sign Services	$0.2 m	Trade sale
State Government Insurance Commission	$175 m	Trade sale
State Bank of SA	$720 m	Trade sale
State Chemistry Laboratories	$0.3 m	Trade sale
State Clothing Corporation	$1.4 m	Trade sale
1996/97		
Radio 5AA	$8 m	Trade sale
SAMCOR (Meatworks)	$5 m	Trade sale
1997/98		
Port Bulk Handling Facilities	$8 m	Trade sale
TOTAL	**$1 899 m**	
Total State Governments	**$31 166 m**	
Total all governments	**$61 269 m**	

Source: *Australian,* 27 April 1998

Much of the momentum for privatisation in South Australia has been generated by the Report of the South Australian Commission of Audit. The Commission provided the government with political ammunition to embark upon an extensive privatisation program. The principal weapon used by the government in the privatisation propaganda war was a claim that public debt levels were unsustainable. Claims of a debt crisis have been used extensively to justify public sector job cuts and privatisation. In practice, privatisation is often a product of short-term political expediency and an antipathy towards the public sector, rather than a necessary response to debt (Chapman & Spoehr 1998; Spoehr & Broomhill 1995).

The re-election of the Liberal government in 1997 enabled a second wave of privatisation to take place in South Australia. On 16 February 1998, Premier Olsen announced the government's intention to sell the Electricity Trust of South Australia (ETSA) and Optima Energy, despite pre-election commitments not to sell these assets. Also up for possible sale were HomeStart finance, the Ports Corporation, the TAB and Lotteries Commission. WorkCover and the Motor Accident Commission were to be subject to 'reviews'. The combined value of these assets was at least eight times the value of the combined income from all previous privatisations undertaken by the Liberal government. The value of ETSA/Optima alone was estimated to be around $5–6 billion.

The privatisation proposals have been justified largely on the basis of their supposed financial benefits. *However*, the loss of revenue to the government from the latest wave of privatisation proposals will harm the medium-term financial position of the state. On the basis of modest enterprise performance and likely sale prices, the sale of ETSA/Optima, TAB/Lotteries Commission and Ports Corporation would result in a $1250 million net loss to South Australian taxpayers over a ten-year period (Spoehr 1998). Interest savings would not be expected to exceed the loss of revenue from the enterprises unless sale prices of $7 billion, $2 billion and $500 million respectively were achieved. Sale prices for ETSA/Optima are estimated to be between $4 and $6 billion while TAB/Lotteries is likely to attract around $1.4 billion based on interstate experience. On financial grounds alone the privatisation of these enterprises could not be justified unless the sale price for the combined enterprises exceeds $10 billion.

The Olsen government's approach to privatisation appears to be based on a combination of political pragmatism, a preoccupation with short-term debt reduction and an antipathy towards public ownership. The primary objective of privatisation has not been to improve the efficiency and effectiveness of the enterprises concerned but to reduce public debt. As Chapman and Spoehr demonstrate in chapter 8, there is no imperative for radical debt reduction in South Australia. Indeed the sale of profitable assets will do more to harm the state's financial position than improve it. The reality is that, while short-term revenue-raising from privatisation of public enterprises would enable some public debt to be retired, the interest savings from debt reduction would be insufficient to offset the revenue lost to the government arising from the sale of profitable assets.

The debate on the future of ETSA has largely been confined to the impact of the sale on debt reduction and to issues of risk associated with South Australia's entry into the National Electricity Market. Before addressing these issues in detail it is important to broaden the debate to include a discussion of the contribution of public infrastructure investment to economic and employment growth in South Australia.

INFRASTRUCTURE IN DECLINE – A CRISIS OF UNDER-INVESTMENT

Arguments for the privatisation of public assets such as ETSA flow in part from an unwillingness of the government to invest in the upgrading of infrastructure. Since the late 1970s expenditure on capital works in Australia has been in decline. Reflecting the post-war industrialisation and nation-building strategies of the post-war period and beyond, spending on capital works ranged between seven and nine per cent of gross domestic product over the 40 years to 1992/93, falling to five per cent in 1992/93 (Neutze 1997).

Governments eager to reduce public expenditure often defer the upgrading and expansion of infrastructure and turn to private sector management and provision of infrastructure. Overall, this short-term approach to the management of infrastructure is limiting our growth potential. Like other Australian states, South Australia has not adequately addressed the need to revitalise ageing infrastructure, let alone embark upon the development of a world-class infrastructure that will underpin prosperity in the twenty-first century century.

It is increasingly acknowledged that expenditure levels on social and physical infrastructure can significantly impact on the level of growth within an economy (See Aschauer 1990; Dowrick 1995). It is possible for government to accelerate economic and employment growth rates by increasing the rate of investment in infrastructure. Strategic long-term investment in physical infrastructure was a key plank of the 'Playford' approach to the industrialisation of South Australia in the post-war period. Significant development and expansion of electricity, water and sewerage services throughout the state were designed to underpin large-scale investment in manufacturing industry and result in the establishment of a viable vehicle industry in South Australia.

Higher levels of capital investment will be necessary to avoid further deterioration of our infrastructure. An ageing and tired infrastructure will create bottlenecks that restrict industry development and job growth. There appears to be mounting evidence of infrastructure run-down in areas such as water and sewerage mains and electricity capacity.

Gross fixed public capital expenditure was around 30 per cent less in 1997 than at the end of the previous recovery period. Levels of public capital expenditure have steadily declined since 1990.

The need for substantial infrastructure upgrade has not been recognised in the Capital Works Program. The allocation to that program has remained largely static in dollar terms over the 1993–98 period. At first glance the Capital Works Program appears to be steadily increasing. In reality however, the capital works budget has been consistently underspent. Expenditure in 1996/97 was less in real terms than expenditure in 1993/94. As an illustration of this problem, expenditure on capital works in South Australia has remained at around $1 billion over the last four years.

TABLE 2: CAPITAL WORKS PROGRAM EXPENDITURE, SA, 1993/98, $ MILLION

	Proposed	Actual
1993/94	1 186 758	1 000 465
1994/95	1 173 756	1 086 373
1995/96	1 149 168	1 071 311
1996/97	1 233 549	1 034 255
1997/98	1 291 022	–

Source: SA Budget Papers

If current trends in capital works' expenditure persist, future generations will suffer the social and economic consequences of a deteriorating infrastructure. This is likely to lead to lower levels of economic growth and productivity.

The positive interdependencies that exist between the public and private sectors in Australia have not been adequately quantified in Australia until recently. Does public sector investment in the economy simply crowd out private sector investment and slow down economic growth as many economic rationalists would argue? A growing body of research reveals a positive relationship between public investment in social and physical infrastructure and national productivity (Aschauer 1990; Dowrick 1994). Rather than cut back public expenditure to promote economic growth, there is considerable evidence to suggest that increased public sector expenditure in social and physical infrastructure will promote higher levels of economic and employment growth.

In an analysis of the relationship between public investment in infrastructure and productivity growth in the US economy, David Aschauer has demonstrated a positive relationship between rates of infrastructure investment and productivity growth. He concluded that if the average levels of public sector investment in infrastructure (relative to GNP) over the period 1950 to 1970 had been maintained over the twenty years to 1990, significant improvements in profitability, investment and productivity would have occurred. These potential improvements included:

- The rate of return to private capital would have averaged 9.6 per cent instead of its actual value of 7.9 per cent.
- Private investment would have averaged 3.7 per cent of the private capital stock rather than 3.1 per cent.
- The average annual rate of private sector productivity growth would have been 2.1 per cent instead of 1.4 per cent a 50 per cent increase in the average rate of expansion ... (Aschauer 1990, p. 1).

The implication of this analysis is that public sector investment in infrastructure such as energy, transport and water and sewerage will promote private sector productivity growth as Aschauer suggests: 'The evidence appears overwhelmingly in support of the proposal that public infrastructure directly augments private sector production. Therefore, a valid case can be made for a significant increase in public investment spending' (Aschauer 1990, p. 19). Such public investment will stimulate private sector investment over time resulting in the private sector's investing around 45 cents for every $1.00 of public sector investment (Aschauer 1990). Preliminary studies of Australian data tend to confirm that GDP growth could have been accelerated by higher levels of public capital investment over the 1980s (Dowrick 1994).

The case for higher rates of public sector investment in social and physical infrastructure is a compelling one. In this context, the retreat by the South Australian government from infrastructure investment is of great concern. The proposed sale of ETSA represents a significant acceleration of this trend. If this trend persists it is likely to create a serious crisis of under-investment in infrastructure. The impact of this crisis is likely to be expressed by slow rates of economic and employment growth.

THE ETSA SALE DEBATE

Early in 1998, Premier John Olsen announced that, contrary to previous commitments, the state's electricity industry would be privatised. The state government's initial attempts to sell ETSA proved fruitless, as they were not able to secure the necessary votes to pass the sale legislation in the Upper House of the state parliament. At first it appeared that opposition to the sale by the South Australian Democrats would ensure failure of the sale legislation. Under normal circumstances the Democrats' hold on the balance of power in the Upper House would have produced such an outcome. Unrest in the Labor Party ensured a different result.

Labor MLC Terry Cameron's support for the sale forced the Independent 'No Pokies' MP Nick Xenophon to determine the fate of ETSA. Nick Xenophon's decision to make the sale of the assets conditional on a referendum made the sale impossible. Given the consistently high level of public opposition to the sale it was not surprising that the government rejected the referendum proposal. Nearly 60 per cent of South Australians opposed the sale, while only around 26 per cent supported it (*Advertiser* poll, 1 July 1998). A referendum in this context was futile. After conceding that the sale option was impossible without a referendum, the Olsen government attempted to persuade Nick Xenophon to support a long-term lease of the state's electricity assets.

An attempt by the government to negotiate a compromise with Nick Xenophon failed in December 1998. This result came after a protracted debate around future electricity generation options and an announcement by the state ALP that it would be impossible for it to reverse any lease agreement once it had been agreed. Much of the debate during this period centred around the government's rejection of the option of establishing the 'Riverlink' electricity interconnector. This infrastructure would enable the importation of excess electricity capacity available in New South Wales. In rejecting this option the government announced plans to establish a new privately funded power station at Pelican Point. Concerns about the financial implications of this for business electricity costs reached boiling point when prominent local businessperson, Ian Webber launched a strong attack on the failure of the government to pursue the Riverlink option. He argued that it, rather than the Pelican Point option would result in lower electricity costs. Whatever the relative merits of these options in relation to electricity costs, it was clear that the Pelican Point option was motivated more by the government's desire to maximise the proceeds of a sale or lease by locking out additional interstate competition from alternative electricity suppliers. Subsequent to the government's rejection of the Riverlink option, Nick Xenophon declared he would not support the government's lease legislation. In rejecting the government's second wave of privatisation legislation, Nick Xenophon argued that the proposal represented a de facto sale and would result in higher electricity charges due to the rejection of Riverlink. With the ALP's stated commitment to supporting the lease if it proceeded, he also indicated that he had no option but to reject the lease proposal. He was determined to prevent voters being presented at the next election with a *fait accompli* in relation to ETSA's future.

The following section begins with a brief historical overview of the development of the electricity industry in South Australia. A review of the Olsen government's arguments for the sale is undertaken, together with a discussion of recent developments in the electricity industry. The performance of ETSA under public ownership is discussed. It is shown that the analysis by former state auditor-general, Tom Sheridan, of the financial impact of the sale ignores or undervalues important components of the return to taxpayers from public ownership of ETSA. Finally, a detailed analysis of the fiscal impact of privatisation is presented utilising three scenarios for ETSA's future earnings.

POWER TO THE PEOPLE

An adequate supply of electricity at reasonable rates is of the utmost importance to the community, particularly for the development of industry. The interests of the public in this regard have so far been largely at the discretion of the directors of the Company. Its [the Adelaide Electric Supply Company] claim that the public interest has been and will continue to be studied tends to conflict with the directors' duty to shareholders (Royal Commission 1945).

Any sober analysis of the merits of selling ETSA in the 1990s should reflect upon the reasons for the nationalisation of the industry in 1945. The 1945 royal commission into the privately run industry revealed an irreconcilable conflict between shareholder interests and the public interest as evinced by the reluctance of the privately owned Adelaide Electric Supply Company to make use of Leigh Creek coal reserves for power generation and its failure to restrain dividends to shareholders. The failure of the company to accelerate the electrification of regional South Australia offered further evidence of the lack of regard for the public interest. These factors combined to convince Premier Tom Playford that broad industrial and social objectives would be best met through public ownership of the industry. Playford concluded that the only effective means of ensuring that electricity infrastructure could be utilised as a tool to advance South Australia's social and economic development was public ownership.

For Playford, public control of the electricity industry was an essential prerequisite for the effective industrialisation of South Australia. Under private control, electrification of the state was proceeding slowly and industry needs were not being met. Playford regarded electricity provision as a 'natural monopoly' where the best interests of the state were served through public ownership. This would ultimately enable him to provide the necessary electricity infrastructure to support the development of the passenger motor vehicle and mining industries in South Australia. It would also ensure that regional South Australia had access to affordable power supplies. Private providers on the other hand, saw the electrification of country areas as unprofitable. Playford and his contemporaries claimed a longer-term view of what was profitable and in the public interest.

Many of the issues raised in the debate surrounding the future of the electricity industry in 1945 are relevant today. In particular the potential for conflict between shareholder interests and the broader public interest remains a critical issue.

SHOCK TREATMENT – THE RISK MADE US DO IT

From 1946 until 1 July 1995, the generation, transmission and distribution of electricity in South Australia was undertaken by a state government instrumentality, the Electricity Trust of South Australia (ETSA). ETSA was corporatised in 1995, and subsequently broken up into retail, transmission and energy subsidiaries, with generation being spun off into a separate enterprise, ETSA Generation. These changes were made in response to the development of a national electricity market and to the requirement for competitive reforms under the Competition Principles Agreement of 1995 and the associated federal *Competition Policy Reform Act 1995*, usually referred to as the Hilmer reforms (Hilmer et al. 1993). Under the Competition Principles Agreement, failure by state governments to implement competitive reforms to the satisfaction of the National Competition Council may lead to the withdrawal of financial assistance grants from the Commonwealth.

Hilmer and others have stated on many occasions that the implementation of these reforms does not require privatisation. Indeed, the terms of reference of the Hilmer Committee required their identifying policies that would enable public and private enterprises to compete on equal terms. Nevertheless, the need to comply with competition policy has been used as a pretext by governments wishing to privatise government business enterprises in the electricity industry and elsewhere.

Under the National Electricity Market (NEM), which has begun operation, generators bid to supply electricity to state pools. Large consumers may purchase electricity directly, while residential consumers contract with retailers who purchase electricity from the pool. Transmission of electricity remains a monopoly activity subject to price regulation.

It is important to note that, despite the description of the new system as a 'national' market, it is in reality a set of interconnected state markets. In the past each state operated an independent system. Thus interconnections allowing the transmission of electricity from one state to another have limited capacity. The large distances between major cities in Australia means that expansion of interconnection capacity is an expensive option.

The initial justification for the sale of ETSA hinged on claims that the risks of entering the NEM were too high and that privatisation of the industry would minimise any risk that existed. Whether risks would be better managed or minimised in public or private ownership was in fact irrelevant to participation in the NEM. Much of the debate however, was constructed as if privatisation of the industry were a prerequisite for compliance with competition policy agreements. Nothing could be further from the truth.

The need for structural reform of the electricity industry in preparation for entry to the NEM had been acknowledged at least four years prior to the government's sale announcement. During this period ETSA was preparing for entry to the NEM and fulfilling the requirements of the Council of Australian Governments' (COAG) Electricity Reform Agreement and the National Competition Policy. In a 1994 review of ETSA's financial performance, the South Australian Commission of Audit noted that ETSA had significantly improved its performance over the 1988–93 period and recommended that ETSA be corporatised in preparation for entry to the NEM (Commission of Audit 1993, p. 261). Since this time ETSA has undergone profound restructuring to prepare for the NEM. The performance of ETSA has improved significantly; its dividend payments to the government have been high and productivity high. The ETSA workforce has declined dramatically by nearly 50 per cent from around 3200 to 1700. While the competitive pressures in the NEM will be significant, ETSA has undergone the necessary reforms demanded for participation in the national market.

The question of ownership is not relevant in assessing compliance with competition policy principles and the COAG agreement. The Olsen government's use of the 1997 auditor-general's report to justify reversing its decision to retain ETSA in public ownership had no foundation in reality. The auditor-general's report specified possible risks associated with participation in the NEM and advised prudence through the operation of appropriate risk management strategies but it did not comment on the question of ownership. The government claimed however, that the financial risks to the state of retaining the South Australian electricity industry in public ownership were so great that it was necessary to sell the industry.

The alleged risk of losing Commonwealth 'competition payments' to the value of $1 billion was central to the early debate on ETSA's future in public ownership. This risk arose only where ETSA and the government failed to comply with the Council of Australian Government's electricity reform agreement signed by the state premiers in 1994. The auditor-general had made it clear that there was no immediate risk to the first payment due in 1998/99.

In the 1997 report the auditor-general comments that 'there are many opportunities for the South Australian government, the ETSA corporations and Optima to manage the risks associated with the entry of South Australia into the NEM' (Auditor-General 1997, pp. 3–40). It can be argued that the auditor-general's comments on the risks associated with management of the electricity industry in South

Australia are a basis for moving forward within existing ownership arrangements. Arguments that private ownership will minimise the identified risks have no foundation in either the auditor-general's report or in international and local experience and do not provide justification for the privatisation of the South Australian electricity industry. The question of ownership of the industry was always irrelevant as the COAG agreement makes clear when it says that: 'This agreement is neutral with respect to the nature and form of ownership of business enterprises. It is not intended to promote public or private ownership' (COAG Agreement 1995). Indeed this view was reflected in the Industry Commission's review of ETSA commissioned by the state government in 1996.

The South Australian government would not be prevented from continuing to own the various businesses which would be created by restructuring ETSA along the lines proposed (Industry Commission 1996).

PRIVATISATION – A FATE WORSE THAN DEBT?

The state government's case supporting the sale was based largely upon financial analysis undertaken by former auditor-general, Tom Sheridan and released on 12 March 1998. The report attempted to demonstrate that there would be a net financial benefit to taxpayers from the sale. It focused attention away from the question of compliance with competition policy to broader questions of the impact of increased competition on dividends flows, the relative effectiveness of private or public ownership and the economic impact of the sale on the state Budget. The key conclusion of the report was that 'combined sale prices in excess of $4 billion could well have a significant favourable net impact on the state budget' (Sheridan 1998).

The Sheridan Report provided a range of estimates of possible proceeds from such a sale, ranging from $4 billion to $6 billion. Sheridan argued that, provided the gross proceeds of any sale were in excess of $4 billion, savings in interest on public debt would exceed the flow of income from ETSA to the public sector. This led the government to claim that the sale would result in a net benefit of $150 million per annum.

The critical flaw in Sheridan's analysis was the fact that it focused exclusively on the dividends paid by ETSA, ignoring the fact that about half the earnings were routinely re-invested in the enterprise, as is common practice for both private and public enterprises. No competent analyst seeking to evaluate a private company would make this error. A number of other errors regarding superannuation and the valuation of debt compounded the effects of this fundamental error.

When the errors in the Sheridan report are taken into account, it is clear that a sale price of $4 billion would result in a net loss to taxpayers of around $1.8 billion over ten years. The privatisation consultants advising the government, Morgan and Stanley indicated that a sale price around $5 billion was most likely. At this price the government would lose around $700 million over ten years.

The following table provides summary results for three projections of the impact of the sale of ETSA/Optima over a ten-year period. The table is organised as follows. The first column shows the sale price under consideration. The second column shows the annual saving in interest calculated at a nominal rate of six per cent. For each of the three projections (central, high and low) estimates of the initial gain or loss and the present value of gains or losses are provided. The initial gain or loss is the difference between the annual interest saving and ETSA's income (earnings before interest and tax) in 1997/98 as estimated in each of the projections. The present value calculation is an estimate of the total value of gains or losses from privatisation over ten years, expressed in 1997/98 values.

TABLE 3: IMPACT OF PRIVATISATION ON PUBLIC INCOME FOR A RANGE OF SALE PRICES

Sale price* ($m)	Interest saving ($m)	Effect under Central projection		Effect under Low projection		Effect under High projection	
		Initial	Present value	Initial	Present value	Initial	Present value
4000	240	−123	−1133	−67	−524	−157	−2010
4500	270	−93	−913	−37	−303	−127	−1789
5000	300	−63	−692	−7	−82	−97	−1568
5500	330	−33	−471	23	139	−67	−1347
6000	360	−3	−250	53	360	−37	−1126
6500	390	27	−29	83	580	−7	−906
7000	420	57	191	113	801	23	−685

*Net of sale costs and provisions

The low projection assumes a significant loss of market share of around 20 per cent over ten years. This projection incorporates an immediate five per cent reduction in gross revenue and an annual decline of one per cent in real revenue. The central projection is based on the assumption that the trend of the last few years will continue, with total revenue rising by around one per cent in real terms. The high projection assumes that real revenue will grow in line with gross state product, at a rate of around three per cent per year. This is consistent with experience over the medium term, and incorporates an assumption that any loss of South Australian retail markets will be offset by gains in other markets.

Results for sale prices ranging from $4 billion to $7 billion are provided. Even under the low projection, the interest savings from privatisation are less than the income foregone when the sale price, net of selling costs, is $5.5 billion or less. If the central projection is taken as a 'best guess' estimate, a sale price of more than $7 billion would be required to generate a sustained net improvement in the state's fiscal position. If sale proceeds are between $5.5 billion and $6.5 billion, short-term net benefits will be more than offset by long-term losses. Even at prices as high as $7 billion, there is still a significant risk of loss associated with privatisation, as is shown by the high projection.

Since this analysis was prepared, the actual earnings of ETSA (consisting of ETSA Corporation and the electricity generation enterprise Optima) have become available. The combined earnings before interest and tax (EBIT) of ETSA and Optima totalled $382 million, which was above the medium projection used in the Table and just below the high projection. With net sale proceeds of $5 billion, the profits foregone as a result of privatisation consistently exceed the interest savings. By 2007, the present value of net loss is approximately $700 million.

The Olsen government's financial case for the sale of ETSA is flawed and misleading. Given likely sale prices it makes no economic sense to sell ETSA. Equally fallacious are arguments that the South Australian electricity market will be flooded by the entry of new competitors. The consultants working on the sale of ETSA went as far as to suggest that global competitors in the electricity industry would crush the South Australian industry. These claims were nothing more than scare tactics. The reality is that the global electricity industry is likely to contain as many public as private players. Public electricity corporations are competing successfully in highly competitive markets as the European experience continues to demonstrate. The public sector is set to remain a dominant player in the Australian electricity industry with Queensland, Tasmania and New South Wales strongly committed to public ownership of the industry. Finally, there are practical limits to competition in generation of electricity which ensure that Optima has a near monopoly, ensuring its viability. Our interconnection capacity with Victoria, which enables the export of power from that state to South Australia, is fully exploited already.

The advice provided to the state government on the sale of ETSA should be approached with great scepticism. It needs to be acknowledged that the consultants driving the privatisation process have significant vested interest in the sale. The prospect of a consultant's 'success fee' of around $30 million is a significant incentive to provide the advice that a client wants to hear.

PRIVATISATION – A CONSUMER UTOPIA?

The benefits to consumers of privatisation have been heralded as a further reason to sell ETSA. Lower costs and better service were the catch cries of the privatisation consultants and spin doctors. Will consumers be better off as a result of privatisation? International experience suggests otherwise. A study published by the pro-privatisation World Bank demonstrated that British consumers were up to $8 billion dollars worse off as the result of privatisation.

The study concluded that despite estimated efficiency savings of between 6 billion and 11 billion pounds which translate into potential price reductions of 3.2 to 7.5 per cent, prices did not fall as fast as costs. Indeed consumers were found to have experienced a significant loss from the reforms of between 1.3 and 4.4 billion pounds (Newbery & Pollitt 1997). On the other hand, shareholders were found to have gained significantly with National Power and PowerGen share prices increasing by around 300 per cent since the public float. The study also found that around 25 per cent of the net gains from privatisation were transferred out of the country through the repatriation of profits.

Thus, the companies seem to have unambiguously gained from the privatisation. Power purchasers seem to be paying higher prices than they would have under public ownership (higher company profit margins offset lower costs). And the government has gained from sales revenue, higher taxes on profits, and dividend income, though it has lost the revenue associated with the public sector dividend target for the CEGB (Newbery & Pollitt 1997, p. 4).

Over the 1989–91 period, domestic electricity tariffs in Britain rose by 28 per cent or four per cent above the rate inflation. Perversely, the cost of coal in 1991 was 27 per cent cheaper than it had been in 1988 (Ernst 1994, pp. 130–1). If this decline in coal prices had been translated into a reduction in prices, the unit price for domestic consumers would have been around eight per cent less in real terms.

Since privatisation of the electricity industry in Victoria there has been a doubling of the connection fee for domestic users from around $16.00 to $34.00. A range of services previously provided free of charge or at low cost has been subjected to charges or large increases (Loney 1997, p. 6). Domestic electricity prices were increased by ten per cent prior to privatisation and frozen in July 1993. Since privatisation in 1995 electricity prices have shown no sign of declining.

Recent evidence on water prices following outsourcing of Adelaide's metropolitan water and sewerage supply reinforces consumer concern regarding prices and privatisation. In this case claimed savings of around 20 per cent during the period of outsourcing have not been passed onto customers. Since outsourcing of the service in 1996, bills for average water use have risen by 6.7 per cent (*Advertiser* 27 April 1998). This experience is parallel with international trends following privatisation.

CONCLUSION

Until very recently, the privatisation juggernaut has seemed unstoppable. Despite continuing public opposition, both major parties have sold off public assets, often at bargain basement prices. In 1998, however, the juggernaut was halted. Proposals for privatisation of the Tasmanian HEC, the NSW electricity industry and Telstra were all defeated. Barring another defection, the Olsen government's plan to sell ETSA will suffer a similar fate.

The defeat of the privatisation push has arisen for two main reasons. First, the fiscal case for privatisation, based on the claim that taxpayers benefit from asset sales, has been recognised as fallacious. Errors like those of the Sheridan report have been exposed repeatedly. Even more importantly, long experience of privatisation has convinced voters that their scepticism about privatisation is well-founded. The promises of greater efficiency, better service and lower prices have simply not been delivered.

REFERENCES

Advertiser 1998, Advertiser Poll, 1 July.

Aschauer, D.A. 1990, *Public Sector Investment and Private Sector Growth*, Economic Policy Institute, Washington.

Auditor-General (South Australia) 1997, *Report of the Auditor-General, part A.3 Audit Overview.*

Australian 27 April 1998.

Chapman, P. & Spoehr, J. 1998, 'The debt debate – public debt and growth in the SA economy', Centre for Labour Research, University of Adelaide.

Dowrick, S. 1994, 'Impact of investment on growth: Externalities and increasing returns?' in *Investment for Growth*, background paper no. 39, Economic Planning and Advisory Council, AGPS, Canberra.

Ernst, J. 1994, *Whose Utility? The Social Impact of Public Utility Privatisation and Regulation in Britain*, Open University Press, Buckingham.

EPAC 1994, *Investment for Growth*, background paper no. 39, Economic Planning and Advisory Council, AGPS, Canberra.

EPAC 1994, *Public Expenditure in Australia*, commission paper no. 3, Economic Planning Advisory Commission, AGPS, Canberra.

ETSA *Annual Reports*, 1995–97.

Government of South Australia 1994, *Charting the Way Forward: Improving Public Sector Performance*, report of the South Australian Commission of Audit, v 2.

Loney, P. 1997, 'The Victorian electricity industry: The social costs of privatisation', a background paper prepared by Peter Loney MLA, Shadow Minister for Energy and Resources.

McMahon, J. 1997, 'Submission to Premier John Olsen regarding the South Australian public sector', Community and Public Sector Union, Public Service Association.

Newbery, D. & Pollitt, M. 1997, 'The restructuring and privatisation of the U.K. electricity supply – was it worth it?', Public Policy for the Private Sector, note no. 124.

Optima *Annual Reports*, 1995–97

Public Sector Research Centre 1997, 'Labor Council of New South Wales submission to the Committee of Inquiry into Electricity Privatisation in New South Wales', Public Sector Research Centre.

Quiggin, J. 1994, *Does Privatisation Pay?*, The Australia Institute, discussion paper no. 2.

Quiggin, J. 1994, 'The fiscal gains from contracting out: Transfers or efficiency improvements', *Australian Economic Record*, 3rd quarter.

Quiggin, J. 1995, 'Does privatisation pay?', *Australian Economic Review*, vol. 95, no. 2, pp. 23–42.

Quiggin, J. & Spoehr, J. 1998, 'The financial impact of the proposed sale of the electricity industry in South Australia', a report by the Centre for Labour Research, University of Adelaide for the United Trades and Labor Council of SA.

Self, P. 1993, *Government by the Market? The Politics of Public Choice*, Macmillan, London.

Sheridan, K. (ed) 1986, *The State as Developer: Public Enterprise in South Australia*, Wakefield Press, Adelaide.

Sheridan, T.A. 1998, 'An assessment of issues pertaining to the sale of ETSA and Optima'.

Smith, S. 1997, 'Electricity and privatisation', briefing paper no. 17/97, NSW Parliamentary Library Research Service.

Spoehr, J. (ed) 1998, 'An independent assessment of the implications of the privatisation of public enterprise in South Australia', a report by the Centre for Labour Research, University of Adelaide for the Public Service Association of SA.

Whitfield, D. 1992, *The Welfare State*, Pluto Press, London.

Yarrow, G. 1993, 'Privatisation in the UK', in *Constraints and Impacts of Privatisation*, ed V.V. Ramanadham, Routledge, London.

CHAPTER 10

FINANCING GROWTH AND PROSPERITY

MARTIN SHANAHAN

INTRODUCTION

The art of public finance requires a delicate blend of many hues. There is a need for a blending of economic theory and political reality, a mix of pragmatism and imagination and a combination of realistic assessment and idealistic optimism. Just as an imbalance of perspective or composition results in a poor painting, so a system of public finance that lacks balance or perspective will result in distorted growth and lessened prosperity.

Financing government expenditures requires a delicate balance, not only between taxing, borrowing or selling assets, but also between revenues and expenditures, incentives and impediments, efficiency and effectiveness, creating opportunities for individuals and protecting citizens in the present and in the future.

It takes particular skill and care on the part of the government to create and foster a sustainable level of economic growth that also enhances the capacity of the community to pay for government expenditures. The extreme solutions of massive or minimalist government will not deliver such growth. The first approach is economically unsustainable, while the second is both socially and economically destructive.

As other authors in this book have argued, the current blend of competing interests affecting South Australia's public finance is unbalanced. This imbalance is the result of a number of forces, not the least of which are a lack of imagination and a preoccupation with the current fashions of non-intervention and political expediency.

This chapter argues that alternatives exist that are both financially prudent and positive for the state's growth and prosperity. The first of the four sections provides a brief overview of South Australia's recent financial history, while the second reviews basic government financing 'techniques'. The third section argues that current developments in the art of economic theory support the case for a positive role for government in both the economy and in supporting a civil society. The final section suggests a number of options for enhancing government revenues which do not damage economic growth or the social fabric.

SOUTH AUSTRALIA'S RECENT FINANCIAL HISTORY

For the past several years, the South Australian economy has been in decline relative to the rest of Australia. In relative terms, state gross production has fallen, population numbers have declined, while unemployment remains higher than the national average, and wages lag behind the national average. Structurally, South Australia is more reliant on agriculture than other states and has a relatively smaller mining sector. Our manufacturing sector has been in decline along with manufacturing in the rest of Australia while small 'islands' of elaborately transformed manufactures have done well. The service sector in South Australia is comparatively smaller than that of other states (with lower levels of tourism, fewer corporate head offices etc.), which in turn means the impact of national trends for an expanding service sector have been more muted in South Australia. The average level of prosperity, in terms of general living standards, remains relatively good, although inequality has increased and particular locations in South Australia have high levels of unemployment and increasing poverty.[1]

The net result has been that South Australia has continued to be heavily supported by the federal system, with Commonwealth grants and revenue transfers contributing more than half of the South Australian government's revenue. In 1996/97, for example, Commonwealth grants comprised 53.2 per cent of the state's total revenue while state-owned source revenues, including contributions from public trading authorities contributed 46.8 per cent. (South Australian Treasury 1997). While such a result is consistent with the federal system, it does mean the state government has direct 'control' over less than half of its total revenue. This clearly reduces its financial autonomy and limits the scope for independent action.

With a comparatively small population expecting adequate levels of infrastructure, South Australia has always borrowed against future income. As chapter 8 indicated state debt as a percentage of gross state product (GSP) exceeded 60 per cent after World War II and is now in the region of 20 per cent. Borrowing has always been a significant factor in state finances.

Recent years have seen the use of asset sales as another source of funds. While governments have always bought and sold assets as required, the last fifteen years have seen a marked shift in attitudes, whereby public assets are most valued as a means by which to lower public debt, rather than as instruments for the provision of services.

BASIC TECHNIQUES

The sources of government revenue can be divided into three categories: taxation (including levies, fees, and licences of all kinds) borrowing and asset sales. A brief review of the principles which underlie each category is useful.

A good tax system is one that is simple, efficient and equitable. It should also gather enough revenue to fund the objectives of government. This latter consideration is important, as government expenditures are the 'other side of the coin' of government revenue. A good tax system is also flexible (to allow the government to respond to levels of economic activity) and should promote economic growth.[2]

Implementation of a taxation system consistent with the basic principles underlying a 'good' tax system is complicated significantly by the existence of a federal system of government. It is clear the current system does not meet any of the criteria required of such a system. The tax base available to state governments is narrowly based and as such liable to producing distorting incentives. (For example, a high charge on payroll taxes can result in a disincentive to employ more labour.) The picture is further complicated by the use of 'tax expenditures' (tax exemptions) which are used to encourage specific activities (for example, locating businesses in regional areas) but which also serve to narrow the tax base and represent revenue foregone to the government. In more recent years governments have also engaged in tax hypothecation (linking levies and charges to specific expenditures) which, while aimed at promoting taxpayer acceptance, further limit government discretionary expenditures.

Broadly speaking, at the present time, the state government is restricted to collecting revenues through stamp duties, payroll tax, gambling and betting taxes, motor vehicle taxes and licences, land tax, financial institutions and debits duties and fees and fines.[3] From an economic perspective, those taxes which are (or could be) broadly based are preferred to those fees and fines which are more narrowly based. Broad-based taxes create fewer price distortions and permit a more efficient allocation of resources.

In the 1997/98 budget papers South Australia was recognised as a 'below average' taxing state, as assessed by the Commonwealth Grants Commission. This result is no accident, but rather, the outcome of a serious attempt to demonstrate that the state is a low-taxing, and therefore attractive state in which to do business. The trade-off, however, is lower revenue receipts than the national average. The effectiveness of this strategy for attracting business investment remains unclear.

Government borrowing is a second major source of finance. Again, the basic principles are simple. Government borrowing should be undertaken to finance expenditures that advance the civic and economic capacity of the state and enhance its productivity. It is a valid and reasonable method by which to finance expenditures that cannot, or should not, be financed through current tax collections. For example, large infrastructure projects which enhance the state's productive capacity, which yield long-term benefits, and which will repay their provision over many years, are most sensibly financed by borrowing. Future generations who receive income streams from using such infrastructure can sensibly and reasonably be expected to contribute toward their cost through repaying loans, in the same way that the present generation is repaying earlier loans and enjoying the use of existing assets (Musgrave & Musgrave 1984).[4]

Clearly, borrowing which is not undertaken to finance such projects and which does not, at a minimum, increase the state's civic and economic capacity to the point where such loans can be repaid, is to be avoided. The critical issue, therefore, turns on the community's capacity to repay such debt.

The economic principles underlying the selling price of government assets are straightforward. Government assets should only be sold when the sale price at least equals, or is greater than, the net present value of the future income stream generated by that asset. A sale price that is less than this is, in effect, the price paid by the community to the private sector receiving the public asset. If efficiency gains result from the asset sale, these should be offset against this transfer of public wealth. Even when these considerations are excluded, other authors have shown the loss realised from privatising government business enterprises is greater than the interest savings generated when sale proceeds are used to repay public debt (Quiggin 1995; Walker 1994).

Nevertheless there are other economic issues involved with asset sales, which must also be considered. Even when the sale price matches the net present value of future income streams, many such assets generate significant economic externalities. For example, in the private sector the externalities generated by research and development, learning-by-doing and so on are more likely to be 'internalised' (contained) than in a public sector providing services to business (for example mapping and exploration services provided to the mining industry). Sales of government enterprises to overseas interests, therefore, run the risk of lessening the opportunity for positive spillovers to local businesses. From a community perspective, school land which is sold at market price and subdivided, may in the short run, reduce pressure on government budget entries, but the lost external benefits such land provides, through providing open space, venues for children to play and so on, are a real and significant economic loss to the community. To ignore these losses is to ignore the true (non-budget) cost of such decisions.

Supporters of asset sales and privatisation, in addition to citing the 'State Bank' debt, frequently argue that South Australia has little choice but to participate in such sales, as the nation as a whole is currently engaged in such microeconomic reform. Not to sell assets, they argue, would be both financially and economically ruinous, since the benefits of such reforms are large. This argument has been overstated. Estimates of the total national benefit of implementing the 'Hilmer' reforms are grossly exaggerated. When allowances are made for problems of estimating productivity, the net gain of such reforms are likely to be 'undetectable', with at most a one per cent gain in GDP being partially offset by unemployment, resulting from the reform process. (Quiggin 1997, p. 270). Neither the Hilmer Committee (1993) nor the 1995 Competition Principles Agreement of the Council of Australian Governments (COAG) actually requires governments to privatise.[5]

To date, most of the benefits claimed to arise from privatisation appear to have been overstated. In the longer term, privatisation narrows the government's revenue base and may reduce its ability to raise funds. It also removes entities from potential government influence which can be used to implement user-pays principles of service pricing or subsidisation of disadvantaged citizens. In short, it decreases the potential for government to enhance growth and prosperity.

CURRENT DEVELOPMENTS IN THE ART OF
ECONOMIC THEORY

While the focus of this chapter is on financing growth and prosperity, the really difficult task in the government's balancing act between promoting and inhibiting economic growth depends upon establishing a virtuous circle of growth and increasing revenue capacity. Recent developments in economic theory establish a strong case for government intervention, and consequently the need for revenue-raising.

It has long been acknowledged that technological progress assists long-term growth. It was not until the late 1980s however, that economists such as Romer (1986, 1987, 1990) and Lucas (1988) began developing economic theories of growth that could successfully incorporate technological change within their framework.[6] A major consequence of the debate stimulated by 'new growth' theorists is the recognition that governments do affect growth.[7] Appropriate institutions and policies can enhance growth, while inappropriate policies and institutions can inhibit growth.

While there are several different strands to new growth theory, elements that have been identified as important in driving technological progress are investment in physical capital, human capital and research and development.[8] While recognition of the first of these is not particularly new, it is the realisation of the complementarity between human capital, technology and growth that provides a new perspective. This operates at two levels. In narrow, firm-specific terms, the operation of new machinery or advanced technology, the responsiveness to market signals, even the production process used, depends on the stock of skilled and knowledgable people in the firm. In broader, economy-wide terms, the flexibility of the economy to respond to price signals, the ability of the economy to shift resources in response to perceived opportunities, in short, the growth of the economy, depends in great part, on the total stock of skilled and knowledgeable humans. Human capital is thus a crucial component of growth.

Human capital (particularly productive human capital) is dependent on a wide range of components. These components include 'know-how' from education and training, learning-by-doing and general knowledge and experience. Both the quality and quantity of these are important (Schultz 1961, 1975). Importantly for the models, and for government policy, investment in human capital is seen as resulting in externalities (Lucas 1988). That is, as individuals and groups in the economy are better educated, better trained and better skilled, 'spillover' benefits result, such as more investment in companies which require skilled workers, more downstream companies supplying components requiring skilled labour, more institutions supplying education and knowledge and so on.

An important implication of the focus on human capital is that factors beyond narrowly defined workforce skills are also important. For example, investment in general education (Schultz 1961, 1975), human health and nutrition (Pomfret 1997), and market access (Palmer 1995) are also linked to the enhancement of human capital. Complementing this focus, the work of Ashauer (1989), Barro (1991), and Otto and Voss (1994) has shown a positive correlation between government expenditure on infrastructure such as streets, sewers, water supply, public transport and so on, and growth. More specifically, they demonstrate a positive link between public works and private sector productivity.

The answer, however, is not simply to 'throw money' at public works. Rather, it is to recognise that many factors interact to produce a growing and prosperous community. Expenditures in areas such as education, enhancing market access for all citizens, communication technology, infrastructure, environmental improvements and public services, complement and reinforce private sector productivity in addition to themselves assisting growth.[9]

These observations are consistent with the work by Porter (1990) and Thurow (1993). A critical mass of competitive, rather than comparative advantage is important. The competitive advantage in turn depends on individuals', groups' and businesses' ability to respond to opportunities. Governments support and enhance this ability through expenditure in education, infrastructure and social capital.

This final component of expenditure is under-emphasised in most of the growth theory literature. The work of Fukuyama (1995) however, makes explicit the link between trust, a healthy social community, social capital, and economic success and prosperity. Economic success relies on groups of people cooperating.

A combination of many factors produces a trusting society. Governments and their institutions deliver a range of services that directly and indirectly affect the level of trust in the community. For example, government institutions should deliver protection and justice to all citizens. They should institute rules and provide agencies to ensure equal opportunity and access. They should design and enforce regulations that promote certainty and consistency, as well as providing opportunity for initiative and energy. They should provide services that supply citizens with economic support, protection against poverty, basic housing and the opportunity to participate. In short, an important task of government is to enhance those factors that result in a civil society.

Governments therefore, do have an important role to play in influencing prosperity and growth. Conditions such as social infrastructure, a civil and just community, public works and a skilled and educated workforce, in combination with economic opportunities and signals, private business energy and risk-taking undoubtedly produce growth and prosperity.

ALTERNATIVE PERSPECTIVES

There are alternatives to the current mix of instruments used to finance state government expenditures.[10] It is important, therefore, to distinguish between what cannot be done, from what governments choose not to do. The South Australian government has a very limited influence on national macroeconomic policies, or on national financial arrangements. It is not, however, totally impotent in this area. It could, for example, do more to promote cooperation and coordination between the states and Commonwealth in the area of taxation.

Even if increased coordination between the states is not achieved, there is a variety of options available to the South Australian government which could increase government revenues. Simply increasing taxes and charges across the board, or imposing a head tax, are not among them. As with expenditures, care must be taken to ensure prices are not inadvertently distorted to produce inappropriate market signals. At the same time, governments should consider taxes and charges that are designed to alter relative prices and produce socially desirable, long-term incentives.[11] A number of options are discussed below.

One of the major criticisms of any general consumption tax is that it is regressive. People on low incomes with no capacity to save are taxed on their entire income, while people on higher incomes who are able to save (either immediately or via superannuation) pay a lower proportion of their income in tax.

Supporters of consumption taxes frequently argue that, given the difficulties inherent in identifying and defining income for tax purposes, together with Australia's current disproportionate emphasis on personal income tax, it would be far simpler, and fairer to tax consumption. It is also implied (though rarely articulated) that income and consumption are virtually the same, with the difference between the two being savings. Represented symbolically: $Y = C + S$, where Y is personal income, C is consumption and S, savings. Such a definition, while probably originating in macroeconomics is, not one generally accepted by tax economists. In 1938, Henry Simons defined personal income as: $Y = C + Wt - Wt\text{-}1$, where Y and C are as before, but $Wt - Wt\text{-}1$ represents the change in wealth that occurs over the observed period. Thus personal income is actually 'the market value of rights exercised in consumption' together with 'the change in value of the store of property rights' over the period in question.[12]

The implication for consumption taxes is profound. Wealth, as well as consumption, should be taxed if a consumption tax is considered to be the equivalent of income tax. If a consumption tax were introduced at a Commonwealth level, complementary wealth taxes could be introduced at the state level that would improve the progressiveness of the overall tax system. If the states cooperated, such a tax would have no impact on interstate relocation incentives. Failing state cooperation, wealth taxes levied on immovable assets (such as land) would minimise interstate migration.

Other forms of wealth tax can be levied. Examples include annual taxes on net wealth and taxes on wealth transfers (including gift and estate duties).[13] Of these, gift and estate duties existed in Australia for several decades at both Commonwealth and state levels before their progressive abolition between the late 1970s and mid-1980s. A re-introduction of the gift and estate duties which existed in the mid-70s would generate, in 1998 terms, more than $90 million per year for South Australia.[14] To quote the 1985 White Paper, 'In general, it seems unlikely that wealth taxes would have a significant effect on economic behaviour relative to any alternative tax that might be imposed (or increased) to raise the same amount of revenue'.[15] If 'taxation is the price we pay for civilisation' then perhaps estate duties are the price we pay for passing civilisation on to our children.[16]

One group of taxes the state government has already begun levying, and which could be significantly expanded with beneficial results, is a set of more comprehensive environmental taxes.[17] Again there are several different forms this tax could take, depending on the degree of interstate cooperation. In theory, such taxes promote economic efficiency by closing the gap between marginal private costs of production and marginal social costs, resulting in more accurate market information.[18] Market signals would more accurately reflect the environmental cost of production, transportation, energy and water supply, top-soil etc. while simultaneously providing incentives to conserve and create alternatives. It has been estimated, for example, that a national carbon tax would yield $6.3 billion per year (1992/93) and permit the abolition of payroll taxes.[19] Failing the introduction of a national tax, there would appear to be scope for a state version of the tax which would add to government revenues while also encouraging conservation of carbon-based production methods.[20]

Economists dislike narrowly based taxes, since they produce price distortions and increase inefficiency. Broadening the tax base, (a *prima facie* argument used to support consumption taxes) is seen as an important component in the design of a good tax system. From this perspective, Albon (1997) has recently argued for an expansion of state payroll and land taxes. Freebairn (1993) shows the long-run effect of a comprehensive payroll tax is effectively the same as a consumption tax. Removing the exemptions to payroll tax would increase its efficiency and state revenue.[21] Similarly, benefits can flow from a more comprehensive, but lower-rated land tax. This is not a radical recommendation. Such a broadening of the land tax base has been recommended by several previous inquiries such as that conducted by the Productivity Commission (1993).

There is a range of other revenue-raising measures, which if carefully targeted, would actually improve economic efficiency by removing externalities while also raising revenues in a progressive manner.[22]

Careful consideration should be given to the current pattern of tax expenditures. They represent revenue foregone to the government, and their actual effectiveness in generating benefits to the state greater than this cost should be carefully assessed.

Expanded and alternative taxation measures are one option available to the state government which would enable it to finance expenditures that promote growth and prosperity. Borrowing funds and a changed approach to state-owned assets are others.

The suggestion for borrowing funds is not equivalent to promoting financial imprudence. On the contrary, borrowing requires administrative prudence and careful judgement. Nonetheless, the need to finance long-term projects will require measured borrowing to ensure the necessary human and physical capital is in place to maintain long-term growth.

The current fashion of selling state-owned assets should be revisited. Rather than disposing of assets in a manner which underestimates their true worth and lessens their potential as revenue producers for government, a policy should be developed which seeks to re-invigorate government business enterprises, and to promote both efficiency and effectiveness. Such a policy would realise significant benefits to the state and assist it in stabilising its long-term revenue-raising capacity.

A further dimension frequently overlooked is the impact government can play in promoting growth through its demand for services and products. The policy is not, however, simply 'buy local'. To promote the production of goods and services with a competitive advantage, state governments should specifically demand those goods and foster those market structures which support the industry networks which lead to competitive advantage. This involves both enhancing existing economic clusters and assisting the development of emerging areas. Current ad hoc approaches to attracting capital investment, such as providing government assistance of a form and quantity that 'outbids' other states is both ineffective and expensive (Productivity Commission 1996).

The art of public finance is not easy. It is possible, with an approach from government different from that currently in vogue, to envisage a prosperous and expanding future for South Australia. To return to our opening image – the creation of such a fine landscape will necessarily demand skill, a substantial understanding of perspective and an imaginative and inspired vision.

REFERENCES

Aiken, M. & McCrae, M. 1992, 'Full cost pricing and public sector reporting: Alleviating undisclosed short-run measurement biases of "user to pay" policies', *Financial Accountability and Management* , vol. 8, no. 1, pp. 13–34.

Albon, R.1997, The efficiency of state taxes, *Australian Economic Review*, vol. 30, no. 3, pp. 273–87.

Aschauer, D.A. 1989, 'Is public expenditure productive?,' *Journal of Monetary Economics*, vol. 23, pp. 177–200.

Australian Bureau of Statistics 1998, *Adelaide: A Social Atlas*, AGPS, Canberra.

Barro, R.J. 1991, Economic growth in a cross section of countries', *Quarterly Journal of Economics*, vol. 56, pp. 408–43.

Brown, C.V. & Jackson, P.M. 1990, *Public Sector Economics*, 4th ed, Blackwell, Oxford.

Crowe, M. 1996, An assessment of the impacts of restructuring payroll taxes, paper presented to the 25th Conference of Economists, ANU, Canberra.

Freebairn, J. 1993, 'The GST and payroll tax abolition', in *Fightback! An Economic Assessment*, ed J.G. Head, Australian Tax Research Foundation, Sydney.

Fukuyama, F. 1996, *Trust: The Social Virtues and the Creation of Prosperity*, Penguin, London.

Groenewegen, P. 1990, *Public Finance in Australia: Theory and Practice*, 3rd ed, Prentice Hall, Sydney.

Grossmann, G.M. & Helpman, E. 1989, 'Product development and international trade', *Journal of Political Economy*, vol. 97, pp. 1261–83.

Grossmann, G.M. & Helpman, E. 1990, 'Trade innovation and growth', *American Economic Review*, vol. 80, May, pp. 86–91.

Harrison, J. 1996–97, 'Total tax review: major reform issues', *Current Issues*, brief 7, Parliamentary Library, Canberra.

Industry Commission 1993, *Impediments to Regional Industry Adjustment*, 2 v., AGPS, Canberra.

King, J. 1998, 'A taxing problem', *Arena*, vol. 34, April/May, pp. 43–5.

Lucas, E. Jr 1988, 'On the Mechanics of Economic Development', *Journal of Monetary Economics*, vol. 22, no. 1, pp. 3–42.

Mathews, R. 1985, *Comparative Systems of Fiscal Federalism: Australia, Canada and the USA*, Centre for Research of Federal Financial Relations, reprint series no. 69. ANU.

Musgrave, R.A. & Musgrave, P.B. 1984, *Public Finance in Theory and Practice*, 4th ed, McGraw-Hill, New York.

Otto, V. & Voss, G.M. 1994, 'Public capital and private sector productivity', *The Economic Record*, vol. 70, no. 209, pp. 121–32.

Owen, A. 1995, 'The environment: The role of economic instruments', *The Australian Economy*, ed P. Kreisler, Allen & Unwin, Sydney.

Palmer, I. 1995, 'Public finance from a gender perspective,' *World Development*, vol. 23, no. 11, pp. 1981–6.

Pomfret, R. 1997, *Development Economics*, Prentice Hall, London.

Porter, M.E. 1990, *The Competitive Advantage of Nations*, Macmillan, London.

Productivity Commission 1993, *Taxation and Financial Policy Impacts on Urban Settlements*, vol.1, AGPS, Canberra.

——1996, *State, Territory and Local Government Assistance to Industry*, AGPS, Canberra.

Quiggin, J. 1995, 'Does privatisation pay?' *Australian Economic Review*, vol. 95, no. 2, pp. 23–42.

——1997, 'Estimating the benefits of Hilmer and related reforms', *Australian Economic Review*, vol. 30, no. 3, pp. 256–72.

Reform of the Australian Tax System (1985) Draft White Paper, AGPS, Canberra.

Romer, P.M. 1986, 'Increasing returns and long-run growth', *Journal of Political Economy*, vol. 94, no. 5, pp. 1002–37.

—— 1987, 'Growth based on increasing returns due to specialisation', *American Economic Review*, vol. 77, Papers and proceedings, pp. 56–62.

—— 1990, 'Endogenous technological change', *Journal of Political Economy*, vol. 98, no. 2, pp. S71–102.

Schmandt, J. & Wilson R. (eds) 1990, *Growth Policy in the Age of High Technology*, Unwin Hyman, Boston.

Shaw, G.K. 1992, 'Policy implications of endogenous growth theory', *Economic Journal*, vol. 102, pp. 611–21 reprinted in Snowden and Vane (1997).

Schultz, T.W. 1961, 'Investment in human capital', *American Economic Review*, vol. 51, pp. 1–17.

—— 1975, 'The value of the ability to deal with disequilibria', *Journal of Economic Literature*, vol. 13, no. 3, pp. 827–46.

Snowden, B. & Vane, H.R. (eds) 1997, *A Macroeconomics Reader*, Routledge, London.

Simons, H. 1938, 'Personal income taxation, Chicago', *Public Finance in Australia: Theory and Practice*, ed P. Groenewegen, 3rd ed, Prentice Hall, Sydney.

Solow, R.M. 1956, 'A contribution to the theory of economic growth', *Quarterly Journal of Economics*, vol. 70, no. 1, pp. 65–94.

South Australian Council of Social Services (SACOSS) 1998, An agenda for action, state budget submission 1998/99, unpublished.

South Australian Treasury 1997, Budget Papers 1997/98, Government Printer, Adelaide.

Stretton, H. 1987, *Political Essays*, Georgian House, Melbourne.

Swan, T.W. 1956, 'Economic growth and capital accumulation', *Economic Record*, vol. 32, pp. 334–61.

Taxation Review Committee 1975, *Full Report*, K.W. Asprey, Chairman, AGPS, Canberra.

Thurow, L. 1993, *Head to Head: The Coming Economic Battle Among Japan, Europe and America*, Allen & Unwin, Sydney.

Walker, R. 1994, 'Privatisation: A reassessment', *Journal of Australian Political Economy*, vol. 34, pp. 27–52.

NOTES

1   See for example, ABS (1998); SACOSS (1998).

2   Taxation Review Committee *Full Report* (The Asprey Report) 1975, See also Reform of the Australian Taxation System, 1985 (Draft White Paper from the tax summit). Attempts have also been made to articulate a 'good' system in the federal context (for example, linking taxation and expenditures more directly with the responsible tier of government). See Matthews 1985.

3   Before World War II, the states also levied income taxes. This power was taken over by the Commonwealth during the war and confirmed by the High Court in *South Australia and Others v The Commonwealth and Others* (1942) 65 C.L.R. 373 and *Victoria and New South Wales v The Commonwealth* (1957) 99 C.L.R. 575. In theory, states are still able to levy income taxes. Judicial interpretations of Section 90 of the Australian Constitution have also limited the scope of state governments to impose sales taxes. Recent High Court rulings have further narrowed the states' revenue-raising options.

4   For a more detailed discussion of the accounting issues see Aiken and McCrae (1992).

5   For a recent application to the proposed privatisation of the South Australian electricity industry, see chapter 9.

6   The older neoclassical growth models based on Solow (1956) and Swan (1956) treated technological change as exogenous (outside) their theories.

7   Earlier theories, such as the Harrod–Domar model, did have a role for government, as budgetary savings could substitute for domestic savings and thus effect capital investment. The Solow–Swan model, however, removed the importance of government fiscal policy, by linking growth to the rate of population expansion. For a summary see Shaw (1992). See also Schmandt and Wilson (1990) and the report of the Industry Commission (1993).

8   Other factors which are highlighted include trade policy (Grossman &
     Helpman 1989,1990), and the existence of imperfect competition
     (Romer 1990). In the Australian context, these issues are more
     appropriately considered within the purview of the Commonwealth
     government.

9   Stretton (1987) also identified the complementarity of business and
     government.

10   Under the Constitution, with the exception of customs and excise duties
     (which has been ruled to include business franchise licences) states can
     legally utilise a variety of tax bases.

11   A clear example of such taxation is a high tax on tobacco products,
     designed in part, to decrease consumption, especially among the young.

12   Groenewegen 1990, p. 146.

13   For a discussion see Reform of the Australian Tax System (1985).

14   Calculated from estimates provided in Reform of the Australian Tax
     System 1985, p. 181 and indexed for inflation.

15   As above, p. 178.

16   Attributed to Peter Groenewegen in J. Harrison (1996–97).

17   For example, the state government already imposes property levies to
     fund the Patawalonga and River Torrens Water Catchment Boards and
     environmental licence and discharge fees.

18   For a discussion see Brown and Jackson (1990, pp. 37–46).

19   Hamilton, Tundlow and Quiggin, in King (1998, p. 45).

20   See also Owen in Kreisler (1995, pp. 191–213).

21   For example, Albon (1997, p. 281) cites the work of Crowe (1996) who
     has estimated that increasing the comprehensiveness of payroll tax in
     New South Wales would result in substantial benefits.

22   These include a broadening of stamp duties and resource rents.

PART 2

TRANSFORMING THE CONTRACT STATE

CHAPTER 11

TACKLING THE JOBS CRISIS

Looking for ideas that work

JOHN SPOEHR

INTRODUCTION

... It is scarcely that there is no work to be done in the world; but the creation of 'jobs', something diminished and desultory without purpose is not going to rescue them. It must start with a more honest and open discussion about where we have come to ...

Jeremy Seabrook, Journalist, *New Statesman* and *Society*

The dimension of the jobs crisis in South Australia was starkly illustrated at the end of 1998 when 2300 people lined up outside Employment National in Salisbury to apply for just 65 jobs. Images of the Great Depression were conjured up when 'people of all ages began queuing outside ... the office at first light. Three hours before the interviews were due to start at 11am, the line of jobseekers snaked more than 600 metres from the office to a nearby carpark' (*Advertiser* 13 October 1998, p. 1).

To say that the outlook for any significant reduction in unemployment is bleak was to acknowledge an unwelcome reality in a battle-weary state like South Australia. Now the reality can no longer be denied. The South Australian labour market is in crisis and the short-term outlook for jobs growth is poor, as other chapters in this book demonstrate. The scale of deterioration of the labour market became clear in 1997 with the appearance of a growing gap between South Australia's and Australia's performance on jobs growth. Over the twelve months to August 1998 the South Australian labour market actually contracted at a time when jobs growth was gaining momentum in Australia. The unemployment rate in South Australia also went against the national trend resulting in a significant increase of the unemployment rate by the end of the 1990s.

In the short term, unemployment will not recover to levels achieved at the end of previous economic recovery periods in 1980 and 1990 when South Australia's unemployment rate had declined to around seven per cent. As the full impact of the global financial crisis begins to be felt in Australia, there is no prospect of a similar outcome at the end of the 1990s. In the absence of significant policy changes, double digit unemployment will be the norm rather than the exception in South Australia.

Public sector job cuts, low relative rates of economic growth and investment, the impact of tariff phase-down and population outflow have combined to sustain high rates of unemployment in South Australia throughout the late 1990s recovery period. The dramatic decline in public sector employment and the sustained longer-term decline in manufacturing employment have contributed significantly to unemployment in South Australia. In an environment of slow economic growth where the state has consistently under-performed relative to national rates of economic growth, the loss of around 25 000 people from the public sector has starved the South Australian economy of an important source of demand. As the once-off effects of separation payments on purchase of local goods and services evaporates, so does the ongoing demand generated by larger numbers of public sector workers. The impact of this has been felt most by many small and medium-sized businesses which have experienced a decline in demand for local goods and services. Less demand means less economic growth and less capacity for employment in the private sector.

Federal government funding cuts to labour market and regional assistance programs have narrowed the range of responses available to organisations seeking to support the unemployed. In particular, the abolition of employment programs like New Work Opportunities and the Land Environment Action Program has torn apart the safety net once available to long-term unemployed people. The Work for the Dole program is a poor replacement, lacking accredited training components and broader linkages to regional development strategies. Meanwhile, the privatisation of the Commonwealth Employment Service is proving to be a monumental policy failure. The new JobNetwork is one of the worst examples of neoliberal ideology prevailing over practicality.

The neoliberal economic obsessions with balanced budgets, privatisation and competition are fueling unemployment and creating greater hardship and insecurity. Substantial productivity growth has not translated into a jobs boom or wages growth. Instead, productivity improvements are being achieved at the expense of jobs, job security and wage rises (Bryan & Rafferty 1999, pp. 78–82). Overcoming persistent double digit unemployment in an unregulated global economy will be difficult. The failure to curb the growth of speculative investment through global and national financial regulation is one of the most significant impediments to jobs growth in Australia. To move towards the development of a productive, job-generating economy rather than a speculative, job-destroying one, policy-makers will have to adopt policies that counter the speculative excesses of 'casino capitalism'.

There is no panacea for the jobs crisis in South Australia. Significant policy shifts will be required at global, national and local levels to significantly reduce unemployment. While global economic and political conditions greatly constrain the options available to small and open economies like that of South Australia, governments can make a difference.

This chapter focuses attention on the need for the state government to work with the South Australian community to develop a sophisticated and comprehensive policy response to unemployment. The role of the public sector in tackling the jobs crisis is discussed and the medium-term prospects for the South Australian labour market detailed. Recent employment policy responses by the Liberal government and the Labor Opposition are canvassed. Finally a range of strategic alternatives for tackling the jobs crisis is outlined. Any effective response to unemployment at a state level will require significant national and international policy shifts as other chapters in the book highlight.

THE CHALLENGE AHEAD

The capacity for bringing down unemployment in Australia and South Australia has been constrained by the prevailing view that substantial reductions in the size of the public sector will improve economic performance. History reveals otherwise. Higher rates of public investment in social and physical infrastructure have underpinned prosperity and jobs growth in South Australia.

Dramatically reducing the size of public sector workforce has not brought about a revival of the South Australian economy as neoliberal economists consistently claim it would. On the contrary, it has led to slower economic and employment growth rates. Economic modelling of the impact of the state government's approach to debt reduction undertaken in 1994 revealed that a more moderate debt reduction strategy would have resulted in an additional 5300 jobs by 1999 and increased annual gross state product (GSP) by up to 0.6 per cent (NIEIR 1994).

Contrary to the state government's commitment to no further loss of public sector jobs, losses will result from outsourcing and privatisation over the course of the next few years. Outsourcing and privatisation are resulting in the loss of full-time jobs and the growth of contract and part-time jobs. Attempting to reduce government outlays through such strategies tends to lower local consumption levels as job security and real wage levels decline. This in turn leads to reduced employment in the private sector.

The performance of the South Australian economy over the last four years has been poor relative to other mainland states and the nation as a whole. Growth rates during the late 1990s recovery period have not been sufficient to bring down unemployment. Deteriorating economic growth rates over the 1995–97 period have led to lower employment growth and higher unemployment. The outcome for GSP growth for the 1996/97 period was nearly 50 per cent less than the forecast rate of 2.25 per cent. After a short 'burst' of growth in 1995, GSP growth steadily declined and contracted at the beginning of 1997. In contrast, national rates of growth in gross domestic product (GDP) rose by 2.8 per cent over 1996/97 (Budget Results, 1996/97). According to economic analysts BIS Shrapnel, South Australian economic growth has been around 1.2 per cent per annum less than national rates of growth. Tasmania is the only state to experience lower growth over this period.

Employment growth rates remain well below those required to make any significant inroads into unemployment in South Australia. Indeed the 1988/99 state budget forecasts of 0 per cent employment growth over 1997/98 and one per cent in 1998/99 are an admission that unemployment will remain very high. Improving employment growth rates will be made much more difficult as the full effects of the Asian financial crisis impact on South Australia.

While modest reductions in unemployment were expected over the course of 1998 as the national economy gained momentum, recent performance suggests that these gains will fall well short of the state government's budget projections. Combined with the effects of the global financial crisis, South Australia's economic and employment growth prospects remain poor.

It is now urgent that a comprehensive policy response be developed by the state government to attempt to boost jobs growth to enable the unemployment rate to decline to seven per cent within the next three years. This is the benchmark set at the end of the previous recovery period when the unemployment rate in January 1990 fell to 7.1 per cent.

Improving the performance of the South Australian economy and bringing unemployment down over the course of the next few years will require a revitalised public sector and strategic investment in public infrastructure to help drive higher rates of productive investment by the private sector. It will also require the development of coherent industry development strategies financed in large part by the federal government.

The challenge for government at all levels is clear. Significant inroads must be made into unemployment in South Australia over the next few years. A comprehensive employment strategy is urgently required in South Australia. While the failure to make significant inroads into unemployment has been the central focus of the employment debate over the last few years in South Australia, there is a pressing need to broaden the debate to encompass the future of work and the quality of our working lives.

POLICY DIRECTIONS FOR JOBS AND PROSPERITY

At a state level the jobs crisis has forced the Liberal government to take the first tentative steps towards acknowledging the need for policy change. Since 1995 there has been a growing chorus of organisations calling for the development of a comprehensive state employment strategy. Organisations such as the University of Adelaide's Centre for Labour Research, the United Trades and Labor Council of SA, the Public Service Association of SA, the SA Council of Social Service and the Youth Affairs Council of SA have continually stressed the need for urgent action to tackle the jobs crisis.

The release of a Youth Employment Statement in 1997 was the first attempt by the Liberal government to specifically address chronically high rates of youth unemployment. While the statement supported a number of important initiatives (such as the expansion of the 'UpSkill' program now requiring contractors on government-funded projects to employ a minimum number of young people in training positions, expansion of the Regional Labour Exchange program to help meet seasonal labour shortages in regional industries and the introduction of a 'Community at Work' program to fund innovative employment projects on a dollar-for-dollar basis), the central problem of a lack of demand in the labour market for young people was ignored.

A near defeat at the 1997 state election caused in part by persistently high unemployment forced the re-elected Liberal government to take further action on unemployment. During the election campaign the Labor Opposition announced a range of policies which attempted to integrate industry, regional and employment policies into a more coherent strategy to tackle the jobs crisis. Significant components of the policy included a 'First Start' apprenticeship and traineeship program for 6000 young people over three years. This program was additional to the ongoing Youth Training Scheme which provided around 1000 trainee positions in the public sector. Related to these employment policies was a number of important industry development policies including the establishment of a Centre for Industry which would 'include and expand' the Centre for Manufacturing while providing support for the development of service industries. The new centre was also intended to be a focus for the development and implementation of job-retention strategies, skill formation, innovation, product development and marketing. Additional support was to be made available to expand the Industrial Supplies Office to enable it to more vigorously promote and support import replacement. Labor also promised to provide greater support to local firms competing for government purchasing contracts. Regional impact statements were to be introduced requiring assessment of the social as well as the economic impact of any proposed change to levels of service provision in regional South Australia.

Labor proclaimed jobs growth as its highest priority during the 1997 election. 'With the right policies', it asserted, 'South Australia's economy can grow at the same rate as the rest of Australia and produce more jobs as the result' (ALP Election Statement 1997). While there is little likelihood that state-based policies alone could produce such a result, the more integrated policy package proposed by Labor would, in all probability, have slowed down the growth of the gap between South Australia and Australia's economic growth and unemployment rates. The convening of a Jobs Summit and the establishment of a tripartite Jobs Commission offered prospects of a more integrated institutional framework for tackling the jobs crisis. Moreover, a commitment to the development of an 'Agreement for Growth and Jobs' represented a meaningful outcome of Labor's Jobs Summit proposal.

The range of policy proposals put forward by Labor in the 1997 state election was a positive contribution to the debate on unemployment in South Australia.

The South Australian Liberal government on the other hand, has failed during four years of government to develop an explicit employment strategy. Instead it has relied upon the neoliberal financial agenda recommended by the South Australian Commission of Audit. In response to growing community concern about unemployment and near defeat at the election, Premier John Olsen invited industry, community and trade union leaders to participate in a 'Partnership for Jobs' forum. The forum has proved to be a poor imitation of Labor's Job Summit proposal. The objective of the forum was to provide employment policy advice to the government in the lead-up to the 1998/99 state Budget. The members of the forum consistently called for the development of a comprehensive employment strategy. An employment statement did emerge in the budget but it failed to address the central strategic question – poor and deteriorating economic and employment growth rates relative to the nation. While the bigger questions were ignored, a number of important concessions were made. The most significant of these was the expansion of the State Government Youth Training Scheme from 1200 to 2500 places per annum and the introduction of the Community at Work scheme.

After sustained community pressure on the state government for a 'Jobs Summit', a series of 'Job Workshops' was proposed by the Minister for Employment, Mark Brindal. Workshops were held around the state throughout November 1998. The government also gave a commitment to a full day of parliamentary debate on an employment strategy before the end of 1998. This commitment evaporated after the government failed to secure support for the sale or lease of ETSA/Optima.

As each set of poor ABS monthly unemployment figures are announced over the next few years, the government will have no choice but to turn its attention to the urgent need to tackle the jobs crisis. The challenge for South Australians will be to ensure that governments pursue alternatives to the failed neoliberal economic policies of the past.

THERE ARE ALTERNATIVES

There are no easy solutions to the jobs crisis but there are alternative policy ideas to those currently being pursued by the state Liberal Government. While the primary objective should be to increase the available pool of jobs, it is also critical to address skill shortages in a range of industries. More broadly, the government should commit the state to a high-wage, high-skill employment strategy. Such a strategy must acknowledge the importance of both the public and private sectors. In particular, it is clear that it will take more rather than less public sector investment to drive higher rates of employment growth in South Australia. The prudent use of debt to achieve this end would be an intelligent policy choice as other chapters demonstrate.

Tackling the jobs crisis will require the development of a well-funded State Rejuvenation Program (SRP) to underpin new investment in the development and expansion of productive local industries and infrastructure. Inevitably this will require that the state government develops a comprehensive case for a substantial federal government contribution to the SRP. A federal government contribution to the SRP would acknowledge the differential impact of 'globalisation' and federal policies on states and regions. In this respect there is an urgent need to broaden and strengthen South Australia's employment base in the face of declining industry protection levels. Given the poor outlook for South Australia's economy, the case for federal assistance is overwhelming. Without significant assistance, further structural decline and social dislocation will be inevitable.

There is much that the federal government should do to assist South Australia to tackle the jobs crisis. This will require a new political consensus on the need for strategic government engagement in social and economic development.

NATIONAL RESPONSES

A federal government with a commitment to full employment could assist South Australia by:

- participating with other nations in efforts to appropriately regulate financial markets and promote higher rates of productive investment (including a more strategic approach to the application of superannuation funds for infrastructure and industry development purposes)

- providing a regional assistance package to help South Australia strengthen and diversify its economy
- increasing levels of public finance to support social and physical infrastructure development, in particular, increased funding under the Commonwealth/State Housing Agreement
- broadening the national tax base by closing loopholes and distortions in the tax system to eliminate corporate tax evasion and promote productive job generation rather than speculative investment
- developing a comprehensive, national industry innovation policy including a comprehensive network and cluster development program targeted at small and medium-sized enterprises
- developing a national import replacement strategy to help underpin export potential
- introducing a comprehensive Regional Development Program and providing greater financial support to regional structures that respond to local needs and harness local commitment to state and national objectives
- introducing a comprehensive Commonwealth Public Sector Traineeship Program to mirror the state government's Youth Training Scheme
- replacing the Work for the Dole program with comprehensive, high-quality, award-based and accredited labour market programs linked to emerging industry needs
- developing an integrated and collaborative national system of employment assistance to replace the highly fragmented JobNetwork.

STATE RESPONSES

The South Australian government should pursue a range of institutional, policy and program reforms as part of the development of a comprehensive economic and employment development strategy. The strategy could include the following elements.

Institutional reform

The separation of employment and training policy from economic and industry policy is a fundamental flaw in public administration in South Australia. Under successive Liberal and Labor governments this separation has led to a lack of integration between supply-and-demand-side policies. To overcome this problem, the industry, trade, employment and training portfolios should be more closely integrated. To provide a focus for integrated strategic planning, policy development and stakeholder participation, a 'multi-partite' Employment and Economic Development Council (EEDC) should be established. The EEDC would report directly to the premier and be serviced by a well-resourced secretariat drawn from the industry, trade and employment and training portfolios. The new structure should take a whole-of-government approach to the development of employment policy, providing short- and long-term policy advice to the premier. The EEDC would relate closely to state-funded Regional Development Boards which would be reconstituted to promote a whole-of-government approach to regional development, linking local, state and federal government institutions together with industry, community and union representation. A key objective of this would be to overcome excessive parochialism and nepotism in regional development.

The EEDC should be supported by specialist policy development focusing on the particular needs of women, young people, indigenous people, people with disabilities and people from a non-English-speaking background.

Promoting regional collaboration

Changes in the organisational structure of local government in South Australia have resulted in the establishment of larger regional councils which are better suited to playing a broader, and more active role in regional economic and employment development. While the potential for stimulating jobs growth at this level is prescribed and limited by state, national and global policy settings, there is much to be gained from the development of closer relationships, or indeed the integration of the activities of Regional Development Boards and larger councils. This potential is emerging in southern Adelaide where the formation of the City of Onkaparinga from the Noarlunga, Willunga and Happy Valley Councils has led to the establishment of a significant economic and employment development unit within the amalgamated council. To accelerate this process and promote closer and more strategic collaboration between local government and regional development organisations, the state government should introduce a Regional Development Partnership Program (RDPP) which facilitates the development of comprehensive regional employment strategies. The RDPP should support a more collaborative and integrated approach to regional employment by sponsoring the development of integrated regional employment strategies linked to a statewide employment and economic development strategy.

Regional employment pacts

To assist regions to put new ideas into practice, the state government should establish a program to encourage the development of Regional Employment Pacts (REPs). Such an approach has been operating successfully throughout Europe over the last few years. Like the former Commonwealth-funded Regional Development Program, European Territorial Employment Pacts encourage the establishment of local partnerships and strategies.

A key aim of regional employment pacts is to support the creation of new jobs by focusing on the development of existing infrastructure, businesses and community organisations. The development of new products and services to replace imports and the promotion of networking would be key objectives of such a program.

The REPs could build on the existing Local Employment Partnership Project and the state government's Community at Work program funded as part of the Youth Employment Strategy. The REPs would involve the provision of funding to innovative employment strategies which are closely linked to emerging training and employment opportunities and have clearly identified performance indicators supported by a business plan. The program should be available to all age groups and promote the development of community infrastructure which underpins the development of skills to accommodate future growth in information technology, tourism and housing and construction industries.

Infrastructure development

As Frank Gelber and Mathew Jones demonstrate in chapter 3, there is an urgent need to increase rates of investment in social and physical infrastructure in South Australia. This is important both as an employment generation strategy and as a measure to boost productivity and economic growth elsewhere. The spin-offs from such investment warrant government review of taxation and expenditure policies to ensure much higher rates of infrastructure investment. While a national approach to this is required, the state government could moderate its debt reduction strategy to ensure that infrastructure upgrade is a priority. In the absence of such a re-orientation of priorities, the consequences of under-investment in infrastructure will be measured by declining productivity and service quality. The failure to upgrade infrastructure contains significant risks as the Bolivar Sewerage Treatment Plant 'Big Pong' crisis outlined in chapter 9 illustrates.

Public sector jobs, skills loss and ageing in the public sector

Sustained reductions in public sector employment combined with low levels of recruitment have led to a significant ageing of the public sector (Commissioner for Public Employment 1997). More than 60 per cent of the public sector workforce is over the age of 40. In June 1997 the median age for the public sector workforce (41.4 years) was 3.5 years higher than that for the South Australian workforce as a whole (38.1 years).

The proportion of 15-to-24-year olds in the public sector declined from 8.2 per cent in June 1996 to 7.6 per cent in June 1997. This compares poorly with the proportion of 15-to-24-year olds in the South Australian labour force as a whole (16.9 per cent).

South Australia's industrial and social development has depended upon the development of a sophisticated public sector characterised by a highly skilled and competent workforce. Continued public sector employment reductions in the context of high levels of unemployment have fuelled population loss resulting in a loss of vitality, creativity and expertise – some of the key ingredients necessary for economic recovery and prosperity.

For South Australia to develop and maintain world-class infrastructure and take full advantage of opportunities for the export of services and expertise there is a need to provide greater stability and security in public sector employment. This will only be achieved by a moratorium on public sector job losses and through an expanded public sector recruitment program. A public sector revitalisation strategy should be introduced to provide new public sector employment opportunities. This should be part of a broader strategy to rejuvenate some of South Australia's ailing regional centres. In addition to specific youth employment targets in the public sector, the state government should make a commitment to the creation of 2000 new public sector positions per annum over the next five years.

Youth recruitment

To help redress the ageing of the public sector workforce and reduce youth unemployment in South Australia, successive governments have provided entry-level training positions to young people through the Youth Training Scheme (YTS). The scheme is a proven success leading to levels of ongoing employment which are twice the average of many other labour market programs. According to the Commissioner for Public Employment (1997), approximately 70 per cent of young people involved in the scheme over the last four years were successful in securing ongoing employment in the public and private sectors.

The number of traineeships offered through the YTS is, however insufficient to meet the objective of redressing the ageing profile of the public sector workforce and contributing significantly to reducing high levels of youth unemployment. In 1996/97, 1500 traineeships were provided to school leavers and young unemployed people. Despite the continued decline in the proportion of 15-to-24-year olds in the public sector workforce, the number of traineeships has been cut by one-third in 1997/98. To help redress the negative consequences of large-scale public sector job losses, the YTS should be expanded to provide 3500 places per annum.

Strategic local sourcing

A significant opportunity exists for the encouragement of growth of local firms and employment through strategic import replacement and procurement. Successive governments have recognised the importance of encouraging local sourcing of goods and services through funding of the Industrial Supplies Office. A further enhancement of this service could include the development of a strategic local sourcing strategy and the establishment of a number of metropolitan and regional industrial sup-plies extension services which would provide a focal point for pro-moting and actively supporting local sourcing of goods and services. Such services could be co-located with existing state-funded Regional Development Boards and some larger councils.

Local sourcing clauses should be incorporated into all government contracts along with a commitment from contractors to employ a minimum number of local people in training positions. This commit-ment should also involve the establishment of targets for the employ-ment of particular groups suffering specific disadvantage in the labour market.

National agreement on investment and industry development

High unemployment throughout the course of the 1990s has accelerated competition between states for new and existing investment. There are few net gains for the nation associated with attracting business from other states. Poaching business from other states is an expedient industry development strategy which encourages firms to play states off against each other in a location-bidding wars. Firms operating in such an environment tend to become more 'footloose' and vulnerable to relocation if incentive packages fail to incorporate strategies which 'tie' down and embed new investors in the local economy. Bidding wars also inevitably favour the larger and more wealthy states. South Australia's prospects of winning bidding wars with the eastern states are likely to be poor.

South Australia should follow the United States example where a group of states has established a legislative framework to develop basic standards in relation to firm location and re-location.

Innovation and workplace change

Encouraging local firm development and new investment are key ingredients to boosting employment growth in SA. The challenge is to approach this in a more strategic way by harnessing local expertise and skill. Various attempts to achieve this include Commonwealth-funded Cooperative Research Centres and Key Centres of Teaching and Research. Expertise has been harnessed through Technology Park in northern Adelaide, Science Parks in southern Adelaide and the Thebarton Research and Commerce Precinct in western Adelaide. A more collaborative approach between each of these centres of technology and innovation should be fostered through the establishment of a national centre for workplace and industry innovation. Such a centre would foster industry and public sector collaboration throughout the state and nationally and internationally. The centre would be the nucleus of an internationally respected cluster of research and development organisations, acting as a focal point for applied research on industrial innovation, workplace organisation, skill formation, product development, marketing and performance measurement. The new centre would help to underpin and support the work of the Business Centre and the Industrial Supplies Office by providing strategic research to support local firm development and new investment. The centre would provide ongoing strategic industrial development support services such as industrial mapping and supply chain identification, skills audits and network/cluster development support, identification of national and international best practice and emerging opportunities. The centre would also provide valuable strategic industry policy advice to government and monitor industry trends. Such a centre could be an extension of the existing Centre for Manufacturing.

A key task for the centre would be to extend some of the recommendations of the Karpin Report relating to management in Australia by working with organisations to develop strategies to modernise management practices and promote the development of successorship planning.

CONCLUSION

This chapter highlights the urgent need for the development of a comprehensive employment strategy in South Australia. It argues that the government must play a more 'activist' role in seeking to tackle the jobs crisis. A commitment to a high-wage, high-skill and knowledge-intensive strategy is essential to ensure that South Australians have access to a high standard of living. A low-wage, low-skill path to jobs growth is a formula for increasing inequality and declining living standards. South Australia cannot afford to engage in a global race to the bottom over wages and job security. It must avoid entering into bidding wars with other states to attract new firms. To counter some of the instability inherent in an unregulated global economy, the government must attempt to more effectively 'embed' domestic and foreign firms into the local economy. It must also utilise the public sector as a tool for social and economic development. Tackling the jobs crisis will require a commitment to the revitalisation of the public sector.

In the absence of new policy initiatives at a national and state level, unemployment rates in South Australia are set to remain in double digit figures. The scene is set for South Australia to enter the twenty-first century with unemployment rates that ratchet ever upwards with each economic downturn. While the international and national forces influencing South Australia's economy are powerful, this outcome is not inevitable. The current obsession with neoliberal economic solutions to the jobs crisis is clearly not working. It is time to embrace ideas that work.

REFERENCES

Australian Bureau of Statistics (ABS), Cat. 5242.0.

—— Cat. *Labour Force*, 6202.0.

Australian Labor Party (ALP) 1997, Jobs for our regions, election policy statement, 1 October.

—— 1997, Labor's Jobs Summit and Jobs Commission, election policy statement, 1 October.

—— 1997, Existing industries: building on our strengths, election policy statement, 1 October.

ANZ Job Advertisement Series Database.

BIS Shrapnel 1997, *State Economic Prospects 1997 to 2002*.

Broomhill, R., Chapman, P., Donato, R., Genoff, R., Juniper, J., McBride, G., Shanahan, M., Sharp, R., Spoehr, J. & Statton, P. 1996, *An Assessment of the Economic Policies of the South Australian Government, 1993–96*, prepared by the Regional Research Network for the United Trades and Labor Council of South Australia

Bryan, D. & Rafferty, M. 1999, *The Global Economy in Australia*, Allen & Unwin, Sydney, pp. 78–81.

Stillwell, F. 1998, 'How to cure unemployment', in *Unemployment: Economic Promise and Political Will*, eds E. Carson, A. Jamrozik, & T. Winefield, Australian Academic Press, Brisbane.

Commissioner for Public Employment 1997, *Annual Report and Workforce Information*, Office for the Commissioner of Public Employment, South Australia.

Dowrick, S. 1995, 'The Determinants of long run growth', in *Productivity and Growth*, Reserve Bank of Australia.

Midwest Center for Labor Research 1989, *Intervening with Ageing Owners to Save Industrial Jobs*, a report to the Strategic Planning Committee of the Economic Development Commission Foundation of Chicago.

The National Economic and Social Forum 1997, *A Framework for Partnership Enriching Strategic Consensus Though Participation*, forum report no. 16, Dublin.

National Institute of Economic and Industry Research (NIEIR) 1994, *Medium Term Prospects for the South Australian Economy*, Regional Research Network, University of Adelaide.

PSA/CPSU 1997, Renewing South Australia: Economic growth, industry development and social equity, 1996/97 state budget submission.

Regional and Industry Development Research Network and National
    Institute of Economic and Industry Research 1995, *Sustaining Growth*,
    University of Adelaide, Centre for Labour Studies.

South Australian Government 1994, *Capital Works Program, 1994/95,
    1995/96, 1996/97, 1997/98.*

—— 1997, *Budget Results*, 1997/98.

—— 1997, *Estimates of Payments and Receipts*, 1997/98.

—— 1997, *Youth Employment Statement*, 1997.

Spoehr, J. 1997, *South Australian Labour Market Briefing*, vol. 2, no. 2.
    University of Adelaide, Centre for Labour Research.

Spoehr, J. 1997 *Regional Youth Unemployment Profile*, 1988–96, vol. 1, no. 1,
    University of Adelaide, Centre for Labour Studies.

CHAPTER 12

INDUSTRY STRATEGIES FOR SOUTH AUSTRALIA

A whole-of-government approach

RODIN GENOFF AND GRAHAM SHEATHER

INTRODUCTION

Both Aristotle and Newton believed in absolute time. That is, they believed that one could unambiguously measure the interval of time between two events, and that this time would be the same whoever measured it, provided they used a good clock. Time was completely separate and independent of space. This is what people would take to be the commonsense view. However, we have had to change our ideas about space and time. Although our apparently common sense notions work well when dealing with things like apples, or planets that travel comparatively slowly, they don't work at all for things moving at or near the speed of light.   **Stephen Hawking, *A Brief History of Time***

Scientists have long since lost their fascination with falling apples, although some may still make the occasional pilgrimage to the leaning tower of Pisa to retrace the steps, antics and experiments of their predecessors. Not so for many of our economists. They still apply the simplistic tenets of supply and demand derived, for example, from the sale of apples in a village market, to explain the complexities of the modern economy where the drivers of prosperity are innovation and technological change. Locked in a time warp, neoclassical economists see technical change as exogenous or 'residual' to their model! And no wonder, their model was developed over two centuries ago. As far back as the end of the nineteenth century, Leon Walrus, one of the world's leading economists of the day urged his colleagues to pay greater attention to the role of science in economic and industry development. His pleas fell on deaf ears.

A modern global economy is not dominated by small individual

businesses selling fruit but by multinational corporations which operate
in a complex global network of business activity and account over half of
the world's trade in goods and services. Robert Reich (1992, p. 113),
President Clinton's former Labour Secretary observes:

In such global webs, products are international composites. What is traded
between nations is less often finished products than specialised problem-solving
(research, product design, fabrication), problem-identifying (marketing, advertising, customer consulting), and brokerage (financing, searching, contracting)
services, as well as certain routine components and services, all of which are
combined to create value.

Global intellectual and financial capital combine to activate the
innovative capacity and capability of firms and regions in which they
operate. The economic transformation we are witnessing is accelerating
and will deliver prosperity to regions and their communities which can
effectively tap into this drive for technological change. The industrial
transformations of Emila-Romagna in Italy, Baden-Wurttemberg in
Germany or the mid-west of the United States are such regional success
stories.

The challenge for South Australia's government is to develop a
working definition of a strategic, pro-active national industry policy
which incorporates directives on: tariff reductions; microeconomic
reform; structural adjustment; taxation; industry development and
adjustment programs; overseas assembly provisions; explicitly deliberate strategies to encourage growth and investment; programs to
support products manufactured from sustainable and energy-renew-
able production processes; and finally, reciprocal rules to counter the
'uneven playing field'. Three factors influencing a change in Australia's
manufacturing paradigm between 1990 to 2010 must be born in mind
in shaping South Australia's relationship to this national industry policy.
They are: globalisation of the manufacturing industry and the change in
business positioning required for international markets, responsiveness
and customisation of manufacturing operations to customers, and
finally, participation in global vendor pyramids of componentry supply
chains (Australian Business Chamber 1997). Guided by such a strategic
national industry policy, initiatives to re-engineer South Australian
manufacturing can avoid the accusations that industry is simply making
protectionist demands for tariff regimes, is inefficient, or that industry

policy becomes a substitute for tax breaks and 'picking winners', driven by politically dominant ideologies and sectoral interests.

Some of this thinking was developed through the A.D. Little Report initiated by the former state Labor government. It lives on in various ways through the state's industry cluster development program, and research being undertaken by the Department of Industry and Trade. But to be successful, a whole-of-government approach is required. Debt reduction strategies alone cannot address South Australia's structural problems. Rebuilding manufacturing and increasing the state's competitive advantages by focusing policy on our industrial strengths are required.

The following chapter begins with an overview of the new economic thinking on the dynamics of growth and innovation. We then explore some of the key policy pathways which can inform industry policy settings in South Australia. The final section of the chapter conjectures on how an expanded role for the South Australian Centre for Manufacturing could contribute to the growth of best practice, industry clusters and industrial renewal.

INNOVATION AND ECONOMIC DEVELOPMENT

So in terms of the new thinking, can a sophisticated economy of the future survive without a dynamic manufacturing sector? International research and new thinking on economic growth and technical change suggest that the answer is no.

Manufacturing currently accounts for 65.4 per cent of all research and development (R&D) in Australia, and exhibits a 'technological innovation propensity three times the non-manufacturing industry average' (ABF 1997, pp. 9.5–9.8). A high-wage, high-growth, knowledge-intensive economy has its roots deep within a sophisticated and diversified manufacturing sector, with strong links to the rest of the economy. This new economic thinking also suggests that economic and industrial growth is path-dependent. In other words, the industry structure we have today will influence the type of jobs and industries we have in the future, and the level of prosperity we enjoy. Governments which fail to take this simple premise into account do so at their peril. They condemn citizens and industry to declining living standards and lost opportunities. Those governments which are forward-thinking and which develop strategic industry policies to encourage knowledge-based industries, can directly influence a region's future growth trajectory and income security.

The alternative to a simplistic free market view of industry policy involves questioning the efficacy of markets in achieving an optimal structure for the Australian economy. It acknowledges broader goals, including the pursuit of full employment and an equitable distribution of income. The question posed by the new economic thinkers in the current industry policy debate is how to devise a supply-side policy aimed at overcoming the balance of payments and capital capacity constraints. Thus long-term growth and jobs will be boosted by increasing exports and replacing imports. The answer, more so now than at any previous point in our history, lies in the development of a high-skill, high-productivity manufacturing sector (Genoff & Green 1998).

The fact is that elaborately transformed manufactures (ETMs) have for some time been the largest and fastest-growing segment of world trade (Genoff & Green 1993). While international trade in services is also increasing rapidly, it is insignificant by comparison, and in many cases is related closely to the growth of manufacturing technologies. Economies that are locked into primary commodity exports are those which have experienced the sharpest fall in their terms of trade in recent years. They have also been vulnerable to an overvalued exchange rate, which in turn has reinforced the domination of resources production by pricing even the most efficient manufacturers out of both domestic and international markets. The old doctrine of comparative advantage, based on a country's factor endowments, has been superseded by the notion of 'competitive advantage', which may be *created* through the concerted application of knowledge and ingenuity (Porter 1990). This parallels the findings of the 'new growth theory' which, by contrast with static neoclassical models, treats technological change and associated spillover effects as an endogenous component of dynamic growth models (Romer 1990; BIE 1992). It is the pursuit of competitive advantage, not textbook orthodoxy, which has underpinned the post-war 'miracle' of Germany, France and Japan, and more recently that of East Asian economies such as that of South Korea and Taiwan (Rodrik 1995). While Australia's manufacturing export performance has also improved dramatically in the past 15 years, the balance of trade in high-value-adding, knowledge-intensive ETMs continues to deteriorate.

The new economic thinking further elaborates the role of innovation and knowledge-intensive industries (ABF 1997). This approach, which has come to be known as 'evolutionary economics', may be traced to the Schumpterian notion of 'creative destruction' in the growth of capital accumulation (Foray & Freeman 1993; Freeman 1994). It seeks to understand the dynamics of the economic system and industrial structure in relation to three key observations: 'that innovation drives the growth of nations; that the free market alone will not maximise innovation performance; that policy needs to focus on generating knowledge and promotion of the efficacy of the flows of knowledge' (ABF 1997, pp. 2–4). The cumulative and self-reinforcing effects of innovation are often highly concentrated and integrated into industrial districts. For example, the investment pull of Silicon Valley and other high-technology 'nodes' continues unabated. National and regional economies with sophisticated physical, educational and information technology (IT) infrastructure as well as governments that place a premium on research and development and leading-edge industrial and service sectors build the fundamental characteristics of long-term sustainable growth paths and first-mover advantages (Genoff & Green 1993; Green & Genoff 1998). These competitive advantages consolidate investment opportunities that feed back into banking and finance, marketing and innovation. As Cohen and Zysman (1989) have pointed out, 'high tech gravitates toward state-of-the-art producers'. This results in a vibrant manufacturing sector and, since embedded within manufacturing, is a knowledge infrastructure essential to a dynamic economy.

These processes taken together have come to be known as national systems of innovation and are the focus of research by evolutionary economics. As the ABF (1997, p. 3.15) observes:

It is clear from recent work [of the OECD] that one reason why countries vary in their capacity to innovate is that the influences in innovation are *systemic*. These national systems of innovation are composed of relationships among firms themselves, which one may consider the 'glue' of the system, but also of broader institutions such as government rules, public sector research and training organisations, labour relations, publicly available infrastructure and so on … The functioning of a national innovation system is limited by past practices and existing industrial structures. This is because what happened in the past determines, [path dependency] to a considerable extent, present opportunities unless strategic policies are implemented to shift the direction of development.

Getting the economic fundamentals right – low inflation and low interest rates – is only the first step of an integrated policy framework aimed at developing our industries of the future. And to do this we need a more informed understanding of the role technology plays in economic and industry development.

HIGH TECHNOLOGY MATTERS

This new thinking about industry development also informs how one views the contribution high-technology industries makes to economic and industry development. And concomitantly, why sophisticated national industry development strategies are required to nurture and develop these industries of the future.

Broadly speaking, high-technology industries include: computers and information electronics, telecommunications equipment, computer-integrated manufacturing, precision and electrical machinery, bio-science and biotechnology products, multi-media products, medical and pharmaceutical products, industrial organic chemicals and production of synthetic materials (see Larcombe & Brain 1998; Tyson 1992). South Australia's defence industries are by far the state's most important high-technology sectors. In turn, the fabric and dynamics of high-technology industries are supported by the critical role that medium, high-technology sectors such as the automotive and chemical industries play in their development (see Sheehan 1995).

Professor Laura Tyson (1992, pp. 32–9), President Clinton's former chief economic adviser, argues that high-technology industries are essential to any advanced economy because they account for the vast majority of R&D spending, and social returns or spillovers arising from 'R&D spending far exceed the private returns'. This diffusion of new ideas, technologies and the knowledge-intensive research undertaken by scientists, engineers and technicians, combine to develop the intellectual capital necessary to activate high-tech opportunities. For instance, in the United States, high-technology industries, while comprising only 18 per cent of manufacturing employment, account for the employment of one-third of all its engineers and scientists. Even production workers employed in these industries enjoy wages 22 per cent higher compared to ordinary manufacturing production workers.

Path dependency is particularly evident in high-technology industries. Lags in the international diffusion of knowledge mean that first-mover advantages accrue to innovative firms, industries and the regions in which they trade. Knowledge is often embodied in company-specific production processes and tends to 'cluster around similar activities generating self-reinforcing localised externalities through the germination of 'specialist inputs and informational networks' (Tyson 1992, p. 41). This 'experience and know-how' accumulates to develop the dynamic, competitive advantages of industry clusters. As Tyson observes:

Studies of technological change demonstrate that technological capabilities develop in conjunction with production. In other words, they cannot be acquired simply by purchasing a product, rather they are 'hands-on' or 'tacit' capabilities that depend on active involvement in the production process itself.

Such dynamic path dependency also has important implications for direct foreign investment. As Tyson (1992, p. 42) concludes:

… when a country has its own indigenous technological capacity in a particular industry based on its own firms and workforce, foreign investment is more likely to enhance local economies. In contrast, if the host country has limited technological capabilities in an industry, foreign investment is more likely to drive out local competitors and further reduce such capabilities.

Clearly, high-technology industry development strategies are essential to develop high-wage and knowledge-intensive sustainable employment opportunities and prosperity for the community, not only because of the spin-offs they generate, but because the developed nations we compete with have a raft of industry development strategies to develop core competencies in research and development and skills to activate first-mover advantages. For example, a snapshot of interventionist policies used by other countries is outlined below.

EXAMPLES OF INTERVENTIONIST POLICIES:

Singapore => tax relief for investment, achieving export targets, pioneer status

=> active investment campaign via Economic Development Bureau

=> Trade Development board seeks out markets

=> targeted government equity investment

Taiwan => Industrial Development Bureau implements industry development component of Six Year National Development Plans

	=>	incentives for investment, low interest loans, tax deductions
	=>	import licensing
	=>	government procurement preference
Malaysia	=>	tax holiday for investment, export achievements
	=>	government supplied infrastructure
	=>	import licensing etc.

Source: Gosman 1998

The message from these countries, especially Taiwan is that 'success comes through highly disaggregated sectoral policies with successive reinforcing measures maintained until a targeted level of export share is attained' (Brain & Spencer 1993). For example, Taiwan's tooling industry now competes head on with Japanese and German manufacturers. As anyone with an engineering background would acknowledge, a successful tooling sector underpins a vibrant and competitive manufacturing sector (Manning 1993; 1996). Targeted sectoral approaches undertaken by the Taiwanese have been both successful and strategic.

A WORKABLE ALTERNATIVE: PATHWAYS OF DEVELOPMENT

While an uphill battle, the problems facing South Australia are not unique. They are challenging but equally they are surmountable. The solutions developed must have an eye to the long term while generating the energy and vision to develop, legislate and implement policy in the short to medium term. And it is paramount that the policy framework is informed by the new economic thinking and not influenced by ideological zealotry. It is also necessary to recognise the limits to what state governments can achieve and also the imperative to marshal sufficient Commonwealth government resources necessary for nation-building and industry development.

Our outline of an alternative industry strategy framework therefore begins with the focus squarely on Canberra. The premier of South Australia should work with the premiers of the other manufacturing states of Victoria, New South Wales and Tasmania to develop national industry development strategies and priorities. These states should press Canberra to restore the $4 billion cuts to valuable industry development measures such as the R&D tax concession. There are promising and successful precedents for interstate collaboration supported by peak industry and trade union organisations such as the campaign to prevent the acceleration of tariff reduction for the automotive industry – a victory for common sense.

In parallel, the manufacturing states should support and mirror at this level the broad industry policy structure and pathways identified by the Australian Business Foundation (1997) in *The High Road or the Low Road* summarised below. Regional and industrial renewal must be firmly embedded in nation-building principles which reduce the destructive competition between the states by developing industry development strategies on the basis of competitive strengths. It is up to the premiers of the manufacturing states and their industry ministers to forge an appropriate industry strategy framework with the prime minister and relevant industry and regional development ministers.

PATHWAY ONE: Acknowledge the importance of the structure of the Australian economy

PATHWAY TWO: Integrate trade and industry policies

PATHWAY THREE: Shift the economy towards greater knowledge and innovation intensity

PATHWAY FOUR: Improve cooperation and linkages

PATHWAY FIVE: Target key productivity drivers

PATHWAY SIX: Ensure programs are performance-based

PATHWAY SEVEN: Build global distribution channels and capability

PATHWAY EIGHT: Invest in education and research infrastructure and training

PATHWAY NINE: Focus public and private sector attention on innovation and knowledge as the basis of competition

PATHWAY TEN: Deal with real industries and their dynamics

Source: Australian Business Foundation 1997

The policies of the Australian Business Foundation (ABF) are broadly consistent with those of the Metal Trades Industry Association (MTIA 1997) and the Australian Manufacturing Workers' Union (AMWU 1997) industry policy recommendations to the federal government, the latter being most pro-active in calling for the establishment of a $3 billion national investment fund three times larger than the $1 billion investment fund announced by the federal government in *Investing for Growth* (Commonwealth Government 1998). The policies advanced by the ABF, MTIA and AMWU are practical and innovative and seek to ensure that Australian industry is not injured by the interventionist policies employed by other countries or the new innovation and technology policies being planned by the European Union.

The challenge for the South Australian government is a complex one. Its strategies relating to cluster development and the targeting of key industries all point in the right direction (EDA 1997). They build upon the Bannon/Arnold A.D. Little Report (1992) and provide some consistency in relation to the state's industry development approaches. This consistency is essential for planning and will, as new investment opportunities materialise over time, build investor and business confidence. While individual industry and regional departments do their best on modest budgets, a whole-of-government approach is necessary.

To accurately and discretely target industry development dollars requires the activation of pathway one as identified by the ABF acknowledging the importance of the structure of the (South) Australian economy – and will involve in-depth research on the structure of the state's economy. In short, 'informed policy making is critically dependent on the quality of research and information about a nation's structure and its system of innovation' (Genoff & Green 1998). Without this sophisticated industry intelligence one is left to second-guess the underlying strengths and weaknesses of an economy's industrial structure. A key task therefore in activating pathway one is to map institutional structures, human resource flows, industry clusters and innovative firms.

By way of illustration – the South Central Regional Network (SCRN) and City of Onkaparinga, in partnership with the Centre for Labour Research and the National Key Centre for Social Applications of Geographical Information Systems of the University of Adelaide are undertaking such an exercise and mapping existing and potential supply chain linkages in the southern region of Adelaide. The study will map the industrial capacity and capability of manufacturing networks and develop new industry-auditing techniques to enable policy-makers to more discretely target industry development measures. The project, through strategic partnerships with key service providers such as the South Australian Industrial Supplies Office, will identify new import replacement opportunities. New opportunities for local manufacturers to produce inputs into the export sector will also be explored. Further, the SCRN's recently developed network of banks, financiers and accountants can be employed to activate new investment opportunities based on discrete and targeted industry development strategies. From the banks' perspective, good industry intelligence allows them to make more-informed decisions about commercial lending based on the underlying strengths and weaknesses in the region. Knowledge reduces risk, uncertainty and increases business confidence. On the other side of the coin, the financial sector, by having a more informed understanding of adjustment pressures, is able to manage firms which are exposed. And in the case of small and family businesses, instituting business planning approaches prevents families from losing their homes and perhaps even having to leave their communities.

At a metropolitan-wide level, the Department of Transport and Urban Planning has undertaken some significant and pioneering work in the area of industry mapping. It has completed an audit of industrial activity by location, the most comprehensive stocktake of its kind ever undertaken in South Australia. This research forms an important base from which to undertake more detailed research such as that undertaken in the south of Adelaide. The combination of research results can inform the development of new cluster and networking approaches.

The completion of pathway one enables the activation of pathway two – integration of industry and trade policies. Under both the former Labor government and the current Brown/Olsen governments, competition between ministers and departments has often resulted in duplication and waste, a situation which increases the cynicism of the community and industry leaders. Meanwhile senior bureaucrats and their staff working with industry – who have to build and maintain links between government and industry – are left in an extremely difficult situation. This political failure has hidden costs.

Without the effective integration of trade and industry policies, it is unlikely that pathways three to ten could be satisfactorily developed, let alone implemented as policy. Intergovernmental coordination and extensive industry involvement are critical to the success of such a strategy. Adelaide is a small-to-medium-sized city that lends itself to effective networking and partnerships between the community, business, trade union and government sectors. To make progress on this front, the government must make a strong commitment to the process of partnership-building. In the end this will require adequate resourcing at an industry level.

The SA Employers' Chamber of Commerce and Industry, in

partnership with the state government, is developing *SA Business Vision 2010*. The current 2010 plan for industrial renewal, based on a partnership between the chamber and the government and other stakeholders is a practical step in the right direction – especially in the current political environment where service provision is increasingly being devolved to industry providers (see Mortimer 1997). Key project areas in this partnership between the public and private sectors include industry cluster and network development and the creation of export and investment opportunities. The strength of this project is that it is driven by the needs of business. For example, the success of the recently established defence cluster has resulted in new contracts worth $50 million (O'Neill 1998). The challenge for the government is to situate outcomes in terms of a whole-of-government approach that is truly tripartite in nature (Green & Genoff 1993).

In short, the application of these new ideas is aimed at strengthening contemporary principles of nation-building. Success can be demonstrated through government support for projects which have the capacity to activate new investment opportunities, create new industry networks, generate new import-replacement opportunities, encourage and strengthen links between industry and universities in a manner which is common in countries such as Germany.

South Australians must work smarter, a strategy which requires a whole-of-government approach. For example, the current Liberal government, along with its predecessor has placed great faith in the contribution that the IT sector can make to the state's prosperity. This is true. However, from a policy perspective, is South Australia in the race? The fact is that NSW has developed a natural and national industry cluster in the IT sector. Three-quarters of the nation's IT firms are headquartered in NSW (NSW Government 1998). Not having corporate headquarters located here has not prevented South Australia from entering new industries in the past, and nor should it do so in the future. However a more realistic task for South Australian policy-makers may be to encourage the development of discrete IT applications for industry and end-users, while encouraging the uptake and diffusion of new technology by industry. This will lead to the strengthening of the state's industrial fabric. As we shall see later in this chapter, the state government's outsourcing of public sector IT requirements may prove counter-productive in this respect, as it relies heavily on contracts with footloose multinational firms.

As outlined earlier, Tyson (1992) argues that direct foreign investment (DFI) by multinationals must be embedded into the fabric of the local economy otherwise industry assistance used to attract DFI through multinationals increases the dividends of its shareholders rather than the long-term needs of industry or the community. The rule of thumb is, the stronger the local industry, the greater the local spin-offs. Government assistance should also (by rule of thumb) promote the spin-offs of an industry sector as a whole rather than the bottom line of an individual firm. In other words – minimise picking individual winners. But should this strategy prove necessary, governments should ensure that performance indicators are in place to guarantee that spin-offs conform to state and regional industry development objectives.

Under pressures of economic globalisation, firms' industrial location decisions are playing a more critical role in relation to the internationalisation of their competitive strategies. Nation–states are deliberately pursuing policy regimes incorporating direct foreign investment (DFI) strategies as leverage points in attracting transnational or multinational corporations (Marsh 1997). As a means of reducing costs in global markets, firms are seeking to reconstruct their industries in innovative ways by obtaining material and financial incentives and concessions. Because the next generation of international economic policies is expected to focus on investment opportunities rather than trade (Drucker 1997), attracting DFI will be a parallel priority to states' development of domestic export and import replacement capability. All Australian states are promoting inward investment through aggressive marketing campaigns to position themselves as preferred locations for international and regional business activities (NSW SRD 1998). Any strategies for revitalisation of South Australia's nascent manufacturing industries must seriously revisit these policy regimes to construct national competitive advantage. There are excellent models for attracting multinational corporations such as those employed by both leading industrialised countries such as Singapore, Ireland, Wales and Scotland, and the newly emerging economies of the 'Asian tigers', initially in Indonesia, Malaysia, and Thailand, and more recently in the Philippines, Vietnam and China (Marsh 1997, p. 2).

The wisdom of the Brown/Olsen 'king hit' approach to IT-outsourcing as a tool for industry development remains to be seen. However, this not to say that outsourcing has the potential in some instances to be employed as a tool for local development through targeted and discrete procurement policies in order to develop dynamic small-to-medium-sized enterprises. With hindsight it is easy to be critical, but the key fact remains that in an era of uncertainty where infant industries can no longer be developed behind high tariff walls, it is incumbent upon governments to explore new and innovative approaches to industry development. There are no easy solutions. This is especially true of the venture-capital-hungry IT sector. With persistent unemployment, many governments are throwing caution to the wind in their attempts to encourage regional investment by multinational corporations. The Brown/Olsen government is no different: it seeks to boost its business credentials through timely accolades in the financial press. But are such deals really good for business?

Good policy and economic outcomes need to be grounded in a sophisticated understanding of the issues of industry development. Desperation should not drive any government to sell or lend the crown jewels when the likely costs and benefits of such an approach are poorly understood. And what encourages accolades in the financial press one day, may bring disapproval the next. A more cautious approach would instead be warranted.

Nonetheless, South Australia's future prospects, despite many negative predictions, are positive. Overcoming our structural imbalances is possible. South Australia had to diversify its predominantly agricultural base to manufacturing in the 1940s and once again the state has the capacity to transform itself.

Nor should South Australia resile from the challenge. The manufacturing mid-west in the United States was written off in the 1980s as part of the unproductive 'rust belt' which was holding back the national economy. Neoclassical economists argued for a switch to service-sector industry development. They have been proven wrong! A change in economic conditions, assertive industry and procurement policies, together with a more informed understanding of the dynamic role manufacturing plays in the economy, based on the new economic thinking, has resulted in unemployment there dropping to 4.5 per cent, industry experiencing problems in the supply of labour available to meet industry needs and recovery of CBD and residential property values in previously depressed markets. The engine room of the economy has also increased demand in the upper high-wage end of the services sectors such as banking, finance, marketing, IT and R&D (see *Financial Times* London, 22 May 1998).

In the meantime the South Australian government has been exposed to a number of simple-minded theories about how to develop jobs for the future and reduce unemployment. For example, one theory contends that policy should target the domestic economy as it offers the greatest prospects of employment growth resulting from contracting-out, gardening, cooking, cleaning and child care. These new jobs are, it is argued, being driven by the growth of double-income families, individuals preferring to work part time rather than full time, while a new generation of individuals are choosing to be self-employed. In the meantime the IT sector is expected to produce high-wage jobs to drive demand. This vision we argue is flawed and not in the interests of South Australians. It holds out the prospects of a bleak future. A divided future.

Economically, South Australia has significant competitive advantages underpinned by world-class infrastructure and a highly skilled workforce. South Australia can emulate the US mid-west experience through building on what it does best – being innovative. But turning these advantages into growth, investment and new, knowledge-intensive and high-wage jobs will require a whole-of-government approach and new institutional structures to encourage new pathways of industry development.

MANUFACTURING AN ICON

South Australia desperately needs an 'icon' for manufacturing. It needs a new institution that will drive innovation and excellence. Despite having some of the largest and most exciting manufacturing firms in the nation, we do not have a world-class institution or icon to incubate and develop these competitive strengths. Such icons exist in Germany and contribute to manufacturing that country's prosperity. An immediate priority for the state government should be the development of such an icon, which can build on current industries and manufacture confidence in the future.

The South Australian Centre for Manufacturing in Woodville could be refurbished into a world-class facility designed by the state's leading architects and engineers. Its name should be changed to the Centre for Australian Manufacturing. This national manufacturing icon would be:

- a centre of excellence in providing extension services to industry
- a centre with strong links to universities, TAFEs and R&D institutions and technology parks

- a centre for the uptake and diffusion of advanced manufacturing technology
- a centre providing an interface between the services and manufacturing sectors
- a centre showcasing the state's manufacturing achievements
- a centre housing a significantly expanded Industrial Supplies Office to maximise new investment, local import replacement opportunities and local inputs into export goods
- a centre building on practical outcomes and demonstration effects arising from the Business 2010 Industry Cluster Development project.

Such an icon would remind South Australians and the rest of the world that this state is the manufacturing innovation state of Australia and that it leads the nation in the growth of manufacturing exports.

There is no point in promoting South Australia as the manufacturing state without an icon. Without a centre of gravity or hub to promote the state's manufacturing achievements and to showcase new local and international advances in technology, industry is left to its own devices to wander the trade fairs of other manufacturing centres of the world, including Melbourne and Sydney. The energy and ingenuity of our manufacturers, researchers, scientists and engineers need to be concentrated in promoting and realising new opportunities. The creation of a manufacturing icon has the potential to maximise such synergies.

There are two key exemplars that can provide operational insights. First, the Fraunhofer Gesellschaft, which employs and trains university graduates, providing a pool of highly qualified engineers and scientists for industry, government and research organisations. This is an effective innovation transfer strategy via the skills it applies to its numerous research contracts. The many agencies of the institute also utilise franchising as an avenue for assisting small-to-medium-sized enterprises (SMEs) to adopt latest industry standards and new technology innovations, often using prototyping and piloting programs to minimise take-up risks. As a non-profit, innovation and applied research organisation it has been influential in generating employment in economically depressed regions in Germany. Employees form self-organised, self-optimising project groups to compete for research contracts with universities, private organisations and other institutes. They establish networks between universities, industries and their own affiliate institutes, ultimately transferring graduates into the marketplace (DIST 1997).

Second, a local example of innovative development and transfer of technology is Australian Technology Park (ATP) in Sydney. Through the use of incubator cells it provides time-capped subsidised assistance to start-up ventures. Creative synergies are achieved through serendipity and mixing established R&D centres with the entrepreneurial energies of new firms seeking 'first-entry' technology advantages. The ATP is at world's best practice level, regularly on the itinerary of countries establishing technology parks, and currently being used as a model for China's Nasha economic region and Hong Kong's forthcoming technology park. The Advanced Manufacturing Centre supported with $2.5 million of NSW State and Regional Development and Federal DIST operational funds, was established at the Australian Technology Park in 1997. Its key objective is to assist the ATP achieve its business vision of 'Growing New Business' by matching the technology needs of SME manufacturers with suppliers of Advanced Manufacturing Technology, acting both as a clearing house and broker of innovative technology. Its business plan is built around a number of industry focus groups concentrating on developing world's best practice capability amongst NSW SMEs – a model that could be rolled out for South Australia.

CLUSTER DEVELOPMENT AND BEST PRACTICE MANUFACTURING

The proposed Australian Centre for Manufacturing could build on the significant networking opportunities which exist in South Australia. Tooling International and Asia Pacific are two world-class tooling networks comprising 13 firms which have contributed significantly to the state's industrial fabric. These networks will also contribute to the development of the metals casting precinct in the north-west of Adelaide. The precinct will provide, 'an engineering rich environment for additional networking opportunities in the future. Together, state-of-the-art tooling and foundry and casting are capital-and knowledge-intensive "foundational industries"' (Genoff & Green 1998; see also Manning 1997).

An Australian Centre for Manufacturing would also focus on major clusters in the South Australian economy in areas such as microelectronics, defence, the automotive industry, wine, health, food processing and the medical, scientific and equipment sector. It could also underpin the development of the environment management, products and services industry, a $7 billion industry in Australia, but which is nonetheless at the early stages of development. It is quite conceivable that South

Australia could develop first-mover advantages in water and waste management through government leadership in this sector.

However, activating networks within these industry clusters will require strategic assistance to manufacturers to enable them to meet the challenges facing their industries. This will involve the leadership of the proposed centre providing the mix of best practice, continuous improvement and big-step changes to optimise and leverage the manufacturing capability of firms.

To be competitive in global markets requires a practical understanding of the link between performance and best practice. The *Made in Europe* project which benchmarked best practice by European manufacturers found that only two per cent of European sites achieved best practice. However 50 per cent were well positioned to achieve world-class criteria. From this project and the latest Australian government *Review of Best Practice*, six key strategies have been identified as necessary to re-engineer manufacturing. These could form the basis for the strategies and service delivery of the proposed Australian Centre for Manufacturing (Sheather 1998).

The first strategy is to provide leadership in developing a congruent industry development framework necessary to encourage innovation.

The second strategy involves recognising that the rebuilding of South Australia's manufacturing base requires an increased commitment to the development of those sectors producing elaborately transformed manufactures and in turn, a strategic commitment to building growth based on productivity enhancement, not labour-intensive employment recovery strategies. Unemployment reduction should not be the responsibility of the proposed centre.

The third strategy involves the centre developing institutional mechanisms to facilitate the uptake, transfer and diffusion of new technology, a strategy which will increase the overall knowledge-based competencies within industry and encourage innovation in production processes, which over time would lead to increased research and development, and ultimately the commercialisation of new technology. While commercialisation is important, ensuring adequate diffusion of new technology is a critical first step in increasing productivity and capital efficiencies.

The fourth strategy is focused on ensuring that the management and organisational strategies match networks being developed, markets pursued and joint ventures entered into. Traditional measures of increasing performance such as total quality management (TQM) programs or time-based management may be inappropriate to the new demands of a global economy, where outsourcing, flexibility and one-off contracts are often the order of the day.

The fifth strategy is designed to prevent uniformity. The centre would encourage innovation and diversity with manufacturers becoming leaders in their own right. Best practice is appropriate for industry leaders, but benchmarking competitors as an end in itself can lead to second best, a finding which is emerging in research being carried out on Japanese industry.

The final strategy involves utilising new strategies based on a 'priorities by capabilities' approach. South Australian manufacturers can 'enhance and differentiate their competitive priorities targeted at specific global market opportunities, through appropriately selected technology investments, management and control systems, human capital developments, and participation in collaborative networks' (Sheather 1998).

A whole-of-industry approach, the judicious use of industry intelligence and the establishment of a manufacturing icon are ways through which the less desirable aspects of industry development – throwing valuable taxpayers' dollars away at any company willing to relocate in this state – in South Australia may be avoided. This approach, in an era of high unemployment, has been the hallmark of the Brown/Olsen governments and would undoubtedly characterise a Labor government as it has in the past (Chapman 1993). But such an approach is neither strategic nor in the long-term interests of the state. More than ever both sides of politics need to draft a whole-of-government approach to industry development based on pathways such as those identified by the Australian Business Foundation and underpinned by the thinking of the new economics.

CONCLUSION

As South Australians we must become more confident about our role and place in the world. But in the difficult climate of change and uncertainty, confidence flags. Simplistic solutions and inward-looking policies addressing complex problems appear attractive in the face of change and job insecurity, making the formulation and implementation of policy to meet new challenges exceedingly difficult.

Failures like the multi-million dollar Multifunction Polis reinforce the community's ambivalence towards jobs of the future. Qualitative polling by Rod Cameron and Hugh Mackay suggests that people are interested in real jobs. For politicians developing policies this may mean looking to the past rather than the future (*Australian Financial Review*, 22 August 1997). But we must look to the future and we must embrace change – nations and regions which fail to do so will be accorded second-class citizenship in the international arena. This means developing appropriate economic counter-cyclical and industry development policies to drive investment and the rebuilding of manufacturing.

South Australia has an abundance of opportunity anchored in significant competitive advantages. It is therefore not surprising to find that South Australia is home to some of the nation's most dynamic and forward-looking manufacturers such as Mitsubishi, GMH, Solar Optical and F.H. Faulding. Art, science, innovation and a culture of egalitarianism are the cornerstones of South Australia, however, a whole-of-government approach is required if we are to prosper in the twenty-first century.

REFERENCES

A.D. Little 1992, *New Directions for South Australia's Economy*, final report of the Economic Development Strategy Study, vol. 1, Adelaide.

AMWU (Australian Manufacturing Workers Union) 1997, *Rebuilding Australia: Industry Development for More Jobs*, AMWU, Sydney.

Australian Business Chamber 1997, *Industry Communication Inquiry: Australia's TCF Industry*, Sydney.

ABF (Australian Business Foundation) 1997, *The High Road or the Low Road? A Report on Australia's Industrial Structure*, Australian Business Foundation, Melbourne.

BIE (Bureau of Industry Economics) 1995, *Beyond the Firm: An Assessment of Business Linkages and Networks in Australia* , AGPS, Canberra.

Brain, P. & Spencer, M. 1993, 'Prospects for industry and growth', in *Making the Future Work: Crisis and Change in the South Australian Economy* , eds R. Green & R.Genoff, Allen & Unwin, Sydney.

Cohen, S. & Zysman, J. 1987, *Why Manufacturing Matters: The Myth of the Post-Industrial Economy*, Basic Books, New York.

Commonwealth Government, 1998 *Investing for Growth: The Howard Government's Plan for Australian Industry*, Canberra.

DIST (Department of Industry, Science and Tourism) 1997, *International Best Practice in the Adoption and Practice of New Technology*, Canberra.

Drucker, P. 1997, 'The global economy and the nation state', *Foreign Affairs*, vol. 76, no. 5, pp. 159–72.

Economic Development Authority (EDA) 1996, *Annual General Report*, SA Government.

Freeman, C. 1994, 'The economics of technical change', *Cambridge Journal of Economics*, no. 18.

Genoff, R.1997, 'Manufacturers and fewer impediments', *Australian Financial Review*, 17 February 1997.

Genoff, R. & Green, R. (eds) 1998, *Manufacturing Prosperity: Ideas for Industry, Technology and Employment*, Federation Press, Sydney.

Gosman, A. 1998, '*Telecommunications – Future Policy Options*', in *Manufacturing Prosperity: Ideas for Industry, Technology and Employment*, eds R.Genoff. & R.Green, Federation Press, Sydney.

Green, R. & Genoff, R. 1993, 'Challenge of industry policy', in *Making the Future Work: Crisis and Change in the South Australian Economy*, eds. R. Green & R. Genoff, Allen & Unwin, Sydney.

Larcombe, G. & Brain, P.1998, 'Competitive advantage in the regions', in *Manufacturing Prosperity: Ideas for Industry, Technology and Employment*, eds R. Genoff & R.Green, Federation Press, Sydney.

MTIA (Metal Trades Industry Association) 1997, *Make or Break*, a report for MTIA by EIU Australia, MTIA, Sydney.

Manning, B. 1997, *Making Provision for Foundries in Our Future – The SA Cast Metals Precinct*, SA Centre for Manufacturing, Adelaide.

Mortimer, D.1997, *Going for Growth: Business Programs for Investment, Innovation and Export*, Commonwealth of Australia, Canberra.

OECD 1997, *National Innovation Systems*, OECD, Paris.

Porter, M.1990, *The Competitive Advantage of Nations*, Macmillan, London.

Reich, R. 1991, *The Wealth of Nations*, Vintage, New York.

Rodrik, D. 1995, 'Getting interventions rights: How South Korea and Taiwan grew rich', *Economic Policy*, no. 20.

Sheather, G. 1998, 'Re-engineering Australian manufacturing', in *Manufacturing Prosperity: Ideas for Industry, Technology and Employment*, eds R. Genoff & R. Green, Federation Press, Sydney.

Sheehan, P.J., Pappas, N., Tikhomirova, G. & Sinclair, P. 1995, *Australia and the Knowledge Economy: An Assessment of Enhanced Economic Growth Through Science and Technology*, Centre for Strategic Economic Studies, Victoria University, Melbourne.

Tyson, L. 1992, *Who's Bashing Whom? Trade Conflict in High Technology Industries*, Institute for International Economies, Washington, DC.

CHAPTER 13

SCHOOL REFORM AND 'HOWARD'S WAY'

Running away from a socially just future

ROBERT HATTAM

Recently, the future of the school has been a question for serious consideration (Deakin Centre for Education and Change 1994). The question, what is the future of the school? – is not being asked by those predicting doomsday, but by those contemplating what might happen to schools as a consequence of a number of significant influences already having an impact. The reality of the neighbourhood school is now very much under threat from at least two sources: information technology and economic rationalism. In what will be a short reading of the contemporary scene, I do not intend to contemplate the possibly of 're-tooling schooling' (Green & Bigum 1998) through information technology, but instead to concentrate my deliberations on the impact of government-sponsored school reform. I guess I'm assuming that information technology will not mean a de-schooling of society – we will still be sending our children to a place called school, at least in the near future. Given that assumption, I'm interested in what is happening to schools as a consequence of government-driven reforms.[1]

In South Australia this means considering models of 'local school management'.[2] What is being considered is the possibility of devolving more responsibility for what goes on in our public schools to local school communities. Sounds good doesn't it? What I want to do in this paper is provide a reading of what's going on in and around this proposal to push responsibility downward, at a time in which education budgets for public schools are being slashed.

What seems clear, given the profound changes in our society, is that classroom life is becoming increasing complex. Children's complex lives are negotiated by teachers every minute of the school day. It is teachers who are making the crucial decisions about what is appropriate for (our) children. So, in contemplating the future of the school, it is essential to ask whether or not contemporary reforms to schools are helpful to teachers. Is recent educational policy sensitive to the increasing complexity of classroom life? Is it supportive of teachers?

WHAT DOES THE TERRAIN LOOK LIKE AND WHERE ARE WE GOING ... LET'S LOOK AT THE AVAILABLE MAPS!

Some commentators argue we live in post-modern times (Lyotard 1984; Jameson 1991), or new times (Hall & Jacques 1990). Claus Offe (1996) puts it most sharply when he refers to 'modern barbarity'. Given the dramatic impact of media culture on everyday life, we might even refer to them as 'dumbing-down times' – dumb and getting dumber. Political debate is collapsed to the ten-second sound bite. But some of us refuse the reading position offered by tabloid newspapers or the shock jocks of talk back radio, or current affairs on commercial television, or some political project that reduces to one notion. Some of us want to continue to grapple with complexity – not opting for simple solutions or accepting common sense.

What I want to do is provide a reading of the contemporary scene in schools. My reading begins with this struggle to grapple with complexity in making sense of what is happening to schools. To carry my argument I want to invoke the metaphor of the map. We are being bombarded with maps of the contemporary scene and maps for the future. Perhaps the most significant maps are those which assert their influence on public policy and law, and more importantly are realised in the material conditions of our lives. But before I take the opportunity to interrogate the maps which are navigating a future for schools, I want to playfully set up my argument by spending a few moments pondering the nature of maps. To establish the metaphor, I want to consider the question: What do we know about maps?

THE MAP IS NOT THE TERRITORY!

Maps themselves are metaphorical. But from the outset we need always to remember that a map is only a representation of the world, it's a view, it's someone's view, it unavoidably leaves off important details, it's an approximation. Maps need to be understood as 'socially situated knowledge' (Harding 1993, p. 53), always developed by real bodies, embodied, always perspectival, riven with values and interests. No map is developed with an infinitely mobile vision or 'god-trick of seeing everything from nowhere' (Harraway 1991, p. 189). As such map-makers at least need to be humble.

SOME MAPS (RE)PRESENT A 'DANGEROUS INCOHERENCE' (MAX-NEEF 1991) BETWEEN THE MAP AND THE TERRITORY.

It seems as though many maps are informed by what Vaclav Havel (1991, p. 15) refers to as 'evasive thinking ... a way of thinking that turns away from the core of the matter to something else'. Havel characterises 'evasive thinking' as 'an immobile system of intellectual and phraseological schemata which ... without our noticing it, separate[s] thought from its immediate contact with reality and thus cripple[s] its capacity to intervene in that reality' (p. 11). As an example, the reality of poverty is no longer named in federal government education policy. The problem has been renamed as literacy. Of course the issues are related, but evading poverty cripples the capacity to develop educationally powerful strategies in schools in which poverty is a daily reality.

MAPS NOT ONLY REPRESENT THE PAST AND THE PRESENT BUT ALSO CONSTRUCT THE FUTURE.

Maps can remember or forget. They not only indicate what the present terrain 'looks like', but also constitute the future, that is, maps are productive. Maps need to be considered as 'a way of working the world' (Willinsky 1990, p. 6). Some maps offer an interpretation of the 'lie of the land' (Carter 1996) and also possible futures – they can envisage utopian potential.

MAPS MIGHT BE UNDERSTOOD TO ILLUMINATE.

The social theory literature refers to vulgar theories – to keep the metaphor – vulgar maps. To be vulgar is to reduce complexity to a single overarching principle. So we have vulgar Marxists – those who continue to argue that life can be understood through the narrow lens of political economy. Ironically, today we have vulgar economic rationalism that basically wants to do the same. For a powerful illumination, for our maps to carry complexity, then we need a constellation of features; that is, a 'juxtaposed rather than integrated cluster of changing elements that resist reduction to a common denominator, essential core, or generative first principle' (Jay 1984, p. 15).

WHAT'S GOING ON, IN AND AROUND CONTEMPORARY SCHOOLING?

Historically speaking, at least during the past twenty years or so, the practice of teaching and learning in schools has been broadly defined in terms of an 'educational settlement' (Freeland 1986; Reid 1998) which often goes by the title of a 'general liberal' education. A settlement can be understood in this instance, as an 'unwritten social contract ... [or] a bargain, a historic compromise ... struck between the different conflicting social interests in society' (Hall 1988, p. 36). The 'general liberal' education settlement has occurred around broad agreements such as:

- adequate funding for public schools
- not contesting government funding of private schools
- pursuing a 'general' education for all – which in effect has meant supporting a competitive academic curriculum formulated around knowledge deemed important for everybody's children
- pursuing policies that advance the educational attainment of groups that are widely recognised as 'educationally disadvantaged'; for example, those affected by poverty, girls and Aboriginal students.

It is possible to gather evidence that under a welfare state settlement, public schools have been able to make ground on advancing an egalitarian view of schooling. Largely worked out in schools, but supported by the federal government and state governments, the idea of schooling for a fair go was given expression in a myriad of ways, including:

- reforms to the post-compulsory credentials and the opening-up of curriculum options for a large group of students who had been denied meaningful and credentialled educational experiences (Teese, Davies et al. 1995; Dusseldorp Skills Forum 1998);
- school-based reforms largely developed under the auspices of the Disadvantaged Schools Project (DSP) (Connell 1993) and the National School Network (NSN) (Ladwig, Currie et al. 1994) that aim to improve student learning by providing more meaningful curriculum;
- programs to improve the learning outcomes of girls, especially in areas of the curriculum traditionally stereotyped as boys only (Australian Education Council 1993; MCEETYA 1997);

- revamping the studies of Australian history that have promulgated a racist view and simultaneously degraded Aboriginal and Torres Strait Islander cultures (Groome 1995; Nakata 1995; McQueen 1997);
- taking seriously the need to develop cultural understanding and particularly learning of languages other than English, and the importance of nurturing languages for those children who have a non-English-speaking background (Singh 1998);
- developing inclusive approaches to teaching and learning based on collaboration, negotiation and assessment designed to give feedback on what has been achieved rather than odium for what has not (Hannan 1985; Boomer, Lester et al. 1992).

HOWARD'S WAY ... DISEASED REASON

Given that the welfare state is crumbling fast – that the market is now wrenching itself free of government – schooling is once again a site of an unsettling contestation about its purpose. This contestation might be characterised by a struggle between two rationalities. Those working in schools have two maps to work from – the one they have developed through experience and the one being imposed on them. One I want to refer to as 'Howard's way' and the other as an 'educator's sensibility'. Howard's way I believe is a 'diseased reason' (Horkheimer 1947) that privileges individualism over community, instrumental reason over ethics and private ownership over common wealth. Having a federal government whose policy formulations,[3] broadly speaking, are about letting loose in a completely unfettered way, the rationality of the market into education and training is a cause for alarm, given the effects noted in countries such as New Zealand (Gordon 1994; Kelsey 1995; Wylie 1995), England (Ball et al 1996) and the United States (Apple 1993), countries that have already felt the blunt end of economic fundamentalism.

IT IS IMPORTANT TO CONTEMPLATE THIS LAST POINT CAREFULLY.

Why would we want to go down the same path – or use the same 'diseased reason' as the countries mentioned above – when their market-driven school reforms are proving to be such a disaster? What now seems clear from those countries which have preceded us in hurtling towards a neoliberal future, is that the social democratic imagining of schooling – that schooling might ameliorate economic inequalities in society – is undermined when the logic of the market is let loose on schooling. Instead, the combination of economic and cultural capital is reasserted as the significant determinant for success in schools. Under the logic of the market, schooling unabashedly reasserts itself as a site of social reproduction: schooling contributes without embarrassment to the rich getting richer and the poor getting poorer and larger in number. If all schools are forced to compete for 'market share' we will end up with public schools that are funded across a gradient that reflects the socio-economics of the community – a few rich schools and lots of poor schools. Why would we want to produce such a future?

MARKETISATION OF SCHOOLING

The marketisation of schooling is well underway and involves a double dose of infection: public schools are being forced to compete for students (Marginson 1995) and the school curriculum is being infected by the market (Kenway, Bigum et al. 1994). The local public school now has to spend increasing amounts of time and resources on marketing image (rather than improving teaching and learning). The school curriculum is also now a site for commercial markets to seek out new consumers and for industry to develop employment-related and entrepreneurial (enterprise) competencies (Collins 1996; Hattam & Shacklock 1997). But the marketisation of the schooling sector has a significant and deleterious effect on teachers' work. As a consequence, the contemporary scene in schools is characterised by public school teachers who are, by and large, increasingly demoralised by what is happening. Such a demoralisation involves the following:

- Intensification of teachers' work, in part due to a reduction of real resources; including time, class size increases, expectations for training and developing, and increased level of administrative workload, pushing all responsibility for balancing the declining education budget into school communities and calling it self-managing schools or devolution;

- Associated with intensification is deskilling or redefining teachers work, not in terms of educated professionals or intellectuals but as competent practitioners or technicians (Knight, Lingard et al. 1994; Ball 1995). Teachers are now expected to implement imposed curriculum frameworks, and increasingly teach to the test;

- Deskilling is also promoted by increasing levels of imposed surveillance, often referred to as 'accountability measures'. Examples
  include, standardised testing (or Basic Skills Testing and 'benchmarking') measuring student achievement according to numerical
  levels, and being evaluated by external quality assurance teams;
- The trend towards vocationalism of the school curriculum (Seddon
  1994). Schooling is being asked to play a more important role in
  vocational skill formation and to prepare job-ready, flexible and
  multi-skilled workers, but at a time when the labour market is
  characterised by increasing levels of part-time work, creeping
  credentialism, the almost complete disappearance of the youth
  full-time labour market, and a large pool of unemployed labour
  (Spierings 1995).

  At a time when it would have been more appropriate to be concentrating on schooling as a means of increasing Australia's 'social
  capital' (Cox 1995), and hence developing more competent learners
  and active citizens, the educational discourse is being colonised by
  the logic of the competent worker. Those working in schools are
  now expected to design curriculum using employment-related key
  competencies. One might ask why not 'competencies for (re)making
  the social fabric, which might entail such things as developing a
  durable network of more or less institutionalised relationships of
  mutual acquaintance and recognition' (Bourdieu 1986, p. 248);
  developing trust, reciprocity, mutuality (Cox 1995); skills for participation in ceremonies and rituals (Luke 1993); and solidarity,
  civic participation, and integrity (Putnam 1993).

- Schooling is a prime target for the use of moral panics or manufactured crisis. Manufacturing crises generates a discourse of deviancy
  to deflect the public attention from the broader structural questions.
  The deviants are the workers (especially trade unionists) who want
  to be paid too much, who aren't productive enough, and teachers
  who don't teach the right things well enough. Schools have had
  to wear responsibility for our economic problems, the deviancy of
  youth and the 'literacy crisis.'
- Closing down spaces for debate: In the education and training sectors,
  state governments became 'managerial husks' (Seddon 1995) during
  the years of the Keating government and hence educational leadership shifted to the federal arena. The spaces for debate about policy
  issues in state education systems almost completely disappeared

when state systems closed down most of their advisory and curriculum officer positions (Bartlett 1994). Leadership positions have also been changed to short-term positions and this too has ensured a silencing of critique from those working in the field.

The closing down of government-sponsored spaces for debate in state education bureaucracies has also most significantly meant an institutional silencing of teachers' voices. It now seems clear that educators' knowledge is ignored when developing policy on schooling (Taylor, Rizvi et al. 1997). It is not only teachers' voices that have been marginalised: it appears also that recent policy development on schools has been ideologically deaf to the best researchers in this country. Take for instance the recent debacle about literacy standards in Australia (Comber, Green et al. 1998).

- Perhaps more insidious has been the blatant muting of social justice discourse (Lingard & Garrick 1997; Luke 1997). The category, 'social justice' has all but disappeared. As examples, the Disadvantaged Schools Program has been renamed the Commonwealth Literacy Program, with its future now under a cloud, and the funding for the National Schools' Network has ceased. To undermine a commitment to equal outcomes and hence affirmative action, neoliberal governments retreat to a 'blaming the victim' position by marshalling such arguments as the need for freedom of speech. The empirical evidence however, overwhelmingly supports the view (Teese, Davies et al. 1995; Dwyer 1996) that the outcomes of schooling are still very much skewed in favour of those groups who are already advantaged in society. The already disadvantaged or disenfranchised continue not to be served well by the schooling system and the present confluence of reforms is only making things worse.

TEACHERS SUSTAINING AN EDUCATOR'S SENSIBILITY

Teachers are not automatons, who simply implement education policy maps (Bowe & Ball 1992; Ball 1994). Rather, they struggle to make sense of – and hence to unite into a coherent practice – the interrelationships, contradictions and profound differences between education policy and their own internally persuasive maps. At its most sophisticated, the internally persuasive discourse of teachers – a view about teaching and learning that I want to refer to as an educator's sensibility – develops in an independent, experimenting and discriminating way through ongoing rigorous examination of what works in the material conditions of schools (Zeichner 1993; McTaggart 1994).

Teachers now find themselves working in 'devolved schools', where devolved means being whipped into shape by a policy process that simultaneously has a fetish for decreasing inputs into schools, while instituting crude measurements of outcomes and failing to make any significant contribution to a debate about the nature of teaching and learning.

Devolution now means that teachers are having to struggle, at the school level, to have an educator's sensibility which informs school reform. The school reform literature and our own case studies indicate that school reform is 'largely worked out locally'. The most successful stories also indicate that school reform needs to be considered as 'whole school reform;' that is, holistic and integrates (re)structuring, (re)culturing, and changes to pedagogy ('teaching and learning') (Ladwig, Currie et al. 1994). Quoting Harradine (1996, p. 4) on these three is instructive:

- restructuring – structural and organisational reforms such as changing the use of time and space, groupings of staff and students, staff roles, organisation of curriculum, and use of technology;
- reculturing – changing values, beliefs, assumptions, habits, patterns of behaviour and relationships in school organisational culture; and,
- changing pedagogy – concentrating on classroom 'instructional practice', the teaching and learning process and student learning outcomes.

Importantly, schools that take school reform seriously, consciously engage in ongoing work on the school culture. If the system is to support an educator's sensibility, then it is essential to have a well-developed understanding of the nature of school culture(s). If teaching and learning is to be improved, then schools need support to develop social capital at the school level.

How might we understand or map school culture? School cultures are dynamic and the diagram below aims to provide a rough map of school cultures. I want to suggest that, although these descriptions are caricatures to some extent, they do seem to strike a strong resonance with teachers. It is also apparent that, in any particular school, more than one of these descriptors might be applicable, but one of them tends to dominate. Within this framework school reform can be seen as an attempt to move from the 'stuck' state in the direction of the collaborative and socially critical culture.

Stuck	Collaborative	Socially critical
■ Low levels of teacher	■ Coherent school planning	■ Social justice emphasis
■ Deficit view of students	■ Student-centred	■ Critically reflective teachers
■ Teacher privatism	■ Curriculum development	■ Promote critical literacy
■ Little of no debate	■ Collaborative Teaching	■ Celebrate difference

What follows is a further elaboration of the caricature of these types of school cultures.

Stuck

A stuck school culture is characterised by having few of the structures and planning processes to promote collaboration and the development of educational dialogues in the community and hence seems to be 'stuck' (Rosenholtz 1989) when it comes to school reform. In such schools, teaching is either individualistic, where teachers work in isolation, or is balkanised, where teachers associate with colleagues only in particular groups. In the absence of educational debate with teachers, students and parents, such schools allow their agenda to be driven from outside and end up being trapped by their own inertia.

Collaborative

Other schools have developed collaborative practices and various forms of collegiality as part of the process of advancing teachers' learning and whole school reform. Ideally, collegiality is not contrived where joint teacher planning is mandated but the whole staff is willing to work together in the pursuit of improved student learning. The big question in such school communities is: How is student learning best enhanced in this place? In such schools, a large number of the teachers realise that it is important to be continually testing the adequacy of their theories about teaching and learning. The school culture supports and encourages such investigations.

Socially critical

'Socially critical' school cultures have moved beyond the comfort zone
of collaboration to a culture of learning where teachers confront their
own teaching practices and begin to 'critically' reflect on the moral and
ethical dimensions of teaching and learning. 'Critical' here refers to a
school culture that promotes an ongoing debate with parents, students
and teachers about the curriculum and the purposes of schooling.
Critical then, means critique with practical intent in collaboration with
students and parents. So the question – how is student learning best
enhanced in this place – is still important but is balanced against other
questions such as how might schooling make a difference to persistent
social inequalities? In such schools, a large number of the teachers is
investigating the adequacy of their theories about teaching and learning,
with a view to introducing their students to the 'representational
resources' (New London Group 1996) needed to 'read the word and the
world' (Freire & Macedo 1987) in these 'new times'.

At this point it might be asserted that my vision of the socially
critical school represents some fanciful ideal which is well beyond the
reach of school communities. I don't want to downplay the formidable
nature of the barriers to school-based reform, but some teachers and
school communities are working to sustain a broader view of teaching
and learning – a view with a more expansive horizon, with a more courageous vision than that provided by neoliberal education policy.

In a context of devolution, some schools are managing to successfully work against the grain of marketisation and the concomitant
effects of intensification. Some schools have managed to sustain a
'culture of innovation' (Kress 1993) by applying strategies of reform
developed through such programs as the Disadvantaged Schools
Program and the National Schools Network. Taking 'whole school
reform' (Connell & White 1989) seriously means the school is viewed as
a site for an 'actually existing democracy' (Fraser 1997) – places which are
about 'teaching democracy democratically' (Worsford 1997).

Some schools continue to struggle to enact a vision of a school as a
site for negotiation of interests. Teachers in such schools reject the view
that the interests of their school communities have been incorporated into
the policy formulations of outside experts. Instead, such schools maintain a view that curriculum-making is largely worked out locally. These
schools are committed to a struggle to actively involve the whole school

community, including groups who have been constantly marginalised or silenced, to ensure all students are actively engaged in learning. The socially critical school, I believe, has the potential to function as a genuine public sphere where students (citizens) can come together to deliberate and construct alternative visions of society.

STRUGGLING FOR SOCIALLY CRITICAL SCHOOLS

What is recognised in those schools still struggling for a socially critical alternative to the shallow and marketised school on offer by neoliberal policy, is that teachers are the most important actors in educational reform and it is their efforts which ultimately determine the success of any moves to change schooling practices (Zeichner 1993). In such schools an educator's sensibility is nourished rather than silenced. Pragmatically this means supporting a school culture that nurtures teachers' learning for the following reasons:

Pursuing a courageous educational vision with the school community

I'm using the term 'socially critical' to name a courageous educational vision, but others sometimes refer to such a vision by terms such as 'democratic schooling' (Goodman 1992). Such a vision is courageous because it means working with the 'tension between individuality and community' (Goodman 1989, p. 41): that individualistic goals are balanced by values of compassion (Greene 1991) and civic responsibility. Such a view 'implies a moral commitment to promote values of economic and social justice and actively inhibit racism, sexism, classism, ethnocentrism and other forms of oppression' (p. 41).

Sustaining a culture of debate in which teachers can (continually) test the adequacy of their theories about teaching and learning that also develops collaboration

Would you continue to send your children to a school if you found out that most of the teachers were not reflective about their teaching or if the school sustained a culture that frowned on rigorous examination of teaching practice? What might a rigorous examination of teaching and learning look like? A socially critical version – critical reflection or action research – has three key elements: a research spiral, a critical community and critical reflection. As an example of a research spiral, Smyth (1989) recommends these elements:

1. Describe ... what is it that you do as a teacher?
2. Inform ... what does this mean?
3. Confront ... how did I come to be like this?
4. Reconstruct ... how might I do things differently?

Working on 'critical instances' (Tripp 1992) forms the basis for further investigation and improvement. Ideally, critical reflection is sustained with other interested teachers, forming a community of critical learners to develop some clearer understandings about how people talk about and categorise teaching and students, what counts as learning and participation and how people relate to each other (the nature of power and authority relations) (Kemmis & McTaggart 1988). In the contemporary scene, teachers are having to struggle to incorporate moral and ethical criteria into their practice of reflection. Critically reflective teachers ask:

... which educational goals, experiences, and activities lead toward forms of life which are mediated by concerns for justice, equity, and concrete fulfilment and whether current arrangements serve important human needs and satisfy important human purposes. Here both the teaching (ends and means) and the contexts which surround the teaching are viewed as problematic, as value-governed selections from a larger universe of possibilities.

Zeichner & Liston 1986, p. 67

Promoting a dialogue with the local community with a view to incorporating the existential struggles of the local community into curriculum

Democratic schools promote a dialogic relationship (Shor & Freire 1987) with the local community. What this means is a commitment to having a two-way interchange.

One begins with the assumption that the other has something to say to us and to contribute to our understanding. The initial task is to grasp the other's position in the strongest possible light. One must always be responsive to what the other is saying and showing ... There is a play, a to-and-fro movement in dialogic encounter, a seeking for a common ground in which we can understand our differences. The other in not an adversary or an opponent but a conversational partner.

Bernstein 1991, p. 337

Not only is the (socially critical) school keen to ensure the community knows what is happening at the school, but the school is also keen to know about the local community. It is essential to recognise the need to craft curriculum responsive to the context: that it takes into consideration the nature of the local community. Knowing about the local community involves understanding the political economy, and the cultural geography, and especially having a clear understanding of the significant issues the community is struggling with. Dialogue with the community can reveal 'generative themes' which are unresolved social problems in the community, good for generating curriculum based on the integration of the 'personal concerns of students and their communities and the larger issues facing our world' (Beane 1990, p. 40; Shor 1992, p. 467).

Promoting a 'student voice' capable of integrating personal concerns and the larger issues facing our world

Why is it, in spite of the fact that teaching by pouring in, learning by passive absorption, are universally condemned, that they are still entrenched in practice?   **Dewey 1916, p. 38**

More than eighty years later, didactic teaching is still prevalent even though most educators agree that 'new knowledge is produced (constructed) through a process of cognitive change and self-regulation' (Kincheloe 1993, p. 107); that is, a constructivist view of learning is now well regarded. Such a view 'maintains that the knower personally participates in all acts of knowing and understanding' (p. 107). Schools might involve a student voice in the school's development plan (McInerney, Smyth et al. 1997), in designing curriculum from generative themes (Shor 1992) or assisting students develop a 'critical sensibility' 'as in the ability to critique a system and its relations to other systems on the basis of the workings of power, politics, ideology, and values' (New London Group 1996, p. 85).

Promoting debate about the content of the curriculum that is responsive to concern for social injustice and that encourages the development of critical literacies (Fairclough 1992)

Critical literacy education pushes the definition of literacy beyond the traditional decoding or encoding of words in order to reproduce the meaning of the text and society until it becomes a means for understanding one's own history and culture, and for fostering an activism toward equal participation for all the decisions that affect and control our lives.   **Shannon 1991, p. 518**

Socially critical teachers reject approaches to curriculum which treat knowledge as deposits or as sanitised and non-controversial. Society is not assumed to be fair and just. Instead socially critical teachers devise curriculum that opens up a space for students to develop 'resistant reading' (Janks & Ivanic 1992) positions that encourage students to 'check and criticise the history [they] are told against the [one they are living]' (Inglis 1985, p. 108).

TOWARDS A POLITICS FOR DEMOCRATIC SCHOOLING

It is usual in the conclusion to a chapter such as this to make some form of recommendation for policy development. In the present context, I can only predict that such recommendations will fall on deaf ears, as educational policy is being developed by a neoliberal government that cares little for a democratic imagining of schooling. Playing the policy game seems pointless at this time. However, now is not the time to be silent. Rather it is necessary to find ways to support teachers in schools who struggle to realise an egalitarian view of schooling. Those teachers need to be supported to:

- resist the worst of devolution – of giving away a centrally funded and supported public school system to produce a user-pays system that relies on the economic capital of the local community. Resisting the savage cuts to the public school budget is a high priority;
- minimise the damage due to the introduction of testing/benchmarking that is ahistorical, culturally insensitive, reductive, incongruent with the practised curriculum and uninformative for teachers who hope to make a difference for their students;
- reclaim the spaces to debate the nature of good teaching and learning, and to re-institute a well-funded dialogue between classrooms and the policy development process. The public school system needs an 'advisory group' that can sustain a significant debate about the nature of good teaching and learning;
- resist 'caging teachers in elaborate, centrally dreamed-up curriculum frameworks' (Collins 1996, p. 11);

- properly fund the professional development of teachers. The state, as employer of teachers, needs to take responsibility for providing resources for teachers to be engaged in high quality professional development.

If you believe that schooling plays a role in the formation of our society, then it now seems essential to support the struggle to sustain a socially critical educator's sensibility in schools.

REFERENCES

Apple, M. 1993, *Official Knowledge: Democratic Education in a Conservative Age*, New York, Routledge.

Australian Education Council 1993, *National Action Plan for the Education of Girls*, Curriculum Corporation, Carlton, Vic.

Ball, S. 1994, *Education Reform: A Critical and Post-structural Approach*, Buckingham, Open University Press.

Ball, S. 1995, 'Intellectuals or technicians? The urgent role of theory in educational studies', *British Journal of Educational Studies*, vol. 43, no. 3, pp. 255–71.

Ball, S. et al. 1996, 'School choice, social class and distinction: the realisation of social advantage in education', *Journal of Education Policy*, vol. 11, no. 1, pp. 89–112.

Bartlett, L. 1994, 'Qualitative research in Australia', *Qualitative Studies in Education*, vol. 7, no. 3, pp. 207–25.

Beane, J. 1990, *A Middle School Curriculum: From Rhetoric to Reality*, National Middle School Association, Columbus, Ohio.

Bernstein, R. 1991, *The New Constellation*, MIT Press, Cambridge.

Boomer, G. et al (eds) 1992, *Negotiating the Curriculum: Educating for the 21st Century*, Falmer, London.

Bourdieu, P. 1986, 'The forms of capital', in *Handbook of Theory and Research for the Sociology of Education*, ed J. Richardson, Greenwood Press, New York.

Bowe, R. & Ball S. 1992, *Reforming Education and Changing Schools*, Routledge, London.

Carter, P. 1996, *The Lie of the Land*, Faber and Faber, London.

Collins, C. 1996, 'What teachers need to know? The competencies debate', *South Australian Educational Leader*, vol. 7, no. 4, pp. 1–12.

Comber, B. et al. 1998, 'Literacy debates and public education: A question of "crisis"?', in *Going Public: Education Policy and Public Education in Australia*, ed A. Reid, Australian Curriculum Studies Association, Deakin, ACT.

Commonwealth Schools Commission 1987, *In the National Interest: Secondary Education and Youth Policy in Australia*, Canberra Publishing and Printing.

Connell, R. 1993, *Schools and Social Justice*, Pluto, Leichhardt, NSW,

Connell, R. & White, V. 1989, 'Child poverty and educational action', in *Child Poverty*, eds D. Edgar, D. Keane & P. McDonald, Allen & Unwin, Sydney.

Cox, E. 1995, *A Truly Civil Society*, ABC Books, Sydney.

Deakin Centre for Education and Change 1994, *Schooling What Future? Balancing the Education Agenda*, Deakin Centre for Education and Change, Geelong, Vic.

Dewey, J. 1916, *Democracy and Education*, repr. 1966, Free Press, New York.

Dusseldorp Skills Forum 1998, *Australia's Youth: Reality and Risk*, Dusseldorp Skills Forum, Sydney.

Dwyer, P. 1996, *Opting Out: Early School Leavers and the Degeneration of Youth Policy*, National Clearinghouse for Youth Studies & Youth Research Centre, Hobart.

Fairclough, N. (ed.) 1992, *Critical Language Awareness*, Real Language Series, Longman, London.

Fraser, N. 1997, *Justice Interruptus: Critical Reflections on the 'Postsocialist' Condition*, Routledge, New York.

Freeland, J. 1986, 'Australia: The search for a new educational settlement', in *Capitalist Crisis and Schooling: Comparative Studies in the Politics of Education*, ed R. Sharp, Macmillan, Melbourne.

Freire, P. & Macedo, D. 1987, *Literacy: Reading the Word and Reading the World*, Bergin and Garvey, Massachusetts.

Goodman, J. 1989, 'Student participation and control for democratic schooling: Towards a connectionist power structure', *Curriculum and Teaching*, vol. 4, no. 2, pp. 39–59.

Goodman, J. 1992. *Elementary Schooling for Critical Democracy*, SUNY Press, Albany.

Goodman, J. & Kuzmic, J. 1997, 'Bringing a progressive pedagogy to conventional schools: theoretical and practical implications from Harmony', *Theory into Practice*, vol. 36, no. 2, pp. 79–86.

Gordon, L. 1994, ' "Rich" and "poor" schools in Aotearoa', *New Zealand Journal of Educational Studies*, vol. 29, no. 2, pp. 113–25.

Green, B. & Bigum, C. 1993, 'Aliens in the Classroom', *Australian Journal of Education*, vol. 37, no. 2, pp. 119–41.

Green, B. & Bigum, C. 1998, 'Re-tooling schooling? Information technology, cultural change and the future(s) of Australian education', in *Schooling for a Fair Go*, eds J. Smyth, R. Hattam & M. Lawson, Federation Press, Sydney.

Greene, M. 1991, 'Retrieving the language of compassion: The education professor in search of community', *Teachers College Record*, vol. 92, no. 4, pp. 541–55.

Groome, H. 1995, 'Towards improved understandings of Aboriginal young people', *Youth Studies Australia*, vol. 14, no. 4, pp. 17–21.

Hall, S. & Jacques, M. 1990, 'From the manifesto for new times', in *New Times: The Changing Face of Politics in the 1990s*, eds S. Hall & M. Jacques, Verso, New York.

Hall, S. 1988, 'The toad in the garden: Thatcherism among the theorists', in *Marxism and the Interpretation of Culture*, eds L. Grossberg & C. Nelson, University of Illinois Press, Urbana & Chicago.

Hannan, B. 1985, *Democratic Curriculum: Essays on Schooling and Society*, Allen & Unwin, Sydney.

Harding, S. 1993, 'Rethinking standpoint epistemology: What is "strong objectivity"?', in *Feminist Epistimologies*, eds L. Alcoff & E. Potter, Routledge, London.

Harradine, J. 1996, 'What research tells us about school reform', *National Schools Network Newsletter*, vol. 2, no. 2, pp. 4–5.

Harraway, D. 1991, *Simians, Cyborgs and Women: The Reinvention of Nature*, Routledge, New York.

Hattam, R. & Shacklock, G. 1997, Investigating enterprise culture in schools is a socially critical enterprise education possible?', paper presented at Australian Education Union (S.A.) conference on vocational education.

Havel, V. 1991, *Open Letters: Selected Writings 1965–1990*, Alfred Knopf, New York.

Horkheimer, M. 1947, 'Reason against itself: Some remarks on the enlightenment', *Theory, Culture and Society*, vol. 10, 1993, pp. 79–88.

Inglis, F. 1985, *The Management of Ignorance*, Blackwell, London.

Jameson, F. 1991, *Postmodernism, or the Cultural Logic of Late Capitalism*, Duke University Press, Durham, NY.

Janks, H. & Ivanic, R. 1992, 'Critical language awareness and emancipatory discourse', in *Critical Language Awareness*, ed N. Fairclough, Longman, London.

Jay, M. 1984, *Adorno*, Harvard University Press, Cambridge, Massachusetts.

Kelsey, J. 1995, *Economic Fundamentalism: New Zealand Experiment – A World Model for Structural Adjustment*, Pluto Press, London.

Kemmis, S. & McTaggart, R. 1998, *The Action Research Planner*, Deakin University Press, Geelong, Vic.

Kenway, J., C. Bigum, et al. 1994, 'New education in new times', *Journal of Education Policy*, vol. 9, no. 4, pp. 317–33.

Kincheloe, J. 1993, *Towards a Critical Politics of Teacher Thinking: Mapping the Postmodern*, Bergin & Garvey, Westport, Conn, & London.

Knight, B. et al. 1994, 'Reforming teacher education policy under Labour governments in Australia, 1983–93', *British Journal of Sociology of Education*, vol. 15, no. 4, pp. 451–66.

Kress, G. 1993, 'Participation and difference: The role of language in producing a culture of innovation', in *Literacy in Contexts: Australian Perspectives and Issues*, eds A. Luke & P. Gilbert, Allen & Unwin, Sydney.

Ladwig, J., Currie, J. et al. 1994, *Towards Rethinking Australian Schools, The National Schools Network*.

Lingard, B. & Garrick, B. 1997, Producing and practising social justice policy in education: A policy trajectory study from Queensland, Australia, paper for the International Sociology of Education Conference, Sheffield, UK.

Luke, A. 1993, 'Genres of power? Literacy education and the production of capital', in *Literacy in Society*, eds R. Hasan & G. Williams, Routledge, London.

Luke, A. 1997, 'New narratives of human capital: Recent redirections in Australian Educational Policy', *Australian Educational Researcher*, vol. 24, no. 2, pp. 1–22.

Lyotard, J.-F. 1984, *The Postmodern Condition: A Report on Knowledge*, Manchester University Press, Manchester.

McInerney, P., Smyth, J. et al. 1997, *Sustaining Teacher Learning as a Dialogic Encounter: Conversing with Pieces of the Puzzle at the Pines School*, case study no. 4, Flinders Institute for the Study of Teaching, Adelaide.

McQueen, H. 1997, *Suspect History: Manning Clark and the Future of Australia's Past*, Wakefield Press, Adelaide.

McTaggart, R. 1994, 'Participatory action research: issues in theory and practice', *Educational Action Research*, vol. 2, no. 3, pp. 313–37.

Marginson, S. 1995, 'Markets in education: A theoretical note', *Australian Journal of Education*, vol. 39, no. 3, pp. 294–312.

Max-Neef, M. 1991, *Human Scale Development*, Apex Press, New York.

Ministerial Council on Education, Employment, Training and Youth Affairs (MCEETYA) 1997, *Gender Equity: A Framework for Australian Schools*, Department of Urban Services, ACT Government, Canberra.

Nakata, M. 1995, 'Cutting a better deal for Torres Strait Islanders', *Youth Studies Australia*, vol. 14, no. 4, pp. 29–34.

New London Group 1996, 'A pedagogy of multiliteracies: Designing social futures', *Harvard Educational Review*, vol. 66, no. 1, pp. 60–92.

Offe, C. 1996, 'Modern "barbarity": A micro-state of nature?', *Constellations*, vol. 2, no. 3, pp. 354–77.

Putnam, R. 1993, *Making Democracy Work: Civic Traditions in Modern Italy*, Princeton U.P., Princeton, N.J.

Reid, A. 1998, 'Regulating the educational market: The effects on public sector workers', in *Going Public: Education Policy and Public Education in Australia*, ed A. Reid, Australian Curriculum Studies Association, Deakin West, ACT,

Rosenholtz, S. 1989, *Teachers' Workplace: The Organization of Schools*, Longman, New York.

Seddon, T. 1994, 'Reconstructing social democratic education in Australia: versions of Vocationalism', *Journal of Curriculum Studies*, vol. 26, no. 1, pp. 63–82.

Seddon, T. 1995, Educational leadership and teachers' work, paper presented at conference: Educational Leadership: Political, Cultural, Critical and Gendered Perspectives, Flinders University, July, 1995, Flinders Institute for the Study of Teaching.

Shannon, P. 1991, 'Questions and answers: critical literacy', *The Reading Teacher*, vol. 44, no. 7, p. 518.

Shor, I. 1992, *Empowering Education: Critical Teaching for Social Change*, University of Chicago Press, Chicago.

Shor, I. & Freire, P. 1987, 'What is the "Dialogical Method" of Teaching?', *Journal of Education*, vol. 169, no. 3, pp. 11–31.

Singh, M. G. 1998, 'It is not easy being Australian: Education in a multicultural and multi-racist society', in *Schooling for a Fair Go*, eds J. Smyth, R. Hattam & M. Lawson, Federation Press, Sydney.

Smyth, J. 1989, 'A critical pedagogy of classroom practice', *Journal of Curriculum Studies*, vol. 21, no. 6, pp. 483–502.

Spierings, J. 1995, *Young Australians in the Working Nation. A Review of Youth Employment Policies for the 1990s*, Social Justice Research Foundation, University of Adelaide, Adelaide.

Taylor, S., Rizvi, F. et al. 1997, *Educational Policy and the Politics of Change*, Routledge, London.

Teese, R., Davies, M. et al. 1995, *Who Wins at School? Girls and Boys in Australian Secondary Education*, University of Melbourne, Department of Education Policy and Management, Melbourne.

Tripp, D. 1992, *Critical Incidents in Teaching: the Development of Professional Judgement*, Routledge, London.

Willinsky, J. 1990, *The New Literacy: Redefining Reading and Writing in the Schools*, Routledge, London.

Worsford, V. 1997, 'Teaching democracy democratically', *Educational Theory*, vol. 47, no. 3, pp. 395–410.

Wylie, C. 1995, 'Contrary currents: The application of the public sector reform framework in education', *New Zealand Journal of Educational Studies*, vol. 30, no. 2, pp. 149–64.

Zeichner, K. 1993, 'Connecting genuine teacher development to the struggle for social justice', *Journal of Education for Teaching*, vol. 19, no. 1, pp. 5–20.

Zeichner, K. & Liston D. 1986, 'An inquiry-oriented approach to student teaching', *Journal of Teaching Practice*, vol. 6, no. 1, pp. 5–24.

NOTES

1   The content of my paper is in part derived from the work of the Teachers' Learning Project. As such I want to acknowledge the other members of the Research Team: Professor John Smyth, Dr Michael Lawson and Peter McInerney.

2   Other issues that are also significant include: falling retention rates in post-compulsory years; implementing middle schooling; and being able to ensure students in the early years are learning appropriate literacies.

3   The policy formulation I'm referring to includes policy that has: opened up the market to establish new schools; began to undermine the federal government's commitment to funding equity programs in schools; abandoned the funding of professional development of teachers; the youth allowance; 'benchmarking' literacy; and, decreased access to higher education through increases to HECS.

CHAPTER 14

A NICE PLACE TO VISIT, BUT CAN YOU AFFORD TO WORK THERE?

Working life and industrial relations in South Australia[1]

BARBARA POCOCK AND ANTHONY PSARROS

In recent years South Australia has very often been a follower rather than a leader when it comes to shaping and reshaping the industrial relations system. It was not always so. On 12 December 1890 Charles Cameron Kingston introduced a bill into the South Australian parliament which provided a model of key provisions later enacted in New Zealand's and Australia's conciliation and arbitration systems. Many features of Kingston's original, comprehensive bill were eventually made law in South Australia, some years after the birth of a system of conciliation and arbitration nationally, and in several states. But the reach of this powerful and visionary South Australian reformer was much wider: 'The original [Kingston Bill] stands … as the earliest version of the classical form of Australasian compulsory arbitration presented to any parliament' (Mitchell 1989, p. 87).

South Australia's system of industrial regulation evolved from the 1912 act to result in a system of conciliation and arbitration where industrial disputes were generally less frequent or severe than in other states, and both employers and unions were generally supportive of its shape and existence. As late as 1985, South Australian legislators were still adopting innovative approaches to questions like unfair dismissal and the role of an industrial court, and by the early 1990s, the system retained some distinguishing features: it was alone in Australia in offering some legal protection to employees and unions who took strike action; it allowed employers to make agreements outside the award system with registered or unregistered associations; and it permitted individual employees to find redress against unfair dismissal and seek reinstatement or compensation (Stewart 1998, p. 135).

More recently, Labor governments and subsequently their conservative successors have followed the footsteps of their federal peers along the path of reform, so that a South Australian approach is no longer clearly distinguishable. This chapter summarises the nature of the system today, analyses the recent fortunes of South Australian workers under it, and argues that far from mimicking – once again – the current conservative direction of Australian industrial reform, the direction of change in South Australian arrangements should be the reverse: a strengthened safety net and steps towards greater employment security in the interests of a more equitable labour market and a more productive state.

SOUTH AUSTRALIAN REFORM IN THE 1990S

Two waves of legislative reform have reshaped the South Australian system in the 1990s. Firstly, Labor introduced two amendment bills: the *Industrial Conciliation and Arbitration (Commonwealth Provisions) Amendment Act* 1991 and the *Industrial Relations (Miscellaneous Provisions) Amendment Act* 1992 that effectively responded to federal Labor reforms. These amendments allowed dual appointments to the federal and state tribunals, and permitted certified industrial agreements (mirroring the federal provisions) alongside the existing state provisions for industrial agreements. Stewart concludes that 'in two short years the two systems had been brought much closer together', mostly in the image of the federal system (1998, p. 138).

The election of a Liberal government in December 1993 gave rise to a new pace and direction of reform, although not to the same degree as the radical changes in Victoria and federally. While the Liberals took steps to privilege the goals of productivity and efficiency, to encourage workplace bargaining and constrain unions, they ran against the tide of individualism characteristic of the Victorian and federal systems since 1992 and 1996 respectively, by stopping short of allowing individual contracts. Collective bargaining remains a cornerstone of the South Australian system – so far. As Stewart puts it, the *Industrial and Employee Relations Act* 1994 'attempts to combine the old with the new: to encourage regulation through workplace bargaining without abandoning the established framework of conciliation and arbitration' (1998, p. 139).

The 1994 act introduced several important changes nonetheless. It encourages a shift to enterprise bargaining through the negotiation of enterprise agreements, underpinned by an award system which – while left intact and not subject to a clipping back to 'allowable matters' – is expected to become a mere safety net beneath the processes of enterprise negotiation.[2] Enterprise agreements must provide wages and conditions that, when considered as a whole, are at least as good as the relevant state award, and include existing legislated standards with respect to annual, sick and parental leave and some other conditions. A majority of employees who vote, free of coercion and properly consulted, must support the terms of the enterprise agreement. An important exception to this exists where an employer's economic difficulties are significant and two-thirds of employees agree to lesser conditions which seem likely to make a material difference to the firm's chances of survival. In such circumstances an inferior agreement may be approved by the Full Commission. Predictably, this provision is not without its controversies (Stewart 1998, p. 144; Employee Ombudsman 1996, p. 37). The act also reduced the appointment of commission members to renewable six-year terms, rather than appointment to retirement. As Owens has pointed out, 'the possibility for political interference in the workings of the commission is most inappropriate' (Owens 1995, p. 138).

During 1997 the state Liberal government further 'harmonised' the state system with the federal *Workplace Relations Act* 1996 through two amendment bills. However, it was unable to convince the Democrats (who continue to hold the balance of power in the Upper House) to support the extension of individual Australian workplace agreements into the state system. Instead it secured changes to unfair dismissal systems and freedom of association laws (Department of Industrial Affairs 1997).

This active program of legislative reform suggests that industrial relations continues to attract headlines in Australian political life and remains an important front upon which parliamentary political fortunes can be made or broken. In recent decades at least, South Australia has not been a site of aggressive public industrial confrontation, as witnessed on the waterfront nationally in 1998 (where events in the state played a relatively small part). However, the main parties continue to differentiate themselves electorally on industrial issues, and both Labor and Liberal nurture plans for continuing change to the system. On the conservative side, various options are occasionally canvassed: firstly, following the Victorian example, the referral of the state's industrial powers to the Commonwealth; secondly, a further round of reform to permit individual contracts, confine awards to a limited range of allowable matters, further constrict and confine unionism, and complete the project of mirroring the federal law in all its conservative fullness. The South Australian government's introduction of further reforms in 1999 all move in these directions. While there might be some economies in the absorption of the state system into the federal arrangements which administrators and some conservatives may find attractive, relatively few politicians at state level are generally drawn to the voluntary surrender of state-level instruments of control and law-making which provide opportunities for the construction of ministerial reputation and advancement. So the likelihood of this surrender may rely upon the size and attractiveness of inducements offered by the federal government.

On the Labor side, in a fairly minimalist offering to reverse some aspects of recent change, the opposition talks of maintaining a strong independent Industrial Relations Commission, and support for common rule awards with decent wages for all, not just those who can bargain for themselves (South Australian Labor Party 1997).

WORKING LIFE FOR SOUTH AUSTRALIANS

While politicians reshape the industrial system around them, how have South Australian workers been faring in terms of income, bargaining and quality of working life? In late 1995 the Department of Industrial Relations (now Workplace Relations and Small Business) conducted its second, large survey of Australian workplaces, making available a wide range of information about the state of Australian workplaces (Morehead et al. 1997). These data show that South Australians are close to the Australian average on many workplace characteristics. But while the state once had something of a reputation as a good place to work, there are now sure signs of growing stress and shrinking rewards for workers in the state – leaving aside the important issue of shrinking employment opportunities for future generations (discussed elsewhere in this volume).

Based on data from workplaces with twenty or more employees,[3] the survey shows that, after the Northern Territory, South Australian workers reported higher levels of increased stress over the 12 months to late 1995 compared to other Australian workers. Over half of South Australian employees (53 per cent) in these larger workplaces said that the stress in their jobs had increased, slightly above the Australian average of 50 per cent. Sixty per cent said that the effort they had to put into their jobs had increased (compared to 58 per cent nationally), and 48 per cent said the pace of their work was increasing (46 per cent nationally) (see table 1).

South Australian workers also had more negative assessments of their chances for promotion, on average, than in any other state: 19 per cent felt that their chances of a more senior job had gone down in the past year, compared to a national proportion of 15 per cent. And more felt insecure: a third of South Australian workers in the survey felt insecure in their workplaces compared to 29 per cent nationally.

TABLE 1: QUALITY OF WORKING LIFE, SOUTH AUSTRALIA AND AUSTRALIA, 1995 – PROPORTION INDICATING 'GONE UP' OVER THE PAST 12 MONTHS

	SA (%)	Australia (%)
Stress in job	53	50
Effort into job	60	58
Pace at which you do your job	48	46
Your chance to get a more senior job	16	18
Satisfaction with job	27	30
Satisfaction with work family balance	12	14

Source: unpublished AWIRS data

On the other hand, a smaller proportion felt that their job satisfaction had gone up (27 per cent compared to 30 per cent nationally). In terms of balancing work and family, only a small proportion felt that things were improving in this area: the balance had improved for only 12 per cent, while it deteriorated for 28 per cent (the national figures were 14 and 26 per cent respectively).

While these differences are slight, the trend is persistently in the negative for the state. South Australian workers consistently place themselves at the worst end of the spectrum in terms of work pressure. This occurs against an overall background of growing pressure in Australian workplaces where half of all workers report increases in stress. It seems that the quality of working life on a range of indicators is deteriorating for many South Australians, and appears to be doing so at a slightly faster rate than in other states. Turning to the question of financial rewards, there are few signs of any compensating increases in earnings.

WAGES AND BARGAINING

A number of significant trends emerge from an analysis of wages and bargaining in South Australia over recent years. Each of these is contributing to a widening dispersion in earnings: between South Australian and Australian workers, between women and men, between those in the state and federal systems, those in differing industries and occupations, those in actively bargaining, unionised workplaces, and those who are not (and even within these, between those who are assertive, well organised and union-active, and those who are not, and are confronted by assertive employers).

Overall earnings in the state have fallen behind those in other states. Alongside this, a sizeable proportion of the working population in the state is effectively excluded from meaningful pay rises, leaving them vulnerable to declining real incomes. Of those within the actively bargaining sector, a growing proportion are engaged in some form of enterprise agreement-making, increasingly within the federal system, and less and less in the state system.

Examining these trends in turn, figure 1 shows the ratio of South Australian to Australian average weekly ordinary-time earnings of full-time adults. While the ratio tended to rise in the late eighties, and peaked at 99 per cent for all of 1993, since that time it has steadily declined and in the last quarter of 1997 reached a fourteen-year low of 93 per cent. In dollar terms, in late 1997 South Australians were earning $666 per week on average, while nationally the average was $47 higher at $713.

Data available from AWIRS confirm that South Australian workers have been lagging behind in terms of the extent of bargaining in the state, and the size of pay rises won through such bargaining. Just over half of South Australian workers in workplaces with more than 20 employees (55 per cent) said that their average weekly pay had gone up in the 12 months to late 1995, compared to 59 per cent nationally; this compared to a high proportion of 68 per cent in the ACT. South Australia had the highest proportion of workers who said that they had not received any pay rise in the period (36 per cent).

AWIRS results suggest that agreement-making – with concomitant pay rises – was much less widespread in South Australia than in most of the rest of Australia: no new written or verbal agreements were negotiated in 42 per cent of workplaces (with more than 20 employees) between early 1994 and late 1995, compared to a much smaller slice of

FIGURE 1: RATIO OF AVERAGE WEEKLY ORDINARY-TIME EARNINGS, SOUTH AUSTRALIA/AUSTRALIA, 1983–97

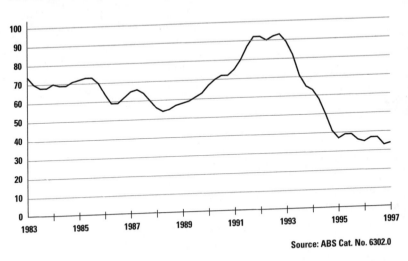

Source: ABS Cat. No. 6302.0

28 per cent in this category nationally. Once again, South Australia was at the bottom of this league after the Northern Territory. This reflects in part the later inception of formal workplace bargaining in the state. Where an agreement had been made, AWIRS survey results show that South Australian employers were more likely to give cost-cutting as a motivation for negotiation: 23 per cent of South Australian managers indicated this as a motivation compared to 18 per cent nationally, perhaps explaining something of the higher sense of rising stress amongst SA workers as described above. South Australian employees were also the least likely out of all states to have been consulted by managers in the process of agreement-making.

Turning to the issue of the size of pay increases, many more South Australian workers received, through enterprise bargaining over the preceeding 12 months, increases smaller than the national average: 17 per cent received less than 2 per cent rise (9 per cent nationally), while 47 per cent were in workplaces with agreements giving over 5.1 per cent increases, compared to a much higher 67 per cent nationally (table 2).

AWIRS data about new agreements being made in South Australia

TABLE 2: SIZE OF PAY INCREASE, ON AVERAGE, IN 12 MONTHS TO LATE 1995, SOUTH AUSTRALIA, AUSTRALIA

	SA	Aust
	(per cent with increase in each band)	
0–2 per cent increase	17	9
2.1–5.0 per cent	36	23
5.1–10.0 per cent	37	53
10.0+ per cent	10	14

Source: Unpublished AWIRS data

between early 1994 and late 1995 suggest that the majority were federal (mostly Certified Agreements, see table 3). Agreement-making through state arrangements was much more widespread in other states at that time: AWIRS survey data suggest that in South Australia only 15 per cent of employees were located in workplaces with a registered state agreement, compared to 28 per cent nationally. (Once again, this probably reflects the fact that state enterprise agreements were only available from 8 August 1994.) A higher incidence of unregistered written or verbal agreements also existed in the state.

TABLE 3: PROPORTION OF EMPLOYEES COVERED BY DIFFERENT FORMS OF AGREEMENT IN 12 MONTHS TO LATE 1995

	SA	Australia
	(per cent)	
Certified agreement under federal legislation or enterprise flexibility agreement	57	45
Other EA or enterprise award (federal)	2	5
Registered state agreement	15	28
Unregistered written agreement between management and unions	12	8
Unregistered written collective agreement between management and employees	9	7
Verbal agreements	3	5
Not sure how to classify	1	2

Source: Unpublished AWIRS data

Figure 2 illustrates a second important aspect of the growing dispersion of outcomes. It shows the ratio of female to male average weekly ordinary-time earnings of full-time employees (including juniors and excluding overtime). The figure shows that while the ratio of earnings was slightly higher for women in South Australia compared to women nationally at the opening of the decade, that advantage has been eroded over the past seven years, particularly in the period 1994–97. While there has been no overall national improvement in the ratio in the years since 1992 when enterprise bargaining became more widespread (indeed there has been a slight deterioration), the slide has been quite marked in South Australia. This probably reflects several factors including the predominance of state awards for many female employees (in retail, education, clerical work and so on), delays in the flow-on of safety net adjustments to these awards, breaches of awards and underpayment of wages, delays in the negotiation of state or federal enterprise agreements or low pay rises within them, a relatively low incidence of such agreements in feminised industries, the exclusion of some feminised occupations from some enterprise agreements,[4] and the absence of any wage increase for the many women in South Australia who are outside the award system – whether federal or state – entirely.

In both the state and federal spheres, several industries in which women are concentrated have a low incidence of bargaining, notably retail trade, accommodation, cafes and restaurants, and personal and other services, and in both spheres, wage outcomes in more feminised industries have tended to lag behind the more male-dominated pacesetters. (For comment on the federal system, see for example, Department of Industrial Relations 1996, p. 48.) In the retail sector in South Australia, for example, employees in the large retailing firms are generally covered by federal enterprise agreements while the many who work in smaller workplaces are left outside formal bargaining entirely.

THE CHANGING SHAPE OF FEDERAL/STATE COVERAGE

There has been a general shift of South Australian workers from the state to the federal system over the past several years: in 1990 (the last year in which the Australian Bureau of Statistics released data) 48 per cent of South Australians were covered by a state award or agreement (see table 4). It appears that this has fallen to around 40 per cent at present, while the share covered by the federal system has risen from 33 per cent to around 45 per cent. It is estimated that at least 15 per cent remain

FIGURE 2: RATIO OF FEMALE TO MALE AVERAGE WEEKLY ORDINARY-TIME EARNINGS OF FULL-TIME WORKERS: TREND ESTIMATE

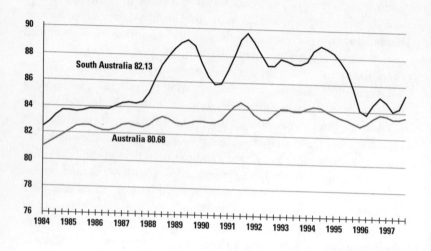

Source: ABS Cat. No. 6302.0

outside the regulated system, not covered by an award or agreement in either sphere.

The shift to federal awards and agreements has affected workers in local government and some in the retail industry, nurses, and fire-fighters. South Australian teachers have also attempted to make the move, without success so far. Employees covered by the federal system have generally benefited from more widespread enterprise bargaining, with higher pay rises than those secured by those left in the state system. Around 65 per cent of workers in the federal system are estimated to now be covered by collectively bargained enterprise agreements, and wage outcomes in these agreements were around the 4–5 per cent per annum level in 1997, compared to increases of only 1.5–2.0 per cent per annum for those left lingering on awards (Buchanan et al. 1998, p. 92). Those in the construction, manufacturing, transport and storage indus-tries are especially well covered and wage increases in some of these sectors are well in advance of either the award or South Australian state sector; for example, the construction industry won pay rises of over 10 per cent in 1997 (to be paid over two years), while manufacturing

TABLE 4: FEDERAL AND STATE COVERAGE OF WORKERS, AND EXTENT OF ENTERPRISE BARGAINING, SOUTH AUSTRALIA

	1990	1998
(per cent)		
In the federal system	33	45
In the State system	48	39
Of those in federal system, per cent with enterprise agreement	n/a	65
Of those in the federal system, per cent dependent upon award or outside regulated system	n/a	35
Of those in state system, per cent with enterprise agreement	n/a	45
Of those in the state system, per cent dependent upon award or outside regulated system	n/a	55
No. of federal enterprise agreements registered in SA in 1997		405
No. of employees covered by federal agreements registered in SA in 1997		39 171
No. of state enterprise agreements registered in 1996/7		301
No. of state employees covered by state agreements registered in 1996/7		58 936
No. of state employees covered excluding the two health and education public sector agreements		21 428

Source: 1990, ABS Cat. No. 6315.0; 1997 based on data provided by Department of Workplace Relations and Small Business and Office of the Employment Ombudsman, South Australia, 1997.

secured rises of just under that amount for the same period (Buchanan et al. 1998, p. 107). Increases were generally lower (around the 4–5 per cent mark) in most other federal sector agreements.

Changes in federal legislation which have encouraged non-union bargaining are now beginning to have some effect, with wage increases in such agreements (which include Australian Workplace Agreements and a growing number of non-union collective agreements) of at least one per cent below those in unionised workplaces. More significantly, these agreements are concentrated in workplaces that are strongly casualised, and contain 'radical changes to working time rights and obligations'; for example, standard hours longer than 38 per week were provided for in 24 per cent of the non-union agreements, compared to 7 per cent of union agreements (Buchanan et al.1998, pp. 102–3).

In summary, in 1997 the 45 per cent of South Australians in the federal system are more likely than those the state system to have received the benefit of a union-negotiated, enterprise-bargained pay rise, which has been higher than the minimal increases in most awards. However, a good one-third of federal system employees remain dependent upon award increases. A small but growing number of workers in this sector are subject to non-union individual or collective agreements which significantly undermine key rights, especially in relation to hours and time, with much lower pay rises (in some cases none at all), through Australian workplace agreements or unregistered agreements.

ENTERPRISE AGREEMENTS UNDER THE STATE SYSTEM

Apart from the scope established for non-union enterprise agreements, the 1994 *Industrial and Employee Relations Act* established the Employee Ombudsman to assist employees bargaining a workplace agreement without the assistance of a union.[5] This served as a model for the federal Employment Advocate, established under the *Workplace Relations Act* 1996 – although his powers are different. The South Australian Employee Ombudsman functions more as an advocate for workers negotiating non-union enterprise agreements, ensuring processes that are free of coercion. The Employee Ombudsman does not formally approve agreements (unlike the federal Employment Advocate); instead, this important capacity remains with the Commission, which must apply the 'no disadvantage' test, with the Employee Ombudsman's assistance where it is relevant or proffered. As we shall see, these aspects of the state system have played an important role in the nature of bargaining that has occurred in the state.

The main workers left in the state jurisdiction are in the state public sector, clerical work (especially in small-to-medium retail, metals and credit union workplaces), hotels, motels and clubs, winemaking, caretaking and cleaning, security, baking, ambulances, cafes and restaurants, child care and teaching. Employees at BHP Whyalla, BHAS in Port Pirie, along with commercial travellers, ancillary professional and general staff in the health sector, approximately one-third of storepersons and packers, and a small number in the state metals and vehicle manufacturing industries, also remain largely within the state system.

State-level enterprise bargaining since 1994 has been very uneven by sector, both in terms of outcomes and the extent of actual bargaining. Fifty-five per cent of those who remain in the state system have not been part of enterprise bargaining and are reliant upon the minimal 1–2 per cent award safety net adjustments, or are outside the regulated sector entirely. By March 1998, 116 500 state sector employees were covered by a state enterprise agreement. Increases for those who remain dependent upon state awards have sometimes been slow to arrive. Some employees have missed out entirely on any pay increases where there is no relevant award, their award has not been varied, or their particular employer has been in breach of it. Many such workers are employed within small businesses and in certain industries where unionism is lower, such as hospitality and personal services. Women and part-time or casual workers are disproportionately represented amongst these employees (Department of Industrial Relations 1997, p. 51).

A sizeable number of workers in the state system are covered by two major agreements (one in health, the other in education) which comprised 64 per cent of all new employees covered by enterprise agreements in 1996/7. Nonetheless, the proportion of workers covered by state agreements has grown significantly since the enterprise agreement provisions were introduced in 1994. Table 5 shows that in 1996/97, 301 agreements were registered, compared to 150 in 1996/96 and 79 in 1994/95 (Employee Ombudsman 1997).[6]

TABLE 5: STATE ENTERPRISE AGREEMENTS, 1994/95–1996/97, SOUTH AUSTRALIA

	1994/95	1995/96	1996/97
No. of state enterprise agreements registered	79	150	301
Per cent of agreements with unions as a party	66	55	43
Per cent of agreements with Employee Ombudsman involved	51	52	33
No. of employees covered by state agreements	10 451	23 489	58 936
Per cent of employees covered by agreements with unions as party	87	82	97
Per cent of employees covered by agreements with Employee Ombudsman involved	61	65	85

Source: Employee Ombudsman 1997

As in the federal system, the proportion of employees covered by union-negotiated agreements remains high: 97 per cent in 1996/97 (although a larger number of non-union agreements covering small numbers of employees has been negotiated in each year since 1994/95). This high result largely reflects the two very large public sector agreements in health and education. Unions are also generally part of bargaining in manufacturing, minerals extraction and building services.

The industry coverage of agreements in the state system is quite uneven, reflecting the activities of some industry bodies (particularly amongst veterinary surgeons, bowling clubs and private schools) and the traditional location of certain industries in the state system (table 6). Small business made up a growing proportion of enterprise agreements in the state in 1996/97, reflecting the role of industry associations. In 1996/97, 60 agreements were approved in independent schools, 57 in social/sporting and recreation, and 44 in veterinary clinics. Each of these three 'sets' of agreements effectively amounts to a form of employer-led pattern of bargaining where the employer association has developed standard agreements which were endorsed at the enterprise level before being approved in batches.[7] These agreements provide an interesting example of the employer acting collectively while, given the low level of unionisation in these sectors and the physical isolation of individual employees, workers are effectively denied the capacity to act collectively. Together, these agreements amount to over half the number approved in 1996/7, but they cover only a small proportion of total employees. Thirty per cent of all agreements approved in the year covered one or two workers: clearly the existing South Australian system offers the capacity, at least amongst small employers, for bargaining that is essentially individual.

Union involvement in these bargaining processes is quite limited, with union participation much greater in larger enterprises. The Employee Ombudsman's office is much more active in relation to smaller enterprises and sees that its activity here is likely to grow:

Increasingly the intervention role played by this Office will become restricted to small enterprises without access to industrial relations expertise whether from unions or employer associations.
                                          Employee Ombudsman 1997, p. 24

Clearly, the role of an active, attentive and interventionist Industrial Relations Commission and Employee Ombudsman are of particular importance to those working in small businesses.

TABLE 6: NUMBER OF APPROVED ENTERPRISE AGREEMENTS
BY INDUSTRY

	1995/96	1996/97
State government	30	14
Food processing	26	18
Manufacturing	24	7
Independent schools	18	60
Hospitality/catering	7	19
Retail/wholesale	7	21
Social/sporting/recreation	5	57
Minerals extraction	0	12
Veterinary clinics	0	44
Other	26	44

Source: Employee Ombudsman 1997, p. 28

In terms of wage outcomes,[8] the provisions in state agreements are lower on average than those in the federal system: where there is union involvement, increases in 1996/7 range between 4–6 per cent per year. In non-union agreements the increases are lower by 1–2 per cent and in some cases are non-existent, with all the emphasis upon greater managerial prerogative in relation to hours and penalty rates. In manufacturing, only two non-union enterprise agreements match the union average of 4.2 per cent, while in the food and wine industry, union agreements have increases of 5 per cent and non-union agreements had only 3.8 per cent. In education, the result is even more marked with union agreements resulting in 6 per cent rises, compared to 3 per cent in non-union workplaces. In the private services sectors, hospitality and catering, service and education, union agreements deliver 5.3 per cent while non-union deals result in increases of 3–3.5 per cent. Agreements in restaurants and catering generally have no union involvement and had the lowest or most ambiguous pay rises. In the retail sector, rises of 5 per cent per year are common in union agreements while the rise implicit in non-union agreements is difficult to discern, linked to future negotiation or productivity increases or delivers only the safety net rise. In contrast, in union agreements, the rises are clearly defined.

Of course, as in the federal system, wage increases in most enterprise agreements cannot be assessed without reference to the total bargaining outcome. It seems from an examination of bargaining outcomes, and discussion with a number of officials involved, that many small businesses have won composite wage rates through their agreements where an all-up pay rate is agreed which averages out penalties and overtime into an average pay rate or an annualised salary. This is especially common in non-union agreements (Buchanan et al. 1998). Medium-to-larger firms have tended to look to changes in the span of hours, to increases in the number of ordinary hours worked before overtime rates apply and to increased flexibility in the way those hours are worked. In many places enterprise agreement pay rises have effectively replaced pre-existing over-award payments.

Changed hours of work are a common feature of bargaining, particularly in non-union agreements in sectors which have a production focus like manufacturing and food. The main changes are to ordinary hours worked, increasing flexibility of hours worked outside the ordinary span, or working a seven-day week roster, and the averaging of hours. Union agreements also reflect the dominance of hours issues, although more than half maintain traditional hours of work arrangements. There is a noticeable focus on increased ordinary hours worked per day, presumably to reduce overtime payments.

Consultation and dispute avoidance procedures are the most common provisions in state agreements after wages, and once again a difference between union and non-union agreements is very apparent. Most union agreements have strong consultation and dispute avoidance procedures that create the possibility of procedural fairness and some transparency of process. In contrast, well-developed procedures are almost non-existent in non-union agreements. Instead, they focus upon managerial authority and individual disciplinary procedures.

Carers' leave for family responsibilities is widespread in all types of agreements and many agreements go beyond the legislative requirements. Commitments to continuous improvement, best practice and key performance indicators are evident in union agreements in the production industries. Waste and energy minimisation, quality control and output are found in areas like food and manufacturing and a number of union agreements note specific changes, indicators and implementation and monitoring arrangements (for example, agreements at Taylors Wines, Hills Industries, and R.M. Williams). Specific references to improving productivity and its measurement through key indicators, along with employer commitment to training and career path development, are much more widespread in union agreements in both the public and private sphere, than in non-union agreements.

Penalty rates are specifically mentioned in 20 of the 31 union and 13 of the 35 non-union agreements analysed. In the union agreements, penalties in relation to overtime and shifts are generally in accordance with traditional rates (although as noted above, changes in the span of ordinary hours are affecting their definition). Variation is much more widespread amongst the non-union agreements, however, where in some workplaces overtime is paid at the manager's discretion, or is fixed at time and a half for all overtime situations. In others, shift penalties are fixed at $1.50 per hour, for example, or an extra $2 and $4 per hour on Saturday and Sunday respectively. It appears that changes to hours of work and penalty arrangements create a major incentive for employers to negotiate agreements, allowing significant movement away from traditional conditions contained in the parent award, particularly where no union is present. It should also be noted that some agreements, particularly in the non-union sector, had no relevant award against which they could be measured for the purposes of applying a safety net test.

In summary, a wide range of wages and conditions outcomes is emerging from enterprise bargaining in the state. The presence of a union – particularly an active union with workplace representatives – is a major factor in the incidence and outcomes of bargaining, both at state and federal levels (AWIRS 1997; Buchanan et al. 1998; ACTU 1998), suggesting that the dispersion of wages between unionised and un-unionised workplaces is set to increase. Agreements which provide increases on a par with federal or community standards, preserve compensation for unsocial hours, involve some consultation with employees, minimise disputes, maximise productive efficiency, improve training and reduce injury, are found almost exclusively in union-negotiated agreements. An example is provided by the Coca-Cola agreement where increases have averaged around 5 per cent per year for the past four years, detailed consultation and dispute avoidance procedures are in place, and strong commitments to teamwork, flexibility, and continuous improvement are made. Employment conditions are clear and training and skill development are a priority.

In contrast, non-union agreements are focused upon cost-cutting (just as the AWIRS results above suggest in 1995), with little attention paid to productivity or procedural fairness. These are especially concentrated in small business, with much more vagueness and employer scope in terms of the organisation of pay, hours and work. The benefits for employees in this slice of agreement-making workplaces are questionable: they are sliding behind community standards in terms of pay, hours and employee consultation and offer little beyond and, in some cases on specific issues, considerably less than relevant awards. Given that only 3 per cent of employees in the state system were covered by non-union state agreements in 1996/7, their direct effect is small. However, as has been noted in the federal system, inferior agreements provide some employers with a new bargaining tactic with which to at least threaten those involved in union-led negotiations (Buchanan et al. 1998, p. 101).

Analysis of these agreements exposes the reality of state-level industrial regulatory change: as a result of non-union, non-collective workplace agreements, the living standards and working lives of vulnerable South Australians are at risk. A fall in real living standards is being experienced by some of the weakest employees in the system: those working alone or in small business, those without the protection of a union, and many women, casual, part-time and young employees.

THE EMPLOYEE OMBUDSMAN

In a series of unusually frank annual reports, Gary Collis, the Employee Ombudsman (appointed by the Liberal government) has openly expressed his views of the state system and the failings of some individuals who make their way within it. His public statements have not endeared him to conservatives or some employers: in his first annual report he criticised an emphasis upon cost-cutting and the failure of agreements to imaginatively address productivity challenges (Employee Ombudsman 1995). The Ombudsman is blunt about the absence of positive change in many South Australian workplaces:

[T]here are still many employers, including those in the Public Sector who are persisting with traditional management practices involving harassment, victimisation, non-payment or underpayment of entitlements, and so on. Such managers seem to be more concerned with maintaining and enforcing their traditional power over employees than in encouraging and rewarding employee contribution to the growth of their enterprises. **Employee Ombudsman 1997, p. 9**

In 1996/97 he forthrightly opposes individual contracts because of their negative effects upon workplaces:

If business 'reforms' result in a reduction in wages, job security or other conditions of employment then any gains achieved through increased flexibility or reduced costs will be cancelled by the consequences of demoralised, dissatisfied or insecure staff. Unfortunately this point appears to have been overlooked by those who advocate individual employment contracts.

Employee Ombudsman 1997, p. 8

He goes on to argue that 'there are few, if any, benefits to be obtained, for both employers and employees, from changing legislation that is already working well', particularly, as he points out, when there is so little public clamour in the state for further reform. He continues his criticism of the use of expensive consultants and legal advisers who sometimes prolong processes and add unnecessary costs, and argues strongly for increased education especially for smaller employers (where so much of his office's effort is concentrated) 'in the actual processes of obtaining an agreement in a cost effective manner' (1997, p. 8).

Adopting his Ombudsman's role with some vigour, he has continued to advise employees on their rights and obligations under awards and agreements, investigate coercion in negotiation, scrutinise agreements and intervene in their registration where necessary, and to represent employees who lack other representation. In 1996/97 the office intervened extensively in only about 7 per cent of cases, although a more minor advisory or facilitative role was adopted in relation to one-third of all agreements (covering 85 per cent of all employees), well down from the 50 per cent in which his office was involved in the previous two years.

The strong positive relationship between the state Industrial Relations Commission and the Ombudsman's office, the careful scrutiny applied to all new agreements by the Commission and the willingness of both the Commission and the Office of the Employee Ombudsman to intervene to protect employees at risk of a serious diminution of conditions mean that the Employee Ombudsman makes a legitimate claim when he notes that the use of agreements to exploit workers has been minimised (Employee Ombudsman 1997, p. 8). Certainly an effective 'no disadvantage' test, in combination with an alert Ombudsman, means that many poor quality or exploitative agreements have been prevented. This experience illustrates the importance of the interpretative scope and stance adopted by an independent appointee like the Ombudsman[9] and an independent Commission.

Most important, however, is the standard maintained in the award safety net and the enterprise agreements against which it is tested. Low safety net adjustments, a general failure to maintain and improve conditions in awards, the absence of relevant awards in many existing and emergent areas of employment, or the stripping-back of common rule awards at state level (mirroring the federal process), promise a deterioration in the safety net. Over time, this might mean that even very poor enterprise agreements will be better than the diminishing safety net standard, and it is into this gap that the future of fair remuneration in the state might drop for many employees.

FUTURE DIRECTIONS

Whether the South Australian Liberal government achieves a further round of legislative reforms, and individualises bargaining and strips back awards, is dependent upon parliamentary political outcomes, and perhaps especially upon the foothold and stance of the emergent One Nation party and independent members of parliament. However, the case for a further round of conservative reform is not established. It is perhaps not surprising therefore, that there are relatively few public calls in the state from employers for radical industrial reform. The realities of high unemployment, a declining industrial base and other forms of economic strain in a small state beset by economic challenge and decline, overshadow the gains that might be expected by further industrial relations changes. In any case, many employers have considerable existing scope to increase the flexibility of local arrangements in their workplaces; relatively few have tested the current system to its limits. For example, there has been virtually no use made by employers of the Enterprise Flexibility provisions written into all state common rule awards in the mid-1990s, suggesting that employers have much scope available to them for local change, although few find the need to pursue it. Such scope undermines any calls for further deregulation.

From the employees' perspective, while the Industrial Relations Commission and the Employee Ombudsman have prevented many possibilities for exploitation, there is evidence of declining standards in some areas. The award system remains the main road to any form of pay increase for many South Australian employees in either the federal or state system. Others are effectively outside the regulated sector, and especially vulnerable. The prospect of widening gaps as the level of protection afforded by the award system falls into decline while others move ahead by bargaining collectively with the help of their unions, must be a real source of concern in this context. We are witnessing a widening disparity in earnings of South Australians relative to the national average, a deterioration in women's earnings relative to men's, a growing gap between unionised and non-unionised workers, and between those employed in larger firms at the big end of town, compared to those in small business.

A reforming Labor government would also face challenges not met within its current policy. How are the working conditions of the growing population of casual workers to be improved and protected? Would a Labor government undertake the kind of pay equity inquiry that the New South Wales government is currently attempting in the face of stalled progress on equal pay? Unless such challenges are met, South Australia faces the prospect of becoming the industrial poor cousin of Australia: a state of low pay, widening inequities, deteriorating working conditions, with an increasingly insecure workforce. This is a long way from what is possible, what has been achieved in the past, and what innovative South Australian policies and action could ensure for the future.

REFERENCES

ACTU (Australian Council of Trade Unions)1998, *Not What We Bargained For, ACTU Report on Enterprise Bargaining in 1997*, ACTU, Melbourne.

Australian Bureau of Statistics (ABS), *Award Coverage Australia*, Cat. no. 5315.0, various years.

—— *Average Weekly Earnings*, States and Australia, Cat. no. 6302.0, various years.

Buchanan, John, Woodman, Murray, O'Keeffe, Shannon & Orsovska, Betty 1998, 'Wages policy and wage determination in 1997', *Journal of Industrial Relations*, vol. 40, no. 1, March, pp. 88–118.

Department of Industrial Affairs 1997, 'Major changes to SA workplace relations laws', Department of Industrial Affairs, Workplace Relations Policy Division, Adelaide.

Department of Industrial Relations 1997, *Enterprise Bargaining in Australia, Annual Report*, Department of Industrial Relations, Canberra.

Employee Ombudsman 1996, *Annual Report 1995/96*, Office of the Employee Ombudsman, Adelaide.

—— 1997, *Annual Report 1996/97*, Office of the Employee Ombudsman, Adelaide.

Industrial Relations Commission of SA 1997, *Third Annual report 1996/97*, Adelaide.

Macintyre, Stuart & Mitchell, Richard 1989, *Foundations of Arbitration: The Origins and Effects of State Compulsory Arbitration 1890–1914*, Oxford University Press, Melbourne.

Mitchell, Richard 1989, 'State systems of conciliation and arbitration: The legal origins of the Australasian model', in *Foundations of Arbitration: The Origins and Effects of State Compulsory Arbitration 1890–1914*, eds Stuart Macintyre & Richard Mitchell, Oxford University Press, Melbourne, pp. 74–103.

Morehead, Alison, Steele, M., Alexander, M., Stephen, K., & Duffin, L. 1997, *Changes at Work: The 1995 Australian Workplace Industrial Relations Survey*, Addison-Wesley Longman, Melbourne.

Owens, Rosemary 1995, 'Legislating for change: The Industrial and Employee Relations Act 1994 (SA)', *Australian Journal of Labour Law*, vol. 8, pp.137–54.

South Australian Labor Party 1997 'A fair go for South Australian workers,' Election statement, Australian Labor Party, Adelaide.

Stewart, Andrew 1998, 'South Australia' in *Australasian Labour Law Reforms*.

NOTES

1   The authors would like to thank the Department of Workplace Relations and Small Business for their assistance in making available the Australian Workplace Industrial Relations Survey and unpublished data arising from it. They would also like to thank Gary Collis and officers of both the Office of the Employee Ombudsman and the Industrial Relations Commission of South Australia for their assistance, along with the Australian Research Council and the Reshaping Australian Institutions Project which supported the research, Australian National University. The usual disclaimer applies.

2   Industrial agreements made prior to the 1994 Act were to be 'converted' into Enterprise Agreements by the parties to them, or if they were unable to do so by 31 December 1996, they would have no further force or effect.

3   AWIRS 1995 is the second largest workplace survey conducted by the federal government to inform analysis of workplace relations. AWIRS consists of several structured questionnaires administered by a range of methods to union delegates, managers and employees at a representative range of Australian workplaces, stratified by location, size and industry.

All industries were included with the exceptions of agriculture, forestry, fishing and defence. While some aspects of the study extend to workplaces with 519 employees, the survey of individual employees did not, and so individual wages data, for example, is available only for employees in workplaces with more than 20 employees. Discussion of AWIRS data throughout this chapter is based on workplaces with at least 20 employees. For details of how the survey was conducted see Morehead et al. (1997).

4   Such discriminatory sex-segmented outcomes are not the result of directly discriminatory agreements (which are illegal), but effectively result from the partial reach of particular agreements and overall outcomes of bargaining.

5   The act also contained other important elements. In terms of the powers and place of unionism, the act prevented compulsory unionism, limited union officials' access to workplaces and reduced unions to bargaining agents rather than principal parties with respect to enterprise agreements. To act as such agents, unions must have at least one member in the affected workplace who confers bargaining authority upon it. The act also allows the establishment of registered enterprise unions (even where an appropriate union already exists) and permits such an association to represent workers 'to the exclusion of any other association, if two-thirds of the group agree'. Any minority who might want to be represented differently hardly has freedom of association (Stewart 1998, p. 147).

6   It seems that the pace of growth has slackened considerably, however, with nearly two-thirds of all agreements for 1996/97 lodged in the first half of that financial year and the rate of increase in people covered slowing from almost 5000 per month on average in 1996/97, to less than 3000 in the opening eight months of 1997/98. The Employee Ombudsman attributes this slowing to uncertainty in legislative arrangements as the state government foreshadowed attempts to introduce individual contracts.

7   This is not to say that unions in some cases where they have a presence have not played a role in attempting to influence bargaining. For example in some private sector education agreements the relevant union was actively involved.

8   In the absence of a comprehensive data base of provisions in South Australian enterprise agreements we have analysed a selection of 66 agreements, drawn from amongst seven industry sectors where bargaining has been concentrated. A range of union (31 in total) and non-union agreements (35) were included, comprising the main public sector agreements, food processing, manufacturing, retail/wholesale, hospitality, services and 'other' industries.

9   Anecdotally, union officials, at least, report quite a different approach arising from their early dealings with the federal Employment Advocate and his state offices, where enthusiasm for getting Australian Workplace Agreements registered has, they report, overshadowed scrutiny with respect to the weaker 'no disadvantage' test they are required to apply.

CHAPTER 15

METROPOLITAN PLANNING FOR ADELAIDE

STEVE HAMNETT AND MICHAEL LENNON

INTRODUCTION: THE SYSTEM IGNORED[1]

In 1992 the South Australian Planning Review[2] proposed a new planning system for the state. Its major components included a metropolitan planning strategy, a new Development Act and proposals for a 'new style of planning', in which strategic planning played a key role. Of central importance was a new set of arrangements within government to ensure that the actions and budgets of individual government agencies were directed towards the agreed purposes of metropolitan development. This was intended to go beyond the coordination of infrastructure planning and the provision of land for new housing which occurred under the established Metropolitan Development Program and to encompass a whole-of-government approach which would integrate economic, social and environmental priorities by placing strategic planning at the heart of government decision-making.

A great deal has changed in six years. The Brown/Olsen governments have presided over a litany of offences against orderly planning in South Australia. A sense of strategy and purpose has disappeared, to be replaced by a series of naive, uncoordinated and contradictory initiatives and decisions by the government which have undermined confidence in the planning system. Ironically, these decisions have often been justified on the grounds of providing certainty to investors and to the community, but such claims seldom stand up to scrutiny. A few illustrative examples follow.

- In 1994, the then Premier, Dean Brown, issued a statement jointly with the general manager of Woolworths announcing the development of a new Woolworths' supermarket at Paralowie. Mr Brown was also reported as saying that Woolworths would be announcing other supermarket proposals for South Australia within the next year.[3] And so they did. Woolworths were revealed as the major tenants intended for a neighbourhood shopping centre proposed on Burbridge Road at Hilton. Variants of this proposal went to the Development Assessment Commission on two occasions in 1994 and 1995 and were turned down on each occasion, principally because the proposal was thought to be too large and inconsistent with the approved Development Plan and the government's adopted 'Centres Policy'[4]. The Development Assessment Commission's second rejection of the Hilton shopping centre proposal came in November 1995. The following month[5] a public meeting to discuss the proposed shopping centre was shown a letter written by the Premier in which Mr Brown expressed his sympathy with those who were frustrated by having such a 'worthwhile development and facility' rejected.

The membership of the Development Assessment Commission changed substantially at the beginning of 1996 as the government sought 'to create an administration that is more supportive of development'. The Hilton proposal was resubmitted to this reconstituted Development Assessment Commission and approved. However, in May 1996, the Supreme Court quashed the approval on the grounds that the proposal was inconsistent with the authorised development plan for the area and represented 'overdevelopment' of the site. The proposal was resubmitted and approved on two more occasions by the Development Assessment Commission and each time the Supreme Court quashed the approval on appeal. In April 1997 the relevant section of the development plan – the 'City of West Torrens Neighbourhood Centre (Hilton) Zone' – was amended with the specific purpose of permitting the proposed shopping centre to go ahead and the development was cleared to proceed. It is hard to see how certainty in planning policy is secured by the government facilitating, in this way, development which is repeatedly found to be contrary to its own approved policies.

- Woolworths was also the developer of a large distribution centre on Main North Road at Gepps Cross on land previously intended to form part of a major public sports complex. Woolworths sought this site as an alternative to land which was required by the government as part of the proposed Multifunction Polis project. There was no shortage of alternative sites available in the private market in the north-western suburbs of Adelaide. But the development plan was changed to accommodate this non-conforming proposal and it proceeded quickly. Woolworths was also involved in controversial development proposals at various times at Gawler and Whyalla. It is scarcely surprising in the circumstances that some commentators concluded that the government was in favour of these developments proceeding 'regardless of process or planning requirements'.

- Local traders became concerned in the latter part of 1996 about a proposed 'bulky goods' retail centre at Walkley Heights intending to sell furniture, carpets and similar items. The traders' concerns were shared by the Mayor of Salisbury, whose council had planned a housing development on adjacent land. There were broader concerns, also, that the government, in selling the land to a Victorian company, had apparently given a guarantee that the land would be rezoned from its existing residential zoning to permit a bulky goods centre to be developed. The land had been owned by the Urban Land Trust before its sale and the increase in value which followed its re-zoning would have been realised by the purchaser, not by the community.

- The Southern Expressway is probably the most outrageous use of large public capital funds in recent times. One hundred and twenty million dollars have been committed with little evidence of traffic or economic benefit deriving from the expenditure. A reduction of travel time for commuters of about seven minutes is likely to be achieved by this project which may well further erode the economic base of the southern suburbs, rather than improving it, since it will facilitate the distribution of goods from existing industrial areas, particularly in the north-western and inner-western suburbs. Ironically, the first major development which followed the committal of these funds was the expansion of the Marion Regional Centre, well located close to the northern end of the expressway, and a threat to the value of the government's own asset, the Noarlunga Regional Centre.

There are also well-grounded concerns that the expressway will increase pressure for urban development of the Southern Vales. (The expressway figures prominently in the advertisements of local real estate firms.) As Peter Ward wrote in the *Adelaide Review* in 1994: 'You don't really have to have a degree in town planning to see ... the inevitable effect of the [expressway] ... will be relentless suburban pressure on the Willunga Basin'.

Recently, Dean Brown, a strong supporter of the building of the expressway during his period as Premier, issued a press release in his current capacity as Housing Minister, expressing his deep concern at Adelaide's continuing outward sprawl: 'The great challenge is to stop the spread and sprawl of Australian cities and look at ways of achieving greater density and a mix of density that works for people; to stop expanding at the fringe and look at the renewal of inner suburban areas – already well-served by transport, education, community services, facilities and near to work'.[7] Notwithstanding the government's belated acknowledgement of the problems of fringe expansion, the second stage of the Southern Expressway was announced in the May 1998 state budget.

Rather than creating certainty in the planning process, these examples suggest a willingness on the part of the government to subvert the process for its own partisan reasons, undermining the confidence and livelihoods of those who had taken the government's approved plans and policies at face value and had invested accordingly.

The present government has regularly blamed the planning system for inhibiting new investment in the state. In fact, there is little evidence of delay in the planning system, except in cases such as the Hilton example quoted above, where proposals, which can be argued to be in conflict with the government's own adopted policies, are approved and then subjected to judicial review. Members of the Development Assessment Commission who were replaced at the beginning of 1996 suggested that the state government tended to blame 'the system' to cover its own lack of vision and policies. Nevertheless, the desire to speed up development was the principal justification used to support changes to the *Development Act* in 1996. These changes included the protection of certain classes of government decision from the possibility of judicial review and a new system for evaluating major projects under which a Major Developments Panel would determine whether an environmental impact statement would be required in assessing a project, or whether a less onerous level of assessment would suffice.[8]

The first significant test of this system was its application to the 'Capital City' project, a proposal for a $300 million hotel and commercial complex in Rundle Mall, topped by an observation tower, and including, amongst its exciting facilities, a 'sensorium designed to appeal to and stimulate all the senses' on the site of the John Martins department store which was to cease trading. This major development – it would have been the tallest building in the city – was enthusiastically endorsed by Premier Olsen and was approved without requiring a full environmental impact statement. Championing the 'Capital City' project in February 1997, Olsen announced that 'the knockers can move to one side – this project will happen for South Australia'.[9]

The Capital City project soon became the centrepiece of a plan for the 'Torrens Domain', a grouping of 33 supposed development projects around the River Torrens and North Terrace. In May 1997 the Multifunction Polis Development Corporation (MFPDC) was given the responsibility for coordinating these projects (much to the surprise of some of its senior staff). The date of this announcement, 22 May 1997, was to be 'the day that the arguing and negativity stops and the city's positive future begins', according to the Premier.[10] In August of the same year, in an announcement which apparently came as a surprise to several Cabinet members, the MFPDC was abolished.[11] The following month it became clear that the Capital City project was unlikely to proceed and that some of the components announced earlier – a five-star hotel, in particular – had been based largely on wishful thinking. A substantially scaled-down development – a department store – was announced in November and was greeted enthusiastically by the Premier as providing 'a degree of certainty'.[12]

Cases like the Hilton Shopping Centre and the Walkley Heights land sale described above, the government's attitude to the Development Assessment Commission and the tendency on the part of successive planning ministers[13] to be critical of their own planning system, seem to indicate a lack of understanding of the relationship which should normally exist between a government, statutory authorities and processes designed to implement its plans and policies. Rather, it appears that statutory authorities have come under some pressure in recent years to approve projects favoured by government interests. The government's expressed intent is 'to provide greater certainty and better outcomes for proponents and the community at large'. To date it would be hard to say that this has been accomplished. A paper published in late 1997 by the former Chair of the Development Assessment Commission and by a Commissioner of the Environment, Resources and Development Court argued that there was evidence, in South Australia, of 'an obsession with development at all costs; a short-term "cargo cult" which, more often than not results in urban products of doubtful quality'. They further argued that the 'Major Developments' amendments to the

Development Act of 1996 had effectively created two development assessment regimes – 'one for the rich and influential and one for the average citizen' and that this went 'against the grain of long-held community ideals of economic as well as social fair play' (Bunker & Hutchings 1997, p.56).

DOES THE SYSTEM MATTER?

It may be worth reviewing some of the commonly accepted reasons for having a government role in the planning and management of urban development.

The first reason relates to the pursuit of efficiency in the management of public funds in the land development process. A planned pattern of sequential land development allows for the provision of infrastructure and community services in a timely and cost-efficient way. In addition, a government which intervenes in the land market through a land supply agency, such as the South Australian Urban Land Trust, has the potential to reduce the public costs of development to some extent by capturing part of the unearned increment in land values which follows from the conversion of land for urban development purposes. The healthy balance sheet of the Urban Land Trust over many years provides testimony to the success of this approach. Bramley (1997), in a major review of state involvement in Australia in the provision of land for housing, noted recently that bodies like the Urban Land Trust are increasingly relevant to urban redevelopment processes and 'particularly well-adapted to the land ownership, assembly and repartitioning/titling functions'. Also '... they have planning skills (including community planning and consultation expertise) and a generally good reputation with local authorities and other public bodies. This means that the level of trust and cooperation elicited from other public bodies and the community may be greater than with privately led schemes ... From the viewpoint of state governments the LSAs [land supply agencies] have one general advantage which may be perceived by ministers, even those with a general ideological predisposition to withdraw the state from involvement in urban development. Unlike the permanent state bureaucracies, they represent a "doing" arm of the state ... Well-led and effective LSAs offer them a means to make things happen'.[14]

Secondly, there are obvious benefits from taking an integrated view of economic, social and environmental issues. The maintenance and improvement of environmental standards depends upon the incorporation of environmental considerations at the earliest stages of strategic planning. For example, the preservation of Adelaide's water catchment is dependent upon urban growth being minimised across the central hills. Provision for the storage and treatment of waste needs to be made in planned facilities well away from residential areas. The reduction of both transport costs and greenhouse gases may best be achieved by policies which seek to bring together transport-generating activities – jobs, shops, community facilities – in planned centres appropriately sited across the metropolitan area. And so on.

Third, the creation of a climate of investor confidence and certainty can only be secured where the set of policies and rules which influences land values is understood and implemented consistently over a significant period of time, and particularly through cycles of property development. Arbitrary departures from approved plans and policies, of the sorts described earlier, may benefit the government's favoured partners or cronies of the day, but for the majority of investors and financial institutions such aberrations make it impossible to value realistically an existing asset, or to assess the risk involved in a new investment. This is a problem which has recently been created for most owners of metropolitan retail space in the light of the substantial expansion of retail centres by the Westfield group in an aggressive campaign to increase market share at a time when population is almost static and growth in household numbers slow. Retailing in the metropolitan area is underpinned by planning policies which seek to establish a hierarchy of shopping centres of various sizes, ranging from the Adelaide city centre at the top, to small neighbourhood and local centres at the bottom. Three successive state ministers for planning have had the responsibility for reviewing these policies but, at the time of the writing, no new 'Centres Policy' has been adopted. There are those who would question the value of such retail hierarchy, but the fact remains that the government's policy has been based on such hierarchy for many years, and random or inconsistent approvals which undermine it, undermine confidence. Lingering uncertainty about the future deregulation of retail trading hours compounds the problem.

So the system is important. It is in the interests of government, of investors and of local communities to support a system which guides the development process in an easily understood way, which provides consistent rules for all parties, which respects the role of statutory bodies charged with the interpretation and implementation of policy and which acknowledges the fundamental role of the courts in enforcement and judicial review.

THE IMPERATIVES FOR URBAN POLICY PLANNING AND MANAGEMENT

So what needs to change? The first requirement is the restoration of confidence and certainty in the planning system. Reasserting its important role in balancing public and private, long-term and short-term, economic, social and environmental interests may achieve this aim. There are however, a number of more specific actions important for the planning of metropolitan Adelaide in the coming years. Although decisions to privatise infrastructure provision and management and to reduce government control over related services have weakened the levers traditionally available to the public sector for development purposes, some major priorities can be identified.

In recent years, commencing with the Planning Review of 1990–92, considerable progress has been made in devising and articulating a coherent strategy for guiding urban development and redevelopment within and around metropolitan Adelaide. Areas identified in the 1980s for future housing, such as the Southern Vales, and the Sandy Creek and Roseworthy areas are no longer under the threat of imminent urban development. There are good reasons for the planned redevelopment and 'regeneration' of large parts of the inner and middle suburbs and work is proceeding with this.[15]

A positive development has been the establishment of Catchment Management Boards which now provide the scope for an integrated approach to water management and for overcoming the problems caused for many years by the absence of a drainage authority for the metropolitan plains. After a long hiatus, programs for the regeneration of the Adelaide city centre also appear at last to be progressing.

A new version of the Metropolitan Planning Strategy has also been developed, although there is some serious doubt about the extent to which the state government supports such a strategy. It is important that the government understands the potential offered by the planning system through its capacity to send clear signals to communities and to investors about its intentions for the future development of the city. While the first of the recent series of planning strategies contained proposals for major urban projects, now largely implemented (such as the Glenelg redevelopment, the Northern Adelaide Plains Stormwater

Management system, the upgrade of the Elizabeth and Noarlunga centres, the redevelopment proposals for old public housing areas, the Mile End redevelopment, the East End redevelopment, catchment management improvements and so on), the latest planning strategy contains fewer new proposals of this sort. The next generation of strategic development projects needs to be identified and championed. The principal new project canvassed in the draft of the latest planning strategy was the failed Capital City Project.[16]

A major vacuum exists in the present government's organisational arrangements. The scrapping of the Urban Land Trust and the absorption of the Urban Projects Authority by the MFPDC, followed by the dismantling of MFPDC, have left the state with no single effective body to deliver complex and strategic urban projects. Golden Grove, the East End redevelopment and other major projects were successful because of the existence of a body able to draw together public and private interests in a commercial and professional way over the long life of such projects. The present division of these functions, principally between a Land Management Corporation and a Project Delivery 'Task Force', is confusing and seems to relate more to political than to functional priorities. A new corporation is required to coordinate responsibility for assembling and holding land, entering into development agreements and joint ventures and balancing strategic, community and commercial objectives. Such a body should also be able to act on behalf of different ministers and government authorities in the land development market, thereby avoiding the appearance of competing government entities, with the consequential confusion of roles. The government's capacity to achieve 'urban regeneration' would be greatly enhanced by the existence of such an organisation.

The management of the Adelaide hinterland as a productive resource, as an environmental resource and as a recreational and tourism asset for the state is a major priority. From the perimeter of metropolitan Adelaide through to Clare in the north, Mt Barker in the east and Goolwa–Victor Harbor in the south, some of the state's most productive land, previously used largely for grazing and for dairy production, is progressively being transformed for major export uses, including viticulture, horticulture and other forms of niche market primary production. Through careful attention to land management practices, the control of subdivisions, and the firm retention of township boundaries, an opportunity to lift the agricultural production and export earnings of the state currently exists. The coincidence of reduced immigration, low population growth and declining household size means that a significant slowing of outward metropolitan expansion is now evident. This situation should allow a breathing space for a more detailed and subtle focus on the opportunities of the hinterland. There are complex issues to balance – the desire to encourage tourism facilities in the Hills, for example, without compromising environmental or water quality imperatives. Planning policies 'which send very clear signals and guidelines to the community as to the patterns, locations and limits of investment and development in the fringe that are desired and in the public interest' need to be developed (Bunker & Houston 1992, p.232). Ad hoc and partisan transport decisions, such as the Southern Expressway, which create expectations of the inevitable urbanisation of fringe areas and which encourage the opportunistic pattern of development which typifies the urban fringe around most other Australian cities should also be avoided.

Within the metropolitan area, a new Centres Policy is still urgently required. Retailing is changing around us with the decline of department stores, the rise of supermarkets selling petrol and filling stations selling food and household goods, pressures for and against deregulated trading hours, the likely impacts of information technology and a range of other economic, social and technological changes to which the government needs to respond. Despite a commitment to an expansion of the Marion, West Lakes and Tea Tree Plaza shopping centres, a long-term view of the desirable distribution of activity across the metropolitan area should be adopted. The slowing of fringe development and the change of emphasis towards the renewal of inner and middle suburbs have implications for the redevelopment of centres at all levels, not least in the expansion of their economic and social functions beyond retailing. There are also issues to be addressed in the planning and management of new district centres on the metropolitan area's outer periphery – places like Mount Barker and Victor Harbor, for example, which are likely before long, to experience the impact of current transport investments in the South East Freeway and the Southern Expressway. The government's approach to retailing and the development of centres generally in recent years has largely been to support the dictates of the national and international monopoly interests which dominate major shopping centre developments. The viability of other centres, including those in public ownership, smaller suburban centres and the city centre itself, has been threatened by short-term opportunistic decisions, and by the lack of an up-to-date Centres Policy which connects and balances the needs of the city centre with the needs of the suburbs. Some have canvassed the idea of a regulatory regime which would require supporters of new retail developments to demonstrate that their proposals would not undermine the value of existing centres. However, a more positive approach would see the government encouraging new initiatives to re-invigorate existing centres whereby issues of marketing, physical upgrades and urban design, parking, traffic management etc. would be addressed.

CONCLUSION

The Planning Review in 1992 addressed the need to resolve some of the role ambiguities of state government departments, charged with both promoting and regulating development. The Review encouraged some re-organisation of agencies to confine responsibility for the government's urban development functions to a single portfolio. The importance of coordinating the government's management of the public housing stock, the assembly and release of land for new development, the management of major public development projects and the location of the government's own activities were also stressed. In retrospect, the Planning Review was a somewhat heroic enterprise and, no doubt, over-ambitious in its attempt to provide a community-shared vision of the future metropolitan area. But it was important in placing equity considerations firmly back on the metropolitan planning agenda and in seeking to resolve tensions between economic investment and environmental planning within an 'integrated' strategy. In this respect however, the review was hampered by the lack of an explicit state economic development policy, something which successive governments have also neglected. Overall, the Planning Review adhered to South Australia's tradition of a sound public sector framework for private sector investment, allied to an inclusive and socially just focus. The roles of the Urban Land Trust and the Housing Trust were strongly reaffirmed.

What matters, of course, are ends, not means. There is a need for the government to reassert its role in guiding the development of the city although there may well be other ways of achieving this than those proposed by the Planning Review. Public sector institutions need to be reformed and to take on new ideas. As Hugh Stretton has argued: 'New kinds of conditions of both public and private enterprise, new patterns of trade between them, should all be open to consideration on their merits, with reference to the ultimate social purposes which economic policies are supposed to serve' (Stretton 1987, p. 53).

There have been too few voices in recent times arguing for the view that governments do some things well – providing affordable housing and land, for example. It is currently held that: '... instead, governments must abandon the field, manage and facilitate economic change, following behind the rationalisers and the privatisers with a few targeted social programs' (Peel 1995, p. 51). The planning profession itself needs to reconsider its present tendency to shy away from any engagement with fundamental social and economic problems. The Royal Australian Planning Institute is well represented on government advisory and decision-making bodies, but it has not been prominent in recent times in challenging the planning system.

South Australia's broader problems are well-known. South Australia shares the difficulties encountered by other cities and regions as they seek to adapt to a changing international division of labour and new spatial patterns of consumption, to dramatic developments in global communications which have facilitated, amongst other things, increased mobility of financial capital and of firms, and a steady increase in the importance of transnational organisations and corporations. Like some other Australian states, South Australia is also struggling with debt burdens, legacies of the financial crisis of the early 1990s. With its dependence on manufacturing and the car industry, in particular, South Australia remains vulnerable in the short term to the dismantling of tariffs. Attraction of private capital for investment remains a vital priority. This paper argues that the best way to attract investment is not to chase spurious projects by trading off long-term strategic planning aims and established policies for doubtful and transitory opportunities. The need is clear: the establishment of a strong development framework and the implementation of coordinated public sector infrastructure programs to underpin private development which is consistent with this framework.

REFERENCES

Bramley, Glen 1997, 'Direct state involvement in housing land development', AHURI working paper 10, AHURI, Melbourne.

Bunker, R. & Houston, P. 1992, 'Natural resource management meets metropolitan growth', in 'Metropolitan Australia in the 1990s', S. Hamnett & S. Parham eds, *Built Environment*, vol. 18, no. 3, pp.221–33).

Bunker, R. & Hutchings, A. 1997, 'South Australian planning in the 1990s', Planning Education Foundation of South Australia/University of South Australia, working paper no. 6.

Peel, M. 1995, 'The urban debate: From Los Angeles to the urban village', in *Australian Cities*, ed P. Troy, Cambridge University Press.

Stretton, H. 1987, *Political Essays*, Georgian House, Melbourne.

NOTES

1 The authors are grateful to Ian Radbone for comments on a draft of this chapter.

2 Both authors of this paper were centrally involved in the SA Planning Review.

3 Messenger Press 27 July 1994 'New Shops Boost'.

4 The Development Assessment Commission was the planning authority in this case, because of the West Torrens Council's interest in the land, which it owned before selling it to the shopping centre developer. The Council's land dealings in relation to the proposed shopping centre site were alleged to have resulted in a loss to ratepayers in excess of $1 million.

5 Messenger Press, 20 Dec 1995, 'Parties back push for shopping centre'.

6 John Olsen, quoted in Messenger Press, 10 July 1996.

7 Address to the National Urban Renewal Seminar, 27 April 1998.

8 The opposition Labor Party shortsightedly endorsed these changes.

9 Advertiser 19 November 1997 'Olsen welcomes "secure" project'

10 Advertiser, 23 May 1997

11 MFP was a project in some difficulty when it was inherited by the Brown government. The Olsen government's unsuccessful attempts to salvage the organisation, however, led to the demise of the Urban Projects Authority, one of the better-performing project management agencies which the state has had in recent years.

12. In a recent lunchtime address, Roger Cook, the Director of the Project Delivery Task Force, expressed the view that the planning system was not an obstacle to attracting investors and developers to South Australia. The problems, rather, were 'attitudinal'.

13 There have been four since 1993 Oswald, Ashenden, Baker and Laidlaw.

14 Ironically, the Property Council which represents large and small commercial owners and developers has recently called for such direct intervention in the regeneration of the Adelaide city centre.

15 Albeit with some apparent problems, in the case of old public housing areas, in arriving at an appropriate value of the asset in negotiation with the private sector partners involved.

16 The draft issued for public consultation in April 1977 included the hastily inserted proposal for this project, described as a 'landmark icon within the City of Adelaide'.

CHAPTER 16

HOUSING POLICY

The national impasse and alternatives in South Australia

LIONEL ORCHARD

THE NATIONAL IMPASSE

Australian society suffers from far greater levels of inequality and social division than at any time since the 1930s and 1940s. Public policies at both the national and state levels are promoting those inequalities and divisions rather than ameliorating them. A genuinely mixed economy, with separate but related roles of the market economy and government, has been decisively undermined by twenty years of 'reform' or, more accurately attack, on the autonomous role of government and the public sector in Australian society. Public regulation and intervention in the mixed economy to ensure the productive and equitable use of economic resources has been replaced by the ongoing push for competition, deregulation, privatisation and contracting-out in government.

There have been decisive differences in the Australian approach from those in other western democracies. Welfare provision, for example, remains more generous in Australia. Nevertheless, economic rationalism and public sector reform have been relentless in Australia and have enjoyed bipartisan political and intellectual support. Labor and Coalition governments in Australia have pursued sophisticated and crude versions of the same agenda. Intellectually, economic arguments about the virtues and efficiencies of markets have been supported by political and social libertarians on the Left and the Right in attacking and undermining confidence in government and public institutions in Australia's mixed economy.

Through all of these changes, the welfare and other systems which are essential to the good functioning of any decent and civilised society continue to be eroded. The choices and options facing low-income people are narrowing severely, causing individual distress, wasted opportunity and increasing levels of social dysfunction.

Nowhere are these trends more obvious than in our housing system and in the policies which now shape it. While those who can afford good housing still have access to it, the Australian housing achievement of wide and equitable distribution of home ownership is being rapidly undermined. Recent research has shown that access to home ownership is becoming more difficult for lower-income people because of rising unemployment and poverty. Increasing numbers of people can neither afford, nor are prepared to risk the long-term financial commitment, that home ownership requires.

Public housing is becoming even more marginal than it is already. Public housing investment is declining while the problems faced by the system – growing demand from people with a declining capacity to pay, and an ageing housing stock in need of significant upgrading and, in some cases, replacement – outstrip either the capacity or the inclination of governments to respond.

Meanwhile, private rental housing provides for increasing numbers of low-income people who pay well over any reasonable proportion of their income in rent and who face much greater insecurity than they would in the public system. And government now sees private rental housing as playing an increasing role in housing low-income people.

While all of these trends reflect economic and social changes not wholly in the control of governments, they also reflect conscious directions in Australian housing policy. These directions were defined in the 1970s and have gathered momentum since then.

From the 1940s to the early 1970s, there was broad bipartisan agreement in Australia that home ownership and public housing gave people the greatest economic benefits and freedom. It was widely argued that equitable, cross-class access to these housing tenures should be encouraged by government policy through direct public housing investment and regulation of mortgage finance and interest rates.

Since the 1970s, these foundations of Australian housing policy have been strongly criticised across the political and policy spectrum. Orthodox economists, welfare economists, and critics on the Left all began to argue that the Australian housing system was economically inefficient, socially inequitable and too politically conservative to warrant ongoing support. For some economists, it was perceived as over-investment in housing because of explicit government support for home ownership and public housing. For welfare economists, the public housing system was not well targeted to those most in need. It was failing on equity grounds. And many thought that the Australian encouragement of home ownership made us a more conservative society than we needed to be.

'Tenure neutrality' as a new foundation for Australian housing policy began to emerge in response to these criticisms. The main idea was that public policy should not favour any one housing tenure over the others. Efficiency, equity and diversity in the Australian housing system required freer, less-regulated financial and housing markets, receipt of welfare subsidy through direct income assistance, and the encouragement of greater flexibility of movement between the different housing tenures and the building-up of new community and cooperative housing options in the public housing system.

The new thinking in Australian housing policy was consistent with the gathering consensus in the 1980s that freer markets and less direct government intervention in the Australian economy was the best way forward in Australian public policy. The decision to deregulate the Australian financial system in 1983 was the first main outcome of the new emphasis on freer markets. This decision made the access and cost of finance for both individual home buyers and for governments much higher in both real and nominal terms, particularly in the late 1980s and early 1990s.

The early 1990s saw the development of many ideas for Australian housing policy based on the 'tenure neutrality' logic in policy reviews conducted for the Hawke and Keating Labor governments. Two broad areas of reform were the most important. The first was that inequities in the system – public assistance going to both public and private renters – demanded the introduction of a 'housing benchmark' income support scheme. This idea was probably the most important legacy of the National Housing Strategy (NHS) conducted between 1990 and 1992. The idea is still to be implemented.

The second area of reform centred on public housing. It was driven by the Industry Commission's Inquiry into Public Housing in 1993 and merged two broad policy arguments. The first was that decisions about the development, sale and pricing of public housing should be shaped by commercial, asset management criteria, not the cost rental principles of the past. Governments should seek to derive the maximum economic return rather than use public housing, as an asset owned in common, to contain costs and rents at the lower ends of the housing market. Market rents for public housing should be more widely introduced. The second principle was that the criteria of social need and targeting should guide decisions about the allocation of public housing.

In general, the tensions in the Industry Commission's arguments between the commercial and social missions of public housing were difficult to reconcile. The Commission believed that conflict between them could be avoided by dividing the property management and tenancy management roles of the State Housing Authorities into separate agencies. This agenda for public housing reform has been taken up to varying degrees by the states.

Some of the central ideas underpinning the housing reform ideas of the early 1990s – the rationalisation and division of the housing responsibilities of federal government and state governments with the former seeing to the income support aspects, with the states having primary responsibility for funding and managing public housing – have yet to be resolved. Since winning office in 1996, the Howard government has been ever meaner with existing income assistance to low-income renters. It has procrastinated over the introduction of the NHS benchmark scheme mainly because of its projected cost. An interim Commonwealth/State Housing Agreement (CSHA) – the agreement which directs Commonwealth funds to the states for public housing and low-income home purchase – remains in place but with significantly reduced funding. It may yet disappear entirely.

In summary, low-income people in all three major tenures in the Australian housing system – home ownership, public housing and private rental – face major economic and social stress in the late 1990s. Economic restructuring and the resulting increase in unemployment bears much of the responsibility for that. Nevertheless, directions in Australian housing policy over the past 25 years have not helped. Major aspects of the framework of housing policy in Australia have been rationalised and reformed on economic efficiency, social equity and tenure neutrality grounds in ways that have undermined equitable access to home ownership and public housing.

LOW INCOME HOUSING POLICY IN SOUTH AUSTRALIA: A BRIEF HISTORY AND RECENT DIRECTIONS

It is well known that the South Australian history of housing policy and market management is different from that of the other states. In its heyday, the South Australian Housing Trust was the most ambitious Australian expression of public enterprise assisting low-income people with their housing needs. Public housing investment has played a more important role in the economic and social development of South Australia than it has in the other states. Per capita, South Australia has about twice the proportion of public housing of the other states – about ten per cent of the total housing stock compared with five per cent elsewhere. When the numbers of households assisted into home ownership by the Trust are added, about 25 per cent of all housing in South Australia has been built, managed, rented and sold through the public system.

The principles informing the South Australian housing model were also quite different from those of elsewhere. The wider purpose of the Trust's activities was to keep housing and land prices down across the whole market in order to keep costs low and thereby attract private investment to South Australia. It was central to Playford's program of state development. The strategy worked well and enjoyed bipartisan support for a remarkably long period.

The Trust built good-quality, if austere housing on a large scale. Elizabeth was the jewel in the crown. Besides Canberra, it was the only Australian example of comprehensive public planning of a new town. The public competition kept private rents in the lower half of the market 25 per cent or more below equivalent averages even in the smaller mainland capitals. The innovation continued in the Dunstan years when the Trust began to acquire and renovate older inner city housing for public rental, protecting what Hugh Stretton called 'class shares' of housing and space in Adelaide's inner and middle suburbs. The Trust was supported by cheap finance and borrowing from both federal and state sources. The core economic principle was to provide and manage public housing to repay its actual costs, not gear the whole operation to market prices.

From about the mid-1970s, the strategy began to unravel. Economic and social conditions worsened. Manufacturing industry began to decline. Unemployment levels began to rise. A growing number of people relied on welfare. Public finance was scarcer and more expensive. An increasing proportion of Trust tenants could not afford to pay full rents. Subsidy costs began to rise, eating into reserves available to build and maintain the public housing itself. In all, the economic and social foundation of the Trust's activities changed dramatically. The Trust could have been given the mandate and resources to address the new problems, especially given its previous achievements; instead, its legacy and approach were increasingly attacked. In line with the national arguments about tenure neutrality and the need for rationalisation of the Australian housing system, state governments were advised either to fundamentally reform the system or simply to abandon it altogether.

Reformers attacked the Trust as an insular organisation having too much power and not enough accountability to the public and government. Its cost-accounting practices were portrayed as antiquated. Its leadership was seen as excessively protective and defensive about the earlier achievements and not open enough about the need for change. Community and cooperative housing activists challenged the Trust's paternalism in its relations with the people it housed. Reformers argued that the Trust should be made more accountable and responsive both to government and the people it served.

Through the 1980s, the Trust addressed many of the criticisms. New accounting procedures were introduced. A new system of regional administration brought managers and public tenants closer together. At the national level, the Hawke government came to office with a commitment to dramatically increase public housing levels in Australia. This commitment was not matched by a flow of finance to ensure its happening. The Bannon government compensated by extensive borrowing at commercial rates of interest to allow the Trust to invest in new public housing. Later, the South Australian Community Housing Authority was created to develop housing cooperatives and associations as an addition to the overall public housing effort.

Despite these initiatives, the pressure for change continued in the early 1990s in line with the national directions in housing policy. In 1993, the Trust's structure was fundamentally changed to take up the Industry Commission recommendation that the functions of the State Housing Authorities be separated into property management and tenancy management agencies. The position of General Manager of the Trust was abolished. While this pleased the Trust's critics, the need to restore coherence and integration soon became apparent.

Tension remained between the commercial objectives that were introduced into the public housing system and the Trust's social mission to provide affordable housing to low-income people. The Trust is expected to sell houses and redevelop its old estates generating commercial returns to enable quick repayment of the debt left from the 1980s. The sale program is well advanced, the aim being to sell 6000 houses by 2001 thereby reducing the public housing stock from 59 000 to 53 000 units. Redevelopment of the Trust's old estates in joint ventures with private development companies has proceeded at Rosewood in Elizabeth and Mitchell Park. There are proposals for major redevelopment of Trust housing estates at 'The Parks' in Adelaide's western suburbs.

In early 1998, the Olsen government introduced changes to rent-setting and the targeting of public housing in line with those implemented by the Kennett government in Victoria. Kennett has introduced policies to reshape and create a 'sustainable' public housing system, policies which limit the length of tenure for public tenants, establish a segmented waiting list giving priority to the neediest cases, and charge market rents while reducing rental rebates for public tenants. The Olsen government has followed suit. Trust housing will no longer be made available on open access as a general housing option for all lower-income people; instead, it will be targeted to those people in greatest need. Life-long tenure in public housing will be abandoned. Waiting lists and eligibility criteria for public housing have been tightened to reflect the new directions. All new public tenants are to be placed on probation for six months. In summary, the criteria for access to public housing in South Australia are now much tougher while its cost is increasing.

A FUTURE FOR LOW INCOME HOUSING IN SOUTH AUSTRALIA?

In early 1998, the Olsen government was handed a blueprint for the future of public housing in South Australia. The plan is to radically reshape and reduce the system over the next fifteen years and proposes public housing principles and practices opposed to those of years past. The case is outlined in a 'triennial' review of the Trust prepared by Coopers and Lybrand Consultants. Proposals are put on two major fronts – changes to the allocation of public housing and changes to the management of the Trust's housing assets.

In line with the Olsen government's recent changes, the review proposes that eligibility for public housing be tightened considerably. Public housing should be targeted to those who have a range of complex needs not likely to be addressed adequately by other housing tenures. Life-long tenure in public housing should be abandoned in favour of more flexible arrangements in which variations in need at different stages of the life cycle would be a central criterion. Rents for public housing should rise to market levels and be set at higher rates for housing in better, more convenient locations. For low-income people facing the 'simpler' problem of being unable to afford appropriate housing, private renting should be more widely adopted. The Commonwealth Rent Assistance (CRA) scheme provides income support to assist with the payment of private rents.

On asset management, the review proposes that a quarter of the public housing stock be sold off over the next fifteen years. The public stock would be reduced from nearly 60 000 houses now to about 43 000 by 2012. The finance generated by this sell-off will provide some of the resources to upgrade the housing remaining in public hands. The sell-off would be through individual purchase of Trust housing, and through more comprehensive redevelopment of old public housing estates, thereby encouraging higher levels of home ownership, reduced concentrations of public housing and improved amenities. Public housing should be retained in the better-located and serviced, inner and middle suburbs of Adelaide and generally reduced in outer suburban areas and in the country.

Other avenues of housing assistance for low-income people should also be explored, in particular, schemes to facilitate access to home ownership and the development of community housing options.

In all, the review proposes a scaled-down public housing system in both size and scope, and the pursuit of greater diversity in government housing programs for low-income people.

The 'triennial' review argues that the proposed changes are inevitable. Current directions in national housing policy away from support for public housing towards schemes of income support for low-income people mean that South Australia is left out on a limb given our relatively high levels of public housing per capita. In the new era, we are the victims of our earlier success (although the reviewers dispute that success). Commonwealth funding of public housing is declining and the state government doesn't have spare funds to contribute. Mixed with the need for higher levels of subsidy of its tenants, these wider trends mean that the Trust faces a major financial crisis over the coming years. In order for that crisis to be averted, the review argues that there is no other way but to adapt the South Australian public housing system in the ways proposed.

How robust is this vision for public housing in this state? Are there other possibilities?

Firstly it is important to note that the triennial review reflects no understanding of the history of South Australia's approach to public housing and the foundations and principles upon which it was based. As indicated earlier, the South Australian model of public housing in its heyday was based on a mixture of radical and conservative principles in which public housing investment played a central and creative role in underpinning the development of the South Australian economy while serving the interests of low-income people by keeping land and housing prices and rents down. The South Australian experience has shown that the commercial and social objectives can be managed in the interests of all.

It could be expected that a review of the South Australian Housing Trust would at least examine and seek to understand the principles of the Trust's activities, especially since they have been very different from those employed elsewhere in Australia. The greater priority given to public housing investment in South Australia for sound economic and social reasons accounts for the fact that we have a higher proportion of public housing than the other states.

Instead of reflecting on that fact, the review defends the all-too-familiar argument that we need to rationalise our public housing system in line with national directions relating to efficiency in public housing. Alignment to national thinking is reflected throughout the triennial review. It is expressed most starkly in comments about the measurement of housing need. The review notes that:

… it is difficult to understand why a national structure dealing with … issues (of housing need) on a common basis for all Australians is not already in place, with national criteria for assessing need, common programs, similar benefits … to similar households in need, and a more limited role for state governments to respond to specific local and regional differences. The ability of the state to maintain its own traditions would then be met within a national approach. It is difficult to comprehend the rationale for the current policy framework which provides some households in South Australia with different benefits than similar households in Victoria and elsewhere. (p. 107)

Why should we think like that? Why should nationally determined criteria on anything take precedence over local ones, especially if they represent meaner and narrower criteria than those applied locally? This kind of thinking reflects centralist rationalism at its worst. It is quite undemocratic to assume that such issues can be addressed without regard to varying local experience and practices. The most general problem with the approach taken in the 'triennial' review is that it adopts the national line that public housing should be fundamentally rationalised, corporatised and targeted to a point where it loses its function and eventually disappears altogether. There is no mention, let alone reflection, on how we might adapt South Australian public housing policy in a way that acknowledges the unique local achievement and the principles upon which it was based.

That achievement rested on the way in which commercial objectives were reconciled with social ones. The key principle was that public investment in land and housing should be managed on cost rather than market principles. Nevertheless, it was always argued that the public housing system should pay for itself. If managed well, subsidies were not required. By such means, housing prices and rents in South Australia were lower than those in other states for a long period to the advantage of all government, private investors and citizens. Strong, decisive public enterprise in urban and housing development was essential to that success.

Whereas the commercial and social missions of the Trust in its heyday formed a 'virtuous circle', those missions are now fundamentally at odds with one another, indeed have been set against one another in recent years. This is because the commercial mission of the Trust is no longer thought of and practised independently of private housing markets. On the contrary, the management of the Trust's property assets is now actively shaped by private market principles. Market rents for public housing have been introduced. More sophisticated market rents which recognise the varying benefits that go with different kinds of housing in different locations are recommended by the review. The management of the Trust's housing assets is now viewed in terms of how valuable they are on the private market, not in terms of the benefits public ownership and management brings to those the Trust was designed to serve. Asset management, 1990s-style, is about 'gearing up' the public housing asset to produce maximum financial return to the government rather than using it as an instrument of market management to keep housing costs and prices lower than they otherwise would be.

The 'triennial' review's sell-off and redevelopment proposals will take the commercial management of the South Australian public housing assets to another level. The primary aim is to seek the highest returns to the government in the sell-off. On redevelopment, the likely approach will be the increasing use of joint ventures between the Trust and private developers to generate the highest rates of return on the investment, while ensuring some upgrading of the remaining public housing. These objectives are not surprising given the financial constraints that now face the Trust. In the context of the imbalances in the economic position of the Trust – less Commonwealth and state funds, an ageing public housing stock in need of upgrading, and the need for ever-greater subsidy of its tenants – the triennial review proposals seem to have a certain inevitability. But the more the government backs away from its responsibilities and the more that private market principles influence the management of our public housing assets, the greater the limits placed on the Trust's social mission of providing cheap, modest but secure housing to those who need it.

None of this is to say that redevelopment, sale and upgrading of public housing shouldn't proceed. But it should and could do so on the basis of a better, more balanced reconciliation of the Trust's commercial and social roles. Redevelopment projects should not pick the eyes out of the public system using old, well-located public housing estates in Adelaide's inner and middle suburbs as a vehicle to generate high returns to private developers and the government. It might also be prudent to retain poorly located and maintained public housing in outer suburban areas in public ownership with simpler and cheaper upgrades than to sell it off cheaply. Such sell-off might mean that for every three or four houses sold, only one new house can be built or acquired.

In general, the social losses from the triennial review's strategy should be balanced against the economic gains that it might produce. Rather than high-profile, 'gold-plated' (or maybe 'silver-plated') redevelopment in which significant amounts of basically good public housing is lost, the better strategy might be to adopt less ambitious approaches to redevelopment and upgrading which retain as much public housing stock as possible.

The review notes that 'the real value of public housing is that it provides a more expensive and more meaningful benefit to those in need than the payment of an income top-up to assist housing affordability' (p. 108). That comment is meant to support the defence of greater targeting of public housing to those with complex needs over those who face 'simple' affordability problems. Taken at a broader level however, it expresses exactly the reason why a strong public housing system should be retained in South Australia and be made as accessible as possible to low-income people. Hard decisions are inevitable in relation to eligibility for public housing, given the growing need and the decline in the capacity of the Trust to provide it. But the realisation of meaningful benefits rather than a bottom line is a much firmer basis upon which to rebuild a commitment to progressive housing policy and programs in South Australia and beyond.

When releasing the 'triennial' review, the Minister of Human Services, Dean Brown argued that it is 'one of the most significant reviews of the Trust in its sixty-year history'. But its significance is as much for the history it forgets and the public housing principles it ignores, as for the policies it proposes. The positive reconciliation of economic and social objectives in South Australia's public housing system of earlier times is being decisively replaced by policies which set these objectives against one another. None of this is any great surprise given trends in national housing policy, but it is somewhat surprising that the current South Australian government seems so determined to undo so much of what its most significant forebear the Playford government achieved.

CONCLUSION

There is little doubt that any viable, long-term response to the housing crisis facing low-income people in South Australia and elsewhere will require a new wave of national policy innovation and reform. The states cannot do it by themselves. The states rightly argue that the policies currently pursued simply take up reform ideas initially outlined and imposed by national governments of both political persuasions.

Nevertheless, it is increasingly recognised that some of the foundations and directions in national housing policy of recent times are fundamentally limited. 'Tenure neutrality' is increasingly acknowledged as a narrow framework for national housing policy by some of those who earlier defended the concept. On the one hand, they argue that the neutrality concept hasn't been applied comprehensively enough to attack the bias to home ownership in Australian housing policy. They acknowledge however, that the preoccupation with tenure neutrality has tended to suppress consideration of the economic and social benefits of home ownership and public housing over private-rental housing (Yates 1997).

A number of those who have been at the centre of the shift in national housing policy away from financial support for the development of particular housing tenures – public housing and low-income home ownership in particular – towards an income-based housing policy now recognise the limits of this shift. They defend the need for additional national resources to underpin investment in a viable supply of low-income housing while improving income support for low income renters (Ecumenical Housing 1997; Farrar 1997).

None of this is inconsistent with the new agenda emerging in the United States relating to urban regeneration, in particular of old public housing estates. In other western democracies like the United Kingdom, the new ideas about urban regeneration focus on local, 'bottom-up' responses and initiatives and the importance of integrated spatial, economic and social responses to neighbourhood regeneration (Maclennan 1998). In Australia, the task is to successfully graft this approach onto a revived national role in housing investment. As Farrar puts it, we need 'a reform package which ensures that social housing can continue to grow [with] greater attention to the upgrading and reconfiguration of existing public housing stock and the diversification of social housing responses and providers' (Farrar 1997, p. 64). In the absence of that, the new urban regeneration ideas will probably be married to increased privatisation of public housing through joint venture redevelopment projects with private developers – an option that might improve the physical fabric of some old public housing estates, but with more doubtful economic and social consequences for those who live in these areas.

The future of housing policy at both the national and state levels in Australia faces major issues of both principle and practice. Current policy are unhelpful while new ideas with a progressive, redistributive intent and capacity are only very slowly emerging.

REFERENCES

Coopers & Lybrand Consultants 1998, *South Australian Housing Trust: Triennial Review*, vol. 1, Adelaide, February 1998.

Ecumenical Housing 1997, *National Housing Policy: Reform and Social Justice*, Ecumenical Housing Unit, Melbourne.

Farrar, A. 1997, 'The end of public housing opportunities and reforms',
The End of Public Housing? ed R. Coles, a discussion forum organised by
the Urban Research Program held on 25 October 1996, Urban Research
Program, Research School for the Social Sciences, Australian National
University, Canberra, pp. 47–66.

Maclennan, D. 1998, Urban regeneration in Britain: New times, new
challenges, unpublished paper presented to 1998 National Urban
Renewal Seminar: Revitalising Housing Areas, Adelaide,
27–28 April 1998.

Yates, J. 1997, 'Changing directions in Australian housing policies:
The end of muddling through?', *Housing Studies*, vol. 12, no. 2,
pp. 265–77.

CHAPTER 17

PUBLIC HEALTH
AND THE MARKET

The invisible hand and our community's health

FRAN BAUM AND CHARLIE MURRAY

INTRODUCTION

This chapter will describe the changes in philosophy, policies and practices which have characterised public health and community health services in South Australia in the past decade and offer some suggestions for the future direction of the South Australian health system.

Our belief is that the South Australian health system should be shaped to emphasise public health principles to a far greater extent than is the case at present. South Australia made, especially in the 1980s, some significant moves towards achieving this, and has been an important contributor to the international new public health movement. This movement has built on the progressive ideas embraced by the World Health Organisation's Ottawa Charter. The Charter stressed the need for action to promote health in all sectors, the importance of striving for health equity, the crucial role of community participation, and the need to go beyond behavioural strategies to those which focus on changing the environment. South Australian policies developed in the late 1980s have provided an example of local implementation of the principles of the Charter (Baum 1995).

The new public health works for the common good and relies on support from government rather than on market activity. We argue that South Australia has a tradition of policy innovation and that the main thrust of these policies has been diminished under recent market reforms. Case studies at the end of this chapter provide examples of the impact these market reforms have had on community health centres and hospitals, and provide a vision for future reforms in relation to each of these.

INNOVATIVE POLICIES

South Australia has developed innovative policies and practices that have challenged narrow concepts of health as well as supporting equity and public accountability.

The first of these was *A Social Health Strategy for South Australia* (SAHC 1988a). This advocated a social view of health emphasising social, cultural, and economic factors. It stressed 'the need to move beyond the current preoccupation with providing expensive high technology services in big institutions like hospitals'. These, it argued, largely deal with illness once it has already occurred. *Primary Health Care: A Discussion Paper* was produced in the same year. This policy recognised that while a great deal of effort had gone into the area of health promotion and illness prevention 'there remain considerable inequities in both health status and access to the conditions of life which promote good health (for example, adequate housing, income, clean air, transport etc)' (SAHC 1988b). The Primary Health Care Policy approved in 1989 defined primary health care as 'both an approach to dealing with health services and a level of the health system'. It was strongly influenced by the state government's Social Justice Strategy and the Ottawa Charter.

The overriding goal for the South Australian health system's policy on primary health care is 'equity in health'; that is, reducing the current inequalities in health status between different sections of the population and in providing equal opportunities to good health for the whole of the population.

These innovative policies enabled South Australia to experiment with a variety of mechanisms in the implementation of the new public health; for example, the expansion of social planning especially for new urban areas, legislation aimed at controlling health-damaging behaviour (for example, seat belt and tobacco control legislation), the establishment of community health centres, the Noarlunga Healthy Cities project, the Health & Social Welfare Councils Program, and investment in the development of epidemiological data bases (such as the cancer registry) to provide detailed information for planning.

Legislation has been an important mechanism for improving public health. Tobacco control legislation developed in the last decade has focused on availability restrictions, pricing, labelling and advertising (Reynolds 1995). Like some other states, South Australia has used revenue from state licence fees to fund health promotion directly. In

1988 it established Foundation SA (subsequently renamed Living Health) to fund health promotion activities in the areas of health, recreation, sport and the arts. This allowed for public events to be sponsored by a health-promoting organisation, following the ban on direct advertising and sponsorship of tobacco products. In May 1998 the Liberal government announced its intention to dis-establish Living Health.

Community health services have been an important mechanism for implementing the new public health at a local level. During the 1980s South Australia also developed state-wide community-based services covering community child and adolescent mental health, child and youth health services and drug and alcohol services.

The progressive policies, and the new public health movement seem to have had much less impact on hospitals in the 1980s.

HEALTH AND THE MARKET

Other chapters in this collection have pointed to the increasing dominance of the twin ideologies of economic rationalism and managerialism. Both attempt to apply the logic of the market and the workings of the private sector to public services. Public health exemplifies the difficulties with this approach. It is not a commodity that can be 'sold', 'purchased' and 'consumed' like other goods. Health tends to be taken for granted until it is absent. Then it is generally not possible to 'buy' public health measures to deal with a problem. Preventing disease requires planning, foresight and long-term investment. Furthermore, public health is nearly always best provided on a collective rather than an individual basis, a situation in which the market's ability to provide effective public health mechanisms must be questioned. For example an individual can not be protected from the harmful effects of tobacco smoke by purchasing clean air. This can only be assured through legislative intervention and enforcement.

The health market is certainly not the level playing field favoured by neoclassical economists. An increasing body of evidence indicates that an individual's chances of being healthy are dictated by their genetic make-up and by the social, economic and physical environment in which they live (see for example National Health Strategy 1992; Townsend, Davidson & Whitehead 1992; Evans, Barer & Marmor 1994). Recent research indicates that the distribution of income within a country is related to population health outcomes: more equity appears to lead to better population health (Wilkinson 1996). Individuals' ability to purchase health is extremely limited. Their ability to purchase health

care, however, is far greater, but only when the individual has purchasing power. Health care, unlike other goods, is usually a 'product'
people purchase reluctantly and in situations in which they feel little
power or control and are often quite vulnerable. They typically have
limited information on the health care they need and rely heavily on the
knowledge of experts who may often stand to profit from the provision
of services. Such factors demonstrate market failure in health care and
clearly show how the logic of the market can not be easily transferred to
the consumption of health care.

QUASI-MARKET REFORMS IN THE SOUTH AUSTRALIAN HEALTH SYSTEM

The costs of providing health care have been rising for three or more
decades. In Australia, total expenditure on health rose from 4.9 per
cent of GDP in 1960 to 7.3per cent in 1980 and to 8.5 per cent in 1993
(Swerissen & Duckett 1997, p. 26). These figures reflect Australia's
ageing population. Diseases are therefore more likely to be chronic,
requiring longer care. At the same time, increasingly expensive medical
technology and drugs are being developed in spite of the absence of convincing evidence that high-technology clinical medicine will improve
population health outcomes except at the margins (Burns 1996 quoted
in Hindle & Degeling 1997). Governments around the world have
been moving to control costs of health care. South Australia is no exception. The budget of the SA Health Commission (when taking inflation
into account) has stayed more or less static in the past five years. This
contrasts with earlier periods in which health service costs rose. The proportion of the total budget spent on the metropolitan hospitals has
risen a little from 49.8 per cent in 1992/3 to 52 per cent in 1997/98
(SA Health Commission 1992; 1997). This has meant there has been a
smaller proportion to spend on primary health care services, such as
community health services. In an attempt to control costs in the health
system, Australian governments, like their overseas counterparts, have
moved to introduce a series of quasi-market reforms. In South Australia
the most notable of these have been:

- introduction of case-mix funding into the public hospital system
- establishment of funder, owner, purchaser, provider (FOPP) split
  into the health system
- privatisation and contracting-out
- pressure to measure health outcomes

CASE-MIX FUNDING

Case-mix funding was introduced in July 1994 as a basis for determining the amount of funding hospitals receive. Previously hospitals were funded on the basis of historical funding. Case-mix funding provides a payment for each particular procedure so that hospitals receive their budget based on the 'throughput' of patients. This funding model encourages hospitals to decrease patients' length of stay in hospital and increase admission rates and the throughput of patients. Case-mix funding also acts as an incentive for hospitals to maximise activities for which they are paid, and to minimise those activities, while of significant value (such as health promotion and illness prevention), which cannot be priced and therefore do not attract payment. A report from the Victorian Auditor General (1998) suggests that in that state case-mix funding has lead to a decline in the quality of care.

FUNDER, OWNER, PURCHASER, PROVIDER SPLIT

The establishment of a funder, owner, purchaser, provider, split by the SA Health Commission was a way of introducing an artificial market within the health system. This effectively opened the way for the introduction of changes modelled on the private sector.

Following the example of New Zealand and the United Kingdom, South Australia moved in 1995 to 'realign' the SAHC so that market principles underpinned the model of funding for hospitals and community health services. The SAHC established a Purchasing Office which had the responsibility to establish contracts (called 'service agreements') with these agencies and to specify the services supplied by the agencies in return for their budget. The purposes of and principles behind purchasing were never clear. Issues such as the role of the community in informing decisions and the balance between community views, market and political priorities have not been openly debated. In May 1998 the newly established Department of Human Services (combining the SA Health Commission, Family and Community Services and Housing) announced a new structure for the department which meant the Purchasing Office no longer existed.

Studies of the impact of the contracting culture on community health agencies in South Australia and Victoria (SACHRU 1996; Hughes 1996; Lewis & Walker 1997) have suggested the following:

- Relationships between central agencies and service provision agencies become based on legalistic arrangements rather than trust.

- Competition between providers does not encourage, and in some cases can actually undermine the collaboration so essential to effective health promotion and public health practice.
- Contracting favours simple, quantifiable units of service which can be monitored easily and provide short-term outcomes. It is easier to specify a contract for direct service provision (medical, podiatry or physiotherapy services) than for a health promotion campaign such as supporting a local environmental group or developing a self-help group with indigenous peoples. Work that is developmental and based on community participation requires trust-building and takes more time than a short funding cycle allows.
- Contracts have focused on the monitoring of quantitative aspects of service performance often neglecting quality of service provided, or actual or potential impact on health status.

PRIVATISATION AND CONTRACTING-OUT

Contracting-out and privatisation of services have been applied to health as they have to other sectors of government. The justification in terms of the government's role being 'steering not rowing' (Osbourne & Gaebler 1992) has also been applied in health. The impacts for public health are two-fold: impacts on health care services and the potential health impacts of privatisation of services outside the health sector such as water.

Within the South Australian health sector, the government has contracted out the management of Modbury Hospital, and a private hospital is being built adjacent to Flinders Medical Centre (a major public teaching hospital). Services within hospitals such as catering, security and cleaning have been contracted out to private sector companies. The government had also intended to privatise the management of the Queen Elizabeth Hospital. This plan met with significant public opposition and, despite putting the management out to tender, the hospital has been retained under the public management of the North-West Adelaide Health Services. It is difficult to assess the effect on Modbury Hospital and the services it offers, of the introduction of private management, because no formal evaluation process has been agreed upon. The government has also sought to deny Freedom of Information requests for vital contract information on the basis of 'commercial in confidence' arguments. This lack of transparency radically diminishes public accountability of a major public health facility.

One feature of the introduction of market reforms on the South Australian health system is that they are very rarely subjected to any systematic evaluation.

Evans (1997) in reviewing the claims for the introduction of competitive mechanisms into health 'markets' points out that, in fact, little real competition exists. He describes the complexity of the provision of health care and cautions against the simple assumption that competition will result in a more efficient and effective health service. This is supported by the fact that the health system which consumes the highest proportion of GDP is that of the United States; and this is also the most market-based health system. In 1995, Australia paid 8.5 per cent of GDP on health services, while the United States spent 14.1 per cent. Life expectancy for Australian males is 75 compared to 72 for US males and for Australian females 81 compared to 79 for US females (Duckett 1998). A comparison of the Australian and US health systems indicates that the Australian system offers universal and more equitable care (Duckett 1998).

HEALTH OUTCOMES

Market ideologies have also affected the health field in the 1990s by applying pressure on providers of health services to 'prove' the benefits of their treatments in terms of 'health outcomes'. The logic of this seems impeccable: money is expended on health services and consequently those services should be in a position to demonstrate the resultant health gains. In practice, the situation is far more complicated. As noted earlier, health services can have only a minor influence on population health outcomes. A range of other factors also make a very significant impact on health for individuals and populations. For instance, social support is a key determinant of how people both recover from illness and how healthy they are (Rosenfeld 1996). Employment status, education level, income, access to goods and services such as transport, all make a significant difference to health. While there is certainly value in evaluating and tracking the impact of health services and medical procedures, an emphasis on health outcomes can be taken to extremes and applied when it is not appropriate. There is little sense in attempting to measure outcomes precisely when the various contributing variables are unpredictable.

A further example of the introduction of quasi-market mechanisms has been the application in hospital and community health centres, of a budget management system derived from health economics, called program budgeting and marginal analysis (PBMA) which attempts to assess and compare the outcomes from different health programs and shift resources accordingly. The technique was originally designed to be applied across large-scale areas of expenditure, but in South Australia it has been adapted to compare programs in small expenditure areas such as mental health programs in community health centres. PBMA can only work where there are 'margins' with flexibility to shift around funds. When funding is tight, especially in small programs, PBMA cannot be used effectively. While the technique had some benefits in terms of encouraging a more reflective approach to planning, its capacity to achieve efficiencies and improved effectiveness has not been proved and its use has not spread.

HEALTH IMPACTS OF ECONOMIC RATIONALISM AND MANAGERIALISM OUTSIDE THE HEALTH SECTOR

There is growing evidence that the overall impact of privatisation may be questionable for the health of a population. A key aim of the new public health is achieving equitable health outcomes. Hutton (1995) reviews the impact of the privatisation of housing, transport and education in the UK and concludes that it has had particularly bad consequences for the poorest part of the population. Hutton cites Ferreira, a World Bank economist, who argues that even when privatisation is designed to be egalitarian, it may lead to increases in inequality and possibly poverty, impacting on groups who are already disadvantaged, and likely to translate to poor population health outcomes over time.

The conservative and prestigious medical journal *The Lancet* has indicated a concern for the potential health effects of the privatisation of water supply in the UK (1995, Editorial). The journal noted how the report to the Chief Medical Officer describing the health problems resulting from the increased number of water disconnections occurring after water supply services were privatised, had been suppressed. The editorial noted an increase in water-borne disease and, while recognising that this could not be directly linked to the disconnections, commented that both personal hygiene and the sanitary disposal of faeces would be extremely difficult with a disconnected water supply.

The trend towards privatisation has also been accompanied by deregulation which may also threaten public health (Baum 1998). In the case of the labour market it tends to undermine conditions of work such as penalty rates, occupational health and safety standards and permanency of employment. The monitoring and surveillance role of public health may also be undermined if the powers of regulatory authorities are reduced, which, in turn may affect the safety of substances and products. Food safety, which has not been a major issue for public health for years, has become significant. In South Australia the death of a young girl from Haemolytic-uraemic syndrome has highlighted the importance of government regulation (Beers 1996). Surveillance is a government function which society can not afford to leave to market forces.

Managerialism brings with it spates of re-organisations. These have certainly characterised the South Australian public service in the 1990s. More staff are on contracts and work-to-performance agreements and do not have the stability and security that was experienced by earlier generations of public servants. A longitudinal study from the UK indicates that this kind of instability has direct health effects. A comparison of civil servants who had experienced change to a more private sector style of management, recorded and reported significantly more morbidity (Ferrie et al, 1998). They conclude that the health consequences of job insecurity should be taken into account by policy-makers when considering the efficiencies of changes in employment policy.

The following three case studies illustrate the impact of the changes in three different settings: Health and Social Welfare Councils, Community Health Services, and Hospitals.

CASE STUDIES OF CHANGE
Health & Social Welfare Councils

The Health & Social Welfare Councils Program provides a good example of how difficult it is for participatory democratic programs to survive when the public sector is heavily influenced by objectives derived from market models. The program was established in the late 1980s by the SA Health Commission to support the development of community participation in health and welfare issues. Their objectives provided a mandate for increasing the accountability of the health and welfare systems and for strengthening local action to prevent social and health problems.

HSWCs were established in four areas as pilot projects (two in the city and two in the country). They each received approximately $85 000 per year enabling them to employ one full-time and one part-time staff member as well as maintaining a small goods and services budget. After three years the program was evaluated and found to be operating effectively. Consequently it was recommended that the program be expanded to establish a council in each region of South Australia. As the result of cuts made to the health budget, the program was not expanded. The four councils continued to operate until the end of 1995, when their funding was discontinued. The SA Health Commission claimed they could no longer fund a program that covered only four regions in the state, and that funds ($1.3 million) were not available to extend the councils to all regions.

Priorities and activities of the HSWCs were determined by the community membership in each council, resulting in a wide range of issues being tackled including the environment, mental health, disability, issues for people from non-English-speaking backgrounds and transport for people living in rural areas. The councils supported a broadening of the areas of concern, moving from the individual problems of community members to identifying broader issues and developing strategies for change. The councils provided a link between community members and the system. They also drew attention to the range of factors that impact on people's health, many of which lay outside the health system, such as air pollution and access to interpreter services.

In the early days of the HSWCs, ministers for health from both ends of the political spectrum considered the HSWCs to be an important public accountability mechanism, an ear to the ground about community issues. In the later years however, ministers from both Labor and Liberal governments indicated less support for them. In 1995 the relevant minister no longer responded to their correspondence. The councils' founding principles of equity, social justice and participatory democracy did not fit within the economic objectives of the mid-1990s (Murray & Tatyzo 1995). A market approach favours market research over genuine community participation in decision-making.

South Australia still supports policies which encourage community participation but an alternative to the Health & Social Welfare Councils has not been developed. Our vision is for the establishment of an independent community participation mechanism to advise health services on how to integrate community participation into their practice. Such a body could also act as an umbrella organisation for community groups raising broader health issues. It should also provide a voice for disadvantaged groups.

Community Health Services

Women's and Community Health Services in South Australia have produced some of the best examples of primary health care in Australia. Their activities have included:

- providing services to individuals based on strong interdisciplinary teamwork (nutrition advice, physiotherapy, counselling, podiatry, and in some cases medical services)
- support groups based on clear principles of self-help, mutual aid and partnership (stress management, dealing with violent behaviour, parenting skills, and health promotion)
- community development based on principles of community empowerment and equity (supporting groups and taking action on issues such as domestic violence, and environmental issues).

A strong emphasis was placed on community participation in the activities of the centres and historically, planning was based on extensive consultation and involvement. Until 1996 metropolitan women's and community health centres were managed by local boards of management that included local community members. Community involvement in management was at the core of community health – an important way of ensuring that community health centres were accountable to local communities, and working with them in ways that were empowering (Legge 1992).

In the 1990s, Women's and Community Health Centres have struggled in an environment far less favourable than that of the 1980s. They have suffered cuts to their budgets at a time when demand for their services has increased, and they have also struggled to justify their existence as managerial reforms to the health system have introduced an emphasis on market economics.

For several years community health centres have faced budget cuts which have led to a reduction in positions and services (SACHRU 1996). In 1995/6 the cuts were equivalent to ten per cent for many services. When Women's and Community Health Services were established their services were available to all living in the locality of the health service. A reduction in funds has forced women's and community health services to prioritise services to those most in need. It has also reduced the centres' capacity to respond quickly to community initiatives.

Managerial reforms include the introduction of the funder, owner, purchaser, provider split, described earlier. As part of this move, the 12 separately incorporated Women's and Community Health Centres were de-incorporated and three amalgamated community health services were established in their place. This has inevitably meant less emphasis on local planning and local participation as a regional focus is developed. Service agreements were also introduced, and while most community health services found the agreement a useful planning tool, some expressed apprehension about its potential to become too directive or prescriptive. Other concerns have been raised about the difficulties of contracting-out work which does not fit within a short-term contract model, such as community development.

Reduced funding, amalgamations of the metropolitan community health services, and the constant changes in structure and personnel in the health bureaucracy, have made the 1990s a disruptive and difficult period for community health. Nonetheless they have survived and continue to deliver quality services and undertake innovative community work.

A major strength of community health services is that they adopt a population perspective to health far more readily than health practitioners who concentrate on treating individuals on a fee-for-service basis. Our vision for the future is that South Australia should develop a network of community health centres, each serving a population of approximately 50 000 in the city and an appropriate population in country areas. These centres would be the focus for a range of local treatment, preventive and health promotion services. They would coordinate care for all practitioners funded from the public purse (including GPs receiving reimbursement from Medicare), develop strong relationships with hospitals and take responsibility for analysing and taking action on local public health issues in partnership with their community. This action would include a range of strategies including health education groups, community development and, where necessary social action.

The centres would also develop links with other sectors such as education, housing, welfare and transport and work with them to assess the potential for changing their practices so that they are more likely to promote health.

The potential for the future of South Australian community health services lies in their ability to build on their strengths as providers of a range of health services utilising a variety of strategies to promote the health of their local communities. More than any other part of the health sector, these services concentrate on positive health promotion.

Changing role of hospitals

The average length of stay of patients in South Australian hospitals has been reduced significantly in recent years. This results from advances in surgical techniques which have made day surgery a possibility, and because of cost pressures which are forcing hospitals to maximise efficiencies. The case-mix funding formula mentioned earlier means that hospitals have a clear cost incentive to discharge patients as rapidly as possible. There are some concerns that this may mean that people are discharged too early and some may subsequently have to be re-admitted to hospital.

Shorter lengths of stay in hospitals and the increase of people with complex chronic health problems have also increased the need for funds for community-based support services and improved coordination of care between hospital and community-based services such as general practitioners, domiciliary care services and district nursing. In recognition of this, the federal government has funded a series of trials of coordinated care. Two of these have been in South Australia: Health Plus and Care 21. Both of these trials aim to improve the care people receive by introducing a care manager to the system. Their role is to assess the person's needs and then organise the coordination of health and support services. These trials are being evaluated and their results should be available in 2000. While much of the government's motivation for funding these trials relates to cost containment, more innovative thinking about the delivery of health care may result.

In the 1990s there has been a drawn-out process of reform with a series of reviews of mental health services. This reform process has been driven by the philosophy of de-institutionalisation but has met an apparent parallel agenda of cost-cutting. The movement of clients from institutions into the community has not been accompanied by adequate funds for community-based care and support. As a result, more responsibility for caring has shifted to the relatives and friends of people with mental illnesses.

Hospitals in South Australia are also moving towards taking a more systematic approach towards health promotion. The three largest teaching hospitals have established health promotion units in the past decade (Flinders Medical Centre, Royal Adelaide Hospital and the Women's and Children Hospital). These units are encouraged to re-orient the work of the hospital to focus on disease prevention and health promotion wherever possible. This trend in hospitals has been an international one, led by the World Health Organisation's Health Promoting Hospitals project. Flinders Medical Centre was the first Australian hospital to be endorsed by the WHO under this program.

A recent study at the Women's and Children's Hospital indicates that the health promotion focus of the hospital is bringing about a shift in organisational culture as indicated by the growth in health promotion activity within the hospital, particularly in relation to public health advocacy. An analysis of media articles on the hospital showed clearly that there had been a shift from 'medical miracle' stories to those with a public health focus (Johnson 1998). This study also demonstrated the ways in which the disease prevention work of the hospital is penalised under the current hospital funding models. The hospital ran a very successful awareness campaign about the risk of children under five years of age choking on particular types of food. The evaluation showed the campaign had effectively reduced the number of children admitted to the hospital for choking. This reduction saved the health system $76 000 in direct costs, but it resulted in a decrease in funds to the hospital under the case-mix funding system. The hospital has taken this issue up with the SA Health Commission, claiming that this system of funding forces hospitals to treat illnesses rather than addressing the question of 'why patients are coming through the door in the first place' (Alexander 1997). This case illustrates not only the inadequacy of market-based models to comprehend a public health perspective, but also how they can actively work against it.

We believe that the future for hospitals lies in their continuing to emphasise the re-orientation of their role from an exclusive focus on treating and caring for people, to one that also includes health promotion. Hospitals in the future are less likely to be perceived in terms of a discrete building, but rather in terms of a service provider facilitating and coordinating networks with other services. In our view hospitals should build strong alliances with community health services and work with them in developing partnerships with communities and other sectors. In this way a re-orientation towards a public and population health perspective could become a reality with major benefits for the population's health and quality of life. The particular challenge for the health system for the future will be to develop mechanisms for providing care for people with chronic conditions such as diabetes, asthma and mental illness. These are complex diseases that will require imaginative and responsive services.

CONCLUSION

This chapter has argued that the moves to introducing market mechanisms into the South Australian health system may have resulted in some efficiencies in the system, but little has been achieved to re-orient the system towards the promotion of a healthy population. In the past decade health policies from the World Health Organisation and from the federal government and state governments urged the desirability of this perspective. Internationally, there have been very few systematic evaluations of the impact of the introduction of market philosophies on health systems. Certainly none has demonstrated that the market is an effective mechanism through which to re-orient the health system to 'health'.

We conclude that the South Australian health system would best be served by strengthening its public management structure so that it strives for efficiency while at the same time supporting the development of an integrated network of health services capable of coordinating care and treatment. The public system should also adopt an overarching role in encouraging social and economic development which promotes health and well-being. Moving beyond the contract state in relation to health implies partnerships across all sectors and with all communities. Health is a public good which is best achieved through public mechanisms.

ACKNOWLEDGMENTS

We wish to thank Danny Broderick, Judith Dwyer, Gwyn Jolley, Paul Laris and Clare Shuttleworth for their helpful comments on an earlier draft of this paper. Thanks also to Denise Daley and Helen van Eyk who assisted by providing information on the budget of the SA Health Commission.

REFERENCES

Alexander, K. 1997, 'Adelaide Hospital queries casemix', *Health Administrator*, issue 42, 22 April.

Baum, F. 1995, *Health for All: The South Australian Experience*, Wakefield Press, Adelaide.

Baum, F. 1998, *The New Public Health in Australia*, Oxford University Press, Melbourne.

Beers, M. 1996, 'Haemolytic-uraemic syndrome: of sausages and legislation', *Australian and New Zealand Journal of Public Health*, vol. 20, no. 5, pp. 453–5.

Clinton, M. & Scheiwe, D. 1995, *Management in the Australian Health Care Industry*, Harper Educational Publishers, Pymble, NSW.

Corbett, D. 1996, *Australian Public Sector Management*, 2nd ed, Allen & Unwin, Sydney.

Duckett, S. J. 1998, *Health Care in the US: What lessons for Australia?* Australian Centre for American Studies, Sydney.

Evans, R. G., Barer, M. L., Marmor M. et al. 1994, *Why are Some People Healthy and Others Not? The Determinants of Health of Populations*, Walter de Gruyter, New York.

Evans, R. 1997, 'The role of competition in the provision of publicly funded health services', *Healthcover*, vol. 7, no. 1, February–March, pp. 32–5.

Ferrie, J. E., Shipley, M.J. et al. 1998, 'The health effects of major organisational change and job insecurity', *Social Science and Medicine*, vol. 46, no.2, pp. 243–54.

Hall, C., & Rimmer, S.J. 1994, 'Performance monitoring and public sector contracting', *Australian Journal of Public Administration*, vol. 53, no. 4.

Hindle, D. Degeling, P. 1997, 'All quiet in the western front? A postcard from the UK's National Health Service', *Healthcover*, vol.7, no.1, February–March, pp. 22–7.

Hughes, D. 1996, 'Coping with contracting: The implications of the contract culture on community service organisations', *Community Quarterly*, vol. 41, pp. 37–41.

Hutton, W. 1995, *The State We're In*, Jonathon Cape, London.

Johnson, A. 1995, Role of hospitals in health promotion Keynote address, Australian Association for Child Welfare and Health, Melbourne.

Johnson A. 1998, Reorientation of a hospital to be more health promoting, PhD to be submitted in 1998, Department of Public Health, Flinders University of South Australia.

The Lancet 1995,'Public health advocacy: Unpalatable truths, Editorial, 345, pp. 597–8.

Legge, D. 1992, 'Community management: Open letter to a new community member', in *Community Health : Policy and Practice in Australia*, eds F. Baum, D. Fry, I. Lennie, Pluto Press/Australian Community Health Association, Sydney.

Lewis, B. & Walker, R. 1997, *Changing Central-Local Relationships in Health Service Provision: Final Report*, Melbourne, School of Health Systems Science, La Trobe University.

Murray, C. & Tatyzo, M. 1995, *A History of the North West Suburbs Health & Social Welfare Council 1988–95*, NWS HSWC, Adelaide.

National Health Strategy 1992, *Enough to Make You Sick; How Income and Environment Affect Health*, National Health Strategy, Canberra.

Osbourne, Dorothy, & Gaebler, T. 1992, *Re-inventing Government: How the Entrepreneurial Spirit is Transforming the Public Sector*, Addison-Wesley, New York.

Raftery, J., 1995, 'The social and historical context', in *Health for All : The South Australian Experience*, ed F. Baum, Wakefield Press, Adelaide.

Reynolds, C. 1995, 'Health and public policy : The tobacco laws', in *Health for All : The South Australian Experience*, ed F. Baum, Wakefield Press, Adelaide.

Rosenfeld, E. 1996, *Social Support and Health: A Literature Review*, South Australian Community Health Research Unit, Adelaide.

SA Health Commission (SAHC) 1988, *A Social Health Strategy for South Australia*.

——1988a, *Primary Health Care in South Australia: A Discussion Paper*.

——1989b, *Primary Health Care Policy Statement*.

——*Budget Summary* 1992/3 and 1997/8)

Sanderson, C. & Baum, F. 1995, 'Health & social welfare councils', in *Health for All: The South Australian Experience*, ed F. Baum, Wakefield Press, Adelaide.

Sanderson, C. & Alexander, K. 1995, 'Community health services planning for health' in *Health for All: The South Australian Experience*, ed F. Baum, Wakefield Press, Adelaide.

Shuttleworth, C., & Auer, J. 1995 'Women's health centres in Adelaide', in *Health for All : The South Australian Experience*, ed F. Baum, Wakefield Press, Adelaide.

South Australian Community Health Research Unit (SACHRU) 1996, *Changing Times*, Adelaide, SACHRU.

Swerissen, H. & Duckett S. 1997, 'Health policy and financing', *Health Policy in Australia* ed H. Gardener, Oxford University Press, Melbourne.

Townsend, P., Davidson, N., & Whitehead, M. 1992, *Inequalities in Health*, Penguin, London.

Victorian Auditor's General 1998, *Acute Health Care Services Under Casemix : A Case of Mixed Priorities.*
http://home.vicnet.net.au/^vicaud1/fr56/ags5600.htm, last updated 12/5/98, accessed 28/5/98

Warin, M., Baum, F., Murray, C., Kalucy, L., Veale, B. 1998, *Not Just A Doctor : Community Perspectives on Medical Services in Women's and Community Health Services*, Department of Public Health, Flinders University of SA and South Australian Community Health Research Unit

Wilkinson, R. 1996, *Unhealthy Societies: The Afflictions of Inequalities*, Routledge, London.

CHAPTER 18

COMMUNITY SERVICES IN SOUTH AUSTRALIA

From contracts to the common good?

ADRIAN VICARY AND MARK HENLEY

It can be argued that the 1970s in South Australia was a decade characterised by welfare state optimism, with an emphasis on expansion of traditional welfare to encompass participation and social development. The 1980s by contrast represented a retreat from the welfare state which has been intensified in the 1990s. The purposes of this chapter are to consider changing demand for community services, examine changes in the provision of social support, analyse more recent policy initiatives in South Australia which have transformed relations between the state and community services organisations and, finally, to suggest some alternative directions.

CHANGING DEMAND FOR COMMUNITY SERVICES

A number of key indicators demonstrate that more South Australians were struggling financially in 1996 than in 1986. During the period from 1986 to 1996 there was a significant increase in the number of households living within $2000 per year of the Henderson poverty line. In 1986 a quarter of the population of South Australia lived in households whose annual income was below 60 per cent of average weekly earnings (AWE) (ABS *SA Yearbook*, 1988, 1997). By 1996 this percentage had risen to 41.9 per cent of South Australian households on low-to-very-low household incomes, an increase of 62 per cent over a single decade. The figures also imply that over the decade there was over 100 per cent increase in the number of households between the poverty line and 60 per cent of AWE benchmark, explained largely by the rapid rise of 'working poor'.

The number of unemployed people in South Australia increased by 18 per cent in the twelve years to 1998. This is reflected as a change of unemployment rate of 9.3 per cent to ten per cent (ABS *Labour Force*, cat. G202). These figures do not include discouraged job seekers who were not actively seeking work. There was also a significant increase in part-time employment, which has occurred at the expense of full-time jobs, reflecting a significantly more casualised labour market. This has reduced certainty of employment and lowered total incomes, leading to lower state demand. Casualisation of the workforce has been concentrated in entry-level jobs, a situation which significantly affects young people. A consequence of this is the postponement of household formation and a reduction in demand with a further dampening effect on the state's economy.

Another indicator of changes in household income is provided by the level of school card approvals. A sharp increase in demand for school card assistance in South Australia reflects the dramatic increase in low and very low-income households with school age children. There has been an increase in the number of school card approvals as a percentage of the total number of South Australian school students in the decade to 1996. For all schools combined, the number of school card approvals as a percentage of the total number of students more than doubled from 18 per cent in 1986/87 to 40.7 per cent in 1995/96.

As the 1998 Industry Commission's *Report on Government Services* notes there has been an increase in the number of people receiving some form of social security assistance over the decade, with 444 336 people receiving a benefit in SA in 1986 and 672 245 receiving some form of benefit a decade later in 1997. Using the Henderson poverty line as a benchmark, there were 162 000 people living in poverty in South Australia in 1997 of whom 60 000 were children.[1]

IMPACT ON COMMUNITY SERVICES

These significant changes in household income over a relatively short space of time have had major impacts on demand for community services. The St Vincent De Paul Society in South Australia reported an 80 per cent increase in demand for emergency assistance over the five years, 1991 to 1996, with 55 700 people seeking emergency assistance in 1996. This is but one agency providing emergency relief, and other SACOSS member agencies providing emergency relief reported similarly large increases in demand over this period.

EMERGENCE OF THE CONTRACT STATE

Given this demand, how did government policy and practice and community service providers respond? In the final days of the Arnold Labor government (as with the Cain Labour government in Victoria), a report on the state of the South Australian economy was received, a report which provided the impetus for reduction of public sector employment and other reforms.[2] In December 1993, the Arnold government lost an election and a Liberal government under Premier Dean Brown took office. Also, as in Victoria, the South Australian Liberal government appointed an Audit Commission which provided an impetus for change.[3] In accordance with new Liberal government policy, the South Australian Department for Family and Community Services (FACS) was reorganised at the end of 1995 to deal with the new policy environment. In 1998 this department was merged with other government functions into the Department of Human Services.

Many of the elements of the Victorian 'contract state'[4] can be seen in the more recent changes in South Australia[5]. Contracting for services was the direction in which FACS began to move in 1995 along with other South Australian government agencies, which were expected by the Liberal government to adopt the government's contracting-out policy.[6] This policy was implemented in the context of the government's economic development plan, a high priority for which was 'to improve government management to reduce debt and increase efficiency of key services'.[7] Economic development, efficiency, effectiveness and 'value for money' in outcomes and quality were the stated goals, and it is significant that the non-profit or voluntary sector was absent from policy documents which heralded the change.

While contracts are not new, the new funder/purchaser/provider model as the basis of contracts in all areas of government places new requirements and demands on parties to the contract. In the community services area this means establishing a new framework, controls and procedures based on the assumptions of economic liberalism. For FACS, for non-government organisations and for peak bodies, new models of funding contain new forms of authority and regulation, or command and control. Monitoring and assessment of contractual arrangements are the responsibility of funders and purchasers. That labour is now more flexible as part of the new arrangements has implications for all community service workers both in terms of conditions and job security.

In a restructure at executive level in 1995, new divisions were created in FACS to correspond to the funder/purchaser split in new funding arrangements. The re-organisation was similar to the restructuring that took place in the Department of Social Welfare in New Zealand in 1991 where four divisions were created: the New Zealand Income Support Service, the New Zealand Children and Young Persons' Service, the Community Funding Agency and the Social Policy Agency which provides policy advice to the government.

Funds allocated under the new arrangements are subject to competitive tendering – successful tenderers will be funded to deliver outcomes determined by the funder in terms of contracts for performance developed by the purchaser. At issue in the new arrangements is not a question of whether governments will fund organisations for the performance of services since this already happens; rather, in Kettl's[8] terms, it is in the nature of the relationship between government and contractors in a field where goals are difficult to define and where relations traditionally have been collaborative rather than competitive. From the point of view of the purchaser, the advantage of the new arrangements is an increase in the accountability of the provider.

Contracting-out, or outsourcing, refers to placing out to tender those functions which have previously been performed by government. In South Australia, FACS has for a number of years contracted-out its responsibility for foster (or alternative) care. Under the funder/purchaser/provider arrangements, the department has developed a new alternative care policy, which incorporates the new ideologies. It is a matter of speculation whether other functions performed by FACS such as youth detention could be contracted-out.

COMMUNITY SERVICES SECTOR REVIEW

The industrialisation of charity, or the movement from charity to industry[9], has been driven by a series of state initiatives to which the community services sector has responded and in some cases been involved. To an extent, the sector itself has taken some initiatives. The Community Services Sector Review is the most recent of initiatives in which the sector has been involved, and it demonstrates the dilemmas and contradictions of the new industrialised partnership. The initiation of the review followed an approach from SACOSS to the then Department for Community Welfare early in 1990 for a 'joint non-government–government review as the basis for the strategic development of community health and welfare services over the next decade'.[10]

Parts of the report documenting the review captured the process of transformation of government–community services sector relations which was already under way, and found much of the sector ill-equipped to deal with the changes. It observed that funding from government to the sector had shifted from a submissions base to needs-based funding, generally of a short term of three years, and that accompanying this shift was a tendency for the government to provide less funds than were necessary to meet the requirements it specified as a condition of its funding. This reflected what the review described as an 'asymmetrical' relationship in which 'non-government organisations are more dependent on funding organisations than the reverse'.[11] Financial problems of the sector were likely to be exacerbated by new industrial agreements for which the sector was not well-prepared, and in many cases, by inadequate management.

Dependence and inadequate funding are long-standing characteristics of the non-government community services sector. To overcome problems associated with funding, the review accepted the introduction of service agreements by FACS, and argued that more formal contracts would enable the development of consistent standards as well as result in improved evaluation of the effectiveness and efficiency of both government and non-government organisations.[12]

From the perspective of SACOSS, the major peak body in the community services sector and a co-sponsor of the review, the report established the social and economic importance of the sector, the diversity of the sector in terms of the numbers and types of organisations, and the need to develop a coherent and sustainable basis of funding. It also legitimated the concept of a partnership with the government based on evidence of the scope of work performed by the sector. For the Labor government of the time, the review provided a rationale for pursuing a new set of funding policies and for rationalising service provision between the state and community services sectors. The review did not speak in the 'reinventing government' terms of steering and rowing.[13] It did however, speak in the terms of the managerialist discourse which was prevalent of the 1980s: performance indicators, performance reviews, measures of outcome, service agreements. It also recommended that purchase of service contracts be explored.[14] A working group representing state government and community services sector interests, established to report to SACOSS and the government, reiterated in 1992, the main findings of the review as well as proposing a structure for implementation.[15]

The final stage in this process was the establishment of the *Serving Communities* Implementation Task Force, membership of which was drawn from the three levels of government[16] and which was funded to carry out its diverse range of tasks until late 1994. An election held in late 1993 resulted in the defeat of the Labor government after twelve years in office and the election of the Brown Liberal government with a large majority in the House of Assembly and with an approach to welfare which emphasised the importance of non-government welfare. As a result, an apparently contradictory political situation existed: a new government was committed to a stronger role in welfare for the non-government sector, but the sector itself was unable to articulate its collective identity sufficiently to take advantage of its potential elevation. Unwilling to adopt the status of industry, the sector remained diverse, with conflicting interests between organisations and divergent approaches to the meaning of 'welfare', a situation characteristic of the sector since its inception.

The most tangible outcome of the *Serving Communities* project was the development of a model service agreement and the elaboration of principles to cover service agreements. However, the final report of the project was also important as an attempt to further refine and develop the notions of 'partnership' and 'industry' in the community services. Partnership, according to the authors of the final report, 'entails the establishment of cooperative relationships between all those involved in the industry – relationships which recognise (and indeed celebrate) the different contributions which the various parties can make but which emphasise a joint responsibility for outcomes for consumers across the industry'.[17] The final report emphasised the necessity of a 'cultural change' towards 'an identifiable industry' and the development of industry structures in the community services if the 'value' of the sector was to achieve appropriate recognition. Nevertheless, the authors understood that there was 'not universal acceptance of the concept of a single Community Services and Health Industry',[18] and that there would be difficulties in the way of the development of an 'industry identity'.

In its strategy of attempted inclusion in the policy community, the non-government sector in South Australia has faced barriers common to the sector throughout Australia and elsewhere. These barriers are both internal and external. The internal barriers are those of disorganisation, divergence and lack of identity, while the external barriers are those of state agendas driven by economic considerations and implemented by administrative and managerial reform. While these reforms include participation in some processes, the determination of policy remains with the state. In these circumstances, partnership in the terms outlined by the Community Services Sector Review and *From Solo to Symphony* is unlikely to receive the assent of the state.

This does not mean, however, that all 'key players' and 'stakeholders' are excluded from the exercise of influence: the role of large organisations and the major peak bodies is crucial. Large, well-funded organisations, with 'private' resources, are not entirely dependent on government funds and have greater flexibility of action than smaller organisations. Peak bodies are valuable sources of policy advice to governments, and they are likely to develop this role at the expense of trying to represent the interests of their diverse constituents, a constituency which, in any case, is undergoing transformation as a result of new contractual arrangements.

FAIRNESS FOR COMMUNITY SERVICES WORKERS AND THE COMMON GOOD

The introduction, through the initiative of the Australian Social Welfare Union (ASWU), now the Australian Services Union (ASU), of an industrial award to cover workers in the community services sector is a further aspect of the industrialisation of charity in the 1990s. Union coverage of workers in the sector historically has been low. Reasons for this low rate of unionisation include the particular characteristics of organisations in the sector, the culture that surrounds work in the sector and the historical indifference of trade unions to the conditions of workers, predominantly female, in what has appeared a chaotic arena for union action. A further factor has been the idea that the sphere of the community services is not an area amenable to description as an industry.

The SACS Award in South Australia was phased in between July 1990 and November 1995. It can be argued that the introduction of industrial regulation in the community services sector was a product of the 'modernisation' of the sector. However, immediately following the introduction of the award in South Australia, a new framework of *deregulation* in the industry emerged which included 'enterprise bargaining' in line with the developments in the more general industrial relations framework in Australia. It is likely that these conditions will further erode working conditions in the community services sectors.

Some of the dilemmas facing community agencies as a result of the introduction of the new arrangements were identified in 1995 by the Northern Suburbs Family Resource Centre, an agency in the northern suburbs of Adelaide. As a result of 'funding restraint, service rationalisation and an increasingly competitive service delivery environment ... agencies [defined] their "core business" in order to maximise the effectiveness of limited resources'. Immediate needs of people in crisis were being met but long-term programs had been shelved. The introduction of the SACS Award compounded

... service delivery issues. While funding bodies are agreeing to fund award conditions for 'core business', some agencies are agreeing to below award conditions for out of hours services. Some agencies are meeting the requirement to pay the award rate by reducing staff hours. This is specially so in the small community based programs.[19]

Competitive tendering has meant that agencies skilled at tendering win service contracts while those which do not have staff with such skills see 'funds slipping away, not because their service is redundant, ineffective or inefficient but because they are not provided with the tools for tendering'.[20]

Since the late 1980s, the industrialisation of charity in South Australia has transformed the community service sector organisations as well as transforming the relationship between state and community services sectors, and between workers and the consumers of their services. While the new emphasis on partnership has the potential to secure the values on which the voluntary organisations have been based, the necessarily unequal relations between the partners mean that the more likely outcome is domination by the agenda of the state.

These changes have a number of implications for the provision of human services. First, state welfare departments may increasingly, as a result of outsourcing, become funding bodies with a concomitantly reduced role in service provision. Thus the number of workers employed in the state sector will inevitably decrease. Work in this sector reduced to 'core' functions with a consequent loss of jobs represents a regulation model of the public sector where the role of government is negative (constraining undesirable activity) rather than positive (doing desirable things). Second, the new imperatives of work in community service agencies will be determined by the specifications in service agreements through models which stress efficiency and accountability. For community services workers this means that a commitment to social justice will be further strained. Third, competitive tendering is likely to result in a restructuring of the sector and reduce the number of organisations. Even though these organisations will be encouraged to 'collaborate' in the tendering process, mergers or takeovers are likely.

Given the growing demand summarised earlier in this chapter, how well do current developments meet the demand? And what does this mean for the 'partnership' and the values espoused by the community services? The South Australian Department for Family and Community Services has been restructured a number of times with the stated aims of providing equitable and better client service with a leaner structure. However, as Healy argues:

Restructuring is a typically managerialist approach, which absorbs considerable staff time and energy, resulting in the new agency concentrating upon its internal problems [and] the unanswered question is whether these restructures eventually result in more effective services for the consumers.[21]

The outcome of the latest restructuring will be fewer services at a time when it can be argued that public organisations need to do more, not less, to meet needs.

It is appropriate in this context to consider the question raised by Oxenberry and Dickey in 1986 about the future of the 'principal state government welfare agency' in South Australia: whether it would be 'once more left as the truncated administrator of resources for a residual set of problems.'[22] There is evidence that this agency has changed more than that envisaged by Oxenberry and Dickey a decade ago. The global political reassessment of the role of the state and the changes to the role and function of the 'principal state welfare agency' over the last decade have transformed it into an administrator of contracts as well as 'the truncated administrator of resources for a residual set of problems' for which it still retains statutory responsibility. To modify the words of Oxenberry and Dickey, it will be worth enquiring the extent to which the current structure of the community services sector in South Australia will remain, and the character of employment within it.

CONCLUSION: WHAT KIND OF PARTNERSHIP FOR THE COMMON GOOD?

The harsh reality is that the social fabric in South Australia is under extreme pressure. There are many acknowledged causes for the growing number of low-income and poor people in South Australia as well as reductions in real wages, loss of jobs, changing family structures, casualisation of the workforce, diminished federal and state government services and market globalisation. Whatever the reasons, there is a significantly increasing proportion of people in South Australia confronting real hardship in their daily lives. The retreat from social policy by governments responding only to the market has dissipated effort and focus from its a primary role of assisting disadvantaged members of society.

To achieve economic and social renewal it is necessary for the state government to adopt a whole-of-government approach to social policy. This would include the active involvement of the community in the formulation and implementation of programs to achieve the required social goals. The creation of a human services portfolio which brings together a number of areas of human service provision by the government is a step in the right direction. However, further planning is needed by the government to ensure that services are accessible throughout the state and delivered in an integrated and effective manner. A whole-of-government approach would enable the articulation of state goals to provide a basis for both the coherent development of social policy and a contribution by the community towards the achievement of these goals. Clear and measurable social indicators are required to ensure that goals are being met and that appropriate and desired outcomes are being achieved. The involvement of community in active and ongoing, and focused dialogue in meeting social policy goals is fundamental. How, therefore is a partnership between government and community services to be achieved?

While the idea of partnership is not new, the contemporary thinking relating to partnership between the state and community services sector is dominated by economic rationalist ideology. In the earlier relations 'partnership' was a rhetorical device employed to recognise the mutual interdependence between the two based on patterns of interaction which had developed from earlier assumptions about the role of welfare.

Although the community services sector may not as a whole embrace economic rationalist doctrines, being a partner in the new relationship requires that it speaks in the terms set by the state, as well as in the older terms of charity, compassion and need. By accepting the new arrangements, this sector is placed in the position of trading its ability to define needs for the position of partner in conditions where, 'nothing is certain but change'. At the same time, becoming an industry places community services in the mainstream of the economy rather than as the backwater of residual support for the poor or disadvantaged, and provides at least ideological recognition of the value of its services. But the dilemma or contradiction for the sector lies in the meaning implicit in the term 'value'. In economic terms, this means measurement and productivity, while in social terms its meaning is taken to be its contribution to social well-being based on a set of values not traditionally the subject of narrowly defined economic measurement. Earlier ideas associated with charity – altruism, voluntarism, helping and caring – and the forms of organisation embodying them, are no longer adequate to meet the requirements of a relationship with a state characterised by a language of performance indicators, results, value for money and productivity.

Social renewal in South Australia through a social policy framework negotiated between the state and community services sectors can be achieved only through a transformation of the partnership between the two sectors. One way out of the dilemma associated with the economic rationalist meaning of 'value' is to characterise the work of the community services as a 'production process' which creates value through the use of resources.[23] The outcomes of the Community Services Sector Review could readily be adapted as the starting point in the transformation of the relationship. The development of indicators based on information such as that presented in this paper is a necessary first step. An implementation program which enables an adequately resourced community services sector to respond not only to social need, but also to extend the capacity of citizens to participate in an equitable, inclusive society would follow. This will be an important part of a mutually agreed, progressive social policy framework which provides for mutual accountability between the state and community service sectors. Partnership can then be reframed as a dynamic and responsive mechanism based on dialogue and renewal to achieve a sense of the common good which moves beyond the individualistic paradigm of the contract state.

NOTES

1   SACOSS, 1998

2   Arthur D. Little 1992, *New Directions for South Australia's Economy: Final Report of the Economic Development Strategy Study*, vol. 1, Arthur D. Little International Inc., Adelaide.

3   South Australian Commission of Audit 1994, *Charting the Way Forward: Improving Public Sector Performance*, report of the South Australian Commission of Audit, Adelaide, April, vol. 1 & 2.

4   Alford, John & O'Neill, Deirdre (eds) 1994, *The Contract State: Public Management and the Kennett Government*, Centre for Applied Social Research, Deakin University, Melbourne.

5   Performance contracts between chief executive officers and their ministers were recommended to the Brown Liberal government by the South Australian Commission of Audit, vol. 2, p. 362.

6   Office for Public Sector Management (OPSM) 1995, *All about Contracting Out: Value for Money for South Australians by Competitive Tendering and Contracting Out*, Department of Premier and Cabinet, Government of South Australia.

7   Brown, Dean, Premier, 'Foreword', in OPSM 1995, p. 3.

8   Kettl, Donald F. 1993, *Sharing Power: Public and Private Markets*, Brookings Institution, Washington DC.

9   The phrase 'from charity to industry' is used as the title of a paper cited in the final report of the *Serving Communities* Project in South Australia. Wiseman J. & Watts, R. 1988, 'From charity to industry', papers presented at a seminar on *The Future of the Social and Community Services Industry*, Phillip Institute of Technology, Melbourne, October, cited in *Serving Communities, Final Report of the Implementation Task Force*, Adelaide, December 1994, p. 63.

10   South Australian Community Services Sector Review 1991, *Report of the South Australian Community Services Sector Review*, Adelaide, 30 September 1991, p. 1.

11   South Australian Community Services Sector Review 1991, p. 17.

12   South Australian Community Services Sector Review 1991, p. 18.

13   Osborne, D. & Gaebler, T. 1993, *Reinventing Government: How the Entrepreneurial Spirit is Transforming the Public Sector*, Plume, New York.

14   South Australian Community Services Sector Review 1991, Recommendation 36, p. 191.

15   Letter to Deputy Premier and Chairperson of SACOSS as co-sponsors of the Community Services Sector Review. Community Services Sector Review Stage 2: Report by Working Group to SACOSS and State Government, *From Solo to Symphony: A Proposal for Reform of the South Australian Community Services Industry*, Adelaide, April 1992.

16   *Serving Communities* Task Force 1994, Appendix 1.

17   *Serving Communities* Task Force 1994, p. 7.

18   *Serving Communities* Task Force 1994, p. 5.

19   Northern Suburbs Family Resource Centre (NSFRC) 1995, *Core Business*, overview presented in *Notes 'N News*, issue 4, December 1995, Northern Suburbs Family Resource Centre, Elizabeth South.

20   NSFRC, 1995.

21   Healy, Judith 1988, 'Packaging the human services', *Australian Journal of Public Administration*, vol. 47, no. 4, p. 330.

22   Oxenberry, Rod & Dickey, Brian 1986, 'Welfare and change since 1965', *Rations, Residence and Resources: A History of Social Welfare in South Australia Since 1836*, ed B. Dickey, Wakefield Press, Adelaide, p. 315.

23   This idea is suggested for the public sector by John Alford 1993, 'Towards a new public management model: beyond "managerialism" and its critics', *Australian Journal of Public Administration*, vol. 52, no. 2, June, p. 138. The suggestion can also apply to the community services.

NOTES ON CONTRIBUTORS

Fran Baum is the Professor and Head of the Department of Public Health, Flinders University, Director of the South Australian Community Health Research Unit and National President of the Public Health Association of Australia. Her research, teaching and publishing are in the areas of health promotion, the political economy of health and social aspects of public health. Recently she published *The New Public Health: An Australian Perspective*.

Ray Broomhill is an Associate Professor of Labour Studies in the Department of Social Inquiry at the University of Adelaide. He is co-author with Rhonda Sharp of *Short Changed – Women and Economic Policy*, published by Allen & Unwin, and co-editor with John Spoehr of *Altered States – The Impact of Free Market Policies on the Australian States*, University of Adelaide, Centre for Labour Research.

Paul Chapman is an economic and industry consultant. Paul is the author of a range of articles on industry and economic policy. He is a regular contributor to the *Adelaide Review*.

Don Dunstan was Adjunct Professor of Labour Studies in the Department of Social Inquiry at the University of Adelaide. He was a former Premier of South Australia. Among Don's many publications are *Felicia – The Political Memoirs of Don Dunstan* and *Don Dunstan's Cookbook*. Don Dunstan died in February 1999.

Frank Gelber is the Chief Economist and Director of the Economics and Property Research and Forecasting Units at BIS Shrapnel. Frank taught Pure Mathematics, Economics and Economic Statistics at the University of Sydney from 1970 to 1980, during which time he also did his PhD in economics. He joined BIS Shrapnel in 1981, becoming a director of the company in 1987. Frank regularly presents BIS Shrapnel's analysis of prospects for the Australian economy at the company's six-monthly forecasting conferences and conducts briefings and workshops.

Stephen Hamnett is Professor of Regional and Urban Planning at the University of South Australia. He was a member of the Steering Committee of the South Australian Planning Review from 1990 to 1992 and has served as Deputy Presiding Member of the Development Assessment Commission.

Mark Henley is an economist with 25 years' experience in providing human services, particularly through youth work and labour market programs. Mark has been involved with the South Australian Council of Social Service for 18 years, most recently as Executive Director. He is currently the CEO of the Blind Welfare Association of SA.

Robert Hattam is the Research Manager for the Flinders Institute for the Study of Teaching. His research interests include: teachers' work, youth, critical pedagogy, policy analysis and school reform. Some of his recent publications include a co-edited book entitled *Schooling a Fair Go*, a chapter in the edited book *The Ethos of the University*, and papers in the journals *Discourse, Teacher Development, Teaching in Higher Education, Journal of Curriculum and Supervision* and the *International Journal of Leadership in Education*.

Graeme Hugo is a Professor of Geography in the Department of Geographical and Environmental Studies at the University of Adelaide. He is Director of the Key Centre in Research and Teaching in the Social Applications of Geographical Information Systems at the University of Adelaide. He has worked extensively on Australian population issues and problems, particularly on issues relating to complications of demographic change for planning the provision of goods and services for the private and public sectors. In 1987 he was elected a Fellow of the Academy of Social Sciences in Australia.

Matthew Jones is a senior economist at BIS Shrapnel. Matthew joined the company in 1998 having worked for the previous ten years in the consulting industry as a transport and business economist. Here he worked on project feasibility studies and economic and financial evaluations for public and private sector clients both in Australia and overseas. Matthew completed an MA in economics at the University of Leeds, England. He has published several articles for journals and conferences.

Michael Lennon is Adjunct Professor of Urban Policy at the University of South Australia and the University of Adelaide. He is a former chief executive of Housing and Urban Development for the South Australian government and was the Director of the Planning Review from 1990 to 1992. Most recently he has worked as the coordinator of the Adelaide 21 Project.

Charlie Murray is a senior research officer at the SA Community Health Research Unit. Prior to this she was the executive officer at North West Suburbs Health and Social Welfare Council, which was a community participation program funded by the SA Health Commission.

Lionel Orchard is a senior lecturer in Public Policy in the Institute of Public Policy and Management at Flinders University. He is co-author with Hugh Stretton of *Public Goods, Public Enterprise, Public Choice*, published by Macmillan in 1994. He is currently writing a book on national urban and housing policy in Australia.

Barbara Pocock is a senior lecturer in Labour Studies, Department of Social Inquiry, University of Adelaide. She has published widely in relation to Australian unionism, the labour market and gender issues. *Strife: Sex and Politics in Labour Unions*, edited by her is published by Allen & Unwin.

Anthony Psarros has had an ongoing involvement in the labour movement for over 20 years where he has worked as a trade union organiser and as an industrial officer and research officer. For the last six years he has worked as a review officer in South Australia's Workers' Compensation System. Anthony is a nationally accredited mediator.

John Quiggin is an Australian Research Council Senior Research Fellow in Economics, based at James Cook University. Professor Quiggin is one of Australia's most prominent research economists. He was awarded the annual medal of the Academy of the Social Sciences in Australia in 1993 and was elected a Fellow of the Academy in 1996. Professor Quiggin is also prominent as a commentator on policy topics including unemployment policy, microeconomic reform, privatisation, competitive tendering and the economics of education.

Martin Shanahan is a senior lecturer in economics in the School of International Business at the University of South Australia. Martin completed his PhD in economics at Flinders University and researches in a variety of fields including economic history, wealth and income distribution, labour markets and cost-benefit analysis. He has published in the *Australian Economic History Review*, *Australian Economic Papers*, *Journal of Income Distribution* (forthcoming), and the *Australian Dictionary of Biography*.

Rhonda Sharp is an Associate Professor in the School of International Business at the University of South Australia where she is also the Director of the Centre for Gender Studies. Rhonda is co-author with Ray Broomhill of *Short Changed – Women and Economic Policy*, Allen & Unwin.

John Spoehr is the Acting Director of the Centre for Labour Research at the University of Adelaide. He is the author of *From Lending Binge to Credit Squeeze – The Failure of Bank and Finance Sector De-regulation*, United Trades and Labor Council of SA and co-editor with Ray Broomhill of *Altered States – The Impact of Free Markets Policies on the Australian States*, Centre for Labour Studies.

Adrian Vicary is Head of the School of Social Work and Social Policy at the University of South Australia. He has a PhD in politics from Flinders University and teaches in the areas of politics and social policy. His research interests are in the structure and organisation of work in the human services, and in civics and citizenship education. His history of teacher unionism in South Australia, *In the Interests of Education: A History of Education Unionism in South Australia 1896–1996*, was published by Allen & Unwin in 1997.

EDITOR'S NOTE

This book was made possible by the generosity and commitment of its contributors. My deepest thanks to all of them.

A period of study leave at the University of Newcastle upon Tyne, Centre for Urban and Regional Development Studies (CURDS) in 1997 provided me with the inspiration and the opportunity to begin work on the development of this book. My thanks go to the staff of CURDS and especially Dr John Tomaney for his generous support during my stay in Britain. I wish also to thank my colleagues at the University of Adelaide, Centre for Labour Research and Department of Social Inquiry for their support. Many thanks to Ray Broomhill, Pat Wright, Barbara Pocock, Elaine Butler, Kate Lawrence, Rodin Genoff, Thalia Palmer and Josie Covino. My thanks also to Janet Wall.

My special thanks go to Michael Bollen and Stephanie Johnston from Wakefield Press for supporting the publication of this book. I am indebted to them for their support and am particularly grateful to Penelope Curtin for editorial assistance and to Clinton Ellicott who designed and typeset the manuscript. Thanks also to Pat Wright for assisting with proof-reading.

I also wish to thank Margaret Pike, Liz Ryan, Peter Spoehr, Jane Rodeghiero, Penny Munro, Leela Anderson, Rhonda Sharp, James Robertson, Jim Redden, Brad Preston, John Rainsbury, Jyanni Steffensen, John Dinham, Ray Di Sessa and Rosa for their love and support. At different times and in different ways they all helped to sustain me throughout this project.

Finally I wish to dedicate this book to Don Dunstan whose commitment to the pursuit of social justice and whose courage continues to be a great source of inspiration for me.

INDEX